THE FISCAL CRISIS OF AMERICAN CITIES

THE FISCAL AMERICAN

Essays on the Political Economy of Reference to New York

Edited by ROGER E. ALCALY

 **VINTAGE BOOKS**

CRISIS OF CITIES

Urban America With Special

and DAVID MERMELSTEIN

A Division of Random House, New York

FIRST EDITION February 1977
A Vintage Original
Copyright © 1976 by Roger E. Alcaly and David Mermelstein

Library of Congress Cataloging in Publication Data
Main entry under title:

The Fiscal crisis of American cities.

   Includes bibliographical references.
   1. Finance, Public—New York (City) 2. Municipal finance—United States.
I. Alcaly, Roger E.,
1941–   II. Mermelstein, David, 1933–
HJ9289.N4F57 1977   336.747'1   76–54679
ISBN 0–394–72193–4

Manufactured in the United States of America

Grateful acknowledgment is made to the following authors and publishers for permission to reprint the selections in this book:

The New York Times: Commentaries which appeared in *The New York Times* of July 30, 1975 under the byline of Israel Shenker. Copyright © 1975 by The New York Times Company.
   Robert Brooke Zevin: "New York City Crisis: First Act in a New Age of Reaction" reprinted by permission of the author. Copyright © 1976 by Robert Zevin.
   Roger E. Alcaly and Helen Bodian: "New York's Fiscal Crisis and the Economy" reprinted by permission of the authors.
   The New York Times Review of Books: "The Last Days of New York" by Jason Epstein. Reprinted from the February 16, 1976 issue of *The New York Times Review of Books.* Copyright © 1976 by Nyrev, Inc.
   David M. Gordon: "Capitalism and the Roots of Urban Crisis" reprinted by permission of the author. Copyright © 1977 by David M. Gordon.
   John H. Mollenkopf: "The Crisis of the Public Sector in America's Cities" reprinted by permission of the author. Copyright © 1976 by John H. Mollenkopf.
   Pantheon Books, a Division of Random House, Inc.: Condensation of pages 165–189, 192–201 of "The Urban Crisis: Who Got What, and Why" by Frances Fox Piven. Reprinted from *The Politics of Turmoil: Essays on Poverty, Race and the Urban Crisis* by Richard A. Cloward and Frances Fox Piven. Copyright © 1974 by Frances Fox Piven and Richard A. Cloward.
   George Sternlieb and James W. Hughes: "Metropolitan Decline and Inter-Regional Job Shifts," excerpted from *Post-Industrial America: Metropolitan Decline and Inter-Regional Job Shifts,* by permission of the editors.
   Random House, Inc.: "Six Pillars of the Southern Rim," a condensation of pages 17–27, 30–35, 38–48 of Chapter 1 from *Power Shift: The Rise of the Southern Rim and Its Challenge to the Eastern Establishment* by Kirkpatrick Sale. Copyright © 1975 by Kirkpatrick Sale.
   Public Employee Press: "The Federal Rip-Off of New York's Money" by Seymour Melman, reprinted from *Public Employee Press,* March 12, 1976 (newspaper of

District Council 37 of the American Federation of State, County and Municipal Employees AFL–CIO).

The Brookings Institution: "Fiscal Problems of Cities" excerpted from *Setting National Priorities: The 1973 Budget* by Charles L. Schultze, Edward R. Fried, Alice M. Rivlin, Nancy H. Teeters and Robert D. Reischauer. Copyright © 1972 by the Brookings Institution, Washington, D.C.

Alfred A. Knopf, Inc.: Excerpt from pages 326–327 entitled "Retrenchment Recalled" from *The Power Broker* by Robert Caro. Copyright © 1974 by Robert Caro. Portions of this book originally appeared in *The New Yorker*.

The New York Times: "Banks Rescued the City in a Similar Plight in '33" by John Darnton. Reprinted from *The New York Times*, May 14, 1975. Copyright © 1975 by The New York Times Company.

Matthew Edel: "The New York Crisis as Economic History" reprinted by permission of the author.

Robert Fitch: Planning New York" reprinted by permission of the author.

The Village Voice: "How the Power Brokers Profit" by Jack Newfield. Reprinted from the April 26, 1976 issue of *The Village Voice.* Copyright © 1976 by The Village Voice, Inc.

William K. Tabb: "Blaming the Victim" reprinted by permission of the author.

Working Papers for a New Society and Robert Friedman: "Pirates and Politicians: Sinking on the Same Ship" by Robert Friedman a similar version of which appeared in Vol. IV, No. 1, Spring, 1976 issue of *Working Papers.* Copyright © 1976 by The Center for the Study of Public Policy, Inc.

Eli B. Silverman: "New York City Revenues: The Federal and State Role" by Eli B. Silverman excerpted from an article by the same title which appeared in the August, 1976 issue of *Empire State Report.*

Peter S. Albin: "Disurbanization and Economic Recovery" reprinted by permission of the author.

David Mermelstein: "Austerity, Planning and the Socialist Alternative" reprinted by permission of the author.

To my parents
R.E.A.

To Mother
D.M.

Preface

Crises beget scapegoats. That lesson of history is nowhere more apparent than in the fiscal crisis of New York City. Depending on your politics and tastes, the culprits include Mayors Beame, Wagner and Lindsay; or black welfare chiselers; or overpaid employees of the city (mostly white) with inflated pensions. Some point an accusatory finger at the opposite end of the income spectrum, at the bankers and real-estate moguls. On occasion such distant devils as Iranian shahs and Arabian sheiks are cited as the real source of New York's woes. Even "inexorable processes" are fashioned into scapegoats: thus the causes of the crisis are attributed to impersonal market forces that led to suburbanization, inner-city decay and regional decline.

Such perceptions of the crisis do not, of course, arise out of thin air. *Effects* on the one hand may be experienced personally as "pink slips," higher taxes or more crowded classrooms. *Causes*, though, are in good part "learned" from the media. Unfortunately, the popular press is not noted for its devotion to serious analysis of social problems. Without neglecting the topical issues of the crisis, this book attempts an investigation of its deeper roots, those slighted by media more concerned with immediate events than with sober and probing analysis. Ultimately, the origins of the urban fiscal crisis lie in the process of capitalist accumulation, in a system of economic growth dictated by capital's needs to seek ever greater profits.

The second section of this book examines the changing role of cities from this perspective. Thus we learn that the pattern of suburbanization found in the United States which so undermines the economic base of the central city is not technologically determined. (In point of fact, European cities exhibit a different geographical configuration and a different pattern of social segregation.) Nor is it primarily the product of economic market forces, of more affluent families with higher incomes using their wealth to purchase more spacious surroundings, or of single-story factories taking advantage of cheaper suburban sites. Rather, the roots of suburbanization are more to be found in an elaborate system of governmental subsidies including federal mortgage guarantees for single-family houses, the tax-deductibility of mortgage interest payments, and most important, the network of highways that link city to suburb. These policies, we suggest, were ultimately created to facilitate private capital accumulation.

The inner-city ghettos of the North are also products of the investment process. Blacks (as well as poor whites) were "pushed" off the farmlands of the South in the post–World War II era by development and application of a new agricultural technology, and "pulled" to the industrial jobs of Northern urban centers. Over time, however, these jobs diminished in number as the thrust of the accumulation process pushed elsewhere. In the first instance, automation wiped out many of these jobs in such heavy industry as steel, rubber and automobiles. Equally important, the change in the composition of output from manufacturing to leisure-oriented services, along with the shift in the basic source of energy from coal to oil, led investment to other, more profitable locations. Among these were not only the Sun Belt of the South but increasingly the greener pastures of Europe and the Third World. Low wages, tax concessions and the absence of effective unions played not a small part in stimulating this extraordinary migration of capital.

Lesser-skilled blacks were thus left stranded in the cities, there to subsist on the handouts of a debasing and bureaucratic system of welfare. Even this miserable existence proved to be a drawing card in the absence of suitable jobs elsewhere, striking testimony to the all-pervasive national prevalence of racial discrimination in schooling, housing and jobs.

The important point about suburbanization and the decline in the industrial Northeast (roughly the parallelogram defined by Detroit, St. Louis, Baltimore and Boston) is that these processes are not to be likened to acts of God. They occurred because those in control of our productive capacity directed it to the pursuit of profit rather than to the meeting of social needs. This point cannot be emphasized too strongly.[1]

If these are trends long at work in undermining the economic base of our Northern cities, a more immediate set of events precipitated the fiscal crisis of New York City, namely the onset of the national

---

[1]We are not arguing that businessmen are particularly evil, uncaring or malicious. Within a capitalist economy they are more or less forced to behave the way they do by the pressures of national and international competition. What is at issue is not morals but the *system* of production itself.

(even international) crisis of the capitalist economy. The latter may be dated from any one of a number of dramatic points, but for the purposes of this discussion the recession of 1969–1970 is an appropriate turning point.

The Vietnam war had helped to create the longest boom in the history of American capitalism. While labor benefited economically, as measured by low rates of unemployment and increases in real wages, capital suffered. From the mid-sixties on, it was a "profitless boom"; that is, profit rates declined under the impact of higher wages, increased rates of interest, and the rising cost of materials. The newly inaugurated Nixon Administration applied the classical capitalist solution of tight money and recession to the problem of a squeeze on profits, the tried-and-true method of disciplining labor. Only this time it failed as the degree of boom-induced dislocation required a recessionary "cure" of considerable depth and duration. Unwilling to jeopardize his political fortunes in the forthcoming election of 1972, Nixon reversed his economic horse in midstream, returning to a stance of easy money instead of restraint.

But for New York City, the recession never ended. The city has lost 500,000 jobs since 1969. The devastating impact of this loss on the fiscal vitality of New York needs no elaboration. On the national level, it is clear that serious problems were being swept under the rug with such gimmicks as the wage-price freeze followed by a system of half-hearted and haphazard controls known as phases two through four. One should not construe these manifestations of "economic planning" as well-intentioned though ill-conceived efforts on the part of government to provide an even-handed solution to economic maladjustments. Arnold Weber, former director of the Cost of Living Council, provides a more realistic though blunt explanation:

Business had been leaning on [Secretary of the Treasury] Shultz and [Chairman of the Council of Economic Advisers] McCracken to do something about the economy, especially wages. The idea of the freeze and Phase II was to zap labor and we did. (*Business Week,* April 27, 1974)

Notwithstanding the intention, Nixon's controls were unable to make inroads on the difficulties described previously which now festered in the form of acute shortages amid repressed inflation. With the termination of these controls and within the context of a four-fold increase in OPEC-produced oil, all hell broke loose on the inflationary front. The response of business units to inflation of this magnitude was to invest heavily in commodities and to accumulate inventories both as a precaution against shortages and as a speculative attempt to cash in on rising prices, thus fueling further the inflationary fires. The bubble finally burst by the early fall of 1974. Recession became the order of the day.

The goal of the Ford Administration and the business community with which it has close ties has been to let the recession run its course and in so doing create a sufficiently large "reserve army" of unemployed workers to put significant downward pressure on wages. Thus can wage costs be held down to a level low enough to re-establish corporate profitability. As of the spring of 1976, this strategy has been highly successful.[2]

Business Week captures the essence of the "game plan" with admirable succinctness: "Yet it will be a hard pill for many Americans to swallow—the idea of doing with less so that big business can have more" (October 12, 1974). We can also expect a snow job: "Nothing that this nation, or any nation has done," *Business Week* adds, "compares in difficulty with the selling job that must now be done to make people accept the new reality." There follow even more ominous words: "Historian Arnold Toynbee, filled with years and compassion, laments that democracy will be unable to cope with approaching economic problems—and that totalitarianism will take its place." Prepare oneself, in other words, for repression in defense of profits.

This, then, is the immediate context within which the urban fiscal crisis must be placed. Its heart and soul is the attempted transformation of the U.S. economy into a generator of high profits, to be achieved at the expense of the living standards of workers and others. In New York City the immediate repercussion of general economic decline has been the loss of tax revenue due to a decline of both corporate and personal income. At the same time, recession creates additional expenses related to higher unemployment and rising welfare rolls. To some extent, then, the fiscal crisis is "merely" a *cyclical*

[2]Interested readers may find it useful to consult the following works for an elaboration and refinement of the above ideas: *Radical Perspectives on the Economic Crisis of Monopoly Capitalism* (New York: Union for Radical Political Economics, 1975); *The Economic Crisis Reader*, edited by David Mermelstein (New York: Vintage, 1975); James Crotty and Leonard Rapping, "The 1975 Report of the President's Council of Economic Advisers: A Radical Critique," *American Economic Review* (December 1975).

problem. The difficulty with such a formulation is that we are witnessing at least in New York such a deep and lengthy decline that
the term "cyclical" implies a temporal understatement.

If the recession-induced imbalance in the budget touched off the
fiscal crisis of New York, there are at least three other aspects of the
national crisis that also bear on the local situation. The first concerns
the banks. The optimism and cost-carelessness of the previous boom
led banks in general, but especially the large New York banks, to
extend a vast amount of loans to credit-unworthy institutions such as
the Real Estate Investment Trusts (REITs), New York City, Third
World governments and illiquid private corporations such as the
bankrupt W. T. Grant, as well as others still functioning, like Pan
American World Airways. Selections in the first and third sections
of the book discuss in more detail the ins and outs of banking as it
applies to the New York fiscal crisis. It is enough to point out here
that the unwillingness of banks to roll over the notes and bonds of
New York City in the spring of 1975 reflected as much the illiquidity
of banks themselves, brought about by the vicissitudes of the national
economy which they in part helped to create, as the fiscal unworthi-
ness of the city of New York.

Nor can the limited federal bailout of New York be seen in isolation from the overall setting of national economic crisis. For example,
Arthur F. Burns, Chairman of the Federal Reserve Board, is known
to fear the inflationary repercussions of a more generous program of
federal aid, financed as it would have to be, by deficit spending. If
New York is eligible, why not Detroit, Cleveland and Boston, not to
speak of cities everywhere in the nation whether needy or not? Thus
would prices and interest rates climb, choking off the recovery and
intensifying the economic muddle of unemployment amidst inflation.

Finally, the wringer New Yorkers are being put through appears
to be the prelude to a nationwide or at least regional squeeze on the
living standards of the urban population. Just as recession created a
desired degree of austerity—the real spendable earnings of nonsuper-
visory workers dropped more than 8 percent between 1973 and early
1975—so too the *urban* fiscal crisis enforces belt-tightening on a local
level. The two crises thus dovetail. Hence we see once again that the
real roots of the urban crisis lie in the uneven nature of capital
accumulation and growth.

A final organizational note. The book is divided into three parts.

The first contains material which introduces the general themes that are elaborated on in the rest of the book. The second section is divided into three parts, which concentrate on the general pattern of urban growth and development, the regional dimensions of these trends, and their economic and budgetary impact on urban America, respectively. The final section is devoted to an in-depth analysis of the fiscal crisis in New York. Each section is preceded by a brief introduction describing its internal organization and basic arguments.

Although we alone are responsible for the organization and contents of the book, we would like to acknowledge the generous assistance and cooperation of friends and colleagues who directed us to material we would otherwise have overlooked, and generally helped us along the way. We are particularly grateful to Peter Albin, Robert Cohen, Matthew Edel, Jason Epstein, David Gold, David Gordon, David Harvey, Cindy Hounsell, Felix Kramer, John Mage, Seymour Melman, Julie Mermelstein, John Mollenkopf, Frances Piven, Robert Reischauer, Leonard Rodberg, Bill Tabb, Robert Zevin, and, most of all, Helen Bodian.

R.E.A.

D.M.

New York City
May 1976

Contents

THE FISCAL CRISIS OF AMERICAN CITIES

Part I
OVERVIEWS

"**W**hat should be done to solve New York City's dilemma? In a crisis that seems fiscal and temporary to some, all-consuming and enduring to others, experts sought and suggested solutions. Some despaired, but others suggested ways to turn red ink into gold." Thus reads the introduction to an article which appeared in the *New York Times* in July 1975. Urban experts spanning a fairly wide range of political opinions offered pithy summaries of their views of New York City's problems. More than a dozen of these brief commentaries are reprinted in selection #1. They provide a useful backdrop for viewing the analyses contained in the rest of this book.

The other material collected in this "overview" section is concerned in greater depth with New York's fiscal crisis and argues, as does this book, that the city's ills must be viewed in the context of widespread economic disorder. These writers understand that a description of one city's most recent symptoms cannot explain the epidemic and its causes, even New York's.

The essays in this section are complementary. Both Robert Zevin, for example, and Roger Alcaly and Helen Bodian (selections #2 and #3) place the New York City fiscal crisis within the larger framework of a worldwide economic crisis. Zevin, an economic historian, assesses the various explanations for New York's demise and finds them to be, at best, only partial truths. He argues that "the New York crisis is both symptomatic and functionally integral to the transition from an era of inflation to an era of disinflation," and suggests that the most interesting question is not "why the city came to its present low estate or what the consequences will be; but rather, why this particular solution has resulted, somewhere between a true default and a complete, happy-ending bailout." He concludes that the New York solution, which has avoided large scale liquidation of shaky debt, is a "razor-edged optimal path. It produces maximum deflationary effects, terrorizing labor and smaller capitalists. At the same time it insulates major institutions from recognizing the losses attendant to actually liquidating any of the paper claims created at the end of the inflationary boom." Nevertheless, liquidation of New York's growing debt, along with other financial claims that cannot be paid, may well produce some five to ten years from now a financial collapse resembling 1929.

Alcaly and Bodian pay particular attention to the cyclical dimensions of the crisis. Arguing that the stop-gap measures enacted to maintain New York City's solvency have been tantamount to default proceedings, they go on to ask why, after a decade of deficit financing, the city's days of reckoning arrived in the spring of 1975. The answer is to be found in the nature of the capitalist business cycle, the enormous increase in debt which accompanied postwar expansions, and the growing illiquidity and fragility of financial institutions.

The banking system and particularly the large New York City banks emerge as major elements in this picture. "Confronted by severe liquidity problems, the banks could not afford to simultaneously perform holding operations on all their ailing debtors. In terms of the magnitude of the risks involved, New York City was the most vulnerable of the bank's dependents. . . . yet the banking system itself remained vulnerable to an outright default by the city, a weakness which the city and its unions failed to exploit." Because of the thinness of the municipal-bond market, the withdrawal of the commercial banks in early 1975 virtually guaranteed the refusal of the New York banks to underwrite additional issues of city notes, thus precipitating the crisis.

Finally, Jason Epstein's essay (selection #4) analyzes the deleterious effects of what he calls the "construction complex—the builders, the autonomous agencies, the federal and state bureaucracies, the banks," on the economic fortunes of New York. Although developed in the specific context of New York City, the basic thesis appears to have wide-ranging applicability (as John Mollenkopf, for example, shows elsewhere in this volume). Epstein notes that the devastating job loss in New York City—500,000 between the employment peak in 1969 and 1976—far exceeds what might have been anticipated on the basis of regional and national trends. This "suggests that forces beyond the ordinary vagaries of industrial devolution were at work here." What was at work, he argues, was a process of massive urban renewal, so ruinous to the economic health and vitality of the city, yet so profitable to the "coalition among the city's building trades, the mortgage bankers, the investment houses, and the politicians" that "nothing short of the city's impending bankruptcy would inhibit it."

1. Urban Experts Advise, Castigate and Console the City on Its Problems

NEW YORK TIMES

JOHN KENNETH GALBRAITH, author of "Economics and the Public Purpose"—I think it's fair to say that no problem associated with New York City could not be solved by providing more money. The remarkable thing is not that this city's government costs so much, but that so many people of wealth have left. It's outrageous that the development of the metropolitan community has been organized with escape hatches that allow people to enjoy the proximity of the city while not paying their share of taxes. It's outrageous that a person can avoid income tax by moving to New Jersey or Connecticut. Fiscal funkholes are what the suburbs are.

ANTHONY DOWNS, urban economist and chairman of Real Estate Research Corporation—New York has been for a long time attempting to redistribute income through an extensive welfare system, through the low-cost university education system, and from landlords to tenants through rent control. The losers are businesses and middle-income people.

In the long run, the city can't redistribute incomes since people who take on the burden will leave, and the result will be the loss of businesses. Attempts to deal with the present crisis by raising taxes further will accelerate withdrawal from New York. Redistribution is a job of the Federal Government, not the city government.

The only thing Mayor Beame can do is decide he wants to solve the fiscal crisis, and not run again. If he wants to run again he can't

Commentaries which appeared in the *New York Times*, July 30, 1975, under the by-line of Israel Shenker.

solve it, because the majority of the people don't want the crisis solved.

ROBERT C. WOOD, president of the University of Massachusetts, former director of the Joint Center of Urban Studies—The prescription you come to in the present time is that the best things in life do cost money. The idea that playing around with tuition at CUNY [City University of New York], and trying to lay off policemen and firemen, and tricks in rolling over short-term notes, will somehow solve the problem is fallacious. There have to be massive infusions of national and state money because cities happen to be national and state assets, and the commercial centers that New York supports between 42nd and 59th Streets and on Wall Street are things important for the nation as a whole.

The second thing is probably more theoretical or egghead. We have to seriously go back to Henry George and consider that the city take over ownership of city land. If, in urban renewal, we had leased land instead of selling it to private developers, most of the cities, including New York, would be better off.

The third thing is that we have to come to grips with the existence of about 2,100 governments—my book was called "1,400 Governments"; but now I think it's about 2,100—in the metropolitan area. You can't simply put burdens on the central city and let the suburbs take the cream.

JANE JACOBS, author of "The Economy of Cities"—I don't know that New York can recover now. A city can't let its skills, manufacturing plants and suppliers' plants wither away and then not suffer the consequences. New York stopped being creative a long time ago. The notion that the city could live on financial and white-collar services was nonsense.

Fifteen years ago New York should have begun garbage recycling, and today it would have had a great business. The heck with saying it's uneconomic. Nothing's economic when you begin it. There wouldn't be an automobile industry today if it had to be economic when it started, or a camera industry, or an industry of anything. A long time ago New York should have begun a mass transit industry, and it would have had an export business now.

What New York could do—maybe it's too late already—is take the lid off transportation. Let anybody who can satisfy authorities that they're a safe driver and a good driver run any kind of transportation they want, any place they want, any time they want. Out of that—in 10 years—would grow some exportable types of transportation. There are still lots of very clever people in New York.

All this talk about *attracting* industries is nonsense. You don't attract industries to a city. Towns attract industries from cities, not cities from towns. Cities can't attract industries—they grow them.

BARRY COMMONER, director of the Center for the Biology of Natural Systems, Washington University—The present situation, with the fiscal operation of New York City controlled by private financiers, is unconscionable. There's no choice but to turn over to the United States Government the problem of New York City cash flow, since there's no reason why a country with the resources of the United States shouldn't provide the credit necessary.

If New York got assurance of United States Government credit, it could undertake projects for improving the city physically in ways that meet its people's needs, rather than having municipal activities dictated by the profit motives of private finance.

This will make more acute the existing problem of transforming the Federal Government from an immoral bureaucracy serving itself and narrow outside interests into a government of service to the people.

MILTON FRIEDMAN, professor of economics, University of Chicago —Go bankrupt. That will make it impossible for New York City in future to borrow any money and force New York to live within its budget. The only other alternative is the obvious one—tighten its belt, pay off its debt, live within its means and become an honest city again. That's a much better solution from the long-run point of view, but whether it's a politically feasible solution I don't know, whereas the first one is.

MICHAEL HARRINGTON, chairman of the Democratic Socialist organizing committee—By the passage of three laws in Washington you could end the crisis immediately—the federalization of welfare, the Kennedy-Corman health-security bill and the Hawkins-Humphrey full-employment bill. Taking off the back of New York City the cost of the failures of George Wallace and others to handle the problem of poverty (by federalizing welfare), catching up with all the other advanced industrial democracies (through a national system of health care) and achieving full employment (through the kind of planning that Hawkins and Humphrey are talking about) would leave plenty still to do in New York, but the fiscal crisis would be over.

Herbert Stein, professor of economics, University of Virginia, and former chairman of President's Council of Economic Advisers —I think that the prescription of New York cutting down its services, cutting down its expenses, and learning to live within its income is the only prescription. New York isn't treated any differently than any other city, and I think they have to adapt themselves to the state of the country.

Edward C. Banfield, professor of public policy and political science, University of Pennsylvania and author of "Unheavenly City" —I don't see what's to stop the unions from shaking the city down for whatever money it can accumulate. The laws have prohibited striking all along, but it's a practical problem—how do you put 30,000 or 40,000 striking teachers or policemen in jail? Obviously you don't, and if you fine them you have to put back in their pockets what you take out.

If the people of New York will tolerate strikes by public employees, against the law, and not tolerate politicians who crack down on strikes, then I can't see that it will be possible to get New York to live within its budget. It would require a fundamental change by the unions and on the part of the middle and upper classes toward the "do-good" activity that New York is more generous with than most cities. I'm afraid that the real trouble is that it's run by the upper and middle classes and they're too moral and too "righteous" to do the painful and sometimes wrong things that have to be done to run a big city. You won't find the policemen striking in Chicago.

Joseph A. Pechman, director of economic studies, Brookings Institution—I've supported countercyclical revenue sharing since the beginning of this recession. This is a supplement to the general revenue-sharing bill that would raise Federal aid to states and local governments when the unemployment rate exceeds 5 or 6 per cent, and then automatically decline when unemployment goes below that level. New York City's revenues would be increased and alleviate the fiscal crisis.

It's such a reasonable proposal that I thought Congress and the Administration would approve, but they seem to prefer public works, although it takes too long to get public works started and they tend to last much longer than the recession does.

RAYMOND VERNON, professor of international business management, Harvard, and former director of the New York Metropolitan Region Survey—There has to be a change in psychology—to see that a decline in population is no indication of failure. There's no reason why eight million should be the optimal population.

What's missing is an institution taking a complicated piece of land and reassembling it into a new package with a different partitioning between public and private. That's perceived as taking a decade or more, and there's no authority capable of accepting that kind of time risk. So these changes take place through slow attrition, including the last stage, during which—as in the South Bronx—the uses of land are wiped out by vandalism, arson and theft.

VERNON E. JORDAN JR., executive director of the National Urban League—Wage freezes, hiring freezes, 4-day work week, and a larger tax on commuters into New York City. Some strong executive leadership by the Mayor and the Governor and more responsible leadership on the part of the labor leaders. I think the Federal Government is not absolved of responsibility in this situation, but I think that city and state initiative should be a condition precedent to Federal help.

NATHAN GLAZER, professor of education and social structure, Harvard—I think there has to be a serious confrontation with the trade unions. The fact is that we're transferring an awful lot of money to the Arabs and everybody has to chip in. We have to figure out a way of providing more services with less highly paid employees. There are presumably hundreds of thousands of people ready to do jobs that city employees are doing—for one-half to two-thirds the salary.

LEWIS MUMFORD, author of "The City in History"—Make the patient as comfortable as possible; it's too late to operate. Stop spending money for the wrong things, and that means stop spending money for genocidal war and nuclear warfare. It's a drain on the national economy, and the state of our cities is a result of the way we've spent our national income.

2. New York City Crisis: First Act in a New Age of Reaction

ROBERT ZEVIN

INTRODUCTION

New York's virtual default confirms long apparent trends: a collapsing private economy, a growing and perversely smothering public economy, a city whose populace and government had rapidly decreasing control over its political economy. New York is not quite dead, but death is clearly inevitable. Death for a city is not physical destruction as befell Carthage or Hiroshima. It is the loss of those things which define a city's vitality: the culture and ferment, material pleasures and comforts, exploration and invention, growth of old activities and creation of new ones which serve as positive attractions for immigrants and produce a flow of ideas and products for export. If these are vital signs, New York is moribund, encrusted with decaying, old West Side Highways and decadent, new World Trade Centers.

A growing portion of its population is ill-housed and ill-fed; badly educated and medically neglected; ill-equipped for most productive work; displaced and disgruntled. To increasing numbers, New York's parks and streets, subways, lobbies, elevators and apartments are places of danger and fear. New York is dying—at a younger age than most great cities, perhaps not much sooner than other cities in the American Empire or than the Empire itself.[1]

So what? A question like that usually means "Who wins and who loses?" Many of the articles which follow deal with who loses. Indeed it seems that virtually everyone and every institution in the city is a loser: taxpayers and welfare recipients, municipal employees and pri-

---

Robert Zevin has taught economics at Harvard, Berkeley and Columbia; at present he is an investment counselor in Boston, Massachusetts. This paper was written in December 1975.

[1] By the American Empire I mean nothing more nor less than that which the innocents among us referred to as "the Free World" until quite recently.

vate-sector workers, museum goers and robbery victims, the largest banks and the smallest delicatessens. The purpose of this article is to step back a little from the crisis and try to see whether there are also some winners in or out of the city; whether New York is only a battle in a larger war; whether New York is only the first victim in a new epidemic.

The most interesting question which this article attempts to deal with is not why the city came to its present low estate or what the consequences will be, but rather, why this particular solution has resulted, somewhere between a true default and a complete, happy-ending bailout.

INFLATIONARY BINGE AND THE MORNING AFTER

The New York crisis is symptomatic of both the legacy of inflation and the tactics of an emerging strategy of disinflation coupled with a regressive redistribution of income, wealth and power. It is an early, perhaps decisive battle in a new war. There are winners as well as losers in that battle. The purpose of the battle, as with all battles, is to show others that what is happening to New York could and in some cases will happen to them.

If the New York crisis is both symptomatic and functionally integral to the transition from an era of inflation to an era of disinflation, then I must digress briefly and discuss the outlines of the most recent inflationary era in the capitalist world, the forces which propelled and accelerated inflation, and the forces which are bringing it to a halt.[2]

The year 1974—and the two, five, ten, twenty, or thirty-year periods ending with 1974—was marked by rates of inflation that rival or exceed those for any period of similar length in all of American history. Inflation has been the salient characteristic of the post–World War II American economy. Until recently it has grown persistently in importance.

Events as sweeping as the recent inflationary trend require explanations of equal magnitude. Such an explanation is provided by the notion that we have just passed the crest of a fifty-year-long great wave of Empire-wide investments based on an expanding complex of devices that generate and utilize energy from mineral resources. Fur-

[2]The following ten paragraphs summarize and frequently quote directly from a longer article that I wrote, "Inflation: Its Roots and Fruits," which was published in the spring 1975 issue of *Working Papers for a New Society*. .

thermore, the last ten years of this process have been characterized by an increasingly intense super-investment-boom in which a growing proportion of investments were superfluous in terms of both need and cost. This view flatly contradicts the prevailing liberal and conservative sentiments that we have in fact suffered from real shortages of petroleum and coal, electricity and food, steel and aluminum, and hosts of other goods. It also contradicts the notion that these shortages result from a growing profligacy of consumption at the expense of the savings and investment required to make adequate supplies of these goods available. While the view I shall describe is implicitly a Marxist view of inflation, it is disturbingly unrelated to anything Marxists have actually said on the subject for the past twenty years.

A long-term investment cycle occurs when a small number of technological innovations lead to a set of investments that are geographically and chronologically extensive, complex, and interrelated. Demand for the resources to make these investments grows markedly over a prolonged period of time, since the technological innovations make the investments appear highly (and increasingly) profitable. But it takes a long time for all the interconnected investments to fall into place and a long time, therefore, for the investment to "pay off" in terms of larger supplies of consumer goods. In the meantime, the prosperity caused by investment activity itself induces still greater investment. So those who control investment decisions typically create new institutions to channel resources away from consumers and into investment. The boom in effect feeds on itself. Prosperity, superprosperity, and inflation, all flow from the investment demand itself.

The unifying theme of the most recent investment cycle might best be described as the conversion of mineral resources into energy. The internal combustion engine is the most spectacular application of this principle, and by itself the original impetus to a massive investment in automobiles, trucks, aircraft, highways, auto-dependent suburbs, and a worldwide complex for discovering, producing, transporting, refining, and distributing petroleum products. The use of steam power converted to centrally generated electricity is another application of the main principle. The electrical and electronic devices that flowed from this development made possible modern communications and indeed many of the characteristics of present-day life. They too absorbed enormous amounts of investment resources and generated a correspondingly large demand for investment funds.

The view that our recent inflationary experience was caused by an excess rather than a deficiency of investment is supported by the statistics. The years 1966 to 1974 constituted a nine-year boom of investment in machinery, buildings, houses, durable goods, and inventories; investment was a higher percentage of total private economic activity than in any other nine-year period since the end of World War I. It is similarly apparent that investment has been a high percentage of total economic activity throughout the rest of the advanced and developing capitalist world.

At the same time, since the early thirties, we have experienced one of those periodic expansions in the relative importance of government economic activity (federal and local) such as those which came to a halt near the ends of previous inflationary cycles shortly after the Civil War and World War I. Some of these government expenditures have gone directly to help finance portions of the Empire-wide investment boom (highways, airports and public power facilities among many other government-financed investments in the domestic United States, and these plus a host of fertilizer plants, steel mills and the like overseas). Another large part has gone into the expansion of the military force and bureaucratic size of various governmental agencies. This expansion can plausibly be explained both by the demands made on government by the investment boom and by the impetus of governments to expand their own power bases in every way possible. A very large portion of increased government expenditures has gone into increased resources devoted to housing, health, education, welfare and direct government employment. A very plausible argument can be made that the primary impetus for this category of increased expenditures was the necessity to deal with the displaced workers created by the rapid growth of productivity in the private sector.

Investment booms big and small have always gone too far, including the most recent one. It is important, before returning to New York City, to briefly explain the systematic reasons for this phenomenon. On the one hand, as already stated, because of the size and complexity of individual investment projects and because of the interrelated nature of a series of investment projects, a long time passes between the making of investment expenditures and the full consequent flow of consumer goods and services. In the meantime these same consumer goods and services appear to be scarce because investments already made have not reached fruition and because investments being made increase incomes and therefore demands for goods and services.

On the other hand, the apparent profitability and desirability of additional investments causes capitalists and governments to extend or create institutions to facilitate an expansion of investment activity. Thus, as the most recent long-term boom expanded we saw an acceleration of public subsidies and tax incentives for investment; of debt financing and bank financing for corporate, government and household investments, as well as other expenditures. Excessive investment demand combined with buoyant consumer demand and a delayed flow of results from investments leads to general price inflation. In effect, those who wish to invest or any other persons or institutions wishing to command a greater share of the economic pie resort to the increasingly available credit facilities to obtain command over resources. Thus monetary claims increase more rapidly than the supply of real goods and services, and the prices of the latter increase.

Inflation reinforces the entire process and causes a further acceleration in inflation itself. Those who borrow funds find that the real cost of repaying them is reduced by inflation. Those who make investments find that their profitability is even greater than anticipated due to an increase in the price of the products produced by those investments, as well as the replacement costs of the investments. Every person and institution contemplating any sort of purchase is encouraged to do so before the price of the transaction increases yet again. Corporations are encouraged to accumulate inventories of the materials (and labor) which they use before the price increases further or the availability is restricted.

Thus the investment boom turns into an inflationary spiral. By the nineteen-sixties the system had evolved to a state of unhealthy addiction to inflation. The burdens of public, corporate and personal debt had grown to the point that further inflation (and debt expansion) was required in order to service existing debt. The Federal Reserve Bank found it necessary to permit larger and larger doses of money-supply increases in order to prevent the whole system from unraveling. The rate of inflation was persistently higher from each cyclical trough or peak to the next. Moreover, in the mid-sixties the great investment boom began to reach a point of natural fruition. Corporate profits began to fall relative to Gross National Product, corporate sales, corporate capital or almost any other measures.

The largest corporations of Western Europe, Japan and the United States began invading each other's markets and searching for new markets and investment opportunities all over the world. A host of leading American corporations became multinational corporations in the sixties. For these and others, an increasing amount of corporate activity was financed by debt expansion. At the same time, an increasing portion of total activity was directed at acquiring other existing businesses, expanding into new countries and new businesses, forming cartels or otherwise protecting the prices of their products as the growth of productivity and final demand both fell dramatically. The most spectacular symptom of this corporate crisis was the creation and dramatic expansion of the Eurodollar market. In 1960 the Eurodollar market did not exist. Today it has created a supply of purchasing power which is roughly comparable in size to the entire domestic money supply of the United States. It is clear from this fact alone that the desire of large corporations to maintain their rates of expansion in the face of declining abilities to do so accounts more for the inflation of the past ten years than any profligacy by governments, unions and individuals, and more also than the war in Southeast Asia.

The crisis of the sixties affected every class and nation and interest group. Specifically, as inflation accelerated, the relative economic position of the United States deteriorated, the relative position of the largest and most powerful corporations deteriorated and the relative position of the wealthiest individuals in all the advanced sections of the Empire deteriorated. Inflation and the new institutions that went with it had the usual classic effects. It became possible for the less rich and powerful to borrow the command over resources with which to invade the domains of others. New entrants in every industry and market multiplied both from within the United States and from overseas. Chemical companies began to explore for petroleum, and petroleum companies began to build chemical plants. The objectives of governments and corporations were increasingly in conflict within and between the two groups. Inflation redistributed wealth and income in favor of the less well-to-do. By the late sixties the entire structure of postwar political stability was collapsing. The sixties also saw the emergence of the crisis of the cities, to which I shall return in a moment.

By the early seventies the very leading government and corporate forces which had fostered the inflation came to perceive inflation itself and all the political-economic institutions that went with it as the major threat to their continued dominance of the Empire. Thus we saw sporadic efforts throughout Nixon's tenure as President to attack inflation and related phenomena. Beginning in the spring of 1974 we saw the emergence of a reasonably coherent, persistent and effective strategy. The period of disinflation began. All of the trends which had threatened the position of the wealthiest countries, companies and individuals were reversed. The growth of the American money supply began to decelerate. The growth of Eurodollars came to an instant halt. Banking deposits all over the world were rapidly reconcentrated in the very largest banks. By 1975, inflation itself began to decline dramatically and the worst recession since the thirties took its full toll all over the Empire. The rate of wage increases declined. The trade position and relative economic strength of the United States improved dramatically. So did the relative strength of the largest corporations as others lost access to credit facilities and securities markets. So finally did the relative economic position of those at the top of the American income distribution.

NEW YORK IN THE BOMB SIGHTS

For the forces which had taken the offensive, the war was still in its early stages in the spring of 1975, and remains so today.[3] A complete victory would require something like the restoration of their former levels of political and economic hegemony. This in turn would mean reimposing strict limits on the abilities of most lesser individuals, corporations and governments to increase their command over resources through debt financing and the like; bringing the rate of wage increase back to or below the rate of productivity increase; freezing or reversing the levels of government health, education, welfare, unemployment and other transfer payments to the less well-to-do consistent with maintaining simultaneous high levels of unemployment and political stability; and finally, imposing the sort of rationalization on the service sector which the previous three quarters of this century has produced in manufacturing.[4]

[3] I do not mean to imply here or anywhere else in this article that I endorse or reject any concrete hypothesis about the conspiratorial nature of the ruling class. I believe that debates about the physical, human embodiment of class actions reflecting class interests has deflected attention from the more interesting questions of what true class interests are and the ways in which impersonal market phenomena signal responses from class actors and their agents. I use expressions like "forces" and "strategies" primarily out of heuristic motives, and they should not be interpreted as a prejudgment about the explicitness with which class interests are considered or defended. In my view, the answers to such questions have virtually no impact on the arguments presented here. I also find such questions personally of little interest.

[4] I know that this proposition remains a sensitive issue for some. It seems to me an obvious historical fact that subsequent to the unionization of the major monopoly and oligopoly manufacturing industries, productivity increased rapidly, nominal and real

New York City presented itself as an exemplary vehicle to further all of these objectives by the spring of 1975. As a consolidated entity the city had amassed over $13 billion of outstanding debt, almost all of it since the early sixties. It had issued more than its per capita or economic share of total state and local debt or of the recent spectacular increase in such debt. It had resorted with increasing desperation to the debt markets over the most recent few years. It had done virtually nothing to restrain total employment, service levels or the seemingly extraordinary levels and rates of increase of wages and pension benefits. The consolidated payroll had nearly doubled in the previous ten years, to approximately 350,000 persons, making the city the largest employer in America after the federal government.

The structure and role of the municipal labor force exemplified all the problems which needed to be addressed before a sense of well-being could be restored in corporate throne rooms. The entire labor force was effectively and militantly unionized. It was very highly paid and had enjoyed rapid wage increases relative to most of American labor. Its excessively generous and woefully underfunded pension benefits were protypical of the ways in which workers had been consoled with questionable paper claims on the future. Finally, the municipal labor force had grown rapidly in ten years while the population of the city and the apparent level of actual municipal services had remained close to unchanged, indicating that the productivity of the city's labor force had *declined* by perhaps 30 percent, while that of American labor generally had increased modestly. The city's labor force was thus the quintessential example of the acute problems in the service sector of lagging productivity coupled with rising labor costs.

In addition, New York was also second only to the federal government as a dispenser of health, education, welfare, unemployment, housing and other benefits. Also, the city typified the targets of the growing new political consensus against profligate politicians and greedy labor bosses. It was clear, or at least it since has been made quite clear, that New York's government and municipal unions enjoyed mediocre levels of support at best even within the city. Even

wages increased relatively rapidly and absolute levels of employment declined significantly while output advanced. Thus far (with the recent exceptions of banking and insurance and the emerging possible exception of retailing), experience in the service sector has been dramatically different. And by now the experience in New York has become yet another major case of conformity to the industrial model.

this list is far from a complete inventory of the lightning rods which New York offered to the growing storm of reactionary and disinflationary purpose and sentiment. I shall return to some others later.

NEW YORK IN THE BINGE

How did New York come to such a pass? It is important to understand what the motives were for tripling city expenditures over the past ten years and who the beneficiaries were, otherwise our understanding of the consequences of the ongoing reductions in municipal expenditures will be obscured. Unfortunately, there are at least four competing explanations for the crisis of the cities in general and of New York in particular. All of them are at least partially true, and little empirical evidence has been compiled with which to assess their relative importance.

First is the argument that New York is uniquely vulnerable. The city is in many ways the cultural and corporate capital of the Empire. Accordingly, it bears many costs of a metropolitan center which are properly allocable to the entire Empire. It provides police and fire protection to the United Nations and innumerable embassies and consulates, all of which provide it with no tax revenues. It is a major port of entry to the United States and hence becomes the final residence for many illegal entrants and underqualified immigrants who become a drain on its resources. It is, for reasons beyond its control (according to this argument), a magnet for immigration from within the United States, and many of these immigrants join welfare and unemployment rolls, which is, again, properly a national expense. All of these arguments have a certain validity, but they seem rather specious as explanations for the tripling of New York's expenditures in the past decade, given no noticeable increase in the severity of these particular problems in the same period.

New York has other unique problems. All of its county and municipal public services—elementary education, higher education, metropolitan public transportation, sanitation, water service, health care, welfare, etc.—are uniquely concentrated in a single five-borough, metropolitan, city government. There are two consequences of this concentration. On the one hand, municipal unions and other pressure groups can concentrate their energy on a single and vulnerable power center. On the other hand, in a period of general municipal financial distress the problems of the weakest components in the conglomerate government structure tend to drag the rest of the structure down much more forcefully than would be the case with a disintegrated structure. New York also shares with all other Northeastern cities the problems flowing from a persistently weak and relatively declining local economy. On balance, all of these considerations may tell us something about why New York became the first victim of disinflation rather than some other city, but they suggest that the fundamental forces which led to the budget crisis are probably typical of most other American cities.

A second argument, not specific to New York City, has been put forth by James O'Connor (*The Fiscal Crisis of the State*, 1973). O'Connor holds that the rationalization of production in the manufacturing sector (in his terminology the Monopoly Capital sector) results simultaneously in the displacement of labor, the displacement of social overhead costs (security, waste disposal, transportation, environmental protection, education, health care, etc.) and the establishment of a competitive wage standard geared to increasing productivity in the manufacturing sector. The burdens of these displaced costs fall on governments, including municipalities. They find themselves faced with increasing demands for production-related services from the manufacturing sector, for the maintenance of the population displaced from useful employment by productivity advances in the manufacturing sector, for the provision of a growing list of services to the population including employees of the manufacturing sector in order to enhance that sector's profits, and with wage demands from their own employees related to the accommodation between labor and capital in manufacturing and the attendant superior increases in productivity. The result is the fiscal crisis of the state (or, in our case, the city).

O'Connor's argument is somewhat more appealing. Still, it suffers by comparison with the realities of New York's actual dilemma. Although municipal employment has doubled, it is dubious whether the actual level of services provided by the city government has increased very much. Although welfare and other transfer-payment burdens have increased over the past ten years, the rates of increase have been far less than the tripling of the city's budget, and furthermore, the modest increases which have occurred seem to be more related to the faltering of the growth of the Monopoly Capital sector rather than its progress.

A third view of the origins of the crisis of the cities including New York was stated by Frances Piven (see selection #7). This view has also been paraphrased recently with some glee by President Ford, Secretary of the Treasury Simon and others of their ilk. The main characters in this version of the drama are the black migrants to Northern cities in the forties and fifties, the existing big-city Democratic machines, the organized municipal employee groups and unions, and the national Democratic Administrations. The blacks came to Northern cities, including New York, and the local machines did not respond, partly because of the peculiar racial hatreds directed at blacks and poorly educated rural Southerners, partly because of some ossification of the big-city machines compounded by the entrenchment of municipal-service provider groups, partly because of the overwhelming numerical magnitude of the black migration.

When the municipal political machines did attempt to respond to the new black immigrants by providing expanded services or entrée into municipal patronage, the reaction from entrenched groups of previous immigrants and municipal employees was decisively negative. In the sixties the political hegemony of the national Democratic party and Administration was threatened by the growing (and increasingly violent) disaffection of the 4 million-plus recent rural Southern black migrants to Northern cities. Accordingly, the federal government intervened directly in municipal politics with a series of programs (Model Cities, War on Poverty, OEO, Great Society *ad infinitum*) designed to increase the share of blacks in urban political power, services and economic rewards. Entrenched municipal-worker groups along with their ethnic and class allies responded by escalating their own wage and working-condition demands. In the end the blacks received modest gains, the entrenched white groups much more substantial gains, and the fiscal crisis of municipalities became acute.

Thus, in Secretary Simon's terms, the main beneficiaries of the increase in New York's level of expenditures were the "middle class." This view is clearly correct in part. Some significant portion of the $8 billion increase in New York City expenditures over the past decade has accrued to those who were already well paid and well treated city employees ten years ago. Moreover, some portion of the additional employees come from the same class and ethnic groups.

A fourth and directly contrary view closer to the first argument is offered by many of the city's politicians and some of its sophisticated bureaucrats. They argue that the increase in the city's expenditures has been primarily directed at increasing economic benefits to the city's most disadvantaged residents, primarily blacks and Puerto Ricans. They maintain that many of New York's existing employees in the mid-sixties and most of the additions over the past decade have come from these ethnic and economic groups. The primary motive for expansion has been a desire to re-establish political harmony by increasing the share of these groups in total economic rewards.

There is no doubt that both of these views are partially correct. It is not possible on the basis of information currently available to quantify the gains which were achieved by competing groups of blacks and whites, service providers and recipients, and so forth.

Most of the differences between these four explanations of the explosions in New York's budget and municipal budgets generally have to do with issues about the relative leverage over municipal government and rewards won by different economic interests. As always these are the most fascinating questions and the most difficult to answer. If we put aside these questions it is still possible to describe an important internal logic to New York's fiscal behavior. Without regard to the degree to which the city's government is controlled by and operated to benefit rich or poor, black or white, new or old, several propositions are nevertheless clear. The city's government, like virtually all institutions in our society, has sought to maintain and expand its own domain of influence. This in turn has necessitated maintaining and expanding the level of economic activity in the city which forms the basis for the city government's ability to command resources for its own use or the reward of its important constituents. In the past decade a precipitous decline in the New York economy, coupled with the proliferation of resource-capturing devices offered by the full bloom of inflation, conspired to make the city's government behave in much the same way as a variety of other governmental and private institutions did over the same decade.

The dimensions of the economic problem are clear. Over the decade ending in 1974, the number of private-sector job holders in the city declined by a spectacular 230,000 persons, or about 7.5 percent of the 1964 figure. Public employment by all governments and agencies, exclusive of the consolidated New York City government, was about unchanged. Not surprisingly, the total value of the city's economic activity before taxes, excluding the city's own budget and adjusted for inflation, also declined over the decade. After a deduction of increased federal, state and local tax burdens, this figure declines even more.

Whatever its intent, the effect of the tripling of the city's budget over the same decade was to substantially counteract the effects of this economic decline. The city alone added at least 132,000 people to its payroll, offsetting more than half the decline in employment which would otherwise have occurred. If we put the impact of the city's own budget expenditures back into the calculation made in the previous paragraph, we find that the aggregate pre-tax, after inflation level of economic activity in the city, actually increased slightly over the same ten years. From the point of view of many New York officials, a political and/or economic disaster was avoided by expanding the share of the city's budget in the total metropolitan economy from roughly one eighth to roughly one quarter. At the same time, the city government expanded its direct share of total employment from about 5 percent to 10 percent.

The new devices which were seductively and abundantly available to pursue these policies are also rather clear. However, I do not wish to belittle the creative efforts of many city officials who played leading roles themselves in developing and refining many of these devices. First there was the proliferation of federal grants and subsidies, beginning with urban renewal and highway programs in the fifties and growing to invade virtually every line of the city's budget during the Johnson and Nixon Administrations. A great deal of the city's remaining autonomy was lost in the process of accepting these funds, and the problem of financing matching portions remained.

One old technique for accomplishing the last task was to convert operating expenditures into capital expenditures. By New York State law the city is supposed to have a balanced operating budget. However, capital expenditures which are deemed to produce a stream of future services may be financed with long-term debt which creates a stream of future demands on operating budgets. In the end the real arbiters of what could be included in the capital budget were the large New York banks who were themselves the largest purchasers of city bonds and served as underwriters for the balance of such issues. The banks accommodated the city much as they accommodated corporations over the same period. Thus, for example, a job-training program heavily subsidized by the federal government and operated as a thinly disguised income-transfer program was financed out of the capital budget on the theory that it would produce a future stream of revenues to the city by reducing welfare rolls and increasing the number of employed taxpayers. Using the same reasoning, the city also added

$120 million of its vocational-education budget to the capital budget. This item alone accounts for more than one quarter of the entire amount of capital budget expenditures which have now been judged "improper."

In addition, the city sought and obtained numerous types of assistance from the state, as did most other cities during the same decade. Direct state assistance to the city's universities, health-care programs, school systems, housing programs and numerous other operations were either initiated or greatly increased. The city also sought, obtained and more than fully exploited the right to issue "budget notes" for the purpose of financing "seasonal" and similar cash-flow disparities. The city also came to be a virtually permanent issuer of several billions of dollars of notes, the repayment of which was pledged from anticipated tax collections or state or federal grants. The city regularly accrued real-estate and other taxes which were due but uncollected in calculating its balanced operating budget. In most cases these properties had been abandoned and the taxes were uncollectable. Nevertheless, notes were regularly sold and resold "anticipating" these tax collections.

The net result was that the city in fact operated at quite substantial deficits year after year and more than tripled its outstanding debt, to $13 billion by the end of 1974. Debt service requirements alone had grown to more than $1.5 billion, or about one seventh of the entire budget.

Aside from a variety of debt financing and outside subsidy devices, the other major device used by the city to expand its activities beyond its obvious means was the pension funds. Printing debt and exchanging it for borrowed money was one way to obtain funds for current expenses. Printing future promises was another way of expanding the rewards which could be used to mollify the city's militant unions and expanding employment faster than would have been possible if the city were constrained to using actual cash. The expansion of pension promises went hand in hand with the expansion of debt throughout the Empire in the last stages of inflation. The worst offender by far was the federal government, which offered such future rewards not only to its own employees but to most of the rest of the population through the Social Security system. None of these accumulating future liabilities was funded with current cash contributions. Rather, the federal government relied on its taxing authority to obtain the funds when they were needed. Indeed, Social Security taxes have risen more sharply than any other category of taxes over the past decade and will continue increasing rapidly if past commitments are to be honored.

To a large extent the city relied on the same future ability to tax. The $7 billion which it has contributed to its pension funds is less than half the amount that would be required to meet future obligations. In effect, the city has borrowed an additional $7 billion from future taxpayers to meet the past decade's payroll.

As was true with most other institutions, the city's grand strategy of the past decade proved to be internally contradictory and ultimately self-limiting if not self-defeating. Debt service itself became a current burden roughly equal to the entire deficit. The size of the city's outstanding debt began to clog the securities markets and make further debt financing increasingly difficult. The increasing tax burdens in the city and the fiercely high wage standards set by the city accelerated the flight of private-sector employers and taxpayers. The decline in real economic activity throughout the Empire caused a sharp acceleration in the decline of the private sector within the city. All of these problems compounded each other in a vicious circle. The city was thus a virtual sitting duck as the Empire-wide disinflation gathered momentum from the spring of 1974 through the spring of 1975.

THE MORNING AFTER

A virtual default has already occurred, as Roger Alcaly and Helen Bodian observe. (See selection #3.) All of the most visible actors seem to have reversed their positions on the question of default at least once since the issue was first raised in the summer of 1975. Only the city's politicians were consistent in their opposition. Yet the compromise which they have achieved relegates them to the role of mere administrators of a policy of retrenchment and discipline determined elsewhere. Their function seems much the same as the newly elected Democratic governors of California, New York and Massachusetts. The politicians seem at the least to have made a tactical error in underestimating the extent to which a precipitously declared default might have threatened the large New York banks and the rest of the power structure. The hasty response to such a fearsome event in February or March of 1975 might have been more generous to the city politically and economically.

The great banks, led by the Rockefellers' Chase Manhattan, have also played a confusing part. Technically, they precipitated the crisis with the questions they began to raise last February. It is not clear to what extent they were implementing a grand ruling-class strategy and to what extent they were protecting their narrow interests as banks against legal liability for their significant role in approving, purchasing and reselling the $13 billion of New York City debt which was outstanding. In any event, they ferociously resisted the notion of possible default throughout the spring and summer in Cassandra-like incantations and rapidly converged to a position of complacency about default by November.

My own guess is that the banks' role in precipitating the crisis was mostly dictated by myopic institutional concerns. They appear to have been the mere instruments of grander designs throughout recent history. By accommodating the increasingly excessive borrowing demands of domestic corporations and governments as well as the Eurodollar demands of overseas customers of domestic corporations, they substantially weakened the underlying economic strength of their positions. In the last five or six years they have been major borrowers themselves in order to finance the services they were called upon to provide for others. In my view their survival has increasingly depended upon the good graces of the Federal Reserve Bank and the major corporations whom they serve. The weakness of their position caused them to yield with less and less resistance to the demands of either regulators or major corporations for further credit extensions to real-estate-investment trusts or electric utilities and others. And these additional credits further weakened the strength of the banks. This analysis of the relative unimportance of the banks is confirmed by an analysis of their profits, employment and stock-market valuations relative to the major multinational manufacturing corporations.

The municipal unions have also vacillated on the question of default. In the spring of 1975 they were basically quiet and unconcerned, although they appeared to be opposed to a default. When default loomed in September and early October they exploited their temporary control over the situation through the pension funds and the apparent apprehension of the banks and politicians to effectively threaten to cause a default. By the congressional hearings in late October they were firmly in the anti-default camp, foreseeing every variety of national disaster if default was not avoided.

Even Gerald Ford and Arthur Burns have appeared to blow with the wind. First they were staunchly indifferent to the side effects of default and enthusiastic about the lesson it would teach the city. Then they appeared to waver. Then Ford reaffirmed his original position with determination. Only a month after that, he accepted the present compromise.

It might be more illuminating to examine what has actually been won and lost by the participants as a result of the quasi-default and what constraints operated on the conflicting forces as they reached the present uneasy equilibrium. Wages have been effectively frozen and a powerful precedent established for the major collective-bargaining sessions of 1976. More significant, the kind of accommodation which emerged after the thirties between major corporations and industrial unions seems already to have become effective in New York. The unions in effect have acquiesced in cutbacks of employment and other steps designed to improve worker productivity in exchange for an implicit guarantee of an organized job hierarchy and the maintenance of existing benefit and working-condition levels.

The city's appetite and ability for additional deficit financing has been severely curbed but not entirely eliminated. Cuts in every variety of service to every social and economic class have been achieved, and more are clearly ahead. Political and financial control of the city has been placed in the hands of the representatives of major private capitalist interests with lesser roles for representatives of the state and federal governments.

Holders of a substantial portion of the city's debt have had a relatively modest diminution in their financial position imposed upon them not too dissimilar from the most favorable terms they might have obtained in a full-fledged bankruptcy proceeding. The relative stature and importance of New York City banks has been diminished by comparison with banks in other money-center cities to the west and south. However, their basic ability to continue functioning has been completely spared.

The critical inflexion point in most of these struggles had to do with whether or not the city would be forced or permitted to actually repudiate part of the nominal value of its $13 billion of debt. In the end, an actual deflation would require that someone actually repudiate a portion of the tremendous debt created over the past ten or fifteen years. However, repudiations of debt have ripple effects in financial markets on vastly greater quantities of similarly situated securities. Moreover, the holders of most debt are the very wealthiest individuals and the most powerful financial institutions in America. Accordingly, the New York solution is not unlike those which have emerged for numerous other marginal debtors of the past decade. Underdeveloped countries and their domestic corporations, unable to repay Eurodollar loans; marginal domestic corporations, real-estate-investment trusts, big-city electric utilities, all unable to repay excessive domestic bank financing; and the major banks themselves, unable to demonstrate solvency by any conventional standard—all have been permitted to postpone and stretch out their obligations, to refinance at longer terms and lower interest rates. In short, all have avoided a direct admission or realization of an actual liquidation of poor credits previously extended.

For those interested in restoring the pre-inflation status quo, this is the razor-edged optimal path. It produces maximum deflationary effects, terrorizing labor and smaller capitalists. At the same time, it insulates major institutions from recognizing the losses attendant to actually liquidating any of the paper claims created at the end of the inflationary boom.

This game may work and appear to work remarkably well for a number of years. In the end it seems doomed by the inevitable re-emergence of the multitude of problems currently being swept under the rug. New York, for example, will have an even greater indebtedness (approximately $15 billion to $16 billion) at the end of its three-year "rescue" plan than it has now. The strength of its private economy is unlikely to be any greater than it is today. The elasticity of its tax revenues is unlikely to be less taut than today. The same might be said for Brazil and Zambia, Chrysler and Lockheed, real-estate-investment trusts and the Chase Manhattan Bank.

What then? One choice would be to bail out the debt with a new round of inflation. The dynamics of our current political direction and the interests of the most powerful institutions would seem to rule out that course. The alternative is to permit the liquidation of financial claims which has been avoided now. In my opinion, the fear of the consequences of such a choice, which constrained policy throughout the sixties and right through the present, was based on correct reasoning. Moreover, that reasoning will remain correct (even if forgotten) five or ten years from now when the paper obligations of the sixties are finally allowed to go up in flames. The conflagration will spread far beyond the confines of the original bonfire and the resulting holocaust will more nearly resemble 1929 than 1975.

3. New York's Fiscal Crisis and the Economy

ROGER E. ALCALY AND HELEN BODIAN

I. INTRODUCTION

New York City essentially defaulted in the spring of 1975. Insufficient funds were available to meet payrolls and debts that had become due, and no one would lend money to cover these immediate cash needs. Ostensibly, it was this "cash-flow" crisis that generated a series of stop-gap measures which were tantamount to default proceedings.

For more than a decade, the city's spending had exceeded its revenues, but it was always able to borrow to cover the deficit. The municipal-bond market had been generally receptive, allowing states and cities throughout the nation to finance expanding budgets through borrowing. Bonds issued by these governmental entities seemed safe, and their interest was tax-free. The banks were especially accommodating lenders. Not only were the tax-free bonds important elements in their portfolios, but as underwriters of the bonds, the banks profited substantially by reselling them at what amounted to a markup.

Over the decade, banks and bond investors continued to gobble up New York City securities, even as the obligations were increasingly converted to short-term paper. The city issued nearly $12 billion in short-term securities in 1971 and 1972 alone, a clear indication of fiscal danger. But it was not until early 1975 that the investment community suddenly lost its appetite, that the banquet turned to fiscal crunch.

This paper was written in March 1976. It is a substantially revised and expanded version of a paper originally written in September 1975. Many of the issues raised in this paper are elaborated on elsewhere in the book. In such instances in particular we have tended not to provide details or references.

Roger Alcaly teaches economics at John Jay College, City University of New York. Helen Bodian is an attorney practicing in New York City.

The first signals of impending municipal fiscal crisis appeared in the fall of 1974 when the city, undoubtedly affected by the acute financial problems of the state's Urban Development Corporation, began experiencing difficulty selling a variety of short-term notes. By December the city was forced to accept a record-high 9.476 percent interest rate for a $500 million loan. By April, city bonds were selling at two thirds of face value, the city's "A" credit rating was suspended by Standard and Poor's, and the city was unable to market a new note issue for $450 million. Only the state's last-minute advance of $400 million enabled the city to meet its debt and payroll obligations for the month. An advance of an additional $400 million kept things going through May.

In June, however, the state's rescue operations assumed a structural form of great significance with the creation of the Municipal Assistance Corporation, which was to function as an interim borrowing agency for the city. "Big Mac," as the agency became known, was authorized to issue $3 billion of its own securities, technically "moral obligations" of the state, with maturities of up to fifteen years and backed by revenues from the city's sales and stock-transfer taxes. The securities were designed to cover the city's borrowing needs through October, and at the same time, transform the city's debt structure in a longer-term direction. Most important, the legislation required the city to balance its budget in accordance with state-approved accounting practices.

II. DE FACTO DEFAULT

Most people believe that the Armageddon of default has yet to occur. Maintaining this illusion has not been difficult, since there was no final catastrophic struggle, only bits of scrapping between the protagonists. But actually, the process of default began on June 10, 1975, the day the state legislature passed the Municipal Assistance Corporation Act. On that day the city went into virtual receivership, and representatives of the city's major creditors took over. During receivership, if the debtor is not liquidated, it can be "reorganized" by its creditors. In New York, the creditors have had all the advantages of receivership without the problems of a technical default. And the city is being reorganized: cutbacks have been made, entire city agencies threatened, home rule has been relinquished, and new agencies and management "panels" are springing up. Predictably, the changes have hurt labor and the city's poor and middle-income residents the most, the creditors the least.

Cutbacks have included wage freezes for city workers, heavy layoffs among the uniformed services, imposition of productivity quotas on civil servants, raised fares for all public transportation, and heavy cuts in the budgets of the city's hospitals, schools and university system. The city is feeling the pressure again, as it did during Rockefeller's term as governor, to abolish free tuition at the City College and to end all forms of rent control.

On the other hand, there has been erratic consideration at best of other possible sources of funds. For example, no examination has been made of the practices of the Tax Commission, which is authorized to reduce real-estate assessments to landlords on the basis of hardship. (Landlords which qualified for this reduction in fiscal year 1975–1976 included the New York Stock Exchange, Morgan Guaranty Trust, Tiffany's, the *New York Times*, Getty Oil, General Electric, Rockefeller Center and the First National City Bank.) Nor was consideration given to a moratorium on service of all city debts (as proposed, for example, by the Ad Hoc Committee of Elected Officials for Social Justice). Moreover, MAC's difficulties in marketing its securities, combined with the expenditure cuts, only increased the burden of the city's debt service (17 percent of its budget before MAC's inception).

During this first phase of the city's reorganization, MAC's leverage in city affairs was derived from its statutory mission to raise $3 billion in an oversaturated and depressed municipal-bond market. In order to market new obligations, a great effort was necessary to convince the investment community that the obligations were secure. For this purpose, it was necessary that MAC be composed of trusted and influential members of the business and financial worlds. In turn these members, as representatives of the investment community, would propose the steps to be taken by the city in order to establish investor confidence. But the catch was that MAC could never assure the city and its relatively submissive unions that each capitulation would obtain a result, namely that investors would in fact buy the new bonds. And as reluctant investors held back, the interest on the bonds skyrocketed.

This initial phase of reorganization served several functions. While maintaining the illusions that default was on the horizon and that the suspension of democratic rule was a fair price to pay for the good offices of the investment community, the creditors bought time to maneuver into positions of greater strength. The city gained only month-to-month survival, while its fiscal plight provided a vehicle for a continued attack on social services and labor unions. And meanwhile, the public became accustomed to their city being managed by creditors.

The surrender of the city's financial management to creditors and the state was sealed on September 9, 1975, when the state legislature passed the Financial Emergency Act. This statute was enacted in response to the closing of the bond market to MAC securities, placing the city once more at the precipice of a "cash-flow" crisis. At the core of these emergency measures was a financing package of $2.3 billion for the city which included purchase of MAC securities by not only the conventional sources, such as banks, insurance companies and private investors, but also by city and state pension funds and by the state itself. (The state's financial situation deteriorated noticeably in the course of borrowing to meet its $750 million commitment to the scheme.) In this manner, the package ingeniously linked the destiny of the city, the state and their employees.

The key element of the legislation was the creation of a seven-member Emergency Financial Control Board dominated by state appointees and essentially empowered to administer the financial affairs of the city.[1] As Milton Friedman stated in early December 1975, "Mayor Beame is no longer in charge of New York, so it [his forced resignation] wouldn't make a difference one way or the other. New York City is now being run by the caretakers appointed by the state of New York. At the moment New York doesn't have any self-government."[2]

Alarms over default thus peaked and subsided in periodic waves,

---

[1] The Congressional Budget Office summarized the EFCB's financial responsibilities as follows:

By late October this board must approve a three-year financial plan that includes transition to a truly balanced budget by fiscal year 1978, a reduction in short-term city borrowing, the removal of expense items from the capital budget, and a growth in controllable spending (all but welfare, pensions and debt service) of not more than 2 percent per year. The board is also given the responsibility for estimating the city's revenues and keeping spending within these revenue limits; reviewing and approving major contracts; approving all city borrowing; extending, if necessary, the pay freeze on city employees through fiscal year 1977; and dispersing city revenues, but only after it is satisfied that the expenditures are consistent with the three-year fiscal plan. The powers of the board extend to the city's semi-independent agencies which provide elementary and secondary education, higher education, hospital, and other services.

[2] In *New York* (December 1, 1975).

while an undercurrent of reorganization processes steadily flowed in the direction of greater control of the city's finances by its creditors. It was this current which was determining the city's course, a course whose direction was clearly revealed by the declaration of a moratorium on the payment of principal on $1.6 billion in city notes maturing after December 10, 1975. The moratorium was part of yet another financial package, this time involving $6.8 billion and including additional purchases of city securities by the pension funds. (The pension funds subsequently suffered losses on the forced sale of other assets in order to make the purchases.) Also included in the package was a "roll over" of $1 billion in maturing city notes held by banks and institutional holders, new and increased city taxes and state aid, and a promise of $2.3 billion of federal "seasonal" loans which were designed to even out imbalances in the city's patterns of expenditures and receipts of revenues within the fiscal year.[3]

Under the moratorium, holders of maturing city notes were given

[3]The details have been outlined by the *New York Times* (November 30, 1975):

Purchase by the pension funds of municipal employees of $2.5 billion in city securities. The pension funds will receive more in interest than they have in the past, perhaps as high as 9 per cent, but they will lose money in liquidating parts of their portfolios to buy the city notes.

A "roll over," or refinancing, by banks and institutional holders of $1 billion in maturing city notes. The interest rate agreed upon is 6 per cent, representing a loss, though not considered large, in that holders would have earned higher interest on the notes as issued and also in the private market. Will the banks raise prices to customers to make up the loss? They have not said.

A moratorium on the payment of principal on $1.6 billion in maturing city notes. . . .

New tax revenues of $500 million through the fiscal year ending June 30, 1978, as a result of the new and increased levies voted last week. They are designed to raise $200 million a year.

The personal income tax for New York City residents will go up an average of 25 per cent, but will be progressive—the burden will fall most heavily on those better able to pay. A married couple with two children and an adjusted gross income of $25,000 a year will pay $437.45, an increase of $93.20. Income taxes will be reduced or eliminated for those earning less than $7,500. The income tax commuters pay will not go up. Estate taxes will rise, as will taxes on banks, cigarettes and various personal services.

An $800 million state advance and $400 million in debt service savings, the savings to be realized in two ways: the holders, primarily banks, of $1.8 billion in M.A.C. bonds have agreed to accept reduced interest rates paid on them. Pension funds have agreed to reinvest in city notes the amount of debt service or interest the city pays them.

Federal aid: it is needed for the $6.8 billion package to help the city bridge the occasional periods when its expenditures temporarily outstrip anticipated revenues. The loans are to be given on a short-term basis over a two-and-a-half-year period.

the "choice" of exchanging their securities for 8 percent, ten-year MAC bonds with the possibility of early redemption, or of keeping their notes at 6 percent interest without payment of the principal for up to three years. The moratorium has been challenged as an unconstitutional impairment of contracts. If the action is sustained, it could precipitate an unambiguous default. But even if the moratorium is upheld, the effects on money markets are likely to be substantially the same. Unilateral alteration of contracts rarely inspires investor confidence.

The ramifications of the city's financial difficulties and the externally imposed austerity program have been similar in kind, if not degree, to what could be expected as a consequence of an acknowledged default. Proposed modifications of the Federal Bankruptcy Act,[4] by clarifying procedures and responsibilities of the parties involved in municipal bankruptcies, might facilitate assessment of the impact of a fully consummated default on various sectors of the economy. But even with this kind of assistance, the multiplicity of factors involved and the fluctuation of their relative importance in any given context frustrates attempts at prediction. Nevertheless, we can identify several key areas of concern and consider some of the likely effects.

New York State and Other States and Localities. New York City's financial imbroglio has reverberated in the municipal-bond market so that other debt-encumbered states and localities have found borrowing to be increasingly formidable and expensive. It is difficult to determine to what degree New York's troubles are responsible, both because other factors have intervened to contribute to the rise in interest rates of municipal securities relative to those in other markets, and because these changes have been accompanied by greater investor selectivity in the market. (This translates into a distinct regional pattern of interest-rate differentials.) It is also difficult to estimate the extent to which the municipal-bond market has already

---

[4]Although we have used the terms interchangeably, there is a technical difference between default and bankruptcy. Default procedures for New York City are covered in the Financial Emergency Act and guarantee that all debts will eventually be repaid. Under the Federal Bankruptcy Act, on the other hand, 51 percent of the creditors must petition the court to initiate bankruptcy proceedings which would determine the precise financial adjustments to be undertaken. This program must be approved by holders of two thirds of all outstanding securities. The virtual impossibility of identifying holders of New York City obligations, however, severely limits the usefulness of the Federal Bankruptcy Act and has stimulated a series of proposed amendments.

discounted state and local fiscal problems so as to assess additional effects of an announced default. It has even been suggested that by reducing uncertainty, bankruptcy might ease access to the municipal-bond market, at least in the long run when immediate psychological effects have played themselves out.

We know that partly because of its financial commitments to the city, the state has not been able to borrow in capital markets since late 1975. But the contribution of the city to this state of affairs cannot be quantified because state agencies and the state itself have had their own budgetary problems. Although the state has taken a greater role in running the city, the financial community in turn has assumed an increased role in the overall affairs of the state as a result of the state's fiscal infirmities just as it has for the city. Thus, no matter where the wheel is entered and no matter which political entity propels it, the financial community is at the axle. As Steve Weisman has written:

> Of all effects of the fiscal crisis on governmental operations, perhaps the most remarkable is the new working relationship between the state and the banks. Not since the Depression has the private investment community had so critical a voice—and stake—in the daily workings of government.
>
> For months their main concern has been two crucial enterprises to resolve the overall emergency: the assembling of a $2.6 billion rescue package to refinance the faltering state construction agencies, and the state's drive to borrow $4 billion in the spring for its own operations and for the huge seasonal aid payments to cities, counties and school districts. Both partners have recognized that, if the state were to fail in either attempt, the banks, whose portfolios are bulging with state and state-agency securities, would be among those hurt most. And yet in both cases the New York City banks have resources to provide only a portion of the financing the state needs.
>
> Most significant about the state-banks relationship has been their combined effort to enlist other sources of financing to help the beleaguered state. Together they put pressure on the reluctant state comptroller, Arthur Levitt, to use pension-fund assets to help bail out the Housing Finance Agency and its sister agencies. Together they sought to persuade the Federal Government to grant mortgage insurance for state-financed and city-financed middle-income housing projects under the Mitchell-Lama program. And now, in an alliance of power and influence that will be tested in coming weeks, they will try to persuade the nation's 50 largest banks, as well as many corporations, to buy state notes for their own portfolios to insure that spring-borrowing needs are met on time. (*New York Times,* March 28, 1976)

Financial Institutions and Other Investors. Investors have already suffered capital losses on New York city, state and other local government securities. If default was actually declared, further losses would undoubtedly result, but the exact amounts and their distribution cannot be known. Precise data on the distribution of holdings of New York City securities by type of holder or income group are not available. However, it is safe to assume by inference from data on holdings of all municipal securities that noninstitutional holders are mostly in high-income brackets. Their losses would be cushioned by other sources of income as well as the tax-deductibility of their capital losses. Lower-income holders would suffer the greatest immediate impact, but they might find some small comfort in the fact that most debts of defaulting municipalities have eventually been covered.

Most attention has been given to the banks as holders of New York City bonds because the manner in which the banks respond to the calling of default could have greater economic repercussions. Banks hold 50 percent of all municipal securities. New York City banks have close to 25 percent of their equity capital and 5 percent of their assets in city securities. (About sixty smaller banks which are not members of the Federal Reserve System have more than half of their capital tied up in city obligations.) These proportions are not recklessly high until they are viewed in conjunction with the overall illiquidity of the banks and with the shakiness of their other loans. It would not take much to topple these storm-weakened structures; it is possible that one more cry in the forest, such as a declaration of the city's default, could cause a run on these banks. (We shall argue later that the financial precariousness of the large New York City banks left them little choice but to cut off additional credit to the city.)

A banking panic is one possibility should a legal default emerge. But the more likely possibility, less distinguishable from the state of affairs under *de facto* default, takes into consideration the declared role of the Federal Reserve System and the Federal Deposit Insurance Corporation. Both have indicated willingness to lend funds to banks endangered by a municipal default and to allow the banks to value city securities at pre-default levels for a period of six months.

The Economy. An overall picture of the economic effects of default combines the individual factors discussed above and their interactions. It is impossible to determine the additional impact of actual default in each of these areas, but already *de facto* default in New York City, combined with widespread state and local budgetary problems, has had significant nationwide repercussions. A recent survey by the Joint Economic Committee found that state and local governments expected to implement close to $8 billion of destabilizing (i.e., recessionary) tax increases and spending cuts in 1975. Although far from uniformly distributed across the nation, these measures are likely to exacerbate the overall recession or retard recovery, and hence further weaken the fiscal position of many state and local governments. Moreover, the tax increases and expenditure cuts imposed on the city in the name of fiscal restraint are likely to erode further the city's tax base. Businesses, including corporate headquarters like those of Union Carbide, Texasgulf and Cowles Communications which have recently announced plans to relocate, and middle-class residents are fleeing the city, thus compounding its fiscal troubles.

III. WHY NOW?

Although the cash-flow problem precipitated the city's spring crisis, it was itself the result of a more fundamental imbalance, a budget disparity between the city's expenditures and its revenues. This disparity persisted for eleven straight years before the city's option of borrowing in the open market was cut off. Even Mayor Beame has emphasized that the financial community always knew that deficit financing and accounting gimmickry were going on:

> The Bond Counsel, representing the banks, knew all these things. It must approve every issue—what it's for and where the revenues are coming from to support it. During this whole period the problem was known. But still the cash flowed in. No question on the part of the banks.[5]

Not only were there no questions from the banks, but the municipal and governmental bond departments of Salomon Bros., one of Wall Street's biggest bond dealers, continued to recommend the city's securities throughout 1971–1972, a period when the city's financial weaknesses were apparent. During that period William Simon—the same William Simon who, as U.S. Treasury Secretary, actively advocated withholding federal aid to New York, claiming that the city's default would create a "relatively short-lived disruption"—was personally in charge of Salomon's municipal and governmental-bond sales. (It can be argued that Simon and a veritable host of others involved in city budgetary manipulations and the marketing of city securities are liable under both civil and criminal statutes.)

The question which arises, aside from the problem of short-sight-

[5]"Interview/Abraham Beame," *Challenge* (September/October 1975).

edness of the financial community, is why, after a decade of deficit financing, it was the spring of 1975 when the city's days of reckoning finally arrived. Here it becomes necessary to view the city's difficulties in a larger context, for the answer to this question cannot be pieced together from an examination solely of recent events or of local fiscal practices.

A. LONG-TERM TRENDS

The United States has been experiencing an almost continual process of urbanization, whether we take that to mean an increase in the fraction of the population living in urban areas or an absolute growth in the number of city dwellers, since at least the first census in 1790. And since approximately 1920 a significant decentralizing tendency has been superimposed on the process of urban growth. There is widespread agreement on this point despite the fact that there are conceptual difficulties and lack of data for measuring "suburbanization" or decentralization of metropolitan regions. For example, as Mills points out,

Suburbanization proceeded rather quickly during the prosperous 1920's, when the use of automobiles for commuting increased rapidly. It proceeded slowly during the depression of the 1930's, and very rapidly during the prosperous war and postwar years after 1940. It is, however, notable that there is evidence of deceleration in the suburbanization process during the latest period.[6]

Conventional wisdom attributes the cities' fiscal debilitation to the character of the urbanizing and suburbanizing populations. Since World War II, large numbers of blacks, other minorities and low-income whites from rural areas migrated to central cities, and large numbers of middle-class city residents as well as businesses, primarily from manufacturing and the retail trades, fled to the suburbs. A clear geographical pattern of class divisions was consequently established,

[6]See Edwin S. Mills, *Studies in the Structure of the Urban Economy* (Johns Hopkins University Press, 1972), especially chapters 2 and 3. The quotation is from page 46. Similarly, he observes that the employment sectors were also suburbanizing steadily before World War I, but that "The most prominent and pervasive characteristic of urban economies in the United States is that residences are more suburbanized than production." Elsewhere he speculates that "the movement of people to the suburbs has attracted manufacturing employment to the suburbs rather than vice versa" (p. 47). For a useful summary of the evidence on suburbanization of employment and population, see Bennett Harrison, *Urban Economic Development* (The Urban Institute, 1974).

complicated somewhat by concentrations of "high level" corporate and financial activities and by the residences of the very affluent in "downtown" areas. For the National Advisory Commission on Civil Disorders, the migrations have been the cause of the "fourfold dilemma of the American city: Fewer tax dollars come in, as large numbers of middle-income taxpayers move out of central cities and property values and business decline; more tax dollars are required, to provide essential public services and facilities, and to meet the needs of expanding lower-income groups; each tax dollar buys less, because of increasing costs. Citizen dissatisfaction with municipal services grows as needs, expectations and standards of living increase throughout the community."

State and local spending have risen dramatically during the past two decades, more rapidly than any other sector of the economy, so that by 1974 they accounted for 11.6 percent of the gross national product, compared to 7.4 percent in 1954. But this increased spending cannot be directly attributed to the "rising needs" of the urban population. Frances Fox Piven has shown instead that while the migration to the cities began seriously after World War II, city expenditures did not rise precipitously until the mid-sixties, and with the exception of welfare, expansion of services to the poor did not account for a large fraction of these expenditures.

Part of the rise in state and local spending can be accounted for by structural characteristics of city-service activities and overall economic growth. The argument is by now well known and widely accepted. If we conceive of an economy whose economic activities can be divided into two groups, one whose productivity is rising relative to the other while wages are equalized between the sectors, then costs of activities in the "nonprogressive" sector will continually rise relative to those in the technologically "progressive" group. A large proportion of government services tend to be relatively stagnant technologically, while pay scales have become increasingly competitive with wages in the progressive sector of the economy. The implication for the cost of providing government services is clear. But in addition, the relative cost position of these activities deteriorates more rapidly the faster the rate of economic growth in the economy.[7]

---

[7]The classic reference for the basic formulation is William J. Baumol, "Microeconomics of Unbalanced Growth: The Anatomy of the Urban Crisis," *American Economic Review* (June 1967). The argument is integrated into O'Connor's more general

To satisfactorily explain the urban fiscal crisis, we need to study more than demographic trends and mere descriptions of technological change. We must also consider the political dynamics generated by these dislocations as well as the reasons for the particular form taken by technological developments. And to approach an understanding of these phenomena, we must examine the imperatives of capitalist economic development in the United States and the role of the state in the process of capital accumulation.

James O'Connor's *The Fiscal Crisis of the State* provides a useful framework for examining the interaction between governmental activity and the process of capitalist accumulation and growth. He argues that capital expansion requires active state participation and continual growth in government expenditures. However, concentrated private appropriation of the proceeds of growth makes it progressively more difficult for the state to finance its participation in the accumulation process.

This approach improves our understanding of the urbanization/-suburbanization phenomena and the fiscal strains which followed in their wake.[8] The massive population shifts of the post–World War II period were largely the result of the growing mechanization and concentration of American agriculture. Although lagging somewhat behind the rest of the economy, the transformation of agriculture has nevertheless attained impressive dimensions, aided by government policy ranging from permissiveness to active financing and encouragement of agricultural innovation as well as promotion of agricultural exports (whose competitive advantages stem in large part from the advanced state of U.S. agriculture).[9]

The Fiscal Crisis of the State (St. Martin's Press, 1973), which divides the economy into a monopolistic sector, a government sector and a "competitive" sector characterized by low rates of technological progress and low wages. In a similar framework, Peter Albin's article "Unbalanced Growth and Intensification of the Urban Crisis," in *Urban Studies* (June 1971), stresses the interaction between urban deterioration and rapid growth. He also shows that given a fixed relative concentration of progressive activities in a city's suburbs, the ratio of the suburb's tax rate to that in the city will fall, in the limit, to the proportion of city employment in the progressive sector and municipal services.

[8]For a more detailed discussion of many of these points, see Manuel Castells, "The Wild City: An Interpretative Summary of Research and Analyses on the U.S. Urban Crisis" (September 1975).

[9]On the recent "agricultural export drive," see R. Boddy and J. Crotty, "Food Prices: Planned Crisis in Defense of the Empire," *Socialist Revolution* (April 1975).

Similarly, the development of factory production and growing affluence among some segments of the working class encouraged the process of suburbanization. This process could not have occurred on the scale it did without governmental and corporate policies which promoted automobile transportation, such as the federal highway program, the construction policies of local public authorities like the Port of New York Authority and Triborough Bridge and Tunnel Authority, and the neglect and suppression of mass-transportation systems. Equally important were the policies which encouraged home ownership:

In the 1930's Congress made two fundamental policy decisions which remain basically intact to this day. The first was the complete restructuring of the private home financing system through the creation of the Federal Housing Administration (mortgage insurance); the Federal Home Loan Bank Board and Bank System (savings and loan industry); institutions like the Federal Deposit Insurance Corporation and the Federal Savings and Loan Insurance Corporation (insurance on deposits of commercial banks, mutual savings banks, and savings and loans associations); and finally, the Federal National Mortgage Association (secondary mortgage market). Creation of these institutions, resulting in the acceptability of the long-term, low down payment, fully amortizing mortgage and a system to provide a large flow of capital into the mortgage market, are probably the most significant achievements of the Federal Government in the housing area.[10]

This pattern of development had a direct impact on aggregate demand, and thus the relative prosperity of the postwar period. It also served to reinforce isolated living styles and wasteful modes of consumption, all of which were amplified by "multiplier" effects and by fragmented local political structures and patterns of local service provision.

The uneven nature of capitalist development was reflected both in the deterioration of cities relative to suburbs and in the dual character increasingly assumed by the central cities, which divided urban populations between the "downtown" areas and the rest of the city. The downtown, central business districts were the centers for top-level corporate activity and related financial and professional services. The isolated, centrally located high-rent residential areas housed some of those engaged in these activities. On the other hand, the outlying areas of the central cities became districts for "competitive" sector

[10]*Housing in the Seventies,* Hearings on Housing and Community Development Legislation, 1973, Part 3, House of Representatives Subcommittee on Banking and Currency, 93d Cong., 1st Sess. (Government Printing Office, 1973). Also cited by Castells.

activities and underpaid workers, as well as the largely nonwhite underemployed surplus population.

The interrelated sets of pressures generated by these divisions prompted, in response, government-financed "downtown" urban renewal and antipoverty programs of all varieties. Rather than leading to urban revitalization and a restoration of fiscal balance, the economic and budgetary impact of these programs proved to be destabilizing.

The mobility of capital and the uneven development which it engenders has not been limited to a suburban/urban framework. The internationalization of capital has a close parallel in regional shifts taking place within the United States, producing relative prosperity for the states and cities of the so-called Sunbelt, and depression and austerity in the Northeast and North Central regions of the country. As in the international arena, the wealth transfers which the "Southern Rim" area has enjoyed could not have attained current proportions without the selective and largely military-related disbursement policies of the federal government, which Seymour Melman has aptly titled "the Federal Connection."

B. THE NEW YORK FISCAL CRISIS AND THE BUSINESS CYCLE—A GENERAL CONSIDERATION

The long-term trends in urban growth and development have taken place against a backdrop of the crisis-ridden pattern of capitalist accumulation.[11] For example, between the Civil War and World War II the American economy experienced at least eleven downturns of significant, if varying, magnitude and duration. In the postwar period we have suffered through seven additional slides in economic activity, the current recession being the worst slump since the Great Depression. "To study crisis" is, as Maurice Dobb has put it, *"ipso facto* to study the dynamics of the system; and this study could only be properly undertaken as part of an examination of the forms of movement of class relations (the class struggle) and of the class revenues which were their market-expression."[12] Similarly, the fiscal crisis of much of urban America can only be understood as part of

[11]Much of the following discussion draws on, and sometimes quotes directly from, R. Alcaly, "Capitalism, Crises and the Current Economic Situation," *Radical Perspectives on the Economic Crisis of Monopoly Capitalism* (New York: Union for Radical Political Economics, 1975).

[12]Maurice Dobb, *Political Economy and Capitalism,* 2nd ed. (Routledge and Kegan Paul, 1972), pp. 80–81.

the class struggle and current crisis of American and world capitalism.

The crisis is rooted in declining profitability, for, fundamentally, capitalism is a system of production for profit rather than production for use. This means, of course, that anything which endangers profits will eventually lead to cutbacks in production and to rising unemployment—in short, to economic crises. Thus, the formal possibility of crises that exists in any economic system in which the acts of purchase and sale are mediated by money and hence are capable of rupture is vastly enhanced under capitalism, in which production will only take place if it expands the value of capital. Moreover, as Marx has emphasized, there are several systematic factors which operate in the course of capitalist economic development to depress profits and consequently aggregate economic activity. These elements turn the formal possibilities of crises into actual crises. And they can be seen to interact with one another in a manner which reinforces the overall crisis tendencies of capitalism.

The principal strands in Marxian crisis theory revolve around the effects of the reserve army of the unemployed on wages and profits, the ability of capitalists to realize full profits on all they produce or are capable of producing, and the generation of profits themselves. These crisis tendencies are generally referred to as crises arising from the exhaustion of the reserve army of the unemployed, realization crises or crises arising from underconsumption, and crises arising from the tendency of the rate of profit to fall, respectively.

In a sense the use of the terms "underconsumption" and "falling rate of profit" to denote alternative crisis tendencies of capitalism is misleading, since, like disproportionality among the various sectors, both occur during a crisis. The real questions in distinguishing among the various crisis mechanisms are whether the fall in the rate of profit is the cause of underconsumption or vice versa, and in the former case, whether the rate of profit fell because of the exhaustion of the reserve army or because of rising capital intensity of production which was not compensated for by a sufficiently rapid increase of productivity.

Despite fairly widespread agreement on the proposition that declining profitability, no matter how it originates, will eventually set off a cumulative process of declining production and employment, there is no such unanimity as to how this occurs. Nevertheless, empirical evidence confirms the development of a squeeze on profits in the course of economic expansion. The prolonged expansion of the sixties was no exception:

The evidence of this period dramatically supports the hypothesis, whether profitability is measured as a share, as a rate of return, or in dollars. Net profits before taxes as a percent of gross product originating in nonfinancial corporations rose steadily from 14.5 in 1961 to a peak of 17.0 in 1965, then fell steadily to a postwar low of 9.8 by 1970. Compensation of employees, on the other hand, declined from 65.1 percent in 1961 to 62.6 in 1965, rising thereafter to 65.1 in 1969 and 67.2 in 1970. As reported by Nordhaus, the rate of return on nonfinancial corporate capital rose from 11.8 percent (before taxes) in 1961 to 16.3 percent in 1965; it then fell steadily to a post-World War II low of 9.1 percent in 1970. Before tax corporate profits for all industries in current dollars rose from $50.3 billion to $82.4 billion between 1961 and 1966. They were $79.8 billion and $69.2 billion in 1969 and 1970, respectively. In real terms, they declined steadily and strongly from 1966 through 1970.

The full employment squeeze on profits means that continuous expansion would undermine the accumulation of profits. It is the profit squeeze, not inflation per se, which motivates capitalists to eventually demand restrictive macropolicies during periods of full employment. The fact that profits are lowest in recession has often been used to argue the preposterousness of the charge that recessions are desired by capital. Indeed they would prefer to avoid them. But the recession is a necessary condition for establishing the basis of the highly profitable first phase of the expansion and for avoiding the highly unprofitable consequences of sustained full employment. Recessions also provide the political context within which the government grants fiscal incentives to capital. Under the impact of recession-induced corporate tax reductions, the post-World War II period has witnessed a secular decline in effective corporate tax rates.[13]

The restorative function of crises is crucial to understanding the apparent irrationality of current government policy for the nation and New York. For Marx, "Permanent crises do not exist." Rather, "these contradictions [of capitalism] lead to explosions, cataclysms, crises in which by momentaneous suspension of labor and annihilation of a great portion of capital the latter is violently reduced to the point where it can go on."[14]

Key elements in the restoration of profits include the restraining

[13]James R. Crotty and Leonard A. Rapping, "The 1975 Report of the President's Council of Economic Advisors: A Radical Critique," *American Economic Review* (December 1975), pp. 797–98. The reference in the quotation is to W. Nordhaus, "The Falling Share of Profits," *Brookings Papers on Economic Activity*, 1974:1.

[14]The quotations are from *Theories of Surplus Value*, Part II (Progress Publishers, 1968), p. 497, and the *Grundrisse* (Penguin Books, 1973), p. 750, respectively.

effects of the recession on the demands of labor as well as the devaluation of capital goods and the consolidation of inefficient and unprofitable units in both the private and public sector of the economy, often but not necessarily a result of outright bankruptcy. Recognition of these central facts would appear to lie behind the present Administration's overriding fear of rekindling inflation and reluctance to stimulate the depressed American economy. By failing to come to the aid of the city at the present time, the federal government is guaranteeing budget policies on the local level which undermine the strength of 1975's tax reductions. At the very time that the New York experience was beginning to poison the credit market for the state and other municipalities, increasing the likelihood that they too will have to curtail spending, President Ford was reaffirming his determination to reverse the upward trend in social spending that "literally threatens our whole economy."

Yet this policy stance is not without its risks. Those who make policy in the interest of capital must balance the restorative effect of cycles on profits against the social unrest which is likely to accompany severe downturns and full restoration of profits. This balancing act, which O'Connor describes more generally as involving the contradictory objectives of maintaining profitable conditions for capital accumulation as well as ensuring the continued legitimacy of a fundamentally exploitative system, constitutes the real problem of "fine tuning" which crops up so often in discussions of government macroeconomic policy. In effect, many of the systems legitimizing social expenses of the sixties are now being pared in the interest of capital accumulation. Or as Richard Ravitch, architect of the rescue operation for New York State's Urban Development Corporation, told *Business Week* in September 1975, "The business of government in the 1970's will be to pay for the decisions of the 1960's." Just how essential these legitimizing expenses were to the maintenance of social harmony remains to be seen in the resistance to their decimation.

Strategies for combating the nation's economic crisis are mirrored in New York City. The exception in New York's case is that representatives of dominant corporate and financial institutions have been brought in specifically to run the city and directly negotiate with the city's unions. Their faces—like that of otherwise exposure-shy Felix Rohatyn—have frequently been gracing the front pages of New York's newspapers. Rohatyn is a former governor of the New York

Stock Exchange, general partner in the prestigious investment bank-ing firm Lazard Frères & Co. and is generally credited with having played a leading role in the growth of the giant conglomerate ITT. Significantly, Rohatyn has also been part of a general movement toward corporate/governmental planning as a means of resolving the current economic crisis.

State and local debt-payment problems have not been unusual in the American economy. And as might be expected, the incidence of payment difficulties exhibits a clear cyclical pattern, at least with respect to the major downturns in the economy. The depressions of 1837–1843, 1873–1879, 1893–1899 and 1929–1937, like the current one (which also contains a strong inflationary component), have exacerbated state and local fiscal problems, leading, in turn, to auster-ity measures which have reinforced the overall declines. In short, the paradoxical nature of New York's current plight is neither unique nor surprising: a national economic recovery would appear to be necessary but not sufficient—recall our earlier discussion of unbalanced growth, regional economic shifts and the plight of cities—for recovery in New York, yet the disciplinary measures being imposed on the city, and their repercussions throughout the economy, decrease the likelihood of an immediate and strong expansion.

Several recent developments may have strengthened the relation-ship between the state and local sector and the economy at large. First, the increased relative size of the state and local sector implies a similarly enlarged economy-wide impact. As already noted, by the beginning of 1975 state and local expenditures had grown to close to 12 percent of GNP; at year-end they were running at about 16 percent of all economic activity compared to approximately 8 percent twenty years earlier. Moreover, state and local employment accounts for about 14 percent of all employment, while many locally provided goods and services like education are crucial for developing the econo-my's growth potential.

Second, the relatively stable pattern of growth in the state and local sector during the postwar period seems to have been eroded by changes in the sources of state and local revenues which have left them more vulnerable to the vagaries of the capitalist business cycle. States and localities have greatly increased their reliance on intergov-ernmental aid: between 1960 and 1973, state and locally generated revenue rose by almost 250 percent, yet federal aid increased almost twice as rapidly and now accounts for about a quarter of state and local budgets; similarly, state aid to local governments increased by 320 percent in the same period. These changes have been accompanied by a transformation in the tax sources of state and local revenues. Local governments have increased their reliance on more cyclically volatile sales and income taxes (as opposed to property taxation), while income taxation has increased in importance for state governments (compared to taxation of sales).[15]

The net result of these twin developments, combined with the severity of the current recession, has been a reversal in the post–World War II ability of state and local budgetary policies to mitigate the effects of recession. And while Citibank takes a relatively sanguine view of the situation, noting that "state and local governments are near the tail end of a famine composed of the effects on tax receipts of a severe national recession and relatively conservative federal policies on aid," a recent survey by the Joint Economic Committee has found that state and local governments will undertake close to $8 billion of destabilizing tax increases and spending cuts in 1975.

As could be expected, the impact of these cutbacks is not distributed uniformly across the country. Eighteen high-unemployment states are being forced to make 85 percent of the cutbacks, while municipalities with higher than average unemployment rates have been forced into budget adjustments five times as severe as those undertaken by cities with less than average unemployment. Those cities and states most severely affected are located in the Northeast and North Central regions of the country, while the "newer" cities and states of the agricultural and oil-rich South and West are enjoying relative prosperity, helped along by federal and defense policies.

The impact of the inflation/recession on New York's fiscal situation was particularly severe. In part this can be explained by the fact that the city's revenues are highly sensitive to the business cycle, although New York's heavy reliance on sales and income taxes means that its revenues hold up relatively better in the face of inflation than do the revenues of cities more dependent on the property tax. Yet the city's devastating job loss—500,000 since 1969—seems to be far in excess of what might have been expected as a result of national

[15]"The Cities and States: Riding a Fiscal Yo-Yo," *Monthly Economic Letter* (First National City Bank), August 1975.

and regional trends. Jason Epstein has argued persuasively that the explanation should be sought in the counterproductive programs of large-scale urban renewal and the "construction complex—the builders, the autonomous agencies, the federal and state bureaucracies, the banks—that generated the patronage, by which the politicians attempted to dominate the city's 'hopelessly split up races and factions.' "

C. Closer to Home—Debt Expansion, the New York Fiscal Situation and the Business Cycle

1. Debt Expansion and the Banking System

"The U.S. economy," *Business Week* proclaimed in its special issue on the "debt economy" (October 12, 1974), "stands atop a mountain of debt $25 trillion high—a mountain built of all the cars and houses, all the factories and machines that have made this the biggest, richest economy in the history of the world." Moreover, the debt explosion is primarily a postwar phenomenon, most highly concentrated in the last fifteen years:

The stunning thing about the Debt Economy is how rapidly it grew. In 1946, the total debt of the U.S., public and private, was only $400-billion, and nearly 60% of that represented U.S. Treasury debt. But in 1946 the U.S. had an economy starved of the good things in life by depression and war. Consumers raced through the liquid assets they had piled up during the war and, having spent them, borrowed so they could keep on buying. To meet their demands, corporations began piling up debt at an accelerating clip. Meanwhile, federal spending—and borrowing—stayed high, and borrowing by local government became a new fact of life for the financial markets.

Yet what happened during the 1940s and 1950s was only a prelude to what happened after 1960. It took 15 years, from 1946 to 1960, for total U.S. debt to double, but only 10 years, from 1960 to 1970, for it to double again. The key economic indicators—gross national product, personal income, corporate profits, and the like—have all grown by 500% or so since World War II. The key debt indicators have all grown by three and four times that amount, and the sharpest gains have come since 1960.

Corporations have tripled their debt in the past 15 years. Treasury debt, which hardly grew at all in the late 1940s and 1950s, has jumped by $180-billion since 1960. Installment debt, mortgage debt, and state and local government debt have all climbed by 200% or more since 1960, and the debts of federal agencies have climbed by more than 1,000%. New demands for money bred new sources: the commercial paper market, which was a nickel-and-dime affair until the 1960s, and the Euro-currency markets, which were not even born until the 1960s. Leasing became a billion-dollar business during the 1960s. The neighborhood bank became a multinational bank holding company that frequently became as voracious a borrower of funds as the companies to which it lent.

It is not the dramatic rise in indebtedness per se which has generated what the *Morgan Guaranty Survey* (November 1974) conservatively described as "a considerable amount of worry in the nation." Rather, it is the fact that the rapid expansion of debt, coupled with the economic downturn and rapid inflation, has produced an increasingly illiquid as well as fragile financial structure, one increasingly dominated by debt obligations of shorter duration. A "healthy" economic system generates sufficient income—profits in the case of businesses and revenues for governmental units—to meet payment obligations, or it contains cash reserves or easily convertible financial assets which are not essential to operations and are ample to meet temporary shortfalls in income. Otherwise, meeting payrolls, making interest payments and fulfilling other commitments requires either curtailing operations or increased borrowing, generally on increasingly onerous terms. Ultimately the process of debt expansion has to validate itself; that is, generate future income which is adequate to meet future obligations, including, of course, the obligations of increasing indebtedness, or else it will precipitate an economic collapse. The debt-ridden American economy is far closer to the latter eventuality than to the former.

In an expanding economy there are certain advantages which accrue to corporations that raise capital by debt rather than by issuing stock, principally increased leverage and tax advantages, since interest payments are tax-deductible to the corporation, while dividends are not. But the opposite would appear to be the case when the economy goes into reverse. Thus, the decline in profit rates for United States nonfinancial corporations which began in 1965 made it increasingly difficult for them to service their growing debt burdens without going further and further into debt. The U.S. economy was caught in a vicious cycle: increased dependence on short-term borrowing and bank loans was both a response to the impending crisis and a factor in its continued development. Growing interest burdens not only add to inflationary pressures as corporations are forced to raise prices in order to meet these and other obligations, but also compel the Federal Reserve to expand the money supply whenever these interest obligations threaten a financial collapse. But such actions can only avert a severe depression at the cost of renewed inflation, growing indebtedness and greater financial fragility, conditions which cannot persist indefinitely.[16]

Parallel to the erosion of corporate liquidity has been a similarly steep rise in indebtedness on the part of banks, consumers and all levels of government. In all cases the process of debt expansion has proceeded more rapidly than the growth in incomes, thus requiring more and more borrowing of an increasingly short-term nature. Nationwide, states and localities have accumulated more than $200 billion in debt, more than half in the last ten years. The recession of 1969–1970 and the current dose of recession and inflation exacerbated fiscal imbalances and increased city and state reliance on short-term capital markets in particular. From the beginning of 1974 through September 1975, close to $50 billion was borrowed short-term.

The increase in short-term borrowing throughout the economy could not have been accomplished without the active participation of the banking system. But this accommodation, profitable as it may have been, has produced a hierarchal structure of financial institutions—weaker elements with more questionable financial practices

[16]On financial fragility and the inflationary constraints it imposes on Federal Reserve policy, see Hyman Minsky, "Financial Resources in a Fragile Financial Environment," *Challenge* (July/August 1975), and Edward J. Kane, "All for the Best: The Federal Reserve Board's 60th Annual Report," *American Economic Review* (December 1974).

In an excellent analysis of recent inflation, Robert Zevin also treats many of the issues considered above. As he put it:

The result of this [debt expansion] process, compounded by inflation, is to increase the financial vulnerability of households, businesses, governments and banks. The further the process continues, the more these paper liabilities and assets become multiplied by serving as the foundation for the creation of still more liabilities and assets; the lower becomes the margin of equity available to businesses, banks and households to absorb any period of economic reversals; and the more the soundness and collectability of debts and other liabilities become dependent on the continued creation of new money and new paper assets, as well as the maintenance of stable or rising commodity prices. The obverse of all this is that the system becomes more and more vulnerable to a major chain reaction of financial disasters and collapses in response to less and less severe moderations in real economic activity or the rate of price increases. Hence government central banks and private banks become more and more determined to make good on their past excesses by extending, reextending and multiplying them in a variety of old and complexly new ways, all of which compound and accelerate the rate of inflation and the financial vulnerability of the entire system. ("Inflation: Its Roots and Fruits," *Working Papers for a New Society* [Spring 1975])

drawing credit from the core—which is increasingly illiquid and vulnerable to "domino" effects.

Harry Magdoff and Paul Sweezy[17] have documented the erosion of bank liquidity, resulting from:

(1) "An expansion of bank lending activity beyond any traditional understanding of the so-called fiduciary responsibility of the banks. . . . While there is no trustworthy guide to the 'proper' ratio of loans to deposits, the persistent rise in the ratio, especially since 1970, reveals that even apart from their responsibility as safekeepers of other people's money, the banks are fast approaching the absolute limit (100 percent) of the deposits that could be loaned out. Thus, . . . by the end of 1974 the large commercial banks had committed 82 percent of their deposits to loans; the same pattern is seen in the large New York City banks—at the heart of the country's main money market. To see this in perspective, it should be noted that the highest ratio of loans to deposits in U.S. banks between 1900 and 1970 was 79 percent (and that in only one year, 1921); in 1929 the ratio was 73.1 percent."

(2) The introduction and expansion of "a new technique of lending, called 'standby letters of credit.' (See *Business Week*, February 16, 1974, p. 120.) For a fee, they guarantee the IOUs issued and sold on the commercial paper market by big corporations. In other words, the banks commit themselves to paying the borrowed money if the corporations default. Since it is the financially weaker corporations that need such bank guarantees in order to sell their IOUs, this type of 'indirect loan' is itself of the shakier variety. These letters of credit are not reported on the balance sheets of the banks. . . . If they were included, the 1974 percentages of loans to deposits would be even larger than those shown."

(3) Increased bank borrowing "in order to enable them to indulge in their furious rush to lend." The sources of these borrowed funds include other banks (Federal funds and Eurodollar borrowing) and certificates of deposit (CDs). "Funds raised in this fashion [CDs] are used to create new loans by the banks which, in addition to being usually of longer duration than the life of the CDs, do not necessarily mature at the same time. This puts the banks under constant pressure to refinance the CDs when they become due, hopefully by issuing still more CDs."

Of particular importance is the fact that large New York City commercial banks are even more illiquid than large American commercial banks in general. Their short-term borrowing, more than 40 percent of which consists of short-term CDs, represents 65 percent of their outstanding loans compared to almost 50 percent nationwide.

Not only are banks alarmingly debt-encumbered, but large quantities of outstanding loans are of clearly questionable character. Martin

[17]"Banks: Skating on Thin Ice," *Monthly Review* (February 1975).

Mayer[18] has identified four major categories of bank loans where substantial losses "must be expected":

(1) "Notes and bonds of New York City, New York State and other New York governmental bodies" represent potential bank losses of "about $2 billion."
(2) "Loans to real estate investment trusts [REITs] and to real estate developers" represent potential bank losses of "about $4 billion."
(3) "Loans to European shipowners and shipyards for the construction of tankers and liquefied natural gas vessels" represent potential bank losses of "perhaps $2 billion."
(4) "Loans to foreign governments, mostly but not exclusively in under-developed countries" represent potential bank losses of "perhaps $3 billion."

To these estimates must be added potential losses on recession-induced personal and business failures such as the celebrated bankruptcy of W. T. Grant, which left banks holding $640 million in Grant's paper, almost half of which was on the books of Chase, Citibank and Morgan Guaranty Trust.

These developments provide the necessary background for understanding the prevalence of widespread fears of a financial panic and the consequent closing of the municipal-bond market to New York City in the spring of 1975. Writing in July 1975, Edward J. Kane summarized the situation:

Whether or not investors' fears are exaggerated, they cannot be called unfounded. A considerable amount of doubtful paper is currently outstanding, much of it concentrated in the hands of large New York City banks. The roster of most seriously troubled borrowers includes New York City, the New York Urban Development Corporation, W. T. Grant, Chrysler, and the bulk of the nation's real-estate investment trusts (REITs), but less spectacular weaknesses characterize a number of other firms. Over the long haul, a substantial portion of the bonds and bank loans of the weakest of these enterprises is going to have to be written off. A general economic turnaround cannot repair the fortunes of firms whose markets have been ruined by shifts in relative prices. The manageable policy problem concerns *when* to realize these write-offs and *how* to prevent such realizations from undermining the faith of self-insuring depositors (whose deposit holdings exceed the FDIC's $40,000 limit) in the commercial-banking system. The banks' own strategy (most evident in their handlings of REITs) seems to be to build up their loss reserves and to carry troubled institutions as long as they can, emphasizing all the while the "valuable" collateral tied up in these firms and how the

[18]"Banking: Good Money on Bad Loans," *New York Times Magazine* (November 9, 1975).

debtors' capital and subordinated debt protect the banks' position. This policy conflicts with the mission of the SEC, which seeks to ensure that investors are provided with an accurate assessment of changes in the recoverability of a bank's loan portfolio. Somewhat unconvincingly, federal agencies responsible for regulating banks have sought to deflect SEC criticism by arguing that banking is a "special" business where facts are hard to interpret and where indiscriminate disclosure of facts has high social costs.

Large New York City banks have roughly $9.2 billion in capital. At the moment New York City has about $6 billion in notes outstanding, about $1.25 billion of this held by large New York City banks (about twice the amount of Penn-Central debt that these banks held in the June 1970 crisis). REITs owe banks about $12 billion, about half of this to large New York City banks. Although the eventual loss on NYC banks' REIT loans may run two to three times the amount of NYC debt to these banks, the $1.25 billion is on a quicker fuse. As a possible point of entry for financial panic, NYC banks' holdings of NYC debt are very threatening. If NYC were to default on its debts, the banks could not control the timing of the accompanying asset write-offs. Under current federal regulations (which authorities have been trying to amend), NYC default would require an immediate revaluation of bank holdings of NYC debt at their post-default market value. This write-down would simultaneously eliminate a substantial portion of these banks' reported net worths and reduce the amount of credit they could raise by offering these questionable securities as collateral for subsidized loans from the Fed. The first consequence increases the probability of a resulting run on these banks by uninsured large depositors, while the second consequence would make it harder for the banks to cope with sizeable deposit outflows.

Unlike the runs of the 1930s, which took place largely through the withdrawal of currency, a modern run would take the form of a "clearings drain." Depositors and sellers of federal funds would become increasingly selective. Both at the domestic and foreign branches of threatened banks large depositors would move demand deposits to other banking connections and let CDs run off.

Even if U.S. government accounting rules were relaxed to allow banks to control the timing of write-downs (e.g., by allowing a six-month grace period), a NYC default would lead depositors to question the continuing ability of the banks to carry slow loans to REITs and such troubled firms as W.T. Grant and Chrysler. ("Why 'Bad Paper' Worries Economic Policymakers," *Bulletin of Business Research* [July 1975])

Before examining the nature of the municipal-bond market and its closure to New York City in more detail, it seems appropriate to consider briefly why such a fragile financial structure developed in the first place. The competitive pursuit of profits appears to be the most plausible explanation for the frenzied expansion in bank lending activity during the sixties and early seventies. Nevertheless, one must still explain why competitive pressures generated such short-sighted and intense pursuit of immediate gain. John Mage has suggested a hypothesis which appears to explain post-1970 behavior. Amendments to the Bank Holding Company Act passed in 1970 eliminated one-bank holding companies and relaxed the conditions under which bank-owned holding companies could acquire other banks. These provisions greatly intensified bank-merger activity, which accelerated the pursuit of short-run profits. The increased pressure to show short-run profits arises because profitability, particularly when amplified by impressive price/earnings ratios, is the key both to making acquisitions and to fending off hostile takeover attempts.

2. New York City and the Municipal-Bond Market

The increasingly precarious financial positions of both New York City and its major banks precipitated the withholding of credit and the crackdown on social services and municipal workers. These financial developments were part of general economic trends in the American economy. Similarly, the attack on workers and living standards is consistent with the relatively passive response to the deepening recession adopted by the federal government. The coincidence of national and local policy does not, however, rest on conspiratorial designs, although the personal and institutional connections between the principals is impressive and the vanguard role of labor in New York is well known. Narrow pursuit of self-interest both with respect to the general crisis of American capitalism and its specific manifestation in New York City provides sufficient explanation.

When placed on a comparable basis, New York City's expenditures are not too different from those of other large cities. Nevertheless, New York does spend more per capita than any other major city with the exception of Washington, D.C. This is primarily because New York provides services which are either financed by other jurisdictions in other cities or not provided by them at all. These jurisdictional and service-provision differences show up in the fact that New York's borrowing, particularly its short-term borrowing, far exceeds that of other local governments.

New York's short-term borrowing has mushroomed like that of no other city. Debt servicing—$1.8 billion in 1975 compared to $644 million in 1969—now occupies nearly 17 percent of the city's budget and costs more than police, fire and environmental protection. Large New York City banks play two important and related roles in the market for the city's securities: they are both underwriters and major holders of city obligations. As has been noted, commercial banks now hold about half of all outstanding state and local securities. But this figure represents smaller participation in the municipal-bond market than was the case only five years earlier. Beginning in 1972, commercial banks and other institutional investors began to reduce their acquisition rate of holdings of a rapidly expanding volume of municipal offerings, and in the first quarter of 1975 they began to liquidate some of these securities. When the commercial banks pulled out of the municipal-bond market in early 1975, it compelled the New York banks to refuse to underwrite further issues of city notes because of the impact of this move on other investors and, more importantly, because of a basic "thinness" in the municipal-bond market.

The attractiveness of the municipal-bond market to investors derives from the tax-free status of interest on these securities. But the value of this benefit varies directly with income; in order to obtain an equivalent after-tax rate of return, the lower-income investor—assuming he or she can afford to purchase securities which are sold in $5,000 denominations—must be offered a higher yield. To attract lower-income buyers, interest rates must be raised, which in turn confers a bonus on more affluent investors.[19] Similarly, large groups of institutional investors such as pension funds, foundations, colleges and mutual savings banks gain little from the tax-free nature of municipal obligations because of low or nonexistent tax burdens. And since most municipal-bond offerings are split into a large number of issues, the resulting loss of liquidity must be compensated by higher yields. All of these factors are compounded in the case of New York City obligations by the fact that interest on these securities is also exempt from city and state taxes for holders who reside in the city.

The creditworthiness of municipalities is thus intimately linked to the availability of lenders and the terms that they require. In addition to the structure of the municipal-bond market, two other factors worked against New York and other hard-pressed localities. On the one hand, these jurisdictions were competing for funds in a rapidly expanding municipal-bond market which permitted greater investor

[19]For an excellent description of the municipal-bond market which elaborates many of the points under consideration, see Sanford Rose, "The Trouble with Municipal Bonds Is Not Just New York," *Fortune* (December 1975). Rose compares the present system of subsidizing municipal borrowing with a more efficient alternative—elimination of their tax-free status combined with direct subsidies—as well as other ways of improving the market.

selectivity. One of the factors contributing to the rise in municipal offerings has been the issuance of pollution-control bonds, which finance pollution-control equipment for private corporations, as a means of attracting industry and manufacturing. Offerings of pollution-control bonds have been estimated at $4 billion to $7 billion for 1975, compared with total municipal issues of $65 billion. At the same time, municipalities whose growing deficits were primarily the result of the recession rather than of stimulative economic policies were also competing for funds with the federal government.

Seen from this general perspective, the significance of commercial-bank curtailment of their purchases of state and local securities seems clear. The reasons for the commercial-bank withdrawal from the municipal-bond market must, in turn, be viewed against the tremendous expansion of their lending operations and their growing illiquidity, which were described in the preceding section. Two points need to be emphasized. First, the development of new, highly profitable (at least in the short run) avenues for bank investments tended to minimize the relative attractiveness of tax-free municipals. For large banks, like other major American corporations, a major recent area of expansion has been overseas. Writing about Citibank in *Fortune*, Sanford Rose put it this way:

Citibank is a different animal because it is far and away the most powerful U.S. bank overseas. The margins on many types of loans are substantially more attractive abroad than in the U.S., where bank lending has long been a low-margin, high-volume operation. During 1973 and most of 1974, domestic margins fell still further as the cost of lendable funds rose dramatically. Large banks that were confined to U.S. bases fared poorly in comparison with those that could roam the world for customers . . . Perhaps the most startling fact of all is that Citibank makes 40 percent of its profits in the underdeveloped world. (March 1975)

Similarly, 1970 amendments to the Bank Holding Company Act enabled banks to engage in highly promising activities like leasing, tanker financing, and consumer financing through credit cards and consumer finance companies.[20]

As these activities, like the budgets of municipalities, soured under the dual assault of inflation and recession, bank-loan losses mounted, lessening further their need for tax-exempt securities. Moreover, confronted by severe liquidity problems, the banks could not afford to

[20]See Louise Billotte and Robert Cohen, "The Role of the Financial Community in the NYC Fiscal Crisis." Unpublished paper, 1975.

simultaneously perform holding operations on all their ailing debtors. In terms of the magnitude of the risks involved, New York City was the most vulnerable of the banks' dependents. No one else but the banks existed to protect their sizable investments in REITs. But the banks could expect, or at least hope, that the state and federal governments would save the city's creditors. Yet the banking system itself remained vulnerable to an outright default by the city, a weakness which the city and its unions failed to exploit. And for this we have all had to pay even as the banks converted their shorter-term, less secure city notes to safer obligations of the Municipal Assistance Corporation.

4. The Last Days of New York

JASON EPSTEIN

Fifteen years ago New York was still mainly a manufacturing city: in fact it had more industrial employees than any other city in the world. Nearly half the people here worked full time and nearly a million of them, or more than a quarter of the work force, worked at the production of goods. Eighty thousand New Yorkers worked in the food trades, baking bread and brewing beer for the city's nearly eight million citizens. A quarter million worked in the apparel industry. More than 20,000 ground lenses and made scientific instruments. One-hundred twenty-five thousand worked in the printing trades.

But New Yorkers did so many other things too that you could live here for years and never think of New York as a manufacturing city at all. Most of the city's industry was tucked away in old lofts in odd corners of Manhattan or in small plants in Long Island City or Brooklyn. There were no great steel mills or automobile factories to dominate the city's economy or its landscape. More than a third of the city's factories employed fewer than twenty people each. New York's industry was nondescript and, like much else that supplied the city's vitality, largely invisible.

It was one of New York's pleasures then that you could stay pretty much in your own compartment, painting pictures or teaching school or selling whatever you sold while the rest of the city became a kind of backdrop, often colorful, often squalid, usually a blur—something you noticed from the window of a bus or an airplane. You didn't have to think about it if you didn't want to, and why would anyone want to? In the outer boroughs there are thousands of New Yorkers who almost never come into what they call the city, by which they mean Manhattan. You can live here for a lifetime and never notice that New York is bounded by one of the world's great rivers or that it is

Reprinted from the *New York Review of Books* (February 16, 1976). Jason Epstein lives in New York City. He is the author of *East Hampton: A History and Guide.*

made up of hundreds of settlements with names like Tottenville, Corona, and Ravenswood or that it has, or once had, dozens of downtowns.

For years the city seemed to run itself by a kind of anarchic common sense. No doubt this was much of its charm for people who came here from smaller, less intimate places. New York lent itself to privacy, to eccentricity, and thus to a kind of freedom unavailable elsewhere. If New York was often a cold city where hardly anyone cared if you lived or died, it was also a city that left you alone to work out your own salvation. The city, for all the socialist talk of its intellectuals and the kaleidoscopic mergers of the alien corporations that had begun to operate here, was still by 1960 or so a kind of living museum of pre-monopoly capitalism: an anachronism as it was to turn out, but still in retrospect the climactic event in the history of those bazaars that arose centuries ago in Venice and Ravenna and moved slowly westward by way of Antwerp, Paris, and London. In New York there was almost nothing that couldn't be bought or sold or made or put together or created or destroyed, including of course the city itself.

Yet as hermetic and various as life here was in those days, it was by no means uniformly so. For all its diversity and toughness, New York, along with the rest of the world, was being drawn up in spasms of conglomeration, as in some great geological shift. Businesses, neighborhoods, whole cities and towns were abolished or fused together in unlikely new arrangements. Sometimes this happened with the help of government, as when new federal and state highways funneled the city's former taxpayers out to the synthetic new suburbs. Sometimes it happened according to the designs of bankers and developers and the brutal logic of balance sheets. But always the cause appeared to be remote, obscure, and autonomous. By the end of the decade, nearly everyone in the city—the landlords, the tenants, the bankers, the welfare clients, even the bureaucrats themselves—complained that something called "they" was running the city and running it badly.

By the middle sixties you could see the city and its people changing all around you. New construction was going up everywhere, herding the old residents and their businesses into ever narrower enclaves, or driving them out of the city altogether. Meanwhile the expanding ghettos were overflowing with refugees driven here by the mechanization of Southern agriculture and by Southern welfare practices that made Northern cities seem deceptively generous by contrast. In the late fifties, Southern legislators joked that the meager welfare programs which they diligently enforced provided one-way bus tickets north for their unwanted blacks. Between 1960 and 1970 the proportion of blacks in the city had risen from 14 percent to 21 percent, most of them trapped here by a city that didn't need their labor and that had, in fact, begun to export its menial and routine work to less costly labor markets, often to the same areas which these new arrivals had recently abandoned.

In the past twenty years the proportion of New Yorkers with incomes beneath the national median has increased from 36 percent to 49 percent. Between 1960 and 1970 a million or more middle-class taxpayers, including 600,000 Jews, had moved out. As the sixties progressed, the city's remaining bourgeoisie was facing extinction as it struggled and fell in the damp embrace of fresh cement, in the transistorized roar of the ghetto and the rising cost of everything, especially the cost of privacy which once could have been had here almost for the asking but which had now increasingly become the privilege of the very rich, more isolated than ever in their midtown compound.

In 1960, 140 of the country's 500 largest corporations had their headquarters here. By 1975, forty-four of them had left, including Borden, Texaco, Allied Chemical, and Nabisco. There are now some thirty million square feet of unrented office space in Manhattan. In 1975 permits to build only 4,400 new housing units were issued in the city, a decline of some 70 percent from the year before, which itself showed a decline of 30 percent from the year before that. The city, which had lost some 250,000 housing units from 1960 to 1970, was losing them at the rate of more than 30,000 a year in the 1970s. The landlords say that the city's rent control laws force them to abandon their properties because their arbitrarily restricted rental incomes can't cover the rising cost of maintaining their buildings. Even so, according to the *New York Times*, controlled rents in the city have risen three times as fast as tenant incomes over the last five years. Building maintenance costs, however, have risen still faster.

The result is an impasse. To decontrol the city's 640,000 controlled apartments will put thousands of needy tenants on the street unless the city itself pays the rent of those who can't afford the higher rates, as it now pays the rent of its welfare dependents. To maintain controls will only increase the rate at which the landlords abandon their properties. In the last ten years the city's subway system has lost 20 percent of its riders, the result partly of higher fares, but mostly of unemployment and decayed neighborhoods.

Since 1958 the city has lost more than 400,000 manufacturing jobs, a decline of some 40 percent, which represents more than $3.5 billion in lost wages. In the year ending June 30, 1975, the city had lost 115,000 jobs in all categories. Employment was at its lowest level since 1950, the year that the city first kept such figures. Not only was the city itself, in effect, bankrupt; the bankruptcy rate for businesses and individuals in the Eastern District of New York, that is, the boroughs of Staten Island, Queens, and Brooklyn, as well as Long Island, increased last year by 72.7 percent against a national increase of 34.3 percent. Among the businesses that failed was the Silvercup Bakery, which had once supplied bread for the city schools. The schools now buy bread from bakers in Connecticut and New Jersey.

The city's printing industry, which produced 18 percent of the nation's printing output five years ago, now produces 12 percent. Since 1960, employment in the printing trades has fallen by a third. One reason for the drop, according to the city's economic development administrator, is that in the 1960s an urban renewal project wiped out 110 printing companies in lower Manhattan.

One million one-hundred thousand New Yorkers are now on relief, many of them the grown children of parents who themselves spent their lives on welfare. Another 400,000 New Yorkers now depend upon the city's $4 billion public payroll to support themselves and their families. Between 1960 and 1974 the number of city employees in New York for every 10,000 citizens increased by 69.9 percent and their average earnings in the same period rose by 129 percent. Of the twenty-four largest American cities, only Washington, D.C., has a higher proportion of public employees. One reason for the increase in personnel was the additional services required by the welfare immigrants. Another was that the city payroll had itself become a form of welfare for many of the city's employees. Between 1961 and 1975 the city's annual contribution to the municipal employee pension funds rose from $168 million to $973 million, by far the highest such increase for any American city.

Felix Rohatyn, the investment banker who contrived the city's temporary rescue from insolvency last year, warned that "the pain is just beginning. New York will now have to undergo the most brutal kind of financial and fiscal exercise that any community in the country will ever have to face. . . ." That Mr. Rohatyn more or less by himself kept the city from bankruptcy suggests the fragility of the institutional arrangements by which the city temporarily survives. That it took Mr. Rohatyn's colleagues in the city's banks until last spring to grasp the city's plight suggests the obtuseness with which they had managed their affairs and the city's all along. Not only had the bankers continued to advance expensive credit to their luckless client when even a waterfront loan shark would have called it quits; for years they had joined the city in backing the wrong horses: office towers that nobody wanted, shopping centers that ruined local merchants, housing schemes that are now tottering toward bankruptcy. Meanwhile, in their private councils, the banks drew red lines around the ghettos, agreeing to deny mortgages to those proscribed areas, no matter what the qualifications of individual borrowers. The ghettos soon collapsed, leaving it to the city's hapless taxpayers to support their miserable inhabitants.

In retrospect history is a record of the inevitable, yet there is little in history that men cannot have done differently. New York's decline is probably inseparable from a general crisis in capitalism, the same crisis that has affected Detroit, London, and Tokyo. More modestly it is a result of the recession of the early seventies, and perhaps too of the gradual westward shift of the American population whose center by 1970 had drifted to the southwestern corner of Illinois. Obviously new technologies and cheaper labor markets have hurt New York's industry. Fifty years ago most of the books published in New York were also printed here. It would be foolish to print them here now.

Yet the rows of unwanted office buildings, the ravaged neighborhoods with their abandoned apartments, the empty factories, the shoals of semiliterate dropouts, the bankruptcies are all partly the result of choices that turned out badly. It was not history alone that ordained the destruction of 110 printing companies in lower Manhattan or that destroyed hundreds of other businesses to build the World Trade Center with its floors of vacant offices or that legislated the welfare differentials that helped stimulate the huge migration from the South to the city's red-lined ghettos or that built expensive apartments on an island in the East River so that the prospective tenants, if in fact there are any, will have to be lofted ashore by aerial tramway to do their shopping. (It costs about five times as much to create a new apartment in such projects as the one in the East River as it would to rehabilitate an apartment in much of the city's old but still usable housing.)

New York is typical of the many old industrial cities that have lost jobs since World War II, but according to Herbert Bienstock, the New York regional director of the federal bureau of labor statistics, New York should have been less affected by changes in industrial patterns and by the recession than other cities. "The industrial structure of New York City, with relatively smaller concentrations of recession-sensitive, goods-producing industries, would suggest some greater relative strength during periods of general economic contraction," he said. "Such strength was not in evidence during the recent period of national employment decline and subsequent recovery." Between 1970 and 1972, for example, the median family income of New Yorkers declined by 3.5 percent in constant dollars.

Since 1969, when employment here was at its highest, New York has lost 500,000 jobs of all kinds, more than the total employment of Cincinnati or Kansas City. Between 1970 and 1973, when the country as a whole gained 7.6 million jobs, New York City should proportionately have gained 466,920. Instead it lost 200,000. That this happened suggests forces beyond the ordinary vagaries of industrial devolution were at work here.

Amid the practical anarchy that characterized New York's economy for more than a century no single industry or group of industries achieved the autonomy that the steel and aluminum makers, for example, enjoyed in Pittsburgh or that gave the auto makers absolute power over the fortunes of Detroit. New York, when it flourished, was never at the mercy of an industrial autocracy or the fortunes of a particular product. Even the huge apparel industry was split into so many competing units that its influence over the rest of the city was slight. It was this lack of a controlling center, according to Mr. Bienstock, that should have supplied New York's resiliency. For Jane Jacobs and her followers it was this same anarchy that had always given New York's economy its unique strength; that supplied the ferment in which one enterprise in New York bred another in the apparently random way that mutations occur in nature.

Thus New York's financial industry helped spawn the specialized printing trades which produced its prospectuses; these printers in turn helped generate the skills that supported the city's graphics and advertising industries, and these supported the complex network of writers and artists and agents and technicians that bred the city's communications industries. New York's economy was a demonstration of the principle that where there is enough genetic activity new forms of life are likely to emerge and the more adaptable of them will survive, producing new species and so on endlessly.

Within this wilderness of economic possibility there emerged, however, a dialectical exception. By 1961 New York employed more than 125,000 construction workers, a more numerous and far more highly paid industrial group than almost any other in the city, including the ladies'-garment workers. Moreover, the construction industry was a uniquely cohesive unit, politically and ethnically, dominated by a handful of politically connected contractors and their captive unions. Its links to the city's financial and political leadership were evident at a hundred Waldorf banquets. The proof of its hegemony was broadcast on thousands of billboards announcing this or that new housing project or highway, usually financed in large part by federal funds and endorsed by the current mayor and his collection of city commissioners. Inevitably there evolved a coalition among the city's building trades, the mortgage bankers, the investment houses, and the politicians. Nothing short of the city's impending bankruptcy would inhibit it.

Much of the construction industry's power over the city and its neighborhoods evolved from the various public authorities that emerged during the depression of the 1930s, particularly the autonomous agencies contrived by Robert Moses which raised huge sums for public works, usually through the sale of bonds guaranteed, as a rule, by the state treasury and marketed by the city's investment banks. These agencies also brought federal funds into the city and state for the construction of public projects whose appeal to the city's politicians was even greater than it was to the citizens themselves. Where the public saw a handsome new bridge or highway interchange, the politicians saw a Niagara of public money with which to employ loyal constituencies and at the same time reward themselves and their companions with multitudes of contracts, architectural commissions, condemnation awards, legal fees, and bureaucratic appointments.

At the same time the politicians could assure the taxpayers that these projects would cost the city little. The money came from Washington or from the sale of bonds whose burden would fall on future generations. The construction industry thus became for the city what aerospace was for the West and the South, the region's major conduit for federal funds and a vehicle for the sale of securities, sponsored by various public treasuries, often in later years without the specific consent of the taxpayers who would eventually have to redeem them.

Within the city's own political structure, the construction industry and its satellites became what the party clubhouses had been for earlier generations—a mechanism for distributing patronage to party workers and for infusing money throughout the political machine. That the industry also constructed buildings and highways was almost incidental, much as the care of the elderly became incidental in many of the city's nursing homes under state and federal medical programs. The ghost within the machine was a system of political preferment and control more powerful than anything the city had known before. A century ago William Marcy Tweed, a Tammany leader whose crookedness was exceeded only by his intelligence, observed of New York that its "population is too hopelessly split up into races and factions to govern it under universal suffrage except by the bribery of patronage and corruption." In our own time it was mainly the construction complex—the builders, the autonomous agencies, the federal and state bureaucracies, the banks—that generated the patronage, by which the politicians attempted to dominate the city's "hopelessly split up races and factions."

When New York first built its subways and its present water supply system, it did so with its own resources and through corporations responsible for their own profits. Though these projects supplied the usual opportunities for patronage, the results were useful public works from which the city still benefits. The wanton construction since the war, on the other hand, has produced public housing that has not only devastated existing neighborhoods but that has itself so deteriorated that much of it is now indistinguishable from the surrounding slums. New public hospitals stand empty while the hospital system as a whole remains 25 percent unused for lack of personnel. Expensive new highways are choked with traffic while mass transit languishes. Yet to criticize the works of New York's builders was, in the 1960s, to criticize America itself and the imperial notions of progress that it promoted. The construction workers who attacked the antiwar demonstrators on Wall Street in 1970 were acting, as it turned out, not only on orders from Washington; they were supporting an absurd war which was yet another manifestation of the same berserk Keynesianism that was devastating the neighborhoods of their own city. Today the construction industry has shriveled, along with the city itself. Last year the city lost 30,000 construction jobs. Of the 75,000 jobs left in the industry, some 40,000 will probably disappear within the year. Like the ghetto leaders of the 1960s, the construction workers were the temporary and fortuitous beneficiaries of governmental programs that no longer interest the parties in power as much as they once did and for which there is no longer as much public support.

What remains in doubt are the city's regenerative powers. In the 1920s the city's Regional Plan Association, a group of high-minded bankers and real-estate developers, advised that an expressway be built across lower Manhattan that would link the proposed Holland Tunnel with the Manhattan Bridge and thus supply a connection between New Jersey and Long Island. Nothing came of this scheme at the time. The plan was revived, however, by Robert Moses in the 1950s, but rejected by the Board of Estimate in response to public protests. The expressway which was to have crossed Manhattan at Broome Street would have destroyed what was still a thriving industrial neighborhood north of Canal Street. It would also have uprooted the city's traditional Italian neighborhood that extends south from the lower reaches of Greenwich Village, and it would have jeopardized Chinatown, south of Canal Street, as well. The threat to the city's living tissue was incalculable.

Apprehensive residents of the area soon recognized that the federally funded expressway was consistent with schemes to redevelop all of lower Manhattan from Greenwich Village to the Battery. Jane Jacobs, for example, observed that Robert Moses' proposal for an extension of Fifth Avenue through Greenwich Village's Washington Square Park was probably intended as the northern link to the new expressway, a link that would have destroyed hundreds of sturdy residences and countless businesses in its path.

The expressway's main sponsor was the Downtown Lower Manhattan Association. Its leader was David Rockefeller, whose Chase Bank had just built a new headquarters in lower Manhattan. Among the other sponsors was the Port of New York Authority, an autonomous bi-state agency which was about to build its World Trade Center in the same area. Harry Van Arsdale, the leader of the city's trade unionists, was another sponsor, and so was Peter Brennan, the head of the city's construction workers who later became Nixon's labor secretary. The American Automobile Association was another sponsor.

Among the expressway's opponents was John Lindsay, then a Republican congressman who was running for mayor. Once he was elected, however, Lindsay became a supporter of the expressway, presumably in response to Tweed's famous rule of city government. The inhabitants of the area were adamant in their opposition. They demonstrated. They protested to the feckless new mayor. They signed petitions and attended hearings, all to no avail. Anticipating the expressway, businesses closed down, factories moved away. Between the late sixties and the early seventies the area known as "The Valley," which extends from 34th Street south to Canal, lost some 85,000 jobs. To quiet the expressway's opponents the plans for the new road were altered. Instead of a surface highway the project's sponsors would build a depressed highway and above it they would build a new school. This scheme was probably their undoing. An environmental study showed that students would be asphyxiated in their classrooms by fumes from the traffic below. One environmental study led to another and the expressway was eventually abandoned on the eve of Lindsay's second campaign for mayor.

Along the western part of the route which the expressway was to have taken were several blocks of abandoned loft buildings, handsome, spacious structures, many of them a century old, with powerful façades of stone or iron. Soon artists driven southward by the redevelopment of Greenwich Village moved into these lofts, at first in violation of the city's housing codes. Since the area was south of Houston Street, they named it SoHo. They opened galleries, restaurants, and bookstores, and they accomplished without having intended to what decades of urban renewal had failed to do. They restored a neighborhood and became its taxpayers. Though SoHo's residents are mainly middle class and the area is anything but the industrial neighborhood that it once was, its revival suggests that the spontaneous generation which once characterized New York's growth remains a possibility.

It was the abandonment of the expressway that led to SoHo's revival and to the continuing vitality of the Italian and Chinese neighborhoods nearby, with their crowds of tourists, their innumerable shops and restaurants, their live poultry markets, their small manufacturing plants, and their surplus electronics and secondhand machinery dealers.

In the area to the south, however, which is now dominated by the two huge towers of the World Trade Center, the outcome was different. Here there were no traditional residential groups to oppose the vast renewal schemes that were proposed for the area in the early 1950s. Though some 550,000 people worked in the government offices, the financial center, and the wholesale markets south of Canal Street, almost no one lived there. The hundreds of small merchants, the radio and electronics dealers, the produce wholesalers who occupied the ancient Washington Market—New York's equivalent to Les Halles—were easily overpowered by the downtown bankers and their companions at the Port Authority, the joint agency of New York and New Jersey which administers the bridges and tunnels that link the two states and whose access to the bond market through the tolls that it collects is practically limitless.

Here the same combination of forces—the Rockefeller bank, the Authority itself, the construction unions—that had been defeated earlier, now prevailed. The Authority's plan was to build a trade center which would become the world's largest office building, two towers of a hundred stories each. Inevitably it would replace the small commercial and manufacturing establishments that had traditionally occupied the area.

In the early 1960s the local businessmen sued the Port Authority, arguing, among other things, that since the vacancy rate in the city's office buildings was already at 9 percent, there was no need for the Authority's new towers. In 1966 the appellate court ruled against the merchants and by the end of that year some 400 commercial tenants left the area. The following summer the Authority opened bids for $100 million worth of construction. Most of these contracts and those that were to follow went to suppliers from outside the city— to Otis Elevator, Borg-Warner, Pacific Car and Foundry, and so on. By December the estimated cost of the project had risen to $575 million. It would eventually go far higher, but the banks that handled the Authority's bonds were happy to supply the money, given the security provided by the taxing power that the Authority had over the city's commuters who used its tunnels and bridges.

The designation of the new buildings as a trade center was disingenuous. Under its charter the Port Authority is supposed to maintain the Hudson River crossings and promote the interests of the Port. It is not supposed to use its borrowing power to erect office towers. However, by calling its new buildings a World Trade Center it could declare them a port facility. Had the Authority invested instead in mass transit it would not only have diluted the income from its bridge and tunnel tolls, it would have offended the banks that marketed its bonds. The banks had no interest in commuter railroads no matter how they might benefit the region and its taxpayers, and thus, in the long run, benefit the banks themselves. David Rockefeller and his Chase Bank were especially eager to have a neighboring office tower to accompany their new downtown headquarters. Typically, the banks were wrong. The Trade Center would find it hard to attract tenants to its lifeless and remote area. Inevitably the taxpayers would pick up the bill for their mistake.

Meanwhile the vacancy rate in Manhattan's existing office buildings had increased still further. As a precaution the Authority arranged to lease 1.9 million square feet of space in the new buildings to the State of New York. The state accepted the arrangement without seeking lower bids elsewhere. Thus the taxpayers were asked to pay twice for the Trade Center, once with their bridge and tunnel tolls and again with their state taxes. Since interest on the Authority's bonds was tax exempt, and thus in effect subsidized by the public, the taxpayers were asked to make a third contribution to the project. And since the Trade Center does not pay normal real-estate tax but makes what it calls "negotiated payments in lieu of taxes," the taxpayers make yet a fourth contribution. How they were to benefit from the Trade Center was unclear.

The Trade Center was completed in 1972 and except for those floors occupied by the state much of it stands vacant. The *New York Times* reported that one of the foremen on the project earned $76,-000 in overtime pay during the final year of construction. The area south of Canal Street has lost 50,000 jobs since 1968. Except for rush hour and at lunch time, a lunar quiet dominates the Trade Center and the streets around it.

Twenty years ago the area where the Trade Center now stands adjoined the old Washington Market, a chaotic jumble of stalls and ancient buildings which housed the city's produce market. In 1959, as plans for the Trade Center were being completed, the city's commissioner of markets announced that the Washington Market, which had served the city for more than a century, was now obsolete and would have to be vacated. The merchants who occupied it were told that they were being moved to a remote neck of land in the southeast Bronx called Hunts Point. The United States Department of Agriculture declared that the new market would save consumers $18 million a year and that it would be built at the geographical center of the city —a center that happened to be miles away from the actual centers where the restaurant keepers and grocers who patronized the produce market had their businesses. Meanwhile the city announced that it had received a federal grant to plan the old Washington Market area as a new complex of office buildings, warehouses, and factories.

By 1961 plans for the new Hunts Point Market were far advanced. So was its estimated cost which had risen from $22 million to $30 million. By the end of the year the Board of Estimate approved a plan to redevelop the old market area at a cost of $100 million and it condemned the existing buildings in which the merchants were still attempting to do business. A few months later the Board abandoned its original plan and approved a new one that would cost $150 million. Except for the demolition of the old buildings, nothing came of either plan. By 1965 the area was devastated, a few stubborn merchants still clinging to their stalls amid the wreckage.

The new Hunts Point Market opened in 1967 with about 150 merchants. It stands behind its grim security fence, a great gray hulk surrounded by the rubble left over from its construction. Since the city has ordered that no merchants can do business outside the boundaries of the market, the adjoining streets promise to remain dilapidated indefinitely. A year after the market was completed the city accepted a new proposal for the old Washington Market area. It was to cost $190 million and would include a community college, middle-income and luxury housing, and an industrial complex. Nothing came of it.

The merchants at the new complex now complain that it takes an extra day for fresh produce to reach consumers, that the new market is too expensive, and that doing business there is less convenient than it was in the old market. "Cheaper?" a radish merchant told a reporter. "It's more dear. Downtown you had a customer for everything. You could get rid of it all there. Here you got to keep it till next morning. We should have what they waste here in a year." A greens merchant agreed. It costs twice as much at the new market, he said. "Here you back a couple of trucks against the platform and the customers can't get in." Edgar Fabber, the city's commissioner of Ports and Terminals, said of the new market. "I think it's the best investment the city has made in the last twenty years."

In fact, the investment was unnecessary. Fifty years ago Americans ate 414 pounds of fresh produce a year. By 1971 they were eating only 239 pounds. In the last ten years deliveries of fresh produce have fallen by a fifth nationally. In New York City they have fallen by a third. The old Washington Market, for all its antiquity, could have accommodated this reduced volume as it slowly expired of obsolescence. Meanwhile it would have sustained the hundreds of downtown businesses that clustered around it, benefiting from the traffic that the market generated and serving its countless incidental requirements.

The abandonment of the Lower Manhattan Expressway and the regeneration of SoHo; the construction of the World Trade Center and the eerie necrosis of lower Manhattan; the failure of the myriad projects undertaken under the Federal Housing and Urban Development Act of 1966 to restore the city's neighborhoods or to create new ones—these events hardly suggest that the current moratorium on capital spending will, in itself, assure the city's future. The city's problems are by now so complex that there may be no solution to them at all. Between 1965 and 1973 the city's expenditures were increasing at a compound annual rate of 13.1 percent while its tax receipts were increasing at a rate of only 6.8 percent. By 1975 the city had used $1.5 billion in capital funds to meet its current expenses, while it was also incurring $4.5 billion in short-term debt, an increase of 700 percent over 1967. For the fiscal year 1975–1976 the city has budgeted $1.784 billion for debt service, more than two and a half times what it spends as its share of direct welfare payments.

The construction complex was not in itself responsible for this disaster nor is New York the only city facing such problems. Yet the Trade Center and projects like it have probably hastened and intensified a decline that might, in other circumstances, have been less precipitous. Certainly the near bankruptcy of the various state construction agencies—particularly the Urban Development Corporation, whose impending collapse last year first alerted the bankers to the shakiness of the city and state generally—could have been avoided had the politicians been more cautious in their commitments to useless new building projects.

In retrospect it now seems clear that what the city needed during the past twenty years were not new office towers and highways, or even urban renewal and slum clearance programs; much less its surfeit of hospitals and such pompous and extravagant confections as the Urban Development Corporation's Welfare Island middle-income housing project—what the politicians call at their ribbon-cutting ceremonies commitments to the city's future. What the city needed instead were commitments to its difficult present and to what could be preserved from its vital past: for example, the abolition of rent control and the provision of rent subsidies to needy tenants, steps that would spare the landlords the impossible choice of subsidizing their tenants out of their own pockets or abandoning their buildings. The political objections to such additional public expenditures are obvious. But the cost to taxpayers would be far less than the cost of lost properties and the more egregious waste involved in supporting such agencies as UDC with public funds.

The few neighborhoods that survived or came back to life during the city's decline—parts of the West Seventies and Eighties, SoHo, Bedford Stuyvesant, Park Slope—were the ones that more or less restored themselves, often house by house, block by block, usually with relatively small loans from local banks and state-financed mortgage guarantees, occasionally with foundation grants; or neighborhoods like Corona and the West Village that resisted the developers, often through years of litigation and public protest.

The industries that typically flourish here and may survive the city's difficulties are similarly resistant to external discipline, self-governing, impulsive, polyglot, mysterious: the diamond market, the fashion and cosmetics trades, the restaurants, the investment banks themselves, the publishers, the port. New technologies, cheap labor, the myriad inconveniences of the city are not likely to make them abandon New York's tolerant and complex environment. That so many corporate headquarters have left could have been predicted.

New York is less amenable than most other places to corporate rationality, cost effectiveness, and the people who value such things, especially if they don't need what the city can offer by way of specialized services and supplies, middlemen, craftsmen, or people with a talent for anticipating fashion.

New York will probably continue to lose its manufacturing jobs and with them the revenues to balance its budget. The city's last two breweries are closing their plants and discharging some 1,100 workers. One of them is moving to Pennsylvania, the other is going to New Jersey, where water, sewage, and electricity will cost the company $1.6 million less. Since the real cost of these utilities can hardly be much less twenty miles away in New Jersey than in Brooklyn, the brewer's gain and the city's loss actually amount to the value of the indirect taxes included in these utility charges. Where the city once exported goods, it now exports jobs—to Indiana and Tennessee, where it makes the books that are published here; to rural New Jersey (where *Women's Wear Daily* and this paper [*New York Review of Books*] are now printed); to California, where the television shows that New York produces are filmed, including *Kojak,* the series about a New York City detective; to garment plants in all parts of the world.

In the unaccustomed space provided by the decline of the building trades, new kinds of work may turn up here spontaneously, growing out of crevices in the city's surface as they did in the past; but they are unlikely to replace many of the jobs or much of the income that the city is losing. The more likely prospect is for a continuing decline in industrial work, a reduced tax base, and higher rates for those who remain. Auditors assigned by the federal treasury to examine the city's accounts have projected revenue losses of $571 million over the next three years. To meet its needs for 1976 alone the city must raise an additional $400 million. To balance its budget by 1978 it must cut its expenses by $1.6 billion over the three-year period, according to these auditors.

The misery that this implies for the city's dependent poor is unimaginable. The *Wall Street Journal* complains from time to time that New York's problems result from its excessive compassion for these people; but if New York's poor were to depend upon the personal good will of their fellow citizens, they would probably starve here as readily as elsewhere. What the city pays its poor, it pays to keep them out of sight and under control. On a per capita basis it doesn't pay much; less, for example, than Detroit, Chicago, and Philadelphia; more than Baltimore, Los Angeles, and Houston, adjusted in all cases for local variations in city, county, state, and federal contributions. Unlike most other cities, New York pays about 30 percent of its welfare costs out of its own revenues, a matter of just over a billion dollars for 1976, which includes direct welfare payments as well as the cost of related social services.

Los Angeles, Chicago, Philadelphia, and many other cities handle welfare more easily; they derive their local welfare shares from a county-wide tax base. For years politicians and editorial writers have talked about extending New York's archaic boundaries to include the suburbs within its taxing area. But the suburbs, which are afflicted by many of the city's own problems, are less likely now than ever to agree to such a scheme.

Still more dim at the moment are the proposals for a national welfare system, for example a negative income tax or a guaranteed wage. Such proposals assume that welfare migrations are a national problem, not a local one. A federal assumption of welfare costs would, in itself, balance the budgets of New York and many other impoverished cities. A uniform federal welfare standard would also encourage the remigration of the unemployable urban poor to regions where they might live more cheaply. But these are likely to be the same regions which encouraged their departure to the cities in the first place. Their political opposition to a uniform national welfare standard can be depended upon.

When Daniel P. Moynihan, as Nixon's first domestic affairs adviser, proposed a national welfare program he was attacked by conservatives who thought the scheme would give the poor too much, while many liberals thought it would give them too little. Nixon himself, whose support for the proposal was never strong, finally abandoned it. Moynihan was soon replaced by John Ehrlichman. Who would now revive his Family Assistance Plan? The constituencies that might benefit from it seem weaker than they were when Moynihan first proposed his plan. Its opponents are stronger. The prevailing wisdom is that New York and the other old Eastern cities are finished anyway. The country's future has shifted westward, to the sunbelt. As New York once carelessly discarded its own marginal neighborhoods, so America may have decided that New York itself can now be junked.

Meanwhile, the poor seem to suffer more or less passively. Their mayhem affects mainly themselves. For all the terror they are said to inspire, the tourist trade flourishes, perhaps for the same reason that it does in Pompeii, but more likely because New York, for all its misery, remains uniquely exhilarating. The restaurants are busy. Hotel rooms are scarce. Cabarets and theaters thrive. Eight new musicals are scheduled to open by spring. Ballet is everywhere. Three and a quarter million visitors came here last year. Wistful champions of the city's well-being contemplate the hordes of tourists and urge that casino gambling be legalized here. Las Vegas showed a profit of a billion dollars last year. New York, they say, can do still better.

In the short run the city's financial problems are unthinkable. How the city will cut its expenses by $1.6 billion by 1978 remains the mayor's secret. Like his fellow citizens he probably expects that something will turn up.

Meanwhile, with the defection of the banks and other traditional markets for its securities, New York now depends upon its public employees' pension funds to buy its dubious bonds. It is a desperate solution, for the undercapitalized pension funds depend in turn upon the city's annual contribution of $1.25 billion for their own solvency. It is a case of two brave old marathon dancers, each holding the other up, with long days and nights of shuffling still to go.

The prospect is dark, but cities don't die easily, much less a city like New York. A Japanese jeweler has just signed the most expensive commercial lease in the city's history for his new shop on Fifth Avenue. The builders report a strong market for luxury housing and are planning a few new buildings. The ghettos are for the moment "quiet," at least for those who don't go there. The Port Authority wants to build a new convention center at the bottom of Manhattan to stimulate its moribund Trade Center and justify its construction of a new hotel in that desolate area. Since the hotels, theaters, and restaurants are in midtown and transportation between the two places is almost impossible except by the dilapidated and dangerous West Side subway, the Authority's proposal is more than normally batty. It may also be illegal, since the Authority's charter makes no provision for building a convention center. That even the *New York Times* has found the wit to oppose the Authority's plan and urges a midtown site for the convention center instead offers another grain of hope. Who knows? We may survive. It's hard to imagine how, but it's harder to imagine that we won't.

Part II

URBAN GROWTH & SUBURBANIZATION, AND THE CHANGING

One can easily imagine opening *Newsweek* or *Time* and coming across a story entitled "New York City in Crisis While Houston Booms." If the title is invented, its message is not. One approach to understanding why this is so is to study each of these cities as *separate* entities operating according to its own secular "laws of motion." While an effort of this sort would undoubtedly yield a number of insights, we believe this approach to be fundamentally erroneous. In our view, Houston's boom is part of the same process that has led to New York's decline, the unplanned accumulation process of twentieth-century capitalism. In other words, it is not merely that the Houstons of America *happen* to boom at the expense of its New Yorks, but that decisions made in pursuit of profits ensure that *both* situations will emerge.

This theme is developed in an article entitled "Capitalism and the Roots of Urban Crisis," by David Gordon (selection #5). Surveying the process of urbanization from a Marxist perspective, he exposes the complex interrelationship between capital accumulation and the distinguishing features of U.S. urban development, including its suburbanization and the dramatic shift in economic production from the Northeast and North Central regions to what is now known as the Sun Belt.

Similarly, John H. Mollenkopf's essay "The Crisis of the Public Sector in America's Cities" (selection #6) analyzes the political dislocations and their resolutions which have accompanied and made possible the pattern of American industrialization that has evolved over the last century. He believes we are at the end of an epoch and mired in a "political crisis [that] bears all the marks of a great defeat

DEVELOPMENT: REGIONAL SHIFTS ROLE OF CITIES

for progressive elements within American politics." In a paper written before the current phase of the crisis came to a head ("The Urban Crisis: Who Got What and Why," selection #7), Frances Fox Piven traces the pattern of urban politics in that epoch as it relates to the distribution of jobs and the production of social services. Blacks were the catalysts for many of the changes which took place, but "it was the organized producer groups in the cities who made the largest gains." With the decline of federal poverty programs, blacks began to lose what little progress they had made.

Gordon, Mollenkopf and Piven present theoretical and historical perspectives; what follows is a series of articles fleshing out some of the more recent empirical details. For example, George Sternlieb and James W. Hughes, Rutgers University urbanologists, examine in the prologue to their recent book, *Post-Industrial America: Metropolitan Decline and Inter-Regional Job Shifts* (reprinted here as selection #8), the underlying demographic and economic changes which took place in and among metropolitan areas between 1970 and 1974 and which have deeply endangered New York City and other cities of the Northeast and North Central regions of the country.

We have previously indicated that the central determinant of the urban configuration is capitalist accumulation. In part this process operates through the "unfettered market." But as various authors point out, corporations manipulate the *political* process as well in their endless quest for profit. Thus, federally financed highways represent political decisions of a kind that undermined the public transportation of the city while simultaneously spurring the profitable construction of suburbs. A second, perhaps less obvious use of state power affecting urban development (or decay) is the military budget. Some have argued that "defense" can be considered America's number-one industry. What is pertinent from our point of view is the geographical pattern of distribution: Department of Defense billions have, in short, helped to promote one region's growth at the expense of others. As Kirkpatrick Sale puts it in his popular book *Power Shift,* "if any one industry can be said to be the backbone of the Southern Rim, it is defense." Sale's colorful description of the six pillars on which Sun Belt expansion is based (agribusiness, defense, advanced technology, oil and natural gas, real estate and construction and tourism and leisure) is reprinted as selection #9.

Honing in on the crux of the question is an additional article, by Seymour Melman, professor of industrial engineering at Columbia University and the author of numerous books on the destructive impact of the military establishment. In "The Federal Rip-off of New York's Money," Melman shows how the civilian parts of the American economy are being milked to support its military enterprise and explores the regional implications of the pattern of military disbursements (selection #10). Melman draws on a study by Monte J. Gordon, vice-president and director of research of the Dreyfus Corporation. Gordon shows that in 1973, New York State generated a total of $32.5 billion in federal taxes but received back only $15.3 billion, less than 50 percent of what it gave. Considered in this manner, Alaska is the number-one federal beneficiary, receiving $2.71 for every dollar it pays in taxes, while New York is pauperized at rank 47.

A final article covers financial and economic issues not previously developed. Staff members of the Brookings Institution explore in much greater detail the fiscal problems of cities by examining their expenditures as well as their eroding base of revenue (selection #11). Writing in a book analyzing the 1973 federal budget, they conclude that the deteriorating fiscal situation at the local level requires a general rescue by the federal "lifeguard," but don't see much hope in current or projected federal programs.

With New York teetering on the precipice of default (and others not far behind?), it is instructive to find out what happened in the past whenever the quality of state and local debt deteriorated under the impact of general economic adversity. A recent study by George H. Hempel, *The Postwar Quality of State and Local Debt,* found "that state and local debt payment difficulties add to the severity of major economic declines rather than occur as a major element leading to these declines." The pattern seems to be holding: current hard times have been exacerbated by state and local fiscal problems. Selection #12 is a compilation of charts and tables from Hempel's study and the work of the Advisory Commission on Intergovernmental Relations depicting state and local defaults over the period 1839–1960.

5. Capitalism and the Roots of Urban Crisis

DAVID GORDON

> [C]apitalism, as a mode of production, is the basic process of most of what we know as the history of country and city. Its abstracted economic drives, its fundamental priorities in social relations, its criteria of growth and of profit and loss, have over several centuries altered our country and created our kinds of city. . . . The division and opposition of city and country, industry and agriculture, in their modern forms, are the critical culmination of the division and specialization of labour which, though it did not begin with capitalism, was developed under it to an extraordinary and transforming degree. . . . The symptoms of this division can be found at every point in what is now our common life.
> —Raymond Williams,
> The Country and the City

American cities are in crisis—budgets splashed with red ink, people protesting cutbacks, unemployment lines extending around the corner. Many of our cities have become the crucibles of general economic crisis. Why are cities experiencing such economic trauma? What sickness has invaded our urban lives? Do our cities have a chance for survival?

Most people I know dislike many aspects of urban life. In varying proportions, many complain about urban chaos and irrationality, about urban inequality and poverty, about urban impersonality and physical control.

Copyright © 1977 by David Gordon. This essay is a short version of a longer work, "Toward a Critique of CAPITALopolis: Capitalism and Urban Development in the United States" (forthcoming, 1977). I have received immeasurable help in that larger project from friends. A list of individual contributors would be too long, so I would like to thank the collective community of radical political economists in this country for providing the context for this work. I benefited from some useful comments on an earlier draft of this essay by the editors of this volume. I was also lucky enough to get some research help from Bob Cohen, Al Watkins, David Kummer and Cydney Pullman along the way. (In the footnotes which follow, the longer essay will hereinafter be cited as Gordon, "CAPITALopolis.")

David Gordon teaches economics at the Graduate Faculty of the New School for Social Research. This paper was written in May 1976.

More important, most people seem to share a sense of inevitability about those urban problems. We regard the urban form as intrinsically determined by the necessities of advanced industrial societies. We may not like our lives in cities, but it often appears that cities must continue to develop as they have if we are to maintain our present standards of living. We shall have to accept our city lives as a cost of satisfying the consumption needs of people all around the world. Think of the need for coordination, for economies of scale, for urban agglomerations, for urban amenities!

This fatalism about our cities resembles an analogous fatalism about technology. That view is often called *technological determinism*. It suggests that our dominant technologies are the *only* kinds of machines which will permit our standard of living. We may not like the alienated, specialized, hierarchical jobs associated with those machines, but we have to accept them as requisites of our current affluence.

Analogously, our views of cities are suffused with a sense of (what I call) *spatial determinism*. This view suggests that there is only one way of organizing economic life across space—generating only one set of community relationships—which is consistent with advanced industrial standards of living. We may not like those urban relationships, but we have to accept them in order to enjoy what we have.

Recent political struggles and social analyses have begun to challenge the technological determinist position. Research has suggested that modern machinery has not only permitted affluence but has also been conditioned by the particular characteristics of capitalist accumulation.[1] As Harry Braverman has recently argued:

> These necessities are called "technical needs," "machine characteristics," "the requirements of efficiency," but by and large they are the exigencies of capital and not of technique. For the machine, they are only the expression of that side of its possibilities which capital tends to develop most energetically: the technical ability to separate control from execution. . . . to subordinate the worker ever more decisively to the yoke of the machine.[2]

---

[1]See Steven Marglin, "What Do Bosses Do?" *Review of Radical Political Economics* (Summer 1974); Harry Braverman, *Labor and Monopoly Capital* (New York: Monthly Review Press, 1975); and David M. Gordon, "Capitalist Efficiency and Socialist Efficiency," *Monthly Review* (July-August 1976).

[2]Braverman, *op. cit.*, p. 230.

We must also begin to reconsider the spatial determinist view. The new view of technology has led us to the conclusion that capitalist machines develop at least partly in order to control us as workers. So may we also conclude, if we look closely enough, that capitalist spatial forms also develop at least partly to reproduce capitalist control, helping maintain the class relationships prevalent in capitalist societies.[3]

This kind of reconsideration has profound political implications. The spatial determinist view treats urban form fatalistically, accepting it as an inevitable concomitant of advanced industrial society. From that perspective, the spatial division of labor appears to be politically neutral, forged outside of the economic system by technical necessities, providing equal benefits to all classes. In contrast, the Marxian analysis of space suggests that the spatial division of labor and the process of capital accumulation are intertwined. Through the process of capitalist development, urban form will be more and more affected by the exigencies of capital accumulation. In particular, for the purposes of this discussion, urban form will be more and more affected by the problems of capitalist control of the production process. If cities do not develop in ways which reinforce capitalists' control of production processes, either they will begin to change or capitalist production will take place somewhere else. *The fate of cities under capitalism, in short, is linked to the control of workers.*

Focused in this way, the conventional view and the Marxian view offer interpretations of urban form which differ sharply on a few critical issues. Keeping those differences in mind, we may be able to clarify our understanding of the links between capitalism and urban form. This essay examines these links in two sections—the first on the historical connections between the capitalist economy and its cities, the second on the implications of those interconnections for the current urban crisis.

CAPITALISM AND CITIES—HISTORY
We cannot reasonably discuss the links between capitalism and urban form without tracing the historical evolution of our cities during the development of capitalism. In this section I explore some of the

[3]This reconsideration is explored on a theoretical level in Gordon, "CAPITALopolis."

historical links between capitalism and urban development in the United States.[4]

In turning toward the history of capitalism and cities in the United States, we quickly confront a common conventional wisdom in the orthodox social sciences. Most urban histories treat the growth of cities as a gradual, evolutionary, ineluctable process. In any developing society, as Kingsley Davis writes, "urbanization is a finite process, a cycle through which nations go in their transition from agrarian to industrial society."[5] Cities become continuously larger, more complicated, more specialized and more interdependent. People are increasingly segregated into separate socioeconomic neighborhoods. City form itself adjusts gradually and continuously to this evolution. Because the United States has become the prototypical advanced industrial society, orthodox historians view urban development in the United States as the perfect reflection of this process of urbanization.[6]

Marxians see that history in a different light. They argue that urban development is not inevitable, but that it is conditioned by the particular system of production under which it operates. They also argue that urban history, like the history of other social institutions, advances *discontinuously* rather than continuously, periodically experiencing qualitative transformations of basic form and structure. During the capitalist epoch in particular, the instability of the accumulation process itself is bound to lead to periodic institutional change. The current economic crisis, from the Marxian perspective, is just another in a long series of such dislocations.

What conditions these changes?

During the capitalist epoch, according to the Marxian view, the process of capital accumulation itself frames the process of economic development in capitalist societies. More specifically, Marxists suggest that capitalist societies have passed through several successive *stages* of capital accumulation. Each stage develops its own dynamic, framed by the structures of production and distribution characteris-

[4]This section depends completely on Gordon, "CAPITALopolis," for much more substantial documentation and further references.

[5]Kingsley Davis, "The Urbanization of the Human Population," in *Cities* (New York: Knopf, 1965), p. 9.

[6]See, for instance, Charles Glaab and Theodore Brown, *A History of Urban America* (New York: Macmillan, 1967), for one of the best examples of this kind of conventional historical treatment.

tics of that period.[7] Although certain details of language and characterization differ, most Marxists agree that we have already witnessed three main stages of capital accumulation in the advanced capitalist countries—the stages of *commercial* accumulation, *industrial* (or competitive) accumulation, and advanced *corporate* (or monopoly) accumulation.[8]

In the schematic view of American urban history which follows, I argue that urban development in the United States has passed through three main stages, each corresponding to and conditioned by the more general dynamics of successive stages of capital accumulation. Within each stage of urban development, I argue that the process of capital accumulation itself was the most important factor structuring the growth of cities. More important—at least for the purposes of this essay—I argue that the transitions *between* stages of urban development were predominantly influenced by the problems of class control in production. Capitalist development in the United States has bred, according to my historical argument, the capitalist city.

COMMERCIAL ACCUMULATION AND COMMERCIAL CITIES

When capitalism first developed, merchant capitalists sought to increase their capital through *commercial accumulation*. Exchanging commodities in the marketplace, they tried to earn profits by "buying cheap and selling dear." They did not directly intervene in the production process, depending instead on their ability to take advantage of differentials between the supply and demand prices for different commodities. They relied heavily on political favors and franchises to strengthen their privileged position in the marketplace. Increasingly through this early period, capitalists' hungry pursuit of commercial profits became the major source of change in societies experiencing capitalist transformation.

Cities served four main political economic functions in this original stage of commercial accumulation:

(1) A Political Capital (and colonial control centers) became the site of the mercantilist government, attracting court followers and mercantile lobbyists eager for commercial privileges.

[7]On stages in general, see Ernest Mandel, *Late Capitalism* (London: New Left Books, 1975).

[8]For further discussion, see *ibid*.

(2) The Commercial Metropolis, often congruent with the Political Capital, housed the discounting, lending, accounting and entrepreneurial functions supporting the commercial exchange itself. (Since commercial accumulation depended on limited competition in the market—and ultimately on some kind of monopoly franchise to prevent competition— the uneven development of commercial power was likely to produce an uneven geographic concentration of these support activities.)

(3) Ports served as Transport Nodes—as collection and distribution centers for commodities being supplied from geographically diffuse points in the hinterland and carried to dispersed markets.

(4) Artisans producing luxury goods also concentrated in cities to gain access to their wealthy customers.

Cities were also influenced by the dynamics of land speculation in the commercial period. Merchants tried to earn profits on the exchange of land as well as the exchange of other, more mobile commodities. Land speculators became active in cities—and their speculation affected urban development—if city populations were increasing rapidly enough to create pressure on land prices. The geographic impact of land speculation therefore depended on the shifting geographic patterns of population settlement. Land speculation had a largely derivative impact, as a result, flowing through population currents generated by deeper economic forces.

With these initial observations, we can quickly review the major links between commercial accumulation and urban development in the United States. The dynamics of commercial accumulation dominated American economic development from the colonial era through the middle of the nineteenth century. Before the American Revolution, British merchants monopolized that process. After Independence, American merchants seized control of older commercial opportunities and created many new ones. The commercial stage lingered in the United States. "Indeed," as Louis Hacker concludes, "mercantile capitalism continued to typify the activity of capitalists in America long after its leadership had been wrested away in England by industrial capitalism."[9]

Our analysis of the spatial consequences of commercial accumulation can most easily proceed in two parts: first, by looking at the forces which influenced the distribution of economic activity and people *among* cities; and second, by examining the forces which

[9]Hacker, *The Triumph of American Capitalism* (New York: Columbia University Press, 1947), p. 202.

affected the structure and content of life *within* the commercial cities.

Among Cities. Before Independence, American colonial cities served few economic functions. The first two general functions of Commercial Cities—as Political Capital and Commercial Metropolis —were firmly lodged in London. Some seaports developed as Transport Nodes. Many artisans gathered in the colonial ports, producing luxuries for colonial merchants, but their numbers were obviously limited by the slow growth of the indigenous merchant class itself.

Because colonial cities were serving such limited functions, their growth was itself constrained. City populations did not grow very rapidly. Although total colonial population increased more than tenfold between 1690 and 1790, cities' relative share of the colonial population appears actually to have declined. Roughly 10 percent of colonial Americans lived in cities and towns in 1690.[10] One hundred years later, the relative urban share had fallen back to only 5.1 percent.[11] Immigrants passed quickly through the ports and fanned out in search of agricultural land. Although the main port cities grew some in absolute numbers, "urbanization" failed to keep pace "with the diffusion of hundreds of thousands of settlers into the back country."[12] There was little to keep them down in the town.[13]

Given the singular importance of the Transport Node functions, there were strong political economic pressures which not only limited relative urban population growth but also limited the *number* of major cities. From the beginning of the period, the British Crown strictly controlled town charters. The Crown feared that British merchants would be unable to control commercial transport if too many port cities developed. (If they could not control transport, in turn, then their monopoly control over commercial activity would itself be threatened.) As early as 1680, according to the governor of Virginia, the King was "resolved as soon as storehouse and conveni-

[10]Glaab and Brown, *op. cit.*, p. 25.

[11]These and other data come from Donald J. Bogue, *The Population of the United States* (Glencoe, N.Y.: The Free Press, 1959), p. 30.

[12]Glaab and Brown, *op. cit.*, p. 26.

[13]This obviously compromises the conventional argument that cities automatically grow in a continuous evolutionary pattern alongside "modernization." The economy was growing and modernizing during the colonial period but cities were not. Analyses of urban growth, this suggests, must focus on much more concrete stages of development than the conventional verities permit.

ences be provided, to prohibit ships trading here to land or unload but at certain fixed places."[14] In the North, these early political constraints limited the growth of commercial ports during the colonial period to just four places—to Boston, New York, Philadelphia, and somewhat later, Baltimore. By 1790, these four ports alone accounted for about two thirds of total urban population.[15] It was nearly impossible for other towns to grow because there was no way for them to secure a niche in the economic tableau.[16]

After Independence, the forces affecting urban development shifted slightly. Commercial accumulation still dominated the pace of economic development, but American merchants were able to gain control over a broader range of commercial functions. As domestic and foreign trade expanded, American merchants quickly replaced British merchants in the middle.

As a result, the growth of American ports exploded. Absolute urban population increased from just over 200,000 in 1790 to more than six million in 1860. More important, the relative urban share of total population *reversed* its decline during the colonial period. Relative urban population began to rise immediately after Independence, rising from 5.1 percent of the U.S. population in 1790 to 19.8 percent in 1860.[17]

With trade rising rapidly, urban merchants competed frenetically to gain control over both the Commercial Metropolis and Transport Node functions. Potential commercial monopolists raced against their peers in other leading American ports. "A complex of city imperialisms arose," as Arthur Schlesinger, Sr., put it, "each scheming for dominion, each battling with its rivals for advantage."[18]

[14]Quoted in Glaab and Brown, *op. cit.*, p. 1.

[15]For the details, see Gordon, "CAPITALopolis."

[16]The importance of this argument is further underscored by the case of the Southern colonies. In the South, the commercial exchange built upon crops grown on plantations. The plantations were usually located on rivers up which ocean-faring vessels could travel. As a result, there was little need for cities to serve even the Transport Node functions. For this reason, Southern cities hardly developed at all. In 1790, only 2.3 percent of the South Atlantic population lived in cities, while 7.5 and 8.7 percent of the New England and Middle Atlantic populations lived in cities respectively. (See *ibid.*, for details.)

[17]Bogue, *op. cit.*, p. 31.

[18]Schlesinger, "The City in American Life," in P. Kramer and F. L. Holborn, eds., *The City in American Life* (New York: Putnam's, 1970), p. 28.

During the first decades after Independence, the battle was evenly fought. Each of the major colonial ports in the North was able to grow more or less apace. Between 1790 and 1810, the populations of Philadelphia, New York, Boston and Baltimore all increased between two and three times. And the absolute growth of these four cities alone accounted for nearly half of total city population increase over those twenty years.[19]

Soon enough, however, tendencies toward uneven development asserted themselves. New York merchants quickly gained competitive advantage over their rivals. Thanks to the Erie Canal and other important commercial innovations, New York commercial capitalists began to control more and more of domestic and foreign trade. Between 1800 and 1860, the New York Port's share of total U.S. foreign trade climbed from only 9 percent to 62 percent.[20] Reflecting its growing role as *the* Commercial Metropolis, New York's population soared. By 1860, it had climbed over one million, exceeding the total population of all seven other American cities with more than 100,000 residents combined.[21] Once again, commercial activity was almost exclusively determining the growth of cities and the distribution of population among them.[22]

Within Cities. The dynamics of commercial accumulation had much less effect on the internal structure of American cities. Commercial accumulation, as we noted above, did not directly intervene in the sphere of production. As a result, the port cities grew within the context of an earlier, largely *pre-capitalist* urban form. In precapitalist cities, social relations "had been dominated," as Oscar Handlin puts it, "by the characteristics of the fair."[23] Life was fluid.

[19]These calculations are based on census data. See Gordon, "CAPITALopolis," for the details.

[20]Raymond Vernon, *Metropolis 1985* (Garden City, N.Y.: Doubleday Anchor Books, 1963), pp. 31, 32.

[21]Bogue, *op. cit.*, p. 35. (The figures include Brooklyn as part of New York; although the two boroughs had not yet been merged, they were already economically integrated.)

[22]Because New York merchants dominated this trade, there remained little role for Southern merchants and therefore for Southern cities. By 1860, the relative urban share in the South had climbed to only 9.8 percent, compared to 28.8 percent and 25.5 percent in the New England and Middle Atlantic states respectively. (Gordon, "CAPITALopolis.")

[23]Handlin, "The Modern City as a Field of Historical Study," in A. Callow, ed., *American Urban History* (New York: Oxford University Press, 1969), p. 11.

People lived and worked around the marketplace in relatively random fashion. Daily life, like the entrepôt around which it centered, was "shot through with chance."[24]

The dynamics of commercial accumulation had two main effects on that pre-capitalist pattern of city life. First, the economic functions of cities specified the groups of people who shared in that random urban life—merchants, a few professionals, artisans, journeymen and apprentices, some servants, and the laborers of transportation, like seamen and draymen. Second, the cities tended naturally to center around the wharves, drawn centripetally to the locus of their main political economic functions.

As the commercial cities grew, then, they began to assume a simple and characteristic urban form.[25]

Most people owned their own property and acted as independent economic agents. Most establishments remained small, making it possible for nearly everyone to live and work in the same place. (Artisans lived in back of their shops. Merchants did much of their work in their homes, occasionally walking to the counting houses.) People of many different backgrounds and occupations were interspersed throughout the central city districts, with little obvious socioeconomic residential segregation. In those central districts, the randomness and intensity of urban life produced jagged, unexpected, higgledy-piggledy physical patterns. Streets zigged and zagged every which way. Buildings were scattered at odd angles in unexpected combinations. (Even in Philadelphia, where William Penn's original street plan of 1681 had projected regular, spacious, extensive city growth, the intensive growth around the wharf had resulted in the creation of many new, unplanned streets around the docks "to break down the size of the original building blocks."[26]) It appears that a vibrant community life flourished throughout this central area. The cities featured "an informal neighborhood street life," in Warner's words, threaded by the "unity of everyday life, from tavern, to street, to workplace, to housing . . ."[27]

Only one group failed to share in this central-district street life.

[24]Loc. cit.

[25]See Gordon, "CAPITALopolis," for documentation.

[26]A. E. J. Morris, *History of Urban Form* (New York: John Wiley, 1974), p. 226.

[27]Sam Bass Warner, *The Private City* (Philadelphia: University of Pennsylvania Press, 1968), pp. 61, 21.

Poor itinerants—beggars, casual seamen—all lived outside the cities, huddling in shanties and rooming houses. They moved constantly. Without enough property to establish themselves stably, moving constantly from town to town, they had little relationship to life in the center and little impact upon it.

By the beginning of the nineteenth century, in short, each of the major ports had acquired a characteristic urban form. Each city was divided spatially into two parts. One part coalesced around the wharf. Within that central district, many different classes lived and worked in intimate, intermingling, heterogeneous contiguity. The second part formed a ring around the central port district. In it lived the transient, homogeneous poor, moving in and out of the city frequently.

Once this basic form was established, rapid urban growth took place within it *as long as* the dynamics of commercial accumulation remained dominant. The cities grew rapidly through the first half of the nineteenth century. Some new economic groups began to enter city life, particularly as some manufacturing began to trickle into the ports. As they grew, the cities retained their spatial forms. The wharves continued to act as magnets, containing urban growth within the central port districts. People pushed toward the wharves as much as possible. Scattered evidence suggests that central-district residential densities probably reached their peak in the port cities in the 1840s and 1850s.[28] "In the area adjacent to the water front," Taylor concludes, "a greatly increased work force lived under intolerably crowded conditions."[29]

And still, the central districts retained their heterogeneity. New immigrant groups were rapidly assimilated into the flowing central city life. Workplace and residence were still connected. Socio-economic segregation did not increase. The ebb and flow of street life, however much more crowded it had become, seemed to continue.[30]

The poor also remained isolated on the outskirts. There is no evidence that the poor had begun to move into the central districts —where we know they later began to live—through the 1840s and

[28]See Gordon, "CAPITALopolis," for details.

[29]George Rogers Taylor, "Building an Intra-Urban Transportation System," in A. M. Wakstein, ed., *The Urbanization of America* (Boston: Houghton-Mifflin, 1970), p. 132.

[30]Gordon, "CAPITALopolis."

1850s. And they continued to shift from town to town.

One major change in city shape did occur, however, but it simply underscores the major themes of this account. Before Independence, urban populations grew relatively more slowly than rural population. As a result, land speculators were most active in the countryside— particularly in rural districts close to the port cities. After Independence, as city populations began to boom, the speculators cast their covetous eyes on urban land. Especially in New York City, where population grew most rapidly, urban land speculation intensified.

The effects of this burst in urban land speculation were not surprising. As Lewis Mumford concludes:

> The ideal layout for the business man is that which can be most swiftly reduced to standard monetary units for purchase and sale. The fundamental unit [became] the individual building lot, whose value can be gauged in terms of front feet. . . . In turn, the lots favored the rectangular building block, which . . . became the standard unit for extending the city.[31]

The map of Manhattan vividly witnesses this effect. Below Houston Street in Manhattan, streets flow in many directions at odd angles. Streets above Houston Street were first mapped in the Commissioners' Plan of 1811. The board appointed to draft the plan was dominated by land speculators, and it plotted rectangular grids all the way up the rest of the island. (The grids had been used before, but "only for unrelated sites," and never so systematically.[32]) Available evidence makes clear that the plan was "motivated mainly by narrow considerations of economic gain."[33] Thus the birth of the "city plan."[34]

INDUSTRIAL ACCUMULATION AND THE INDUSTRIAL CITY

Commercial Cities were obviously short-lived. City life had changed dramatically by the end of the nineteenth century. Why?

Following our application of the Marxian perspective, we can draw our first clues from the pace and pattern of capital accumulation. In

---

[31]Lewis Mumford, *The City in History* (New York: Harcourt, Brace & World, 1961), p. 422.

[32]Morris, *op. cit.*, p. 226.

[33]*Ibid.*, p. 227.

[34]Because the growing cities west of the Appalachian Mountains had not existed before this period of exploding urban growth, they never had the central zigs and zags. The speculators laid them out in grids from the beginning.

the United States, the years between 1850 and 1870 witnessed a transition from the stage of commercial accumulation to the stage of industrial accumulation. During the period of industrial accumulation, capitalists turned more and more toward making profits through industrial production itself—through the manufacture of commodities which people bought in the market.[35] In the United States, as in England before, this consolidation of the capitalist mode of production depended on the final development of the *factory system*.[36] In the capitalist factories, workers—owning so little property that they were forced to work as wage laborers—were combined with capitalist-owned machinery to produce goods under the direction of the capitalist employer.

Once the factory system was solidly established, continued accumulation depended centrally on two main factors. First, problems of cost-minimization and labor discipline both required the continual *homogenization* of the work process. Craft jobs were eliminated, work was characterized more and more by semiskilled operative work, and almost all factory workers were subjected to the same discipline of factory control. Second, the system required the continual availability of a *reserve army of the unemployed*—jobless workers, available for employment, whose presence could help discipline those inside the factory gates. The two forces were mutually interdependent. Employers could not successfully overcome workers' resistance to the degradation of their work unless they could easily replace recalcitrant workers with available reserves. Thus, homogenization depended on the reserve army. And those in the reserve army of labor could not credibly pose as potential substitutes for workers inside the factory unless they were competent to perform the factory jobs; since most new workers were unskilled, factory work had to require such low skills that reserve workers could easily move into it. Thus, the effectiveness of the reserve army depended on homogenization.[37]

Given these arguments, it hardly seems surprising that cities became the central locus for industrial production. Cities provided easy

[35]On these points, see Paul Sweezy, *The Theory of Capitalist Development* (New York: Monthly Review Press, 1942).

[36]See Marglin, *op. cit.*

[37]These points are developed in David M. Gordon, Richard C. Edwards and Michael Reich, "Labor Market Segmentation in American Capitalism," mimeographed, 1976.

access to markets, facilitating the scale of production necessary to support homogenized processes. Cities also provided easy access to pools of reserve workers, much less accessible to employers in the countryside.

But which cities would house those factories? And what would they look like? We haven't yet learned enough to answer those questions fully.

The Transition. During the first stages of industrialization, before capitalist production "took off," manufacturing cities were characteristically modest. "The typical industrial town was at this period still a medium-sized city . . ." writes Eric Hobsbawm; "the typical new industrial region generally took the form of a sort of growing together of separate villages developing into smaller towns and small towns developing into larger ones."[38]

The first major factories in the United States followed this pattern. The textile mills of the 1830s and 1840s were clustered along the rivers of New England in small cities like Lawrence, Lowell, Waltham and Chicopee. The factories were relatively small, and the cities acquired their own particular shape around the factory centers.

When coal replaced water as a source of energy between 1845 and 1870, however, factories were freed from the river banks, cast "footloose" to locate where capitalists found it most advantageous. Where?

Conventional economic historians have argued that factories eventually concentrated in *large* cities for four main reasons: (1) they could be near large numbers of workers; (2) they could be near markets for their goods; (3) they could be near major rail and water transport facilities; and (4) they could be near other factories from which they could secure supplies of intermediate products. All of these factors are captured by the conventional term from locational economics, "economies of agglomeration." The idea is simple: it's to each individual employer's advantage to locate near lots of other factories.

That argument still doesn't fully answer our questions, however. How big will these industrial cities become? When do "agglomeration economies" turn into "diseconomies"? When do the cities become so clogged with industry that no one can move?

There is some more recent evidence that central cities become too

[38]Eric Hobsbawm, *The Age of Capital* (New York: Scribner's, 1975), p. 210.

clogged for manufacturing if they grow much beyond a population of 300,000 to 400,000.[39] Intuitively, this makes sense. If too many factories locate near the center of town, transportation can get jammed. The supplies of intermediate goods can be slowed. The "economies of agglomeration" can be compromised.

Had these considerations of purely *quantitative efficiency* dominated the development of industrial cities in the late nineteenth century, one might have expected that many different industrial cities would grow to medium size as the economy boomed. Few cities would grow beyond half a million, perhaps, because congestion would soon develop. (Scattered evidence suggests, indeed, that "early American cities exhibited [such] congestion."[40]) Many different manufacturing cities would sprout and grow to medium size across the country, knit together by the extending railroad network.

So much for expectations! In fact, just the opposite happened. As the industrial economy boomed, more and more manufacturing was concentrated in fewer and fewer cities. Between 1860 and 1890, the share of total manufacturing employment in the twenty largest cities had grown from under one quarter to nearly two fifths in just thirty years.[41] Just as New York had been the protypical Commercial City, Chicago became the exemplary Industrial City. In 1830 its population was insignificant. It grew rapidly. Did it stop at half a million? Hardly. By 1890 it had soared over a million. By the end of World War I its population had climbed past two million. Rather than experiencing a diffusion of manufacturing employment, as one might conceivably have expected, industrial America was witnessing a rapid centralization of manufacturing employment in *large* industrial cities. Why?

I do not think that this concentration of industrial employment can be explained by conventional interpretations.[42] Cities of both 300,000 and one million afforded access to workers. Cities of both 300,000 and one million provided access to markets. Rails and waterways serviced both kinds of cities. Enough different kinds of

---

[39]These conclusions are based in part on work by David Wheeler and Matt Edel. See the discussion in Gordon, "CAPITALopolis."

[40]Dean S. Rugg, *Spatial Foundations of Urbanism* (Dubuque: William C. Brown, Co., 1972), p. 55.

[41]See Gordon, "CAPITALopolis."

[42]*Ibid.*

factories crowded into medium-sized cities to provide employers with sufficient access to intermediate goods.

Instead, I submit that one reason was more important than any other in explaining the concentration of industrial employment. *It involved the problem of labor control.* As the industrial factory was being established, labor conflict began to intensify. Workers resisted the factory discipline to which they were being exposed. In medium-sized cities, the middle classes and working classes tended to live relatively near each other. When workers went on strike, the middle classes frequently supported them against their employers. As Herbert Gutman writes:

Through its early years, for at least a generation, the factory and its disciplines, the large impersonal corporation, and the propertyless wage-earners remained unusual and even alien elements in the [medium-sized] industrial town. . . . In these years, therefore, the factory-owner symbolized innovation and a radical departure from an older way of life. His power was not yet legitimized and "taken for granted." . . . He met with unexpected opposition from nonindustrial property-owners, did not dominate the local political structure, and learned that the middle and professional classes did not automatically accept his leadership and idolize his achievements. Moreover, the new working class, not entirely detached from the larger community, had significant ties to that community which strengthened its power at critical moments and allowed it, despite the absence of strong permanent labor organizations, often to influence events at the expense of the factory-owner.[43]

In the largest industrial cities, in contrast, employers could more easily achieve labor control. The working classes were segregated into separate districts. The middle classes and upper classes were tucked away safely out of reach. "Unlike similar groups in small towns," Gutman concludes, "the urban middle- and upper-income groups generally frowned upon labor disputes and automatically sided with employers." The employer could rely on the impersonality of the large-city environment to echo the impersonality of the factory. Reserve workers could mingle indistinguishably with employed workers in the working-class housing districts. The effects of homogenization and the reserve army were reinforced.[44]

---

[43]Herbert Gutman, "Class, Status, and Community Power in Nineteenth Century American Industrial Cities . . . ," in B. Cook *et al.*, eds., *Past Imperfect,* Vol. II (New York: Knopf, 1973), p. 11.

[44]Logically, this concentration of workers could have had the opposite effect—forcing workers together and amplifying their individual strikes into broader rebellion.

In short, I submit that the transition to the Industrial City was mediated by the problems of labor control in the capitalist factory. Capitalists had to find *qualitatively efficient* locations for their factories. Medium-sized cities did not fully satisfy this imperative. Larger cities satisfied it much better. And so, more and more, capitalists built their factories in those large cities. Reflecting the domination of the dynamics of capital accumulation, those large cities became more and more characteristic as industrial accumulation proceeded.

The Form of the Industrial City. As a consequence of those forces, the Industrial City was radically different from the Commercial City. Its characteristics can be easily summarized.

First, huge factories were concentrated downtown, near rail and water outlets. These factories were so quickly constructed, in many cases, that the mixed workplace/residential districts of the downtown Commercial Cities were often torn down. (Scattered data suggest that residential densities actually declined, despite the rapid growth of these cities, in those downtown districts during the period of transition and reconstruction.[45])

Second, entirely new segregated working-class housing districts emerged. Located near the factories, so that the workers could walk to their plants, the housing was crammed densely together. In New York, there were tenements. In Philadelphia, there were row houses. In Chicago, there were walk-ups. Whatever the specific features of the housing, it was clustered together in isolation. In these districts, both the employed and unemployed lived together in mobile confusion.

Third, the middle and upper classes began to flee from the center city as fast and as far as their finances permitted. The wealthy and the not-so-wealthy joined in "fleeing from the noise and confusion of the water front, the dirt, the stench, and the intolerably crowded conditions of the old central city."[46] Since the wealthier could afford to travel farther to and from work than the middle classes, residential socioeconomic segregation became more and more pronounced. The middle and upper classes were gradually arrayed in concentric circles

---

At first, however, the segregation of workers effectively subdued them. Later, as we see at the beginning of the next section, the concentration began to backfire and workers began to explode.

[45]Gordon, "CAPITALopolis."

[46]Taylor, *op. cit.*, p. 134.

moving out from the center, with each band reflecting different income levels.[47]

Finally, shopping districts arose in the heart of the city to provide centralized shopping outlets on which the middle and upper classes could converge for their marketing.

Working from this schematic view, we can easily see that the Industrial City represented a clear *reversal* of some of the most important tendencies reflected in the Commercial City. The character of the central city was now shaped by dependent wage earners rather than independent property owners. People no longer worked and lived in the same place; there was now a separation between job and residential location. There was no longer residential heterogeneity; instead, the cities had quickly acquired a rather sharp residential segregation by economic class. In the Commercial Cities, the poor had lived outside the center while everyone else lived inside; now, suddenly, the poor and working classes lived inside while everyone else raced away from the center. In the Commercial Cities, central-city street life involved nearly everyone; in the Industrial City, only the working classes participated and they had little choice.

Was this new urban form destined by technical necessity? Other, more mixed, much smaller cities might well have facilitated equally rapid industrial growth. But capitalism requires workers' submission to their exploitation. Only in this new kind of large Industrial City, it appears, could workers be sufficiently isolated from everyone else that their resistance might be rubbed smooth. In England, Manchester had already pioneered this form—in the first half of the nineteenth century—and Friedrich Engels had already perceived the essential social functions of that shape:

The town itself is peculiarly built, so that someone can live in it for years and travel into and out of it daily without ever coming into contact with a working-class quarter or even with workers. . . . This comes about mainly in the circumstances that through an unconscious, tacit agreement as much as through conscious, explicit intention, the working-class districts are most sharply separated from the parts of the city reserved for the middle class.[48]

[47]These rings were actually lines along a ray from the center of the city, with each ray determined by streetcar trolley lines.

[48]Friedrich Engels, *The Condition of the Working-Classes in England, 1844* (Moscow: Progress Publishers, 1973), p. 84.

Without that separation, the problems of capitalist production would have remained problematic. With the development of the Industrial City, the basis for capitalist production was established.

CORPORATE ACCUMULATION AND THE CORPORATE CITY

We now know—again from hindsight—that the Industrial City was itself short-lived. For about half a century, at least, our cities have been pushed in different directions. A new kind of city form has come to dominate American urban development.

Three main tendencies have characterized this change from the Industrial City.

- The centers of many cities have been more and more dominated by central business districts—by towering clusters of corporate skyscrapers.
- Manufacturing has moved rapidly away from the center of the city, rather than concentrating increasingly in its middle.
- Cities have become politically fragmented, splintered into thousands of separate urban and suburban jurisdictions.

What explains these new developments? Conventional urban historians have some easy answers.

- They explain the growth of central business districts with new versions of the same arguments about "agglomeration." Every complex society needs vast administrative organs coordinating its many interdependent transactions, they argue, and many of these activities are best located near each other to permit "face to face" communication.
- They explain the decentralization of manufacturing by technological change. Somebody invented the truck, they note, and the truck has made it more efficient to locate manufacturing outside the central city. Somebody else invented land-intensive automated processing machinery, they add, which placed a premium on employers' finding cheap land *outside* dense central-city manufacturing districts.
- They explain political fragmentation with a tip of the hat to people's preferences. People began to move outside the city, they argue, and discovered the joys of living together in separate, homogeneous suburbs. All the king's men couldn't overcome those preferences and put the suburbs back together again.

There are grains of truth in each of these explanations. But they are also essentially misleading. They suggest that our new urban form is determined by technical necessity and by people's preferences. There are several respects in which that kind of argument misses the point.

In order to develop a clearer understanding of this new urban form, we have to return to our analysis of the underlying process of capital accumulation. Around the turn of the century—between 1898 and 1920—the United States experienced a transition from the stage of industrial accumulation to advanced corporate accumulation. More and more, giant corporations began to dominate the process of capital accumulation. They still depended ultimately on the production and realization of surplus value. The process still led to both deepening and widening of capitalist control. What was new was that those tendencies were being guided by the decisions of many fewer, much larger economic units. Most important, those economic units—the giant corporations—now had sufficient size to permit a qualitatively new level of rationalization of production and distribution.

The Transition. To appreciate the impact of this transition to corporate accumulation on urban structure, therefore, we have to go back to the very end of the nineteenth century. The central cities had been growing rapidly throughout the second half of the nineteenth century. Factories were piling into the downtown districts. And then, at the very end of the century, something began to change.

Suddenly, around 1898 or 1899, manufacturing started moving out of the central city. Charles Glaab and Theodore Brown summarize the data:

A Census Bureau study of twelve of the thirteen largest "industrial districts" showed that from 1899 to 1904 the number of persons employed in industry in central cities increased by 14.9 per cent while in the outlying zones the number increased by 32.8 per cent. From 1904 to 1909 the increase in central cities was 22.5 per cent while in the surrounding zones it was 48.8 per cent. For the decade, the growth rate was over two times as great for the suburbs—97.7 per cent to 40.8 per cent.[49]

That sudden movement of manufacturing was not invisible, either. New suburban manufacturing towns were being built in open space

[49]Glaab and Brown, *op. cit.*, p. 277.

like movie sets—as in Gary, Indiana, where U.S. Steel constructed an entirely new complex in 1905; in East St. Louis; and in the industrial suburbs of Cincinnati and Buffalo.

This sudden reversal of manufacturing centralization cannot be easily understood by conventional explanations. The truck was not yet providing effective transportation. There is no obvious evidence that there was a sudden rash of new inventions prompting a shift to land-intensive technologies.

Rather, the explanation turns again upon an appreciation of the problems of labor control. The rapid centralization of manufacturing, it turns out, had involved a fundamental contradiction. Large impersonal central-city factory districts overwhelmed workers for a while, but workers eventually began to rebel, anyway. Throughout the late 1870s and 1880s, class conflict in the central cities began to intensify. The contradictions of centralization erupted. Because workers were so densely packed into working-class districts, the struggles at one plant quickly spread to others. Rebellion multiplied. What had once been qualitatively efficient, from the capitalists' perspective, was now inviting disaster.

The solution? Move! In testimony before the U.S. Industrial Commission from 1900 to 1902, employer after employer explained the calculus. Some examples:

- The President of Fraser and Chalmers Co. in Chicago: "Chicago today is the hotbed of trades unionism. . . . We believe here in Chicago . . . that unless something is done in Chicago soon . . . it is doomed as an industrial center."
- The President of Turner Brass Works in Chicago: "This strike which we have had has set us to thinking very seriously whether it would be possible for us to more satisfactorily conduct our business outside of Chicago in a smaller place. . . ."
- Chairman of the Board of Mediation and Arbitration, New York State: "Q: Do you find that isolated plants, away from the great centers of population, are more apt to have non-union shops than in a city? A: Yes. Q: Do you know of cases in the State where they do isolate plants to be free . . . from unionism? A: They have been located with that end in view. . . ."
- President of company in Chicago: ". . . all these controversies and strikes that we have had here for some years have been a great injury to the city. It has prevented outsiders from coming in here and investing their capital. . . . It has discouraged capital at home, and it seeks other markets for investment. It has drawn the manufacturers away from the city, because they are afraid their men will get into trouble and get into strikes. . . . New

industries that would locate in Chicago have been placed outside. The result is, all around Chicago for forty or fifty miles, the smaller towns are getting these manufacturing plants. . . .[50]

If labor trouble had been burgeoning since the 1880s, why did this movement begin so suddenly? (There were some earlier movements, of course, but the pace appears to have accelerated sharply in 1898–1899.) I would argue that the pressures for the decentralization of manufacturing had been building with growing labor unrest for several years, but that the actual movement awaited the great merger wave of 1898–1903. As corporations centralized capital, they acquired enough extra money to be able to finance new plants outside the central cities. Before then, and particularly during the depression of 1893–1897, they could not afford to move.

In short, the great twentieth-century reversal of employment location must be carefully analyzed. It appears that it began because corporations could no longer control their labor forces in the central cities. Once again, as with the transition to the Industrial City, problems of labor control had decisive effects. The emergence of the large corporation—with the transition to corporate accumulation— played a critical role in forging a new spatial dynamic.

What about the growth of downtown central business districts? What explains their emergence?

The major expansion of downtown central business districts occurred in the 1920s. ("By 1929, American cities had 377 skyscrapers of more than twenty stories in height."[51]) Why then? It cannot easily be explained by the "face to face" argument. As far as one can tell, there was no dramatic increase in the "complexity" of transactions in the economy as a whole during that period which could explain the sudden need for close administrative contact. Technical explanations also seem to founder. Although engineering developments were necessary for the boom, the skyscraper style had been perfected for at least fifteen years, and the Woolworth Building in New York, completed in 1913, marked the prototype for the new towers.

The most important reason for the central-business-district boom was that the huge corporations had not consolidated their monopoly

[50]All these quotes come from the *Report of the U.S. Industrial Commission, Washington, D.C., 1900–1902,* 19 vols. For full and detailed references, see Gordon, "CAPITALopolis."

[51]Glaab and Brown, *op. cit.,* p. 280.

control over their industries until after World War I.[52] Once they gained stable market control, they could begin to organize that control.[53] They were now large enough to separate administrative functions from the production process itself, leaving plant managers to oversee the factories while corporate managers supervised the far-flung empire. Having already spurred the decentralization of many of their production plants, they could now afford to locate their administrative headquarters where it would be most "efficient."[54] They chose downtown locations, in most cases, to be near other headquarters, near banks and law offices, and near advertising agents.

From this perspective, there is nothing necessarily destined about central business districts and towering skyscrapers. Those spatial forms develop as the sites for administrative control functions *when power gets very centralized.* During the stage of corporate accumulation, economic power has become very centralized indeed.

The third major change in the transition to the Corporate City involved political fragmentation. Can we explain that fragmentation with reference to people's preferences?

Again, we must be very careful about the timing of events. Up to the end of the nineteenth century, central cities habitually annexed outlying residential districts as people moved beyond the traditional city boundaries. Central cities continued to unify their political jurisdictions as they spread outward. This process of annexation continued steadily until the end of the century. At the turn of the century, however, annexations ended somewhat abruptly in most of the Industrial Cities.[55] Manhattan's "annexation" of Brooklyn in 1898 symbolically marks the end of an era in those cities.

Can this rapid change be explained by a sudden shift in people's preferences? Not at all. As we learned in the preceding section on the Industrial City, people had been fleeing the central city since the 1860s. According to one study, New York City's population had

[52]For details on this argument, see Richard C. Edwards, "Stages in Corporate Stability and the Risks of Corporate Failure," *Journal of Economic History* (June 1975).

[53]See Alfred D. Chandler, Jr., *Strategy and Structure* (Cambridge, Mass.: MIT Press, 1969).

[54]For this argument, see Steven Hymer, "The Multinational Corporation and the Law of Uneven Development" in J. Bhagwati, ed., *Economics and World Order* (New York: Macmillan, 1972).

[55]See Sam Bass Warner, *Street-Car Suburbs* (New York: Atheneum, 1969).

begun to decentralize as early as 1850, and nine other cities had begun to decentralize residentially by 1900.[56] Until 1900, however, those refugees were continually caught in the extending central city web.

What changed at the turn of the century? There was no apparent acceleration of residential suburbanization. There was not yet a sudden increase in the use of the car. There were no identifiable shifts in people's tastes for homogeneous suburban living, since they had been marching on those tastes for fifty years. The electric streetcar developed rapidly through the 1890s, permitting somewhat more distant intra-urban travel, but it represented a simple improvement on a long succession of carriages and trolleys dating from the 1840s rather than a qualitative transformation of city transit.

What changed most dramatically was that manufacturers themselves began to move out of the central cities. Once they established themselves in the Garys and Lackawannas, they naturally wanted to avoid paying central-city taxes (whereas in the earlier period of Industrial City manufacturing centralization, central-city capitalists had obviously encouraged annexation to prevent fleeing residents from escaping the tax burdens which the manufacturers were spatially bound to bear). So, suddenly, it was clearly in their interests to oppose further annexation. Once they succeeded in generating opposition to annexation, others joined them. The sudden shift in manufacturing location seems the only plausible historical explanation to the sudden success of those anti-annexation movements. Once again, the transition to corporate accumulation played a central role in the transition to the Corporate City.

The Form of the Corporate City. Having reviewed these several arguments, we can now review the central political economic features of the Corporate City.

If a city had reached maturity as an Industrial City during the stage of industrial accumulation, its character changed rapidly during the corporate period although its physical structure remained embedded in concrete. Its downtown shopping districts were transformed into downtown central business districts (CBDs), dominated by skyscrapers. (Some Industrial Cities, like Baltimore, never got many headquarters to locate there.) Surrounding the central business district were emptying manufacturing areas, depressed from the desertion of

[56]More detail on this argument is provided in Gordon, "CAPITALopolis."

large plants, barely surviving on the light and competitive industries left behind. Next to those districts were the old working-class districts, often transformed into "ghettos," increasingly dominated by the working poor, locked in the cycle of central-city-factory decline. Outside the central city there were suburban belts of industrial development, linked together by circumferential highways. Scattered around those industrial developments were fragmented working-class and middle-class suburban communities. The wealthy lived farther out.

Many other, newer cities—particularly those in the South, Southwest and West—reached maturity during the stage of corporate accumulation. These became the exemplary Corporate Cities. They shared one thundering advantage over the older Industrial Cities: they had never acquired the fixed physical capital of an earlier era. They could be constructed from scratch to fit the needs of a new period of accumulation in which factory plant and equipment were themselves increasingly predicated on a decentralized model. As a result, there was no identifiable downtown factory district; manufacturing was scattered throughout the city plane. There were no centralized working-class housing districts (for that was indeed what capitalists had learned to avoid); working-class housing was scattered all over the city around the factories. Automobiles and trucks provided the connecting links, threading together the separate pieces. The Corporate Cities became, in Robert Fogelson's term, the perfectly "fragmented metropolis."[57] No centers anywhere. Diffuse economic activities everywhere.

These models of the two cities help underscore the significance of the *reversals* reflected in the Corporate City—reversals of tendencies which had crystallized in the Industrial City. Manufacturing had been clustering toward the center of the Industrial City; now it was moving anywhere across the urban space. Working-class housing had been packed into dense central zones; now it was scattered around the metropolitan area and increasingly segmented. Central business districts had been dominated by shopping centers; now, in at least some cities, they were dominated by corporate headquarters. The middle- and upper-classes had been fleeing but were continually reabsorbed; now, in the older cities, they fled more successfully into

[57]See Robert Fogelson, *The Fragmented Metropolis: Los Angeles, 1850–1930* (Cambridge, Mass.: Harvard University Press, 1967).

separate suburbs. Before, the city had crammed around its center; now, the Corporate City sprawled.

The Corporate City first began to acquire its shape during the 1920s. The Depression and World War II slowed its growth within the consolidating form. After World War II, the Corporate City came into its own. Several important trends helped accentuate some of the most dramatic developments.[58]

- The Cold War spurred a continuation of enormous defense spending. Pork-barrel politics and locational imperatives combined to channel disproportionate amounts of defense money into the South, Southwest, and West—into the "Sun Belt"—and helped reinforce the tendency of the Corporate Cities in those areas to grow more and more rapidly.

- Federal policies, zoning regulations and the construction industry all helped to reinforce scattered sprawling, extensive single-family housing development. Single-family homes helped intensify, in turn, the isolation and separation of individual families from their class and community ties.

- The energy, auto, and highway construction industries combined to promote auto and highway development. Highways reinforced the sprawling, circumferential development of the Corporate City —accentuating some of the disadvantages of the older central cities—and autos reinforced people's isolation within the metropolis.

- Financial and real-estate interests in older central cities reasoned correctly, as they watched manufacturing employment move away, that their vested interests in downtown finance and land would be preserved if and only if more and more corporate headquarters located in their CBDs. "Urban renewal" programs cleared "decaying" districts for "redevelopment." Whether or not the headquarters eventually arrived, these renewal programs almost always had the effect of pushing the poor into more and more crowded quarters and emptying out vast downtown tracts for long ghostly "incubation" periods.

The story of the Corporate City goes on. Because its history is more recent, we know it more intimately. Its details surround us. For the purposes of this essay, however, the details are less impor-.

[58]See, for further detail, the following essay by John Mollenkopf (selection #6).

tant than the major themes. If we look up at the Corporate City from within it, it seems fixed and unyielding. If we view it more critically over a much longer horizon, its form seems much more contingent. The Corporate City emerged as a historical solution to some eruptive crises in capital accumulation. Its form began increasingly to correspond to the pace and pattern of a new stage of corporate accumulation. If we have learned that the Corporate City emerged historically from the disarray of capitalism in crisis, it seems equally likely that the current crises of the Corporate City can best be understood within the context of capitalist accumulation.

THE ROOTS OF CRISIS

Some of the current urban crisis can be simply explained as a product of general economic crisis.[59] When the economy plunges into a tailspin, for instance, city finances suffer badly and many in the cities go jobless.

It would be misleading to stop at that kind of analysis, however, for we would falsely characterize the current urban crisis. We must go beyond that initial response to a more coherent understanding of the particular character of the current urban crisis.

It turns out, at this more particular level, that the current urban crisis is not a general urban crisis at all. Some cities are undergoing a crisis, like New York and Detroit, while others are not. Which ones are being hit the worst?

In order to be more specific, we must find some useful ways of distinguishing between different cities. Here, the analysis of the preceding sections can help. Cities tend to acquire the urban form characteristic of the stage during which they develop to "maturity." Cities acquired the form of the Industrial City if they reached maturity during the stage of industrial accumulation. Cities acquired the form of the Corporate City if they reached maturity during the stage of corporate accumulation. Perhaps we can best distinguish between cities by categorizing them according to the period of their full development.

When does a city reach "maturity"? A city grows rapidly until it reaches the size appropriate to its economic functions and its place within the urban system. When cities reach their own "level," their growth begins to slow. They have passed into the years of their "adult" life. They have "matured."

[59]See the essay by Roger Alcaly and Helen Bodian in this volume (selection #3).

It is possible statistically to detect the point of maturity by tracing the last point at which a city's population growth slowed. Before that point, a city is still maturing. After that point, it has acquired its enduring physical structure.

Into what groups should we divide cities? The preceding analysis suggests that we should separately consider Commercial Cities, Industrial Cities and Corporate Cities.

On second thought, however, it makes little sense to retain a separate group of Commercial Cities. Five cities passed their growth peaks before the transition from commercial accumulation to industrial accumulation—Boston, Baltimore, New York, Philadelphia and New Orleans. (We can recognize these as the main ports of the commercial period.) During the transition from the commercial stage to the industrial stage, however, at least three of these cities—New York, Philadelphia and Baltimore—experienced substantial reconstruction and quickly acquired most of the characteristics of the Industrial City. Boston and New Orleans appear to have experienced much less substantial reconstruction, but they, too, began to reflect some of the same characteristics.

In this more general sense, then, we can consider as "Old Cities" all those cities which reached maturity before the final consolidation of the corporate stage of accumulation after World War I. We might expect that these cities, even today, would continue to reflect some of the characteristically centralized structures which they acquired during the stage of industrial accumulation.

In contrast, we can characterize as "New Cities" all those cities which reached maturity after the end of World War I. We might expect that these New Cities would reflect, on average, some of the basic structures characteristic of the Corporate City form.

Relying on the careful statistical work of Alfred Watkins,[60] we can safely date the decade of maturity of 43 of the 50 largest metropolitan areas (ranked by 1970 population) in the United States. (The remaining 7 are difficult to date because of shifting metropolitan definitions.) Of those 43 cities, 25 are Old Cities and 18 are New Cities.

Twelve of those cities reached maturity during the transitional period between 1910 and 1920, however, and their categorization definitively as either Old or New Cities may be problematic. For the purposes of this brief essay, therefore, we can work more easily with

[60]See Alfred Watkins, "City Age and the Typology of Subemployment," working paper, New School for Social Research, 1975.

31 cities whose categorization seems less ambiguous. Of these, 18 are Old Cities and 13 are New Cities.

A first measure by which to locate the incidence of crisis involves the basic health of metropolitan economies. If employment and the labor force are growing, cities will prosper. If employment and the labor force are shrinking, cities may be in trouble—particularly when general economic crisis strikes. We can therefore examine cities' differential vulnerability to the recent crisis, for example, by looking at the change in civilian labor force over the years from 1960 to 1970.[61] Over that decade, the civilian labor forces of 15 metropolitan areas grew; 12 of those 15 were New Cities. The civilian labor forces of 15 cities declined; 14 of those 15 were Old Cities. (Data were not available in comparable form for one of the 31 in our comparison.) By this measure, in other terms, 12 of the 13 New Cities grew, while 14 of the 17 Old Cities declined.[62] When crisis struck in the mid-seventies, it seems obvious that the Old Cities would be buffeted the most.

If metropolitan economies are stagnating, social problems intensify. Unemployment grows, the jobless seek welfare, crime rates soar, and so on. Richard Nathan has developed (with others) a metropolitan index of social hardship by combining indices of several different problems like unemployment, poverty, and welfare incidence.[63] The hardship index allows an analysis of the severity of these problems in central cities by comparing the magnitude of the index between the central city and the suburbs for each metropolitan area. The higher the index of central-city disadvantage, the more severe the social problems faced by central-city governments. By this standard, once again, the Old Cities are suffering the worst. When metropolitan areas are ranked by this measure of central-city disadvantage, 13 of the 16 most disadvantaged central cities are Old Cities. Ten of the

[61]Changes in the labor force are a somewhat better indicator of overall growth than changes in employment, in certain respects, because they reflect the total response of people to the general state of the economy. If a city is growing, for instance, people may move to it. If a city is stagnating, people may be moving somewhere else. Labor-force figures capture employment effects, labor force participation effects and migration effects.

[62]These data are based on tabulations in the U.S. Bureau of the Census, City-County Data Book, 1962 and 1972.

[63]See Richard P. Nathan, "The New Federalism versus the Emerging New Structuralism," Publius (Summer 1975).

13 least disadvantaged central cities are New Cities. The average index of central-city disadvantage is 58 percent higher in the Old Cities than in the New Cities.

Social hardship means mounting city expenditures. The poor and unemployed may require social services and, given our federal political structure, central cities will often have to bear the costs of those services. A third index of comparison, therefore, involves municipal expenditures in central cities. Most simply, we can compare general municipal expenditures per capita in 1972 between old central cities and new central cities. Within our group of cities, 10 of the 11 central cities with the highest municipal expenditures per capita are Old Cities. The average in the Old Cities is 42 percent higher than in the New Cities.[64]

With declining economies and exploding expenditure obligations, finally, we might expect that Old Cities would be more likely to get into serious fiscal trouble. As employment lags, tax revenues will stagnate. With revenues lagging and expenditures climbing, Old Cities may be forced to borrow in order to balance their budgets. As their debts grow deeper, creditors may become squeamish. Sooner or later the threat of municipal default or bankruptcy may loom. Municipal debt, in this sense, becomes the lightning rod for more general urban crisis. We can compare the severity of this problem between cities by studying the incidence of municipal short-term indebtedness per capita. By this measure, the structural differences between Old Cities and New Cities seem especially dramatic. In 1973–74, 14 of the 16 most indebted cities were Old Cities. The average municipal short-term indebtedness per capita was 6300 percent higher in the Old Cities than in the New Cities.[65]

These several measures make clear that the "urban fiscal crisis" is neither specific nor universal.

On the one hand, despite the headlines, New York City is not the only city with problems. Among the 18 Old Cities in this comparison, New York City is in "better" shape than 8 others on the labor-force measure, 7 others on the hardship measure, and one other on the expenditure measure. (New York City's short-term debt per capita

[64]This particular compilation of city expenditures comes from Charles Schultze *et al.*, "Fiscal Problems of Cities" (selection #11).

[65]The data on debt are based on U.S. Bureau of the Census, *City Government Finances*.

was the highest among the Old Cities.) While crisis has arrived more dramatically in New York City than in other Old Cities, objective conditions make many others equally vulnerable.[66]

On the other hand, the urban fiscal crisis is not universal. It has not spread to New Cities. The current crisis is a general crisis of Old Cities in the corporate stage of capital accumulation. Capitalism has decreed that those cities are archaic as sites for capitalist production. The process of capital accumulation is leaving them behind. Capitalists have found that they can better control their labor forces and make higher profits elsewhere. The logic of capitalism, in this ultimate sense, lies at the root of our current problems.

[66]See several of the essays in this volume for further discussion of the particularities of the New York City case.

6. The Crisis of the Public Sector in America's Cities

JOHN H. MOLLENKOPF

*Budgets are not merely affairs of arithmetic . . . in a thousand ways they
go to the root of prosperity of individuals, the relation of classes, and
the strength of kingdoms.*   —*William Gladstone*

*This is a Republican pincer movement responsible not to the people
but to financial interests using cash as a weapon in an attempt to direct
the social and economic policies of our city.*
—*New York Mayor Abraham Beame, 1975*

*Indeed, as the classical economists up to and including Karl Marx
demonstrated with a clarity that eludes modern economists, the entire
history of civilization is bound up with capital accumulation.*
—BUSINESS WEEK, *special issue on the*
"Capital Crisis," September 22, 1975

If one charted the reasons the *New York Times, Business Week* and
other major news organs offer for the contemporary urban crisis,
three themes would emerge: growing welfare costs, public-sector
worker militance and bureaucratic inefficiency. These sources infre-
quently mention the recession, federal austerity measures, non-local
sources of the capital crisis, and other background factors, while they
treat the crucial impact of corporate-dominated growth patterns (and
their costs) with stony silence.

Yet one basic fact looms through the highly politicized and technical discussion about the "causes" of the crisis: not only did the poor
people and public workers who are being blamed for it not play an
active role in creating the crisis, they hardly understand it. They
understand only its tragedies. However, not only do leaders of dominant city agencies, banks and corporations understand such arcane

Copyright © 1976 by John M. Mollenkopf. This is an edited version of a paper which
was presented to the Conference on the Sociology of Urban and Regional Development, International Sociological Association, Messina, Italy, April 10–14, 1976. Another version has also appeared in *Socialist Revolution* (July–September 1976). John
H. Mollenkopf teaches in the Public Management Program at the Stanford Graduate
School of Business.

matters as "rolling over" bonds, evaluating program effectiveness and financial juggling, they *invented* them. While the current crisis involves public welfare functions and the public work force, its roots can be traced back to the political/economic strategy which created the need for tricky financing and enlarged bureaucracies. As such, it arises from tensions built into the course of metropolitan growth since World War II, and the collapse of the political coalitions and programs which directed that growth.

Post–World War II economic growth required a reshaping of the metropolitan area and therefore the institution of new mechanisms to contain the attendant social and political instabilities. The turmoil of the 1960s gave the costs of these containing mechanisms, in the words of President Ford's 1975 State of the Union message, "a life of their own." The current Administration and its backers are employing the urban fiscal crisis to terminate these claims on the public budget. In doing so, however, they are revealing a crisis not only of public welfare functions but of the political coalitions and growth strategies which created a need for them. At bottom, then, the current crisis is one of growth, of a general strategy for accumulating capital. By no means is it accidental that the current crisis has been most virulently manifested in New York City, the capital of Capital.

I. THE CITY AND CAPITAL ACCUMULATION

Modern analysts tend to view cities as epiphenomena: once economic forces reach a certain level, they argue, urban agglomerations are made possible. Agricultural technology makes food plentiful and cheap, factories require steadily larger work forces, and willy-nilly, cities develop. Yet, exactly the opposite is true. As Lewis Mumford has written:

> The city was the container that brought about the concentrated development of new technology, and through its very form held together the new forces, intensified their internal reactions, and raised the whole level of achievement.[1]

The city is a device for concentrating and controlling political power, and it is this capacity which makes concentrated economic activity possible, not the reverse.

[1] Lewis Mumford, *The City in History* (New York: Harcourt Brace, 1961), p. 34.

But if concentrated urban power is necessary for more intense development, it does not follow that urban social and political structures always smoothly encourage and reinforce it. As with societies as a whole, urban institutional arrangements which originally promoted economic development can evolve along their own logic and become impediments to further growth. The guild structure of English and Continental medieval towns, for example, strongly inhibited the establishment of manufacturing in the transition to the modern capitalist industrial system. It has been a hallmark of the last two centuries, however, that the resolution to this tension between old urban forms and new ways of organizing economic activity has been fundamentally urban. Thus, though early factory production in England took place outside of towns, England ultimately gave us the characteristic modern industrial city in Manchester, Hull, Leeds, Liverpool, and indeed, London itself.

Political, social and economic forces have been concentrated in an urban form as a precondition to any economic leap forward. As a period of growth matures, however, the older urban "prerequisites" frequently become impediments, which must then be broken apart and reshaped if a new stage of growth is to occur. As a result, cities have experienced a cycle of political and social crisis which parallels and is intimately linked to the major economic crises; in both domains, crises have had the effect of clearing away outmoded furnishings. As with any housecleaning, the process has been fraught with conflict, stress, abandonment of the familiar, and forced accommodation to new conditions. But these periods have also allowed the bold and powerful to reorganize their environments along more comfortable and useful lines.

THE INDUSTRIAL CAPITALIST CITY

In U.S. urban history, three such periods can be broadly if schematically outlined. Between 1840 and about the turn of the century, the industrial revolution and the modern city rapidly nourished each other. Industrial capitalism's key need was to amass and discipline large amounts of capital (both in the human and machine senses). Capital was accumulated during this period both through expanding the scale of production and by intensifying work. As the period developed and class antagonisms mounted, capital responded with generous applications of factory power in its many forms: wage cuts, unemployment, Pinkertons, labor-saving technology and an increasingly finely graded division of labor.[2]

Newly forming and re-forming cities catalyzed and multiplied this development. Chicago, a 50-person trading outpost in 1830, sixty years later had swelled to 1.1 million, 80 percent of whom were immigrants, under the impetus of railroad construction, the stockyards, farm-equipment production and the burgeoning steel industry. Fed by streams of migrants from the U.S. countryside, Ireland, Germany, and later Italy and central Europe, the U.S. urban population curved exponentially upward in the latter nineteenth century. Heterogeneity, geographic mobility and the chaos of rapid urban development proved to be high barriers against this newly invented work force's becoming conscious of its collective interests, but above all, the relentlessly unprincipled urban political machines controlled and stabilized these cities.

Indeed, if urban machines had not driven out all alternatives, including both Yankee aristocratic rule and fledgling American socialism, it is doubtful that the industrial revolution could have occurred with such speed and effectiveness. The almighty dollar exercised its reign not only over individual lives but over the rate and type of public investments in roads, real estate, transportation, sewers, public utilities, and indeed over the character of the urban political community.

---

[2]In general this discussion follows Erik Wright, "Alternative Perspectives in the Marxist Theory of Accumulation and Crisis," *Insurgent Sociologist* 6 (Fall 1975), pp. 5–40; Joseph Gillman, *The Falling Rate of Profit* (London: Dennis Dobson, 1957); Robert A. Gordon, *Economic Instability and Growth: The American Record* (New York: Harper & Row, 1974). Every economic historian of worth notes a basic transition at the end of the nineteenth century from industrial to corporate capitalism, with the full emergence of advanced capitalism based on multinational corporations and Keynesian government policies since World War II. Harry Braverman, *Labor and Monopoly Capital* (New York: Monthly Review Press, 1974), and Katherine Stone, "The Origins of Job Structures in the Steel Industry," *Review of Radical Political Economy* 6 (Summer 1974), discuss changes in job structure across this period, while A. D. Chandler, *Strategy and Structure* (Garden City, N.Y.: Doubleday, 1962), remains the best history of the emergent corporation. David Brody, *Steelworkers in America: The Non Union Era* (Cambridge: Harvard University, 1962), and A. D. Lindsay, *The Pullman Strike* (Chicago: University of Chicago Press, 1946), offer excellent pictures of the late-nineteenth-century links between urban structure, urban politics, factory production and class conflict.

THE TRANSITION TO MODERN CORPORATE SOCIETY

In the years after 1900 it became increasingly clear, however, that these once highly functional arrangements were creating difficulties. Intense competition and an increasing substitution of machines for labor tended to drive down profit rates. Together with speculative and fraudulent activity in the capital markets, falling profits triggered a series of sharp fluctuations in the business cycle and a growing wave of monopolization within many areas of production. At the national level, Progressive efforts to achieve greater stability through government regulation culminated finally in the New Deal. At the local level the Progressive era produced a whole series of institutional changes designed to make local government function in a "businesslike" and apolitical manner. Cities thus entered a second, transitional period in which the centralized power of the political machines was fragmented and emasculated.

As working-class ethnic communities built self-help institutions like savings and burial societies, developed enclaves of small-scale property ownership and became integrated into trades or occupations they could claim their "own," the political machine became less critical as an engine of social peace. At the same time, the machine's venality and political inertia made life difficult for entrepreneurs not intimately connected with it. Even for businessmen for whom city political connections were for some reason paramount (public-utility franchises, real-estate development, large factories where worker organization caused difficulty, etc.), the machine represented an immense monetary burden and an uncontrollable political quantity.[3]

Roughly speaking, the New Deal marked a turning point in the evolution from early industrial capitalism through finance monopolization to the modern advanced or "late" capitalism; that is, from a city based on the factory to a city based on administrative functions. The managerial and technical innovations and growing ownership concentration of the 1900–1929 period made possible production beyond the capacity of existing markets and, with continued lack of sound financing practice made possible the Great Crash. The Depression also helped business elites complete their series of local

[3]Samuel Hayes, "The Politics of Reform in Municipal Government in the Progressive Era," *Pacific Northwest Quarterly* 55 (October 1964), pp. 157–169, remains the landmark study of reform in this era.

government reforms, the brunt of which was to depoliticize and professionalize large areas of public policy, thus removing them from the vagaries of the political marketplace. In New York, for example, "the banks agreed to bail out New York, but only if the Mayor took marching orders from the banks and cut the budget drastically."[4] Detroit, Fall River and a score more cities experienced municipal defaults during the thirties, and all endured significant periods during which bankers ran their affairs.[5]

Even relatively sound cities found themselves governed by a growing number of semi-autonomous agencies and subjected to increasing state and federal regulation. Civil service, nonpartisan, at-large elections and the other post-1900 local government reforms emptied city politics of its meaning. And the steady growth of suburbs, which since about 1920 effectively resisted central-city annexation attempts, helped diminish central-city political conflicts' influence on regional affairs.[6]

THE POST-INDUSTRIAL CITY

The third major period of urban growth, characterized by full development of the administrative city with suburbanized production, rested on these institutional foundations. Variously termed "the service society," "advanced monopoly capitalism" and "the post-industrial society," it is characterized by:

- Increasing regional and international diffusion of capital and labor. For central cities, this meant suburbanization and the loss of factory employment.
- A shift in private sector activities from production to administration, and to the service activities associated with administration (research, education, finance, information manipulation, entertainment, etc.). For the central cities, this meant a transition from the factory to the office building as the basic unit of social organization.

[4]"Experts Fear Growth in Costly City Debts," *New York Times* (November 25, 1974), p. 48.

[5]An extremely interesting series of case studies of Depression-era defaults is given in the Advisory Commission on Intergovernmental Relations 1973 report *City Financial Emergencies: The Intergovernmental Dimension* (Washington, D.C.: Government Printing Office, 1973).

[6]For an analysis of these developments, see Ann R. Markusen, "Class and Urban Social Expenditure: A Local Theory of the State," *Kapitalistate* 4 (1976).

- Political and economic incorporation of organized labor. For the cities this was accomplished by a political alliance which actively promoted metropolitan growth and central business district construction.
- State-managed demand, particularly in terms of military spending, fiscal policy, and infrastructural investments. For central cities this meant growing federal intervention, particularly in housing and urban development matters.
- An extraordinary increase in public sector activities, both in terms of the areas affected and the size of employment. For cities, this involved new services, such as manpower training, welfare, etc., and greater activity in old service areas, particularly those related to development.

These features responded to many of the constraints which the nineteenth-century city and its politics had placed on development. Suburbanization and internationalization of factories, for example, put them beyond the turmoil of central-city politics and allowed the introduction of both labor- and capital-saving techniques. Productivity-based wage gains and increasing government demand created markets for a whole new range of products and services, from inflatable swimming pools and the split-level ranch house to the most complex weapons system.

The features of metropolitan political life provided both the framework on which these changes were constructed and much of the muscle to accomplish them. Proliferating semi-autonomous public agencies, including both big-city bureaucracies and suburban governments, mobilized debt for the sake of metropolitan growth subject only to infrequent recourse to the public. The fragmented nature of metropolitan politics encouraged not only the extension of the periphery but the more intensive use of the core, and thus prompted a revolution in land-use regulation. Rapidly growing public and non-profit service institutions, ranging from universities to antipoverty agencies, provided both key informational needs and social control. Finally, the fragmented nature of the metropolitan polity discouraged the formation of any cohesive policy to regulate (and perhaps deter) development; rather, it encouraged the suburban, gray-flannel political apathy which characterized the 1950s. The central cities, which might have provided coherent guidance over growth, were dominated by political coalitions devoted almost by necessity to growth at any cost.[7] The suburbs, for their part, were politically distinguished only by consumerism, individualism and ennui.

New York City provides an archetype for these new urban-growth mechanisms, for which. it is an extreme but suggestive example.[8] . . . Without massive government activity, and the political relationships which it cemented, it is highly doubtful that New York could have functioned as the economic and administrative center of the country and, indeed, the world.

As a net result, New York and other large cities were, in political scientist Theodore Lowi's view, "well run but ungoverned." Highly specialized but politically fragmented and autonomous agencies like the Metropolitan Transportation Authority, the City University, and the urban-renewal administration promoted growth and responded in an ad hoc manner to the cities' needs for transit, educated labor power, urban planning, and the like. No single authority oversaw these activities with any degree of success; oppositional movements (whether from above or below) were simply incorporated, often as parallel and powerless new bureaucracies. Although this arrangement had the virtue of stimulating growth while limiting political opposition, it also rendered cohesive and efficient policy making impossible. The costs of this arrangement set the stage for the current crisis.

THE COLLAPSE OF THE POST-INDUSTRIAL CITY

This situation, with all its costs and improbable political alliances, was not fated to last. The era's touchstones—rapidly growing mortgage and bond debt, extension of the periphery coupled with greater intensity at the center, massively extended government activity, and social control via fragmentation—have faced opposition from below and breakdown from within. Matters have reached the point where *Business Week*, commenting on corporate headquarters' movement from the central city, can editorialize about "The Prospect of a Nation with No Important Cities" (February 2, 1976, p. 66). Not only has the central-city development process entered depressionary conditions, but the metropolitan housing industry, central-city politi-

[7]John H. Mollenkopf, "The Post War Politics of Urban Development," *Politics and Society* 5 (Winter 1976) discusses many of these matters at length. Robert Wood, *1400 Governments* (Cambridge: Harvard University Press, 1961) gives a classic description of the economic consequences of metropolitan political fragmentation.

[8]Robert Caro, *The Power Broker* (New York: Knopf, 1974), provides a wealth of evidence for the New York City case.

cal alliances and the public sector itself face great jeopardy.

The elements of this collapse are a well-known story. Growth strategies of the 1960s created immense antagonisms within the minority and white ethnic neighborhoods which were demolished or invaded by highways, renewal and other developments. Together with urban riots, they sapped the legitimacy of urban government. A host of small commercial and manufacturing firms, and the social and spatial networks which sustained them, fell to the bulldozer. When added to the dubious financing and the failure of anticipated revenues to materialize from the projected replacement activities, this transformation also imposed great political and economic costs on big cities. The loss of political authority opened the way for both old-line public employees (teachers, policemen and firemen) and the new civil servants (in Model Cities, manpower programs and neighborhood planning agencies) to increase their claim on the city budget. More and more, city governments attempted to cover their tracks with borrowing and outside financing, but the burden became so large that it threatened, in the eyes of the business community at least, the stability of the private sector.[9]

The fragmented and insulated main lines of public policy, which had worked so well to promote growth, also generated pluralist irrationality. Independent agencies adopted uncoordinated, sometimes antagonistic, wasteful and frequently ineffectual directions; academic opinion of direct government service provision, which had once been so supportive, turned quite sour.

In case after case, public facilities designed to amortize their own costs through revenues have become liabilities instead. In New York, the Port Authority's World Trade Center holds the world's record for vacancies. In New Orleans, Denver, San Francisco and elsewhere, baseball stadiums which were purported to be surplus operations are sucking millions from city treasuries. Urban-renewal areas, which were theoretically supposed to increase city tax bases, either imposed losses or funneled the increases to public facilities specifically for the

[9]In its special issue on the capital crisis, *Business Week* noted: "The obstacles to raising the required amount of private capital in the economic environment that is likely to prevail in the next decade . . . are formidable . . . but the social and financial consequences of not generating sufficient savings . . . are not pleasant to contemplate." Later it added: "The growth of government spending must be curbed so that surpluses emerge in the federal budget . . . private investment cannot increase as a share of GNP unless government spending declines" (September 22, 1975), pp. 42, 115.

area. Growth, to put it mildly, failed to provide the fiscal bonanza for which its original patrons had hoped.

In short, an entire mode of metropolitan development, with its specific political and programmatic bulwark, was thrown into doubt, conflict and perhaps even economic demise. Even in New York City, which has long prided itself on being biggest, richest and best, political and business leaders "have had to admit to themselves that it is a city which can no longer grow."[10]

II. THE CURRENT POLITICAL CRISIS

The fiscal dilemmas of New York City, Detroit, Cleveland, Boston, San Francisco and other major cities, if the preceding arguments are correct, do not stem simply from aggressive "outsiders" burrowing into the city budget. Rather, they reflect fundamental internal weaknesses with post–World War II metropolitan development patterns. Not only have cities found it difficult to pay off dissident forces, whether city workers or minority neighborhoods, but they have failed to finance the full costs of public and private investments in the built environment. On the economic side, the growth of cities and the shift from a factory-based to an office-building-based economy has required tremendous bonded indebtedness and rising annual expenditures for transit, roads, urban renewal, education of the labor force, police, fire protection, and the like. Central to this pattern of growth, however, and the key to understanding its high public costs, is that it has been a highly political phenomenon. The course of the post-industrial city's seeming collapse, and the key to understanding its possible future, therefore, lies in understanding the city's recent *political* history.

A. URBAN STRUGGLE IN THE 1960s

Metropolitan growth in the 1960s was in many senses the logical projection of the New Deal. Across the nation, activist mayors like New Haven's Richard Lee, New York's Robert Wagner, Boston's John Collins and Kevin White, and San Francisco's Joseph Alioto assembled coalitions which included major corporate officials, central-business-district commercial and real-estate interests, the construction trades (and by extension the central labor councils), city

---

[10]"City Seen Entering Era of Retrenchment," *New York Times* (February 15, 1976), p. 1. It noted that many business leaders thought "New York is a city unable to regenerate itself."

workers, and middle-class professionals in planning, law, management consulting, and the like. Growth provided the glue which bound these composite elements together. In city after city, such pro-growth coalitions put in place the crucial public investments, renewal planning, highways and modern transit necessary to facilitate the rapid transition in urban economics. Just as President Kennedy's promise to "get the country moving again" caught the popular imagination, these alliances experienced considerable electoral strength. The expanding public pie, filled with billions in federal urban-renewal expenditures, billions in subsidized housing and billions in urban freeway expenditures made it possible for quite disparate parties to join in the meal.

During the fifties and early sixties, renewal agencies, highway departments and private developers could plan without interference from public referenda or neighborhood opposition. Within city bureaucracies, they could count on traditional labor relations, with their deference and hierarchy, to maintain authority and efficiency. While the process involved a great deal of waste (and sometimes graft), it did not, at the outset, need to be spread much beyond the traditional elements of the New Deal political coalition.

Urban political struggles exploded this comfortable arrangement not because they stopped growth dead in its tracks—far from it—but because they forced a series of procedural, programmatic and bureaucratic changes in the way growth was administered. At the same time, such struggles tugged at loose threads in urban bureaucracies, and ultimately unraveled their political reliability.

In the course of the sixties, the pro-growth coalition was undermined at almost every turn: as whites packed up and left the central cities, their minority successors came to feel they were being ruled by unrepresentative and unresponsive institutions. The devastating impact of urban-renewal clearance, highway construction and conflicts over neighborhoods that were changing both "downward" and "upward" triggered large-scale neighborhood mobilizations. In Boston, for example, five-year-long battles were fought to defeat highway construction, institute community control over urban renewal, and secure citywide rent control. Black rebellions in nearly every major American city further challenged the legitimacy of public business-as-usual.

Federal policy and local practice instituted a series of devices to accommodate this minority neighborhood unrest. Where planning had previously been executed behind closed doors, in the late sixties it became formally (if rarely substantively) subject to public hearings, project area committee review, relocation procedural rights, intense litigation, environmental impact reports and equal-opportunity hiring. These constraints did not stop development, nor even change its general outlines, but they did slow it down and make it more expensive.

Where welfare had been directly and modestly distributed through paternalistic private social service agencies and well-controlled public agencies, during the sixties it both multiplied and divided. The welfare rights movement and black political unrest stimulated large increases in federal welfare payments. Total transfer payments burgeoned from $37.1 billion in 1965 to $155.9 billion in 1974, or from 7 to 20 percent of all wages and salaries. In most major social policy areas, the Great Society programs of the Johnson era established "rich-poor alliances" in which the wealthy were subsidized to provide welfare services to the poor. Medicare expenditures, for example, shot from $200 million in 1960 to $5.3 billion in 1973. Subsidized housing expenditures amounted to several billion dollars over the 1965–1975 period, but the tax loophole aspects of such programs cost local and national treasuries many billions more. In the important cases, particularly welfare and Medicare, the formal right to service was nearly open-ended, with no cost constraints. More often than not, benefits flowed not to their intended recipients but to wealthy investors, hospital corporations, doctors, and other professionals.

Where civil servants had previously been primarily poorly paid white ethnics accomplishing traditional tasks in structured settings, in the sixties they increasingly became non-whites attempting to accomplish new tasks in unorthodox and politically unsettled agencies like community mental-health programs, Model Cities agencies and manpower planning councils. While these new bureaucracies failed to overcome their social problem targets and often "bought off" dissent, they certainly abolished both the old cost structure and the old political ethos within city government. Under the influence of such pressures, local government employment jumped from 6.1 million in 1960 to 11.6 million in 1974, and provided one in three new urban jobs.

These trends encouraged organization and militancy among workers in the more traditional services. While strike activity and wage gains were particularly noticeable among schoolteachers (who account for 44 percent of public work stoppages), policemen, firemen, hospital workers, sanitation workers and bus drivers followed suit. Public-sector work stoppages grew from 42 in 1965 to 382 in 1974; in 1955 fewer than one million public employees were unionized, while today 2.5 million belong to unions and two million more to associations like the National Education Association. Indeed, public-sector labor has become the most volatile and poorly contained area of class conflict in the economy, parallel in many respects to the early days of the CIO.

The efforts to contain political conflict during the sixties produced the opposite result. They ultimately destroyed the pro-growth political alliance of city workers, the construction trades and old-line political organizations on the one hand, and renewal officials, real-estate developers and major corporations on the other. The costs of incorporating political dissidence and reconciling political clashes within city bureaucracies proved too great; business opinion turned decisively against the old alliances and their new-found centripetal tendencies. Thus, an untenable political situation reinforced the economic costs of ungoverned and uncoordinated investment decision making.

B. THE CONSERVATIVE COUNTERATTACK

To the accumulating sector of the economy, particularly major corporations and the solidly unionized segment of the labor force, the urban fiscal crisis posed a key question: How can we rekindle the growth process while correcting its internal weaknesses and abolishing its many encumbrances? For the Republican party and the principal organs of business sentiment like *Business Week* and the *Wall Street Journal*, the answer has been nothing less than a full-scale attack on the public sector and on pluralist democracy itself, at least as practiced in the 1960s. More moderate sentiment seeks not to abolish government but to gain more centralized and efficient executive control over it through devices like budget cutbacks, national economic planning, management by objective, and benefit-cost analysis.

But the attack on the public sector has developed most effectively at the local level. A liberal Congress has thwarted some of Ford's austerity measures, and threatens to keep the federal budget far out of balance. Locally, however, national policy, constrained revenues, and business initiatives have unlimbered a whole series of political/fiscal crises. Large and small business groups, bankers, and molders of elite opinion across the country are using the crisis to take aim at public-sector labor unions, the size of public employment, the "wasteful" functions of government, the number of welfare clients, and the "poor" regulatory environment for growth.[11] This is not simply playing rough in a well-recognized political game: if possible, these forces would like to torpedo New Deal pro-growth politics and replace it with depoliticized, business-oriented government in a manner reminiscent of the Progressive Era.

Because they have developed the most cohesive political presence, this counterattack has focused on organized public employees and their bureaucracies. *Business Week* put business sentiment on this question concisely in its special issue on public workers:

> The big city governments of the U.S. are overextended and over-manned. They need to shape up and simplify the complex structures they have developed through the years. They desperately need to increase productivity. They need to end once and for all the idea that the city is run primarily for the benefit of its employees.[12]

New York City is only the best-known case where these views are being put into practice. The city's Emergency Finance Control Board, headed by the president of N.Y. Bell Telephone, the chairman of American Airlines and the chief executive officer of Colt Industries, has cut 60,000 employees from the city's payroll and may well close half its public hospitals, eliminate a major portion of the City University system, and even further increase the transit fare. It has already forced city employees to forgo wage gains and pension rights secured through difficult strikes and protracted collective bargaining.

In San Francisco, the local chamber of commerce in 1974 proposed a charter amendment to abolish collective bargaining, reduce employee benefits and limit future wage gains. While vigorous efforts by labor and left groups defeated this initiative, in the wake of a recent and disastrous police and fire strike, similar measures were resoundingly endorsed by the electorate.[13] City-hall budget cutting

[11]See, for example, Attiat Ott and Jang Yoo, "New York City's Financial Crisis," (Washington, D.C.: American Enterprise Institute for Public Policy Research, November 1975), which takes aim at the unions, their pensions, welfare expenditures, and even federal bail-outs.

[12]"Public Employees vs. The Cities," *Business Week* (July 21, 1975), p. 76.

[13]Tom Emch and Gerald Adams, "Four Days in August," San Francisco Chronicle *California Living Magazine* (October 12, 1975), pp. 7–25, gives a strike chronology.

has meanwhile slashed community mental-health positions, neighborhood recreation and school aides, street cleaning, and social welfare services. The police department, by contrast, got $1.4 million for a new computer system, and $5 million was set aside from revenue-sharing money for a Lincoln Center–type performing-arts center.

Many other large cities, particularly those located in the Northeast, have suffered from similar cuts. Detroit, with 21 percent unemployment, faces a $30 to $100 million deficit and has already closed many facilities, ended preventive maintenance and furloughed hundreds of employees.[14] Atlanta, Cleveland, Newark, Boston and others have cut budgets, laid off workers, sacked poverty programs and taken steps to aid business.

Equally important, the fiscal crisis has served as a pretext for a counterattack on practically every major procedural gain established through community struggles during the 1960s. In Massachusetts, real-estate interests have launched a major campaign against the state's 1969 rent-control law, already weakened by administrative and judicial interpretation. The 1974 Housing and Community Development Act abolished the "citizen participation" measures which had been instituted under the old urban-renewal legislation. Studies of revenue-sharing allocations demonstrate that instead of using the money for social policy innovations or new housing policies, cities have invested in capital improvements, completing stalled renewal projects and lowering tax rates. In San Francisco, even after lengthy legal battles and the election of a labor- and neighborhood-backed mayor, the city is going ahead with a widely unpopular sports center/office building complex.[15]

III. The Future Course of the Crisis

History has a disconcerting predilection for side-stepping the neat logical alternatives which analysis poses for it. Any simple extrapolations from the past which fail to search for new, controverting factors therefore run the risk of being greatly misleading. Nevertheless, in a

---

Afterward the *New York Times* editorialized that this strike was "not only the road to municipal bankruptcy, it is the road to anarchy. It is the death knell for democracy."

[14]"How a Budget Pinch Diminishes Amenities in Depressed Detroit," *Wall Street Journal* (May 25, 1975), p. 1.

[15]For a case study of this conflict, see Chester Hartman, *Yerba Buena* (San Francisco: Glide Publications, 1974).

tentative way, three possible outcomes to the current crisis can be delineated: the Pariah City, the Corporatist City and the Primitive Socialist City.[16]

The current political counterattack against the public sector, taken together with business sentiment and private-sector location decisions, is driving events toward the Pariah City. In this form of urban organization, central-city budgets would be pared back to the minimum social expenditures necessary to maintain social peace; the central city would be governed essentially by agents of social control; public and private decision-making institutions would abandon (even more rapidly) their central-city habitat. As *Business Week* put it, in this type of city "corporations are primarily trying to keep a grasp on the benefits the city can still offer while avoiding its problems."[17] (In the last decade, more than sixty *Fortune 500* corporate headquarters have relocated to Fairfield County, Connecticut, from Manhattan.) Throughout the economy, and particularly in metropolitan areas, the market rather than the state would be relied upon to make basic allocation decisions and restore authority relations.

The problems with this course are obvious, given earlier arguments. This strategy would likely fail simply for internal reasons. Cities exist in their present concentrated forms for very real economies of scale. Recent tendencies may have vitiated these scale returns, but certainly have not eliminated them. The social costs of highly diffused metropolitan development cannot be minimized: increased travel times, increased energy consumption, increased costs of servicing less dense land uses and increased communication costs face any such arrangement. From a fiscal point of view, the implied austerity measures would reduce certain burdens on growth but could not eliminate them, since growth *itself* has imposed many of the costs. The poor could be forced to bear some of the burdens, but they could not erase the source of the burdens.

Nor do the political prospects of such an alternative seem particularly promising. The anti-growth movement has already

---

[16]A similar distinction has been made by Rick Hill, "Black Struggle and the Urban Fiscal Crisis," *Kapitalistate* 4 (1976). I have borrowed the term "Pariah City" from Hill.

[17]"Prospect of a Nation with No Important Cities," *Business Week* (February 2, 1976), p. 66.

reached major proportions in suburban areas, and any greater tendency toward regional, as opposed to central, city development would simply further inflame this opposition. In region after region, suburbs have attempted to close their land to office complexes, further factory development, housing for the low-wage labor force which further administrative development would require, and further freeway construction. This strategy poses as well the possibility of a central city in open rebellion. No matter how much the situation may favor marginal decisions to leave the central city, they could never warrant writing off the colossal capital investments they currently represent. Yet even if the Pariah City poses its own economic and political complications, in the absence of new forces to the contrary, it currently seems like the most probable outcome.

The Corporatist City, on the other hand, would deepen but simultaneously restructure government's role. Centralized city government and regional planning would, in this model of metropolitan development, come to grips with the chaotic pluralism of the past. Tools like benefit-cost analysis, operations research and management by objectives would be used to suppress the irrational, political character of current programing, and would eliminate both excess service to clients and the excess influence of "special interests" (e.g., the considerable subsidies to hospital expansion and doctors' wages hidden in the Medicare program.) As with the New Deal's National Recovery Administration, all relevant parties (management, labor and clients) would participate in and be disciplined by the rational planning process. This general approach has been advocated by the most sophisticated elements of business opinion, the professional managers of the public sector produced during the aborted Program-Planning-Budgeting revolution, and the major unions, since the Corporatist City would attempt to provide full employment. Nationally, this conception is embodied in the Humphrey-Javits full-employment and national-planning initiatives. Not by accident, Felix Rohatyn, a political supporter of Senator Humphrey's, not only directs New York City's financial balancing act but has been an outspoken proponent of government planning of credit allocations in the national economy.

The Corporatist City, however, is equally unlikely to provide an effective resolution to the current crisis, but in many respects is simply a rehash of old and discredited measures.[18] From the point of view of capital, the heart of the problem lies in the already excessive political claims on the accumulation process. To impose more claims, in conservative mimicry of the European welfare states, would simply make matters worse. The technical qualities of scientific budgeting and management methods have time and again been swamped by political considerations. In the absence of a considerably more centralized state, capitalist class and labor force, these measures would be no better than spitting in the wind. Nor, given the vigor of conservative opinion, is it likely that a political consensus could be mobilized around such a program. Given current conditions, however, it seems like the next most likely alternative to the Pariah City.

The Primitive Socialist City may sound utopian in many respects. If one bears in mind Communist successes in governing major French and Italian cities, however, it does not seem to lie completely out of the realm of possibility. State entry into actual production in areas formerly dominated completely by private enterprise provides one key to this vision, and running services in a way which responds to the real needs of public workers and public clients provide the other. This idea has obvious and powerful fiscal appeal to local public officials. The city of Palo Alto, California, for example, runs its own utilities system at rates competitive with the private sector and produces 40 percent of its revenue from this source. In North Dakota, a state-owned bank returns a tidy dividend every year to the public treasury. While these enterprises are managed in ways quite similar to private firms, they nonetheless suggest the germ of an alternative development. The journal *Working Papers for a New Society* and the Conference for Alternative Public Policy, a loose association of several hundred left-liberal elected and appointed officials, are currently developing and disseminating ideas of this sort, and in many cities broad coalitions of community organizations, progressive elements of the Democratic party, some union members, and independent socialist organizations are attempting to put them on the public agenda.[19]

The political obstacles facing the development of the Primitive

[18]For an extensive discussion of this point, and firm conclusion that there are no remaining methods of legitimizing accumulation, see Alan Wolfe's forthcoming *The Limits of Legitimacy in Late Capitalism.*

[19]For news of one such effort, see *Common Sense,* newspaper of the Northern California Alliance, 2811 Mission Street, San Francisco, Calif. 94110.

Socialist City, however, are enormous. Minority neighborhoods, rank-and-file city workers, professionals in threatened social services, political descendants of the New Left and Black Power movements, and many other elements of urban society, would seem to offer fertile ground for organizing. Yet opposition from the private sector, the regular political parties, top-level urban managers and politicians, the construction trades and other unions tightly affiliated with current conceptions of growth would oppose them vigorously. But while current trends suggest the Primitive Socialist City may well be the least likely outcome, the nasty and unworkable characteristics of the alternatives may make it more possible over time. Certainly, for progressive activists who would like to prevent austerity and destruction of the remaining qualities of urban life, the time has come to turn to urban politics with renewed vigor. Neighborhoods, public-service clients, and city workers are currently in motion, and the nature of the underlying issues could hardly be more important. If those who seek a more humane city fail to act coherently, they will have suffered a loss which stands in stark contrast to the major gains won in the previous decade.

7. The Urban Crisis: Who Got What and Why

FRANCES FOX PIVEN

For quite a while, complaints about the urban fiscal crisis have been droning on, becoming as familiar as complaints about big government, or big bureaucracy, or high taxes—and almost as boring as well. Now suddenly the crisis seems indeed to be upon us: school closings are threatened, library services are curtailed, subway trains go unrepaired, welfare grants are cut, all because big city costs have escalated to the point where local governments can no longer foot the bill. Yet for all the talk, and all the complaints, there has been no convincing explanation of just how it happened that, quite suddenly in the 1960s, the whole municipal housekeeping system seemed to become virtually unmanageable. This is especially odd because, not long ago, the study of city politics and city services was a favorite among American political scientists, and one subject they had gone far to illuminate. Now, with everything knocked askew, they seem to have very little to say that could stand as political analysis.

To be sure, there is a widely accepted explanation. The big cities are said to be in trouble because of the "needs" of blacks for services —a view given authority by the professionals who man the service agencies and echoed by the politicians who depend upon these agencies. Service "needs," the argument goes, have been increasing at a much faster rate than local revenues. The alleged reason is demographic: The large number of impoverished black Southern migrants to the cities presumably requires far greater investments in services, including more elaborate educational programs, more frequent garbage collection, more intensive policing, if the city is to be maintained at accustomed levels of civil decency and order. Thus, city

---

This is an abridged version of a paper written in 1972 which has appeared in Richard A. Cloward and Frances Fox Piven, *The Politics of Turmoil* (New York: Pantheon, 1974). Frances Fox Piven is professor of political science at Boston University.

agencies have been forced to expand and elaborate their activities. However, the necessary expansion is presumably constricted for lack of local revenues, particularly since the better-off taxpaying residents and businesses have been leaving the city (hastened on their way by the black migration).[1] To this standard explanation of the crisis, there is also a standard remedy: namely, to increase municipal revenues, whether by enlarging federal and state aid to the cities or by redrawing jurisdictional boundaries to recapture suburban taxpayers.[2]

It is true, of course, that black children who receive little in the way of skills or motivation at home may require more effort from the schools; that densely packed slums require more garbage collection; that disorganized neighborhoods require more policing. For instance, the New York City Fire Department reports a 300 percent increase in fires the last twenty years. But fires and similar calamities that threaten a wide public are one thing; welfare, education, and health services, which account for by far the largest portion of big city budgets, quite another. And while by any objective measure the new residents of the city have greater needs for such services, there are several reasons to doubt that the urban crisis is the simple result of rising needs and declining revenues.

For one thing, the trend in service budgets suggests otherwise. Blacks began to pour into the cities in very large numbers after World War II, but costs did not rise precipitously until the mid-1960s.[3] *In other words, the needs of the black poor were not recognized for two decades.* For another, any scrutiny of agency budgets shows that, except for public welfare, *the expansion of services to the poor, as*

[1]This view of the urban problem was given official status by government commissions like the National Advisory Commission on Civil Disorders and the U.S. Advisory Commission on Intergovernmental Relations, scholars and politicians.

[2]As a matter of fact, city revenues have not declined at all, but have risen astronomically, although not as astronomically as costs. Presumably if the city had been able to hold or attract better-off residents and businesses, revenues would have risen even faster, and the fiscal aspect of the urban crisis would not have developed.

[3]It should be made clear at the outset that the costs of government generally rose steadily in the years after World War II. But while all government budgets expanded, state and local costs rose much faster, and costs in the central cities rose the most rapidly of all, especially after 1965. Thus, according to the Citizen's Budget Commission, New York City's budget increased almost eight times as fast in the five fiscal years between 1964 and 1969 as during the postwar years 1949 to 1954. From an average annual increase of 5.5 percent in 1954, budget costs jumped to 9.1 percent in 1964 and to 14.2 percent in 1969 (*The New York Times*, January 11, 1960). It is with this exceptional rise that this article is concerned.

such, does not account for a very large proportion of increased expenditures. It was other groups, *mainly organized provider groups,* who reaped the lion's share of the swollen budgets. The notion that services are being strained to respond to the needs of the new urban poor, in short, takes little account either of when the strains occurred or of the groups who actually benefited from increased expenditures.

In the era of the big city machine, municipal authorities managed to maintain a degree of consensus and allegiance among diverse groups by distributing public goods in the form of private favors. Today public goods are distributed through the service bureaucracies. With that change, the process of dispensing public goods has become more formalized, the struggles between groups more public, and the language of city politics more professional. As I will try to explain a little later, these changes were in some ways crucial in the development of what we call the urban crisis. My main point for now, however, is that while we may refer to the schools or the sanitation department as if they are politically neutral, these agencies yield up a whole variety of benefits, and it is by distributing, redistributing, and adapting these payoffs of the city agencies that urban political leaders manage to keep peace and build allegiances among the diverse groups in the city. In other words, the jobs, contracts, perquisites, as well as the actual services of the municipal housekeeping agencies, are just as much the grist of urban politics as they ever were.

All of which is to say that when there is a severe disturbance in the administration and financing of municipal services, the underlying cause is likely to be a fundamental disturbance in political relations. To account for the service "crisis," we should look at the changing relationship between political forces—at rising group conflict and weakening allegiances—and the way in which these disturbances set off an avalanche of new demands. To cope with these strains, political leaders expanded and proliferated the benefits of the city agencies. What I shall argue, in sum, is that the urban crisis is not a crisis of rising needs, but a crisis of rising demands.

THE POLITICAL DISTURBANCES THAT LED TO RISING DEMANDS

If the service needs of the black poor do not account for the troubles in the cities, the political impact of the black migration probably does. Massive shifts of population are almost always disturbing to a political system, for new relations have to be formed between a political leadership and constituent groups. The migration of large numbers of blacks from the rural South to a few core cities during and after World War II, leading many middle-class white constituents to leave for the suburbs, posed just this challenge to the existing political organization of the cities. But for a long time, local governments resisted responding to the newcomers with the services, symbols, and benefits that might have won the allegiance of these newcomers, just as the allegiance of other groups had previously been won.

The task of political integration was made difficult by at least four circumstances. One was the very magnitude of the influx. Between 1940 and 1960, nearly 4 million blacks left the land and, for the most part, settled in big Northern cities. Consequently, by 1960, at least one in five residents of our fifty largest cities was a black, and in the biggest cities the proportions were much greater. It is no exaggeration to say that the cities were innundated by sheer numbers.

Second, these large numbers were mainly lower-class blacks, whose presence aroused ferocious race and class hatreds, especially among the white ethnics who lived in neighborhoods bordering the ghettos and who felt their homes and schools endangered. As ghetto numbers enlarged, race and class polarities worsened, and political leaders, still firmly tied to the traditional inhabitants of the cities, were in no position to give concessions to the black poor.

Not only was race pitted against race, class against class, but the changing style of urban politics made concessions to conflicting groups a very treacherous matter. Just because the jobs, services, and contracts that fueled the urban political organization were no longer dispensed covertly, in the form of private favors, but rather as matters of public policy, each concession was destined to become a subject of open political conflict. As a result, mayors found it very difficult to finesse their traditional constituents: New public housing for blacks, for example, could not be concealed, and every project threatened to arouse a storm of controversy. Despite their growing numbers and their obvious needs, therefore, blacks got very little in the way of municipal benefits throughout the 1940s and 1950s. Chicago, where the machine style was still entrenched, gave a little more; the Cook County AFDC rolls, for example, rose by 80 percent in the 1950s, and blacks were given some political jobs. But in most cities, the local service agencies resisted the newcomers. In New York City and Los Angeles, for example, the AFDC rolls remained virtually unchanged in the 1950s. In many places public housing was brought to a halt; urban renewal generally became the instrument of black removal; and half the major Southern cities (which also received large numbers of black migrants from rural areas) actually managed to reduce their welfare rolls, often by as much as half.[4]

Finally, when blacks entered the cities, they were confronted by a relatively new development in city politics: namely, the existence of large associations of public employees, whether teachers, policemen, sanitation men, or the like. The provider groups not only had a very large stake in the design and operation of public programs— for there is hardly any aspect of public policy that does not impinge on matters of working conditions, job security, or fringe benefits— but they had become numerous enough, organized enough, and independent enough to wield substantial influence in matters affecting their interests.

The result was that, over time, many groups of public employees managed to win substantial control over numerous matters affecting their jobs and their agencies: entrance requirements, tenure guarantees, working conditions, job prerogatives, promotion criteria, retirement benefits. Except where wages were concerned, other groups in the cities rarely became sufficiently aroused to block efforts by public employees to advance their interests. But all of this also meant that when blacks arrived in the cities, local political leaders did not control the jobs—and in cases where job prerogatives had been precisely specified by regulation, did not even control the services—that might have been given as concessions to the black newcomers.

Under the best of circumstances, of course, the task of integrating a new and uprooted rural population into local political structures would have taken time and would have been difficult. But for all of the reasons given, local government was showing little taste for the task. As a result, a large population that had been set loose from Southern feudal institutions was not absorbed into the regulating political institutions (or economic institutions, for they were also resisted there) of the city. Eventually that dislocated population became volatile, both in the streets and at the polls. And by 1960, that volatility was beginning to disrupt national political alignments,

---

[4]For a discussion of the uses of welfare in resisting black migrants, see Frances Fox Piven and Richard A. Cloward, *Regulating the Poor: The Functions of Public Welfare* (New York: Pantheon, 1971), chapters 7 and 8.

forcing the federal government to take an unprecedented role in urban politics.

By 1960 the swelling urban black population had a key role in national politics, especially presidential politics. With migration North, blacks became at least nominal participants in the electoral system, and their participation was concentrated in the states with the largest number of electoral votes. By 1960, 90 percent of all Northern blacks were living in the ten most populous states: California, New York, Pennsylvania, Ohio, Illinois, New Jersey, Michigan, Massachusetts, Indiana, and Missouri. It was the heavy Democratic vote in the big cities of these states, and especially the black Democratic vote in these cities, that gave Kennedy his slim margin. That narrow victory helped mark the importance of troubles in the cities, especially the troubles with blacks in the cities.

Urban blacks, who had been loyal Democrats for almost three decades, had begun to defect even as their numbers grew, signaling the failure of the municipal political machinery. In 1952, 79 percent voted Democratic; by 1956, the black vote slipped to 61 percent. Kennedy worked to win back some of these votes (69 percent in 1960) by taking a strong stand on civil rights in the campaign.[5] But once in office, his administration backed off from supporting civil rights legislation, for that was sure to jeopardize Southern support. Other ways to reach and reward the urban black voter were needed.

Accordingly, administration analysts began to explore strategies to cement the allegiance of the urban black vote to the national party. What emerged, not all at once, but gropingly, was a series of federal service programs directed to the ghetto. The first appropriations were small, as with the Juvenile Delinquency and Youth Offenses Control Act of 1961, but each program enlarged upon the other, up until the Model Cities legislation of 1966. Some of the new programs—in manpower development, in education, in health—were relatively straightforward. All they did was give new funds to local agencies to be used to provide jobs or services for the poor. Thus, funds appropriated under Title I of the Elementary and Secondary Education Act of 1965 were earmarked for educational facilities for poor children; the Medicaid program enacted in 1965 reimbursed health agencies and physicians for treating the poor; and manpower agencies

[5]See Piven and Cloward, op. cit., chapters 9 and 10, on the impact of the black migration on the Democratic administrations of the 1960s.

were funded specifically to provide jobs or job training for the poor.

Other of the new federal programs were neither so simple nor so straightforward, and these were the ones that became the hallmark of the Great Society. The federal memoranda describing them were studded with terms like "inner city," "institutional change," and "maximum feasible participation." But if this language was often confusing, the programs themselves ought not to have been. The "inner city," after all, was a euphemism for the ghetto, and activities funded under such titles as delinquency prevention, mental health, antipoverty, or model cities turned out, in the streets of the cities, to look very much alike. What they looked like was nothing less than the old political machine.

Federal funds were used to create new storefront-style agencies in the ghettos, staffed with professionals who helped local people find jobs, obtain welfare, or deal with school officials. Neighborhood leaders were also hired, named community workers, neighborhood aides, or whatever, but in fact close kin to the old ward heelers, for they drew larger numbers of people into the new programs, spreading the federal spoils.

But federal spoils were not enough, for there were not many of them. What the new ghetto agencies had to offer was small and impermanent compared to ongoing municipal programs in education, housing, or health. If blacks were to be wrapped into the political organization of the cities, the traditional agencies of local government, which controlled the bulk of federal, state, and local appropriations, had to be reoriented. Municipal agencies had to be made to respond to blacks.

Various tactics to produce such reform were tried, at first under the guise of experiments in "institutional change." This meant that the Washington officials who administered the juvenile delinquency program (under Robert Kennedy's direction) required as a condition of granting funds that local governments submit "comprehensive plans" for their own reform (that is, for giving blacks something). But the mere existence of such paper plans did not turn out to be very compelling to the local bureaucrats who implemented programs. Therefore, as turbulence spread in the Northern ghettos, the federal officials began to try another way to promote institutional change— "maximum feasible participation of residents of the areas and members of the groups served." Under that slogan, the Great Society programs gave money to ghetto organizations, which then used the money to harass city agencies. Community workers were hired to badger housing inspectors and to pry loose welfare payments. Lawyers on the federal payroll took municipal agencies to court on behalf of ghetto clients. Later the new programs helped organize the ghetto poor to picket the welfare department or to boycott the school system.

In these various ways, then, the federal government intervened in local politics, and forced local government to do what it had earlier failed to do. Federal dollars and federal authority were used to resuscitate the functions of the political machine, on the one hand *by spurring local service agencies to respond to the black newcomers,* and on the other *by spurring blacks to make demands upon city services.*

As it turned out, blacks made their largest tangible gains from this process through the public welfare system. Total national welfare costs rose from about $4 billion in 1960 to nearly $15 billion in 1970. Big cities that received the largest numbers of black and Spanish-speaking migrants and that were most shaken by the political reverberations of that migration also experienced the largest welfare budget rises. In New York, Los Angeles, and Baltimore, for example, the AFDC rolls quadrupled, and costs rose even faster. In some cities, moreover, welfare costs were absorbing an ever-larger share of the local budget, a bigger piece of the public pie. In New York City, for example, welfare costs absorbed about 12 percent of the city's budget in the 1950s; but by 1970 the share going to welfare had grown to about 25 percent (of a much larger budget), mainly because the proportion of the city's population on Aid to Families of Dependent Children increased from 2.6 percent in 1960 to 11.0 percent in 1970.[6] In other words, the blacks who triggered the disturbances received their biggest payoffs from welfare,[7] mainly because other groups were not competing within the welfare system for a share of relief benefits.[8]

---

[6] *Changing Patterns of Prices, Pay, Workers, and Work on the New York Scene,* U.S. Department of Labor, Bureau of Labor Statistics (New York: Middle Atlantic Regional Office, May 1971), Regional Reports No. 20, p. 36.

[7] The dole, needless to say, is a very different sort of concession from the higher salaries, pensions, and on-the-job prerogatives won by other groups. For one thing, the dole means continued poverty and low status. For another, it is easier to take away, for recipients remain relatively weak and unorganized.

[8] That poor minorities made large gains through the welfare "crisis" and other groups did not is important to understanding the furious opposition that soaring

But if blacks got welfare, that was just about all they got. Less obvious than the emergence of black demands—but much more important in accounting for increasing service costs—was the reaction of organized whites to these political developments, particularly the groups who had direct material stakes in the running of the local services. If the new upthrust of black claims threatened and jostled many groups in the city, none were so alert or so shrill as those who had traditionally gotten the main benefits of the municipal services. These were the people who depended, directly or indirectly, on the city treasury for their livelihood: They worked in the municipal agencies, in agencies that were publicly funded (e.g., voluntary hospitals), in professional services that were publicly reimbursed (e.g., doctors), or in businesses that depended on city contracts (e.g., contractors and construction workers). Partly they were incited by black claims that seemed to threaten their traditional preserves. Partly they were no longer held in check by stable relationships with political leaders, for these relations had weakened or become uncertain or even turned to enmity. Indeed, in some cases, the leaders themselves had been toppled, shaken loose by the conflict and instability of the times. In effect, the groups who worked for or profited from city government had become unleashed, at the same time that newcomers were snapping at their heels.

The result was that the provider groups reacted with a rush of new demands. And these groups had considerable muscle to back up their claims. Not only were they unusually numerous and well organized, but they were allied to broader constituencies by their class and ethnic ties and by their union affiliations. Moreover, their demands for increased benefits, whether higher salaries or lower work load or greater autonomy, were always couched in terms of protecting the professional standards of the city services, a posture that helped win them broad public support. As a result, even when the organized providers backed up their demands by closing the schools, or stopping the subways, or letting the garbage pile up, many people were ready

---

welfare budgets arouse. Organized welfare-agency workers were competing for the welfare dollar, of course, but were not nearly so successful as the workers in other services, for they were not in a position to take much advantage of political turmoil. They were not nearly so numerous or well organized as teachers, policemen, or firemen, and they could not use the threat of withholding services to exact concessions nearly so effectively. Unlike schoolteachers or garbage men, their services were of importance only to the very poor.

to blame the inconveniences on political officials.

Local political leaders, their ties to their constituencies under-mined by population shifts and spreading discontent, were in a poor position to resist or temper these escalating demands, especially the demands of groups with the power to halt the services on which a broader constituency depended. Instead, to maintain their position, they tried to expand and elaborate the benefits—the payrolls, the contracts, the perquisites, and the services—of the municipal agen-cies.

Nor, as had been true in the era of the machine, was it easy to use these concessions to restore stable relationships. Where once political leaders had been able to anticipate or allay the claims of various groups, dealing with them one by one, now each concession was public, precipitating rival claims from other groups, each demand ricocheting against the other in an upward spiral. Not only did public concessions excite rivalry, but political officials lost the ability to hold groups in check in another way as well; unlike their machine pred-ecessors, they could attach few conditions to the concessions they made. Each job offered, each wage increase conceded, each job pre-rogative granted, was now ensconced in civil service regulations or union contracts and, thus firmly secured, could not be withdrawn. Political leaders had lost any leverage in their dealings; each conces-sion simply became the launching pad for higher demands. Instead of regular exchange relationships, open conflict and uncertainty be-came the rule. The result was a virtual run upon the city treasury by a host of organized groups in the city, each competing with the other for a larger share of municipal benefits. Benefits multiplied and budg-ets soared—and so did the discontent of various groups with the schools, or police, or housing, or welfare, or health. . . .

The cities are unable to raise revenues commensurate with these expenditures; and they are unable to resist the claims that underlie rising expenditures. And that is what the fiscal crisis is all about. . . .

FEDERALISM AS A CONSTRAINING INFLUENCE

If mayors cannot resist the demands of contending groups in the cities, there are signs that the state and federal governments can, and will. The fiscal interrelations that undergird the federal system and leave the cities dependent on state and federal grants for an increas-ing portion of their funds are also a mechanism by which state and federal politics come to intervene in and control city politics. This is happening most clearly and directly through changes in state expenditures for the cities.

In brief, pressures from the big cities were channeled upward to the state capitals, with some response. At least in the big urbanized states, governors and legislatures moved toward bailing out the cities, with the result that state expenditures and state taxes skyrocketed. But the reaction is setting in; the taxpayers' revolt is being felt in state legislatures across the country. And as raucous legislative battles continue, a trend is emerging: The states are turning out to be a restraining influence on city politics, and especially on ghetto politics.

Nor is it likely, were the Democrats to regain the presidency and thus regain the initiative in federal legislation, that the pattern of federal restraint would be entirely reversed. The conditions that made the ghettos a political force for a brief space of time seem to have changed. For one thing, there is not much action, either in the streets or in the voting booths. The protests and marches and riots have subsided, at least partly because the most aggressive people in the black population were absorbed; it was they who got the jobs and honorary positions yielded to blacks during the turmoil. These concessions, together with the Great Society programs that helped produce them, seem to have done their work, not only in restoring a degree of order to the streets, but in restoring ghetto voters to Democratic columns.

In any case, it was not ghetto insurgency of itself that gave blacks some political force in the 1960s. Rather it was that the insurgents were concentrated in the big cities, and the big cities played a very large role in Democratic politics. That also is changing; the cities are losing ground to the suburbs, even in Democratic calculations, and trouble in the cities is not likely to carry the same weight with Democratic presidents that it once did.

To be sure, a Democratic administration might be readier than a Republican one to refuel local services, to fund a grand new cornucopia of social programs. The pressures are mounting, and they come from several sources. One is the cities themselves, for to say that the cities are no longer as important as they once were is not to say Democratic leaders will want the cities to go under. Moreover, the inflated costs of the city are spreading to the suburbs and beyond, and these communities are also pressing for federal aid. Finally there is the force of the organized producers themselves, who have become very significant indeed in national politics; the education lobby and the health lobby already wield substantial influence in Washington, and they are growing rapidly. But while these pressures suggest that new federal funds will be forthcoming, the rise of the suburbs and the parallel rise of the professional lobbies indicate that it is these groups who are likely to be the main beneficiaries.

The future expansion of the federal role in local services has another, perhaps more profound, significance. It means that the decline of the local political unit in the American political structure, already far advanced, will continue. No matter how much talk we may hear about a "new American revolution," through which the federal government will return revenues and power to the people, enlarged federal grants mean enlarged federal power, for grants are a means of influencing local political developments, not only by benefiting some groups and not others, but through federally imposed conditions that come with the new monies. These conditions, by curbing the discretion of local political leaders, also erode the power of local pressure groups. As localities lose their political autonomy, the forces that remain viable will be those capable of exerting national political influence. Some may view this change as an advance, for in the past local communities have been notoriously oligarchical. But for blacks it is not an advance; it is in the local politics of the big cities that they have gained what influence they have.

The general truths to be drawn from this tale of the cities seem clear enough and familiar enough, for what happened in the 1960s has happened before in history. The lower classes made the trouble, and other groups made the gains. In the United States in the 1960s, it was urban blacks who made the trouble, and it was the organized producer groups in the cities who made the largest gains. Those of the working and middle classes who were not among the organized producers got little enough themselves, and they were made to pay with their tax monies for gains granted to others. Their resentments grew. Now, to appease them, the small gains that blacks did make in the course of the disturbances are being whittled away.

There is, I think, an even more important truth, though one perhaps not so quickly recognized. These were the events of a political struggle, of groups pitted against each other and against officialdom. But every stage of that struggle was shaped and limited by the structures in which these groups were enmeshed. A local service apparatus, which at the outset benefited some and not others, set the stage for group struggle. Service structures that offered only certain kinds of benefits determined the agenda of group struggle. And a fiscal structure that limited the contest mainly to benefits paid for by state and local taxes largely succeeded in keeping the struggle confined within the lower and middle strata of American society. Schoolteachers turned against the ghetto, taxpayers against both, but no one turned against the concentrations of individual and corporate wealth in America. Local government, in short, is important, less for the issues it decides, than for the issues it keeps submerged. Of the issues submerged by the events of the urban crisis, not the least is the more equitable distribution of wealth in America.

8. Metropolitan Decline and Inter-Regional Job Shifts

GEORGE STERNLIEB AND JAMES W. HUGHES

The history of the United States can be structured in terms of the ebbs and the flows of migration. The classic analytical works on westward expansion, for example, paralleled by the equivalent detailing of the new flow of immigration and activity into older areas, dominate the history shelf. But the thesis debated in this collection of papers commissioned by the Center for Urban Policy Research is that these flows have changed in character and in substance so vitally as to require a reexamination. Our basic working hypothesis is that many of the traumas of our older central cities, for example, can only be understood within the context of slow or no-growth metropolitan settings. Much of the pattern of unemployment which currently dominates public attention, in terms of its locus and potential longevity, requires evaluation not merely in terms of national policy, nor for that matter in terms of the specifics of the central city, but rather in reference to changing patterns of job types and their regional location.

I. THE PATTERN AND PROBLEM

The pattern which we can observe in the first half of the 1970s is a considerable movement of households from the older, high density urban areas of the Northeast and East North Central states to other regions. The historic problem of the declining central city in most

Excerpted from Sternlieb and Hughes, eds., *Post-Industrial America: Metropolitan Decline and Inter-Regional Job Shifts* (New Brunswick, N.J.: Center for Urban Policy Research, 1976). Many of the references and data referred to in the text are contained in papers in this volume. George Sternlieb is director of the Center for Urban Policy Research at Rutgers University; James W. Hughes is associate professor of urban planning at Rutgers.

parts of the nation has been joined by the stagnant or declining metropolis within America's heartland, the industrial belt from Boston to St. Louis which Wilbur Thompson calls the "American Ruhr." The out-migration from these industrial metropolises is really of two parts. The first is simply an exurban movement—shifts to areas outside of but still adjacent to formally defined SMSAs. This, then, is partly a problem of lagging definition, an extension of the classic exposition of metropolitan growth shifts away from the urban core. This is well within the established literature. But the major movements appear to be regional, to the South and to the Mountain region, areas which Berry terms "the amenity-rich locations of the western and southern 'rimland' on a national scale."

The problem is one of the future of industrial regions in a post-industrial society. As Brian Berry observes,

> Those areas declining most rapidly have been the central cities of the metropolitan areas that emerged during the 19th century, built on productive power, massed population and industrial technology. By the end of the century, these new cities had been credited with the creation of a system of social life founded on entirely new principles. A short half-century later they have become obsolete. These flowers of industrial urbanization—the great manufacturing belt metropolitan areas—are lagging.

Perhaps the problem of these "flowers"—their long term regenerative capacity to survive, adapt, or thrive—is their original function and the way they were put together. Wilbur Thompson offers an insightful explanation:

> We did not, for the most part, build great cities in this country; manufacturing firms agglomerated in tight industrial complexes and formed labor pools of half a million workers. That is not the same thing as building great cities. . . . Our great industrial transformation has left us with a large number of overgrown "cities"—a ramification we have not faced up to.

The momentum of declining cities has been with us for a long time; however when entire metropolitan areas are encompassed by a similar trendline, we must alter our mental model of reality.

THE TRENDLINES

Like pieces of an abstract puzzle slowly fitting together to form the outlines of a final mosaic, post-1970 data are slowly interfacing to reveal new patterns of regional and metropolitan change. The pace of this recognition has probably been slowed by the substantial time gap between full census enumerations. While the 1960 to 1970 census comparisons aroused only limited reservations about the continuities of past assumptions, the possible break in trend, or a peaking, in say 1967 or 1968, is a phenomenon which could very well have been masked by virtue of our benchmarks bounding the climax point. Consequently the drama of the reversal uncovered in the 1970 to 1974 tabulations, and the basic questioning of it, may well be an artifact of our established accounting system.

Nevertheless, the data are revealing patterns which confront us with a new dimension of concern. What shape are they taking? Special tabulations by the U.S. Bureau of the Census have led Director Vincent Barabba to isolate the following tendencies:

The Overall Metropolitan Profile

1. There has been a substantial diminution in the rate of growth of metropolitan areas (Standard Metropolitan Statistical Areas, or SMSAs) between 1970 and 1974.

2. For the same time period, nonmetropolitan areas grew faster than metropolitan areas, representing a sharp contrast to the trends extant to several decades prior to 1970.

3. The reason has been the greater magnitude of out-migration compared to in-migration; the decline in the birth rate means natural population increases can no longer offset negative migration. Metropolitan areas across the United States no longer appear to be gaining net in-migration from nonmetropolitan areas.

4. The largest SMSAs, those of more than 3,000,000 population, have largely accounted for the decline.

5. Those SMSAs with populations between 1,000,000 and 3,000,-000 were still growing, but at substantially reduced rates from the immediate past. For SMSAs of this size, the regional setting appears as an important influence of growth behavior.

    a) In the Northeast and North Central regions, the SMSAs exhibit no-growth or stagnation.

    b) In the West, there is a large decline in the growth rates of metropolitan areas.

    c) In the South, metropolitan areas' growth continues, but at reduced rates.

d) *In the South and West, most of the net metropolitan in-migration occurred in three SMSAs—Miami-Fort Lauderdale, Tampa–St. Petersburg in Florida, and Phoenix, Arizona, all important recreational and retirement enclaves.*

6. *In contrast, the SMSAs of less than 1,000,000 population have experienced increased rates of in-migration since 1970.*

Overall, according to Wilbur Thompson, there is a strong negative correlation between the rate of growth from 1970 to 1973 of metropolitan areas and the proportion of the labor force employed in manufacturing activity. We have passed through the age of manufacturing and the changes we are now experiencing reflect this industrial transformation.

Intra-Metropolitan Area Shifts

1. *In 1960, metropolitan area populations were about equally divided between central city and suburban residence. By 1970, the majority, 54 percent, lived in suburban areas, a percentage which increased to 57 percent by 1974.*

2. *The net out-migration from cities to suburban and nonmetropolitan areas between 1970 and 1974 was equivalent to 10 percent of their 1970 population. Taking into account net natural increase, cities lost 2 percent of their 1970 population.*

3. *About two-thirds of the metropolitan area net out-migration to nonmetropolitan areas originated in their central cities.*

4. *The largest city losses have occurred in the largest SMSAs.*

5. *The mainstays of growth taking place in metropolitan areas are the suburbs. On a regional basis, they account for all the growth in the North and South. Only in the West has there been any measurable increase in the central-city population.*

6. *There has been no change in the proportion of blacks residing in suburban areas. However, the black population in nonmetropolitan areas increased between 1970 and 1974, marking a reversal of the pattern of the last decade. At the same time, black population in cities continued to grow as a result of net natural increases.*

7. *Substantial flux of movement into and out of central cities continued. The aggregate family income in 1973 of families and unrelated individuals who moved out of central cities between*

1970 and 1974 was about $55.3 billion, while for those moving in, it was $25.7 billion, a loss of almost $30 billion due to migration.

8. *The number of jobs is increasing at a faster rate in the suburban areas of SMSAs compared to central cities. Although the number of professional and technical workers did not decline significantly in cities during the past four years, it appears that the increase in their numbers, which was characteristic of the 1960s, has apparently halted.*

In regard to this last phenomenon, Wilbur Thompson poses some vexing questions:

Whatever happened to the post-industrial age that was supposed to strengthen our central cities? Ten years ago, we all talked optimistically about the new age of services. "Post-industrial" does not, of course, tell one what the new age is, but only what it isn't. But we meant this time to be a professional-service age. What happened to this new force that was supposed to come in and rebuild the cores of our aging metropolises? . . . The service age just has not come to the fore to rescue the big cities.

Regional Growth Patterns

1. *Since 1970, the Northeast has lost population through substantial out-migration. Between 1940 and 1970, it had a net out-migration of whites totaling over 900,000; however, this was offset by a net in-migration of 1.6 million blacks. In the four year period since 1970, the net out-migration of whites was 869,000, practically equal to the previous 30 year period, and blacks too experienced a net out-migration from the region.*

2. *There are indications that as many blacks are moving to the South as there are moving from the South. This is a marked shift from previous patterns.*

3. *Overall, there is a major increase in net in-migration to the South.*

4. *In terms of total employment, between 1967 and 1972, the growth rate was more than five times faster in the Southern Atlantic states (a censal division of the South) than in the Middle Atlantic states (a division of the Northeast).*

5. *The most significant changes occurred in manufacturing employment, with the Middle Atlantic states declining by 12 percent and the South Atlantic states increasing by 7 percent.*

6. Other industrial sectors also had greater gains in the South compared to the Northeast. As Wilbur Thompson points out, the South is going through the industrial and post-industrial age at the same time.

7. New York State and Georgia are typical of their respective regions. The latter's rate of total employment growth between 1967 and 1972 was nine times that of New York.

8. Projections by the Bureau of Economic Analysis (of the Department of Commerce) to 1990 indicate a pronounced shift of income away from the Northeast and North Central parts of the country to the Southern and Western regions.

    a) Nearly every major industry in the Mid-Atlantic sector will expand at below average rates.

    b) Employment in the Southeast is projected to grow at a faster rate than the national average; moreover there will be an increase in the number of persons migrating to the area in response to expanding economic opportunities.

    c) The boost in incomes in the Southeast will be a consequence of manufacturing, not only in the obvious textile and apparel industries, but also in chemicals, machinery, fabricated metals, paper, and printing.

    d) Tourism and recreation will expand in the South as will service industries.

9. The metropolitan housing stock in the South is increasing 1½ times faster than in the Northeast.

10. Overall, there is much newer inventory of housing in the South, a more rapidly changing mix of units, and a much lower cost threshold compared to the Northeast. The sales price for a newly built one-family home in the South is 25 to 30 percent less than in the Northeast.

If these emerging directions of regional and metropolitan evolution are not temporary discontinuities, and if our conceptual framework is valid, then we must begin to think about the consequences of grappling with no-growth settings. And this is at a time when we are just hitting full stride in our debate over the implications of growth. Although both concerns are relevant to the trends at hand, since there will obviously be both losers and gainers, we need to divert some of our attention to the critical issues facing areas having substantial net out-migration. But before we attempt to diagnose the prospects of aging metropolises, we would like to speculate on some of the processes giving rise to them.

THE UNDERLYING PROCESS

No one particular development can be singled out as the primary agent facilitating the current regional shifts and the decline of a number of metropolitan areas. The changes taking place, or at least those which have suddenly become visible, are the cumulative result of a number of small scale events and innovations, acting in concert with long-standing cultural predispositions and accumulating market forces, which have finally congealed into the dynamic which now confronts us.

Current trends of metropolitan decline may be a continuation of long-standing processes that began with a more publicized migrational pattern, the resynthesis of American life in suburbia. While conventionally viewed as a post–World War II transformation whose triggering mechanisms were a pent-up housing demand, increased affluence, the widespread ownership of automobiles, and federal mortgage insurance programs, the original foundation for the suburban shift was slowly laid down many decades earlier, piece by piece. For example, the development of the horse-drawn streetcar in the late nineteenth century was the initial instrument which stretched the city beyond its circumscribed pedestrian limitations. The ability to transmit electricity from a central power station to a moving vehicle, and the development of an efficient electrical streetcar motor further facilitated movement to the countryside. But other innovations were necessary before extensive settlement in dispersed residences could take place: the single residence septic tank for areas beyond city sewerage systems, improved well drilling techniques to supply water to unattached houses, and advances in the transmission of electricity economically, including the switch from direct to alternating current. Step by step, these factors, by improving the level of amenities available beyond the cities' edges, gradually made suburbanization economically feasible.

Extensive real-estate promotions, often the offshoot of streetcar enterprises, played on the American ideal of single family homeownership, and publicized the possibility of new lifestyles. Indeed, these developments keyed in on a variety of cultural traits—termed by Brian Berry love of newness, an overwhelming desire to be near to nature, individualism, and freedom to move—that are interwoven in the American character. And by the 1920s, with the advent of the automobile, suburbanization became a significant force. Depression and war in the following two decades were to markedly restrict the full momentum of these cumulative forces but their strength was not diminished, as the rapid suburbanization of the post-war years demonstrates. The post-war decentralization, further stimulated by additional technological developments, which facilitated economic markets to assume new spatial settings, cannot be considered a break in long-standing trends, but rather the later, perhaps more dynamic, evolutionary stages of a transformation which was based on a pyramiding of small scale innovations and underlying social desires.

And in like fashion, a series of individual changes and shifts have brought about an evolution of regional and metropolitan fortunes and potentialities. Perhaps the most significant of these was the transportation revolution of the 1950s and 1960s, which generated an increasing reliance on air and truck transportation, gradually supplanting the dependence on the nation's rail system. As the Interstate Highway network gradually fostered new patterns of connectivity—first visible in suburbia—many parts of the South were opened up to small manufacturing plants which did not have to rely on rail lines. In contrast, the crisis-ridden Penn Central Railroad appears as an aging network upon which the no-growth industrial regions are superimposed. Yet, while this new homogenization of space and time is one of the major stimuli for the shift to net in-migration in the South and to net out-migration in the Northeast, the shift was aided by other developments operating analogously to those which permitted suburbanization via early technological innovations. The requirements of manufacturing industries provide a case in point.

Manufacturing

Historically, the shifting locational patterns of manufacturing industries were based upon a filtering process, with urban centers losing industries as their products evolved and became standardized. As Wilbur Thompson has pointed out, when a new industry matures, and its products become routinized rather than unique, it can become more efficient in its production process and can use less skilled labor; therefore, it seeks lower wage rates than those extant in urban locations. These spin-offs—what Thompson terms filtering down through a national system of urban hierarchies—have not been particularly harmful, until recently, for older industrial areas for two reasons: first, relocations were often to the suburban areas of the same metropolitan region; and second, the stronger cities of the Northeast were able to continuously innovate to more or less replace what they had lost. This is what is known as the "incubator hypothesis" whereby the rich panorama of services and facilities in our older cities provided the spawning grounds for new innovations and products. The New York metropolitan area, for example, "grew by incubating new functions, nurturing them off to other sections of the country, all the while regenerating this cycle."

However, Thompson seriously questions whether the Northern cities are innovating to replace industries as fast as they are losing them, or whether they can hold their own in days to come. Additionally, the filtering process may be accelerating, occasioned by a decrease in transportation costs relative to production costs and a decrease in the economy of scale. This development favors smaller plants decentralized into smaller places away from large final markets. What this has caused is not simply the dispersion about the older manufacturing cities, but a dispersion out of the Northeast region, to smaller places in nonmetropolitan areas made increasingly accessible by truck transportation over the ever-growing highway network.

Attracted by traditionally low wages and cheap electric power, light manufacturing is migrating South. The absence of unionization, the rising educational levels of the southern population, and a surprisingly deep labor pool—the advertisement of a new plant appears to generate the re-migration of natives from the industrial belts of the North—have permitted the shifts to take place. Additively, these factors have facilitated the passing of substantial manufacturing activity out of the Northeast region and its constituent metropolitan areas.

The harbinger of these changing manufacturing parameters was the well-known shift of textiles from New England and the garment industry of New York City to the lower waged and nonunionized South over the past several decades. In fact, these early examples may be the regional analogues of the pre-depression suburbanization movement. Similarly, what we now see happening may be a replication on a regional scale of events which occurred in metropolitan areas in the 1950s.

Residential Choices and Growth Resynthesis

As we have pointed out, shifts of any substantial magnitude also hinge upon a host of enabling developments which permit the transition to take place. So it is with the population flows, the corollary of industrial shifts. Such movements are the end result of the individual locational choices of numerous households and individuals, and several factors may be gaining importance in regard to these decisions.

The social desires which permeated the "long wave" of suburbanization, as stated by Brian Berry, have grown to full national force with the rising consciousness of the environment and quality of life. Their demise, real or imagined, in the Northeast and North Central regions may foster movements to areas which provide more pleasant climates, attractive scenery, and convenient outdoor recreation facilities. And in turn these amenities are predicated upon the leisure opportunities associated with a shorter work week, and the widespread use of air conditioning to eliminate some undesirable elements of climate. Moreover, the cost of living in aging areas—of housing and the like —may be approaching intolerable levels. Consequently, as Thomas Muller notes:

The sharp rise in the cost of energy is likely to encourage further movement of jobs and households from aging areas which already experience high costs of living. . . . It is probably more than mere chance that the five urban areas with the highest cost of living in 1973 all experienced net out-migration totaling 372,000 persons between 1970 and 1973, while four of the five regions with the lowest cost of living had a net in-migration of 173,000 persons during the same time interval.

Thus it is not difficult to see the rationale for households to follow employment opportunities, particularly when it additionally means a higher quality of life—at least as current fashion interprets it—in housing less expensive and newer than that extant in aging metropolitan areas.

Moreover, just as manufacturing shifts have stimulated the movement of jobs and people, so too does the shift of the latter engender the movement of a number of service industries catering to both the needs of manufacturing and residential activities. Thus we may be witnessing the first stage of a vigorous cycle of urban development. Indeed, Wilbur Thompson suggests that the post-1970 trendlines indicate:

not so much the vigor of nonmetropolitan areas as the emerging of new metropolitan areas. There is such great cumulative power to urban growth that each new wave of population decentralization soon crystallizes into new cities.

And in symmetrical fashion, aging metropolitan areas may be slowly decanted of elements that are mainstays of their long-term viability. With the risk of overdrawing the analogy, we might suggest this is what has been happening in central cities the last several decades. The pyramiding of small-scale developments thus permit the working out of basic social contours and market forces in new settings.

These are just some of the elements which may be spurring the emergence of declining metropolitan areas. What we are basically suggesting is that long-term social trends are now playing themselves out all over the geography of this country, just as they have over its metropolitan areas the last several decades. Clearly, much more work needs to be done to adequately specify the trendlines and causal mechanisms and to weave them into a rigorous explanatory framework. Yet, it is still possible to suggest some of the consequences and issues, which will arise if these trends do signify the wave of the future.

Declining Fiscal Postures

Thomas Muller has dissected the web of fiscal complexities and highlights some very alarming perplexities. As a metropolitan area expands, the average cost of providing similar services rises somewhat proportionally. At the same time, growing areas also tend to have above-average gains in income, generally permitting a fiscal balance to be maintained without any serious increases in taxation burdens. However, as Muller points out:

the ten largest SMSAs, all of which are experiencing net out-migration in the early 1970s, have more serious fiscal problems. These and other declining areas experience higher absolute outlays and more rapid rates of expenditure increase (on a per capita base) compared to smaller metropolitan and non-metropolitan urban areas, most of which are gaining residents.

Since the declining SMSAs correspondingly exhibit substantially lower per capita income growth, the heroic proportions of the impending fiscal shortfalls are not difficult to forecast. Indeed, the dynamics underlying both the revenue and expenditure side of the equation, which Muller clearly isolates, provides a panorama of dilemmas. What they all suggest is that the recent crises of New York City may well be prototypical of those facing other declining metropolises, as well as states and regions.

But the obvious solutions to fiscal problems in declining areas appear to be counterproductive. Higher taxation can only serve to enhance the flight of jobs and talent, reinforcing our basic trends. On the other hand, reduction of expenditures and services heightens an atmosphere of impending crisis, signaling further inroads into the quality of life and increasing the impetus for migration. Moreover, declining metropolitan areas are often hamstrung by strong municipal unions; and as New York City's trauma shows, these unions do not quietly accept restrictions on their domains. Their threats and actions publicize the pervasiveness of the deterioration which underlaid the crises in the first place.

Increasing Spatial Competition

Certainly central cities have had declining fiscal postures for a long time. Glazer points out that was not particularly alarming as long as metropolitan areas grew, since the phenomenon could be explained as a political artifact. The wealth was still within the "daily urban system," and somehow all that was required was the means to tap this wealth. However, this reassurance is shaken if the entire metropolitan area is in decline. Moreover, we might even suggest that political boundaries within aging metropolitan areas will stiffen as its constituent jurisdictions scramble to maximize their share of a shrinking pie of resources. This is already happening at a broader geographical scale.

The competition between metropolitan areas, states, and regions for new industry and jobs has grown ever more fierce, particularly since the payoffs of the industrial recruitment drive in the formerly depressed South have become more visible. In fact, the *Wall Street Journal* has recently reported on the redoubling of states' efforts to lure new industry through an array of inducements. Metropolitan areas may be hard put to match the incentives offered by nonmetropolitan places, such as tax reductions, which would aggravate already periled fiscal systems. The *Journal* ominously reveals that New York City is teeming with industrial recruiters, emphasizing the growing role of jurisdictional—regional, state, metropolitan and suburban—initiatives in industrial shifts. Despite the seeming incongruity of recruiting in an era of no-growth, the realities of the employment consequences of no-growth or decline appear to be striking home.

Employment Dilemmas

The wilting of metropolitan areas raises to new heights the crisis of function of the American city. "The city's major historic role in the United States has been as recipient of successive waves in immigrants . . . the city has provided some entrepreneurs with a source of cheap labor, and for the migrant to it, the city has offered employment at levels of skill he could meet." But without jobs, and without the high levels of innovation in new products which create new jobs, the integrative function may pass by the boards. One could argue that the heavy representation of minority groups in governmental jobs indicates the traditional role still is being fulfilled, but in new fashion. Yet the fiscal dilemmas arising from stagnation make such employment precarious indeed, as municipal and governmental job tenure becomes increasingly less secure.

Effects such as these must be evaluated by income class. The less skilled will apparently bear the brunt of the burden of no-growth and decline. Only those in the public sector may, and we stress may, enjoy some measure of protection. But clearly the affluent will probably be the least affected; they have the jobs least likely to be terminated, while at the same time may enjoy the benefits of lessened congestion. And if they have to be, they are much more mobile. Yet their insularity is not unbreachable. As Wilbur Thompson points out, any no-growth context implies:

serious employment problems even for the most talented. Young professionals out West are pushing for no-growth so that the wait at the ski line is *shorter*. They will come to understand that under no-growth, the wait for promotion at the office is going to be *longer*—a hell of a lot longer.

The implications of no-growth or stagnation may be much more far-ranging than its advocates initially envisioned.

Paradoxically, the shift of economic opportunities to the South may not measurably alleviate the extant unemployment problems there. As Wilbur Thompson points out, new manufacturing plants in the South serve as magnets for drawing in higher skilled workers from the North. This easy mobility has the consequence of inflating the local labor force. Towns may grow, yet still struggle with the burden of endemic unemployment. Moreover, Thompson stresses that manufacturing firms are favoring the white South—Northern

Mississippi, the white hill country, and northwestern Arkansas. They are not locating in the black Delta towns. "There are a number of reasons for this new form of racial discrimination . . . Relocating manufacturers find the hill country white workers are free thinkers who reject unions, while black workers seek the protection of unions. With white labor, there is neither a union problem nor a racial problem." Consequently, as suggested by a fashionable platitude, growth does not solve all problems or create opportunities for all. But this is of little consolation for aging metropolitan areas.

II. NEW YORK CITY

In New York City, the average annual change from 1964 to 1969 for employment was a positive 47,700 increment. This growth pattern abruptly shifts as we turn to the next five year period, from 1969 to 1974, with an absolute annual decline of 68,000 jobs.

The city in the last five years has been losing more than 43,000 manufacturing jobs annually. The apparel industries, once the major source of the city's growth, and certainly a major input into its image as the fashion center of the country, represent a very significant component of the manufacturing decline with an annual average employment loss of 12,000. The strides in transportation and bulk shipping technologies may have permitted the sales rooms to remain in the city—but clearly the earlier trends of out-migration of the production facilities have been accentuated. The classic entry level jobs for the relatively unskilled which were once found on Seventh Avenue now are in the South. The printing industry is also suffering equivalent losses with an annual average job loss of 5,600. The city may retain its specialty printers who are attached to the Wall Street complex, where the legal requirements of security issues require overnight service. Clearly, however, the more mobile members of the industry are fast disappearing.

Private nonmanufacturing facilities are suffering job losses averaging slightly more than 30,000 persons per year. More than half of this is in wholesale and retail trade. The declining quality of retail establishments on Fourteenth Street, the increasing challenges even to the classic giants of yesteryear on Thirty-fourth Street—Macy's, Gimbels, and the like—have been paralleled by the decline of some of the older outlying shopping facilities—the Fulton Street area of Brooklyn, the Jamaica area of Queens and the like. The waning of these commercial junctions is partially offset as new in-town branches are opened up, as they have been by Macy's, Alexander's, etc. Certainly less obvious but equally striking is the decline of small-scale retailing in the city, leaving a trail of empty "Mom and Pop" type store facilities behind them.

This has been paralleled by a shift of distribution and warehousing facilities to the new suburban industrial parks as a function of transportation elements, land availability, and the like. Even the finance, insurance, and real-estate bastions of the central city over the last five years have averaged losses in the vicinity of 7,500 jobs annually.

It is *local* government employment which has been utilized to absorb some of this slack. We have emphasized the term local government here because it is evident that federal government employment is actually declining in the city. Between 1964 and 1969 federal employment decreased 2,000 jobs each year. This has increased to a decline of 2,200 jobs per year in the 1969–1974 period. It is state and local government which shows the greatest level of increase; indeed, with one exception *the only increases in absolute average annual employment from 1969 to 1974 in the city as a whole was in just this area. Every other element, with the exception of the relatively small 2,100 job increase in services, was declining.* From 1964 to 1969 state and local employment within the city increased at a rate of 21,700 jobs a year. The pace decreased from 1969 to 1974 but still averaged 9,000 additional state and local employees annually. While this tends to offset federal job losses, the pattern of the latter raises important questions as to the changing function of New York City.

Increasingly, whether it is in regard to the trade association, the law firm, the academic consultant, or the businessman of any and every variety, one finds that it is Washington where the important decisions are made. The New York banker may as commonly be found in the latter city as in his own home office. The federal budget now represents more than a quarter of the gross national product—the regulatory agencies influence every facet of our lives and industry. The Kennedy Center has become a uniquely successful cultural development. The rise of a well-paid bureaucracy after the governmental pay reforms of the mid-1960s and the ever expanding level of employment in and around Washington combined to make it most competitive with New York City. Indeed the growth of the condominium conversion process in Washington, D.C., is generated by the critical mass of affluent households there. In contrast, the co-op housing market in New York City has fallen on hard times.

Certainly, in any case, it is most striking to see the consistent withdrawal of federal employment from New York City. Some of this undoubtedly may represent a substitution of local activity through transfer payments from the federal employment list per se; a great deal of it, however, represents the increasing centralization which has taken place regardless of all the lip service given to getting more Washingtonians out into the field. The dynamic growth of the federal vehicle in Washington certainly does not portend well for the leadership activities centered in New York City.

Growing Employment Sectors

What sectors of jobs are increasing in New York? Among those sectors showing growth, only local government, nonprofit membership organizations, medical and health services, and banking have continued their positive trends into the 1969 to 1974 period. It is unfortunate that we do not have available further detail on medical and other health services which experienced an increase of 38,800 jobs from 1969 to 1974. It should be noted here, however, that we have reason to believe that a substantial portion of these health care activities are at least in part paid for out of the city's exchequer through the municipal hospitals, services, and the like. To the degree that this is the case, the increase in such activity cannot be viewed as more than a redistributive activity.

The local government increase of 37,500 jobs dwarfs the increment in banking, which at 10,200 is less than a third the government increase. Note that the banking industry had grown by some 31,100 jobs from 1954 to 1969. The tremendous growth in the scale of operations of the clearinghouse banks in New York, or for that matter, of the New York Stock Exchange activity—where a rare 10 million share day has given way to a commonplace 20 million share level of activity—has *not* been paralleled by an equivalent growth in human manpower. It is barely five years ago since the stock market was convulsed by the difficulties of clearing 80 million shares per week. Volume far in excess of this is now casually handled. The age of capital intensification in data processing is finally with us; the computer may not have displaced extant employees, but once fully integrated and assimilated into functional areas of business, it provides substantial excess capacity without having to add proportionately more manpower. The Vernon and Hoover analysis of the growth of financial institutions within the city was precise. What was not fully comprehended was the shrinkage in manpower associated with the definite amount of activity as a function of the electronics revolution. *The city has been losing its manufacturing employment just as the rationalization and the automation of paper and information handling has finally come to fruition.* The imbalance thus created is shown by the increasing levels of unemployment and welfare recipiency within the city as a whole.

Declining Employment Sectors

The reality of the loss in apparel employment within the city is clear to anyone who tours the classic garment sections of the city. The loft manufacturing facilities which dominate the streets from the mid-Twenties, to the upper Thirties of the West Side are sadly quiet. It is far from unique for an industry to decline—or for it to move from a specific region. Certainly New York City has gone through a very substantial number of shifts in employment characteristics over time. What is particularly striking, however, is the failure of the loft district, now in many areas substantially deserted, to serve as an incubator for new industries of a small scale which needs the kinds of infrastructure support and external economies which New York can provide. *It is not the loss of old jobs which is the city's employment problem. It is rather the question of securing or generating new ones.*

How viable an atmosphere does the city provide to potential new employers? The topic certainly is a very broad one—requiring much more in the way of insight and analysis than we can provide in the course of this paper.

CONCLUSION

The history of the last half decade indicates a national economy whose growth patterns before the current recession tended to exclude the metropolitan region of which the city is part. And this was at rates of growth far in excess of those that are foreseen for the near to intermediate future. Secondly, the data indicate that within this slow-growing region, New York City itself is faltering markedly. Analysis of the components of change of its economic base reveals that the historic bastions, such as the apparel and printing industries, have substantially shifted away with little indication of return. Equally striking is the failure of substantial growth to occur in the historic nongovernmental, nonmanufacturing industries—or for that matter the rise of new economic activities to offset this decline. We are still just at the beginning of the paperwork revolution; but even the relatively primitive state of its current organization appears to inhibit any growth in jobs commensurate with the vast increase in information processing functions.

The data on government employment are particularly ominous: an absolute decline in federal employment and a vast and very costly increase in local government supported activities. The latter, unless supported by a renewed growth in nongovernmental functions—which are not dependent on taxes—must ultimately falter under their own weight. The city simply does not have the resources to employ so high a proportion of its own population. Additionally there is a very strong possibility that the marked growth in federal government functions, centralized as they increasingly are in Washington, has spawned a vigorous challenger to New York City as the headquarter of major enterprise. Increasingly, private enterprise is dependent upon government funding, sanction, and regulation. And all of these elements find the decision makers in Washington—not in New York.

Is the crisis of New York City one of will, of organization, or, is it rather one of function? Certainly, the erosion of its economic base and competitiveness sketched out in the foregoing material would suggest the latter. The city, historically, has served as an enormously successful, complex staging ground for successive flows of immigrants. It provided bad housing and limited social welfare mechanisms. But these elements were competitive with the alternatives of their time. Whatever additional inadequacies it may have had were more than offset by the vigor of New York as an employment center. The symbiotic relationship between new inflows of poor, yet willing workers and the availability of jobs—which may have exploited these workers but, at the same time, provided them an avenue of social mobility—is a characteristic of its history. The city, in part, flourished as a nexus for inexpensive labor.

But now one must view new patterns of jobs and places, and the competition of alternative regions. The city's current capacity to provide for both newcomers and for the nearly one in seven of its inhabitants who is on welfare, is seriously in doubt, not merely in terms of social services, important as they may be, but for meaningful and competitive job opportunities. The homogenization of the labor force which has taken place through shifts in the location of consumer markets, the vast rise of transportation facilities, and the variety of support mechanisms such as air conditioning, make hitherto inhospitable regions more and more the successful competitors with the region as a whole and the city specifically.

The questions raised in Wilbur Thompson's essay on the decanting of cities become most urgent as we view the largely manufacturing city of yore, a Cleveland or a St. Louis. The very diversity of New York City's job base, its unique mass, and fiscal base have slowed the process which he sketched. The basic issue in each case, however, is the degree to which we can support a city whose infrastructure is geared for a far larger population than is presently the case.

The Future

Economic analysts have been far more successful as historians than as forecasters. With this admonition in mind, there are a number of extrapolations which we would offer from the data shown.

1. *The region will continue to lose both jobs and population.*

2. *There is little in the present allocation of industries within the city to provide any great level of confidence in their reversing this trend.*

3. *In part, this stems from both the factors of decentralization which we have stressed here as well as the new automation which is affecting all systems of information processing.*

4. *Thomas Muller's analysis of the continuing increase in municipal costs in the face of declining population certainly is exemplified by unabated increases in New York City municipal employment. In turn, the impact on the municipal fisc cannot help but result in a loss of competitive status for the city in its efforts to offset the lures of alternative locations.*

5. *We have yet to feel the full impact of the enormous change in both variation and absolute level of energy costs. Certainly, however, preliminary implications are that they pose yet another danger to the city's economic base.*

6. *So while the city's overall competitive position is continually being undercut by these last two factors, the predicted bases of new strength—the information processing and headquarters functions— are being eroded by technology and the growth of a centralized federal bureaucracy.*

7. *What this suggests is that the immediate past—the post-1970 trendline—may be the future.*

New York City is a unique conjunction in space of population, of support structure, and of genius, talent, and activity. The future that we have sketched is a bleak one; the capacity of the city to deflect the current momentum is questionable. But if we accept the reality of New York's endangerment, what then can we say of less advantageously positioned cities, particularly those in metropolitan areas which suffer equally or perhaps more markedly from the regional shifts which have been detailed here?

9. Six Pillars of the Southern Rim

KIRKPATRICK SALE

If the Southern Rim were an independent nation, it would have a gross national product bigger than any foreign country in the world except the Soviet Union—it stood at some $312 billion in 1970, is probably closer to $400 billion today—and bigger than that of the United Kingdom, Italy, Sweden, and Norway combined. It would have more cars (43 million) and more telephones (38 million) than any foreign nation (more than the United Kingdom, France, and Germany combined), and more housing units (22 million), more television sets (25 million), and more miles of paved highway (1.1 million) than any nation except the Soviet Union. It would, in short, be a world power on the scale of the present superpowers.

Which is only one way of dramatizing the enormous economic importance of the Southern Rim, an importance all the more remarkable in that it has come about only in the last thirty years, changing the pleasant little backwaters and half-grown cities into an industrial and financial colossus. The explanation of that remarkable growth is that, to an unusual extent, almost all of the general trends in the American economy since 1945 have been more to the benefit of the Southern Rim than any other section of the country.

The first and most important trend was obviously that of the population migrations. From 1945 to 1975, the Southern Rim underwent the most massive population expansion in history, from about 40 million people to nearly 80 million people in just three decades, giving the area today a population greater than all but seven foreign countries. Thanks to a complexity of factors—a hospitable climate, the development of air conditioning, water reclamation projects, available space for commercial and private building, the new tech-

Abridged from *Power Shift: The Rise of the Southern Rim and Its Challenge to the Eastern Establishment* (New York: Random House, 1974), chapter 1. Kirkpatrick Sale is a writer living in New York City.

nologies of communication and transportation—industries and individuals alike poured into new territories of the Rim. Every single one of the fifteen cowboy states grew during this period, some quite spectacularly—Texas by over 100 percent to become the third largest state, California by 200 percent, to become the largest state of all, Florida by 400 percent, Arizona and Nevada by more than 450 percent—and as a whole they have consistently made up nearly half of the growth that the nation as a whole has undergone. Migrations every year since World War II have poured millions of new people into the area—on average about 650,000 newcomers every year, turning bucolic farmlands into sprawling suburbs and little crossroads cowtowns into gleaming metropolitan centers. The cities have grown unlike any urban areas in the world, 500 and 800 and 1,000 percent in just this thirty-year span—Fort Lauderdale from 18,000 to 150,-000, Huntsville from 13,000 to 140,000, Houston from 385,000 to 1,400,000, Phoenix from 65,000 to 755,000, San Jose from 68,000 to 446,000, incredible urban explosions right across the Rim—and today there are actually more cities over 100,000 people in this area than there are in the Northeast. Nor does this development show any signs of slackening, despite the economic downturn, despite the efforts of "no-growth" lobbies: the most recent statistics show that the Southern Rim continues to grow about three times as fast as the whole rest of the country combined, and even modest projections suggest that the region will have 83.7 million people by 1980. According to the demographers, never in the history of the world has a region of such size developed at such a rate for so long a time.

The second decisive economic trend of this period has been the transformations brought about by the sophisticated new technology developed since World War II. In broad terms there has been a shift from the traditional heavy manufacturing long associated with the Industrial Belt of the Northeast to the new technological industries that have grown up in the Southern Rim—aerospace, defense, electronics—and from the dependency upon railroad transportation to the growth of air and highway transportation, both relatively more important in the Southern Rim. Similarly, in the use of natural resources there has been a development away from coal and heavy metals such as iron and steel, the resources of the Northeast, toward oil and natural gas and the light metals such as aluminum and titanium, the products of the Southern Rim. And in agriculture, new technologies have favored large-scale and often corporate farming, advantageous particularly where space is plentiful, growing seasons are long, and the crops are suitable, and that turns out to be the Southern Rim.

Finally, trends in employment patterns over this thirty-year period have also tended to tilt things toward the cowboy economy. The single most important development has been the gradual decrease in blue-collar industrial workers—these the backbone of the Industrial Belt—and the sharp increase in service and government workers—these the ones most important in the newly populated states with expanding governments and in the tourist-and-retirement areas like Florida, Texas, Arizona, and Southern California; especially in the booming new Rim cities, service employment has enormously increased, in fact by more than 70 percent over the last twenty years, as against 6 percent in the older cities of the Northeast. In like nature, the employment shifts brought about by postwar programs of paid retirement, the expansion of Social Security, and union-won benefits for longer vacations and shorter hours have all meant more earlier retirements to the sunnier parts of the land and more emphasis upon climatic amenities as an inducement for resettlement of the labor force.

In a general sense, then, it is clear enough that mid-century trends have been tilting the country southward, but it is in turning to specifics that the process becomes even clearer still, particularly the six specific industries whose development and importance rank them as the six basic pillars of the cowboy economy: agribusiness, defense, advanced technology, oil and natural-gas production, real estate and construction, and tourism and leisure. Inasmuch as each of them has been absolutely crucial in the growth of the Southern Rim and each has had an ineradicable impact on the economy of the nation as a whole, a rather more detailed examination of them is appropriate.

Agribusiness

At the heart of the economic power of the Southern Rim is the activity that, we often forget, remains what the *Wall Street Journal* calls America's "biggest industry"—agriculture, or, as both friends and critics have come to call it, "agribusiness."

Given the vagaries of weather, crops, markets, and customers, agriculture is bound to be cyclical to some degree. But the remarkable thing about American agriculture in the period since World War II is the extent to which its growth has been steady and sure—and, in the early 1970s, almost meteoric. Assets of what the Agriculture Department calls "the farming sector" have risen from $132 billion in 1950 to $310 billion in 1970 and on to nearly $350 billion in 1975.* Farm income has nearly tripled since 1950, outpacing most other sectors of the economy, and farm profits have doubled, from $13.7 billion in 1950 to $32 billion in 1974, with the once-impossible $40 billion mark expected to be reached well before 1980. Exports alone have risen by an unheard-of 150 percent in the last five years, and now provide more than enough cash to pay off all U.S. deficits on oil imports.

Healthy enough, but even more impressive when you figure that all this money is going to fewer and fewer people as the farm population dries up steadily every year. More than three million farms have folded since 1945 and more than sixteen million people have left the business. That has meant many things for the postwar society—crowded cities, lands put up for the developers—but for the remaining farmers it means only one thing: the average income per person has soared from $570 to $4,260 in the last thirty years. Take cotton, for example. There are today fewer than 40,000 cotton farms, compared to 242,000 in 1960, but there's no need to fret for those remaining, since the average farm now makes $300,000 a year, thirty times what it was making in 1960.

At the same time, agriculture has succumbed to the mid-century phenomenon that has characterized the rest of the economy—the corporate takeover. From 1945 to 1970 the size of the average farm, which is one rough index of corporate growth, doubled from 191 acres to 390; by 1969, at the time of the last agriculture survey, these large corporate operations held nearly 40 percent of all the acreage in the country and accounted for 57 percent of all the sales. A state like California is a perfect example of the agribusiness process: in 1950 it had more than 110,000 farms, by 1969 it had only 78,000; nearly four million acres, and three-quarters of the prime irrigated land, were owned by just forty-five top corporations, accounting for the largest slice of California's $4-billion-a-year farm income.

The agriculture industry, in short, has had fewer and fewer people cutting up larger and larger slices of a bigger and bigger pie throughout the last thirty years. The chief beneficiary, it should come as no great surprise, is that region of the country where agriculture has

*Figures throughout are in current dollars.

always flourished, where the climate permits the longest growing season, where crops suitable for large-scale corporate cultivation are grown, and where there are the greatest spaces and therefore the biggest farms: the Southern Rim. This last factor is particularly important, since the average Rim farm is four and a half times the national average, and in such states as Arizona and New Mexico ten and fifteen times.

The Corn Belt and popular conception notwithstanding, the Southern Rim is *the* great agriculture belt of the United States. It has more farms than the Corn Belt (over a million, compared to 640,000), more tractors and more farm trucks. All of its states have increased their percentage of the agriculture market in the last thirty years, while the Northeastern quadrant and even the Corn Belt have seen their shares decrease, and the value of its farms have increased from $500 billion in 1959 to more than $820 billion in 1969 and an estimated $950 billion today. The Rim accounted for some $16.5 billion in farm sales at the time of the last agriculture census in 1969, the Corn Belt for only $12.5 billion, and that difference has increased during the farm boom of the last few years; in fact, three Rim states alone—California, Texas, and Florida—account for nearly 20 percent of *all agricultural sales*. And the largest farm-lending banks, which are the real mainstay of the agriculture system, are in the Southern Rim: California's Bank of America, the Security Pacific Bank of Los Angeles, and the Valley National Bank of Phoenix.

Dozens of major corporations, reading the growth patterns in agribusiness, have attempted to diversify into this area in the last decade, producing both a greater investment in the agricultural sector year by year and a steady change in the nature of the industry. A good deal of the farm-based wealth thereby gets sucked off into yankee corporate coffers, but much still remains, and the Rim corporations are every bit as productive: one only has to go down the roster of such producers as Southdown (Houston: sugar), Missouri Beef (Plainview, Texas: beef), and Del Monte (San Francisco: fruits and vegetables); such processors as Tropicana (Bradenton, Florida: orange juice), Carnation (San Francisco: dairy products), and Sunkist (California: fruits); or such giant food retailers as Safeway (Oakland: supermarkets, number one in the land), Coca-Cola (Atlanta: beverages), and Southland (Dallas: "convenience" stores).

DEFENSE

Of all the mid-century growth industries, none has been more phe-
nomenal than defense, fed by the apparently inexhaustible funds
from the federal government. All by itself the military arm of government has created and sustained a whole spate of new communities
and almost single-handedly sponsored dozens of new corporations.

The figures are immense, the economic impact equally so, and
nowhere greater than in the Southern Rim. This is a region that was
transformed, and brought into modernity, by World War II, when
the defense establishment moved in to take advantage of its benign
climate, vast open spaces, extensive and for the most part protected
coastline, abundant and cheap labor, and nascent shipping and aircraft industries, altogether pumping in an estimated 60 percent of its
$74 billion wartime expenditures into these fifteen states. And as the
defense installations and contractors continued to grow with growing
defense budgets even after the war—$13 billion in 1950, $50 billion
in 1960—they continued to build up the substructure of the whole
economy, in practically every state from North Carolina to California. Indeed, if any one industry can be said to be the backbone of
the Southern Rim, it is defense.

During the years of Vietnam and the moondoggle the balance of
Pentagon prime contracts shifted sharply to the Southern Rim, with
the percentages mounting every year, until by 1970 its states accounted for 44.1 percent of all the money going to the defense
industry, the Northeast only 38.9 percent. Texas surpassed New York
as the number two state behind California, and those two between
them accounted for 28 percent of the contracts, more than twice as
much as the next two states, New York and Illinois. By 1970, too,
the Rim had five of the top ten states in terms of total Department
of Defense spending (California, Texas, Georgia, Florida, and North
Carolina), four of the top five states in aerospace funding (California,
Texas, Florida, and Alabama), and four of the top five states in
Atomic Energy Commission grants (New Mexico, California,
Tennessee, and Nevada). The number of major defense installations
(military bases, missile sites, etc.) in the Southern Rim had grown to
142, more than all the rest of the nation put together, and 82 more
than were located in the Northeast. Defense Department payrolls by
1970 were also concentrated in the Rim: military salaries went primarily to California, Texas, Virginia, North Carolina, Florida, and

Georgia, in that order, and military and civilian payrolls together amounted to more than $10 billion in the Rim, more than in all the other states combined. And Pentagon research-and-development funds—the seed money that creates new technologies and industries —were concentrated in the Southern Rim, which had 49 percent of the funds as against just 35 percent for the Northeast.

Today the repercussions of military money upon the once-placid Rim are evident everywhere. It is a commonplace that California is a heavily saturated defense area—especially around Los Angeles, where no fewer than seventy firms depend upon Pentagon prime contracts—and that it receives about a quarter of the total defense dollar all by itself; Texas, too, what with the Houston Space Center and major firms like LTV and Convair, has long been identified with the new Washington money. But few realize that even in such states as Louisiana, Georgia, Mississippi, Tennessee, and New Mexico, the defense industry is the single largest employer, an economic presence with enormous ramifications. Take New Mexico, for example. Without defense, it would still probably be a land of Indians and Chicanos —a reversion to which condition those two groups would no doubt welcome—instead of one of the nation's fastest-growing states. It has eight major defense installations (including the White Sands Missile Range, site of the first atomic bomb test), a dozen important research centers (including the Los Alamos and Sandia laboratories), and several dozen corporate defense contractors (including AT&T's Sandia Corporation and United Nuclear). It gets more money from the AEC than any other state and almost as much from the Pentagon, together amounting to some $750 million a year—which works out to about $2,500 for every single family in the state. (The military loves the place so much that even the Navy spends money there— some $11 million a year—even though the state is completely landlocked and there's not even a lake big enough to spit in.) And its industry is dominated by defense work, responsible for half of all employment and by itself the largest manufacturing sector in the state's economy. It seems entirely fitting, if nonetheless gruesome, that one little New Mexico schoolchild after a visit to the Atomic Museum at Kirtland Air Force Base should write to the curator, "You have nice rockets and nice bombs. Thank you."

The industrial aspect of defense spending, though only one part of the total defense cornucopia, has been especially significant in the Southern Rim, inasmuch as it has been largely responsible for building the manufacturing substructure of the region. From 1965, thanks partly to Lyndon Johnson's ascendancy, Southern Rim firms have gotten a greater percentage of Pentagon contracts than any other section of the country, an influx of $15 billion or so a year.

TECHNOLOGY
One part of the defense industry that has been particularly glamorous in recent decades is aerospace and electronics, but that is actually just a part of the whole range of modern scientific and engineering businesses—including computers, calculators, semiconductors, scientific instruments, magnetic recordings, and much else besides—which can broadly be called the technology industry. Given its unquestioned importance now, even more outside of the defense industry than in it, and its assured centrality in any future industrial development, it seems reasonable to regard this as a separate economic pillar.

To take just the aerospace component for a start, this business has expanded from a minor nuts-and-bolts operation after World War II to a $30 billion industry today, with more scientists and engineers than all the universities put together and the largest concentration of research-and-development money of any industry in the nation. In the brief fifteen years of the American space program, federal expenditures quintupled from $900 million to $5 billion, with a peak of $7.2 billion back in 1967, when landing men on the moon was the government's top priority; in all, about $80 billion has been spent by Washington on aerospace development. Most of that money, as any Cronkite-watcher knows, has gone to the Southern Rim, with the industry's headquarters in Houston, its research arm in California, its rocket center in Huntsville, Alabama, and its launching station in Cape Canaveral, Florida—an aero-arc right across the country. It is the Southern Rim whose firms account for 70 percent of the national aerospace production and whose plants employ more than half of all the country's aerospace workers—55 percent, as against 27 percent for the Northeast. Only three states in the nation have thirty or more major aerospace plants—California, Texas, and Florida—and there are ten major firms each in Arizona, Oklahoma, Tennessee, Alabama, and North Carolina, a full sweep of the Rim.

But the technology industry is more than just rockets and missiles; it takes in the vast development of sophisticated post-war science in everything from transistors to lasers, all the varied industries that have grown up in the wake of nuclear physics and modern electronics in the last couple of decades.

Here, too, the Southern Rim has been the main beneficiary. Sprawling scientific complexes have been established over the whole area, in Los Angeles, Phoenix, Dallas, Fort Lauderdale-Melbourne, Durham-Chapel Hill, concentrations of technological power which have grown up right along with the population in areas where the economic climate was as congenial as the meteorological to new enterprises and innovations. Professional and technical employment in the region has mushroomed in the last thirty years, growing by more than 90 percent (202 percent in California alone), while the Mid-Atlantic region, for example, though inevitably sharing in the new sciences, increased by only 41 percent. Today, measured by state government employment, there are more scientists in the top four Southern Rim states (California, Florida, North Carolina, and Texas) than in the top four Northeast states (New York, Illinois, Pennsylvania, and Michigan); California alone has an estimated 28,000 natural scientists, twice as many as Pennsylvania or Illinois, and Texas— long-degraded Texas, home of cattle, oil, and sagebrush—has more scientists than Wisconsin and Indiana combined, in fact more than that famed science-centered state, Massachusetts. Finally, federal research-and-development funds are highly concentrated in the Rim area, which absorbed as much as 60 percent at the last count, and one institution alone—the California Institute of Technology, the Pasadena laboratory-cum-university—is said to get more money in grants from Washington than the entire legislative branch of the federal government, which indicates at least something about the nation's priorities.

Although the Los Angeles metropolitan area has long had the largest number of high-technology businesses in the nation—more than the New York region, more than Boston-Cambridge, more than Chicago-Evanston—the most dramatic proof of the role of the technology industry is provided by a smaller 25-mile strip farther north, Santa Clara County, California. There, on land which used to be orange groves just twenty-five years ago, is located what *Fortune* has called "the densest concentration of innovative industry that exists anywhere in the world," whose more than 800 scientific companies and 150,000 technical employees have "created an innovative ferment on a scale without precedent in industrial history." The base of this phenomenon is Stanford University and the industrial park that it began to put together in the early 1950s to attract high-technology experts and creative scientific minds; soon such electronic giants as Hewlett-Packard, Fairchild, Lockheed, Sylvania, and Admiral located in the area, and they in turn began spinning off highly successful smaller operations with those mysterious machine-made names like Syntex, Itek, Zeocon, Rodal, Litronix, Synetics, and Memorex. Today Santa Clara County has far surpassed the older technical clusters like Cambridge and Ann Arbor and is the world capital in the development and production of semiconductors (transistors, diodes, and the like, fundamental to all modern technology), lasers, and computer disks, the headquarters for the leading firms in medical instruments, microcomputers, magnetic tapes and sophisticated pollution-control devices, the acknowledged leader in all kinds of scientific research and development, the home of at least a hundred technology millionaires, and the center for the kind of advanced research that will stand behind the industrial development of the future.

OIL

Because it is now the single source of energy that America depends upon most, industrially and commercially, oil is obviously a major mid-century growth industry—and just as obviously its benefits have been most spectacularly felt in the petroleum province of the country, the Southern Rim.

We tend to forget, what with our gas-geared economy these days, that for most of this century oil was a weak sister to coal. In 1940 gas and oil supplied less than half of U.S. fuel needs, but by 1950 this had grown to 57 percent and thereafter never slackened: in 1960 it stood at 73 percent of the energy market and in 1975 at nearly 78 percent. "King" coal, the Northeast's only energy resource, provides no more than 17 percent of the nation's needs.

In other words, this country—its cars and planes, its utilities and businesses, its farms and homes—now runs on oil. Oil stands behind the threefold increase in the motor-vehicle market, the multibillion-dollar superhighway system, the proliferation of single-family suburbias, and such new and increasingly important industries as petrochemicals, man-made textiles, synthetic rubber, fertilizers, plastics, asphalt, and airplane travel. Oil stands behind more of America's mid-century fortunes than any other product or service, accounting for no fewer than thirty-three oilionaires with net worths of $75 million or more, according to one count in 1968, and for fully a third of all the multimillion-dollar new-money fortunes made in the first fifteen postwar years, including those of the two richest individuals in the world, J. Paul Getty and H. L. Hunt. Oil stands behind a dozen of America's largest corporations, whose assets of more than $100 billion are greater than those of any single industry in the nation, more than twice as large as the runner-up automobile industry; oil's tentacles reach so far into the corporate world that today it accounts for fully 20 percent of all the stocks traded on the New York Stock Exchange. For all the talk about the Nuclear Age, the last thirty years have in fact been the Age of Petroleum—fusion produces less than 1 percent of America's energy—and the next thirty are likely to be, too.

No one needs to be told that during this period it was upon the state of Texas that the oil gods showered most of their manna. From the discovery of the enormous East Texas field in the 1930s, through the opening up of the Permian Basin in the 1950s, down to the offshore Gulf of Mexico finds of the 1960s and '70s, that state has been at the heart of American oil development. All the great names of oil—Getty and Hunt, Sid Richardson and Clint Murchison, D. H. "Dry Hole" Byrd and R. E. "Bob" Smith, John Mecom and Glenn McCarthy, and all the old-timers who bring faraway looks to the eyes of modern oilmen as the evening waxes moister—belong to Texas. That state alone, as of 1970, produced 35 percent of all the petroleum in the country and 40 percent of all the natural gas, at a value of some $6.5 billion a year—so much money that the millions coming into the state from the cattle business, according to Texas historian J. Frank Dobie, "have come to look like tips." In the last thirty years the city of Houston has become not only the oil capital of the country but also without question the energy center of the world.

But Texas is only the heart of the oil business—though of course its braggadocio has made it the most talked-about—and the industry's arteries (or, perhaps better, pipelines) extend in every direction all along the Southern Rim. Next to Texas, the most important oil-producing states are Louisiana, California, Oklahoma, and New Mexico, in that order, and the five of them together account for an astounding total of 82 percent of all the oil produced in the country, 88 percent of all the natural gas. In fact, if you drew a circle with a 500-mile radius and Houston at its center, taking in the major oil areas of all the states from New Mexico to Florida and most of the offshore fields, you would have a Southern Rim energy kingdom that could probably supply this nation with the *totality* of its energy needs, even at accelerated future rates, for the next fifty years. The Rim, in short, is the gas tank of the American car, the furnace of the American home, the turbine of the American generator, and nothing—not the Alaska pipeline or the Rocky Mountain oil shale, not solar energy or geothermal geysers—seems likely to displace its primacy.

But there is a confusing element in the American oil business, for it has an odd mixture of cowboy and yankee to it. The Rockefeller fortunes, after all, are based upon Standard Oil, the Mellon empire upon Gulf, and no amount of divestiture and trust-busting has done much to change that; and the international giants, the "Seven Sisters" that dominate Middle Eastern production and American markets, are heavily involved with yankee capital even though a number of their executives and some of their bigger investments are rooted in cowboy soil. On the other hand, there are also down-home Texas companies, as cowboy as the Marlboro man, which now operate overseas in the former yankee provinces and behave every bit like their yankee counterparts.

The old distinctions—"international" vs. "domestic," "integrated" vs. "independent"—are simply no help as a way out of this confusion, but it *is* valuable to draw a distinction between the *old* oil companies, those with their roots in the late nineteenth and early twentieth centuries, mostly around the oil strikes of Pennsylvania and Illinois, and the *newer* oil companies, those which grew up after the big Texas strikes of the 1930s, the offshore drillings of the 1950s and '60s, and the advantageous overseas tax breaks of the 1960s and '70s.

In the first group are the Standard Oil offshoots (Exxon, Mobil, the Standards of California, Indiana, Ohio, and Kentucky, and small tendrils like Continental and Marathon), plus other independent giants like Gulf, Texaco, and Shell, and the Northeastern-based firms like Sun and Cities Service. Many of these have brought up oil and gas holdings in the Southern Rim, of course, and have even located division headquarters in Texas or California, but they are not really cowboy corporations: their primary province is generally the Middle East, their markets are as much international as domestic, and their stockholders, their executives, and their interests tend to be yankee-oriented. To take just one example, Mobil Oil, though it has four regional offices and eighteen plants in Texas, a North American headquarters in Houston, some two and a half million acres of U.S. land, and a domestic production of 400,000 barrels a day, is still not primarily a Rim company: its American production is only a quarter of its world-wide gross, its income is more than 60 percent foreign-derived, its stock is owned mostly by yankee banks (22.7 percent) and Rockefeller interests (1.8 percent), and its corporate headquarters, the place where the managerial and money men gather daily, is on Forty-second Street in New York City. Clearly for Mobil there is considerable interest in Rim happenings, the positions of the Texas regulatory commissions or the developments of Gulf superports, and it will have an inevitable effect upon the economy of the Rim, but just as clearly this is not a cowboy corporation.

The second group, containing the newer oil companies and most of the natural gas companies, is by contrast preponderantly Rim-based, though sometimes with outposts elsewhere. There are two different kinds of operators here. The familiar ones are the wildcatters, the so-called independents (who are in reality dependent upon larger corporations for sales, pipelines, and often their very existence, but that's another story), the royalty owners (who are simply landowners who lease out their land and get a percentage of the profits), and various assorted small beasties and roustabouts in between; according to the Liaison Committee of Cooperating Oil and Gas Associations, lobbyists for these people, there are some seven thousand of these independents, more than 90 percent of whom are Southern Rim born and bred. Then there are the much larger new firms which have spread out in recent years on the yankee model, trying to establish vertical monopolies (that means owning everything from the drilling rig to the station pump) and flinging themselves into overseas exploration in areas that the older firms have neglected; most representative here are such companies as Getty, Occidental, Union, Signal (all of Los Angeles), Phillips (Oklahoma), Superior, Tenneco and Tesoro (Texas), all of which are large enough to figure in *Fortune*'s top five hundred industrials but are also of fairly recent vintage. These are firms which, like Getty, have built their dynasties on the offshore drilling operations that became economically significant only in the 1950s, or which, like Union and Occidental, moved into international exploration in the untouched Pacific and neglected North Africa during the 1950s and '60s, when U.S. government tax breaks made it more profitable to find oil overseas than at home.

In fact, it was the irreverent competition from this second group which more than anything else brought on that recent oil panic which went under the name "energy crisis." The instigation was the willingness of the newer oil companies to deal with the Middle

Eastern producing companies on the producers' terms just in order to get a share of the riches, an eventuality which exploded the fat-cat monopoly of the old yankee firms and destroyed their happy hold over Middle Eastern oil. For example, in 1973, when all the other oil firms refused to give up a majority share of their Libyan oil finds to the new military government there, it was Occidental, the California upstart, that first agreed to an unheard-of 49–51 split; this started the round of high-pressure renegotiations by the Libyan government and then by other Middle Eastern states which wanted similar lucrative deals, a flurry that eventually ended up with most of the cards in the producers' hand, their eventual boycott of the United States, and the resultant energy panic. With $3 billion in corporate assets, ranking thirty-second among all American firms, Occidental is surely no cowboy David—but its effect upon the yankee Goliaths was very much the same.

REAL ESTATE

Nothing can be quite as spectacular as the oil boom, but if anything comes close, with perhaps even greater effects on the Southern Rim, it has been the mid-century real-estate boom. Combine an ever-growing population, the extraordinary migrations into the South and West, the insatiable American desire for a home of one's own (and in many cases *two* homes), and you get a buying-and-building spree that is gobbling up 700,000 acres a year and has changed the nature, not to mention the face, of the Southern Rim.

Mid-century Americans seem to have taken to heart that old Will Rogers suggestion, "Buy land, they ain't makin' any more of it," and have produced what is easily the greatest land boom since the Oklahoma Territory opened in 1889. Millions of acres of open land have gone under the plow in the last thirty years in the relentless sweep of "progress," with probably an area bigger than the state of Ohio given over to real-estate development alone. Land prices have gone up every single year since 1945, in the 1970s by 8 percent or so a year, and not even a depressed economy and a downturn in housing starts has slowed that process much; urban Miami Beach in 1974 was going for $450,000 an acre, suburban Palm Springs for $100,000 an acre. A very valuable investment, obviously, and the foundation for some very sizable fortunes.

Building upon this land has been every bit as dramatic, with a relative slowing-down in 1974 and 1975 only after nearly thirty years of headlong prosperity. For complex sociological reasons, American families have tended to split up into smaller groups in recent years, and each of those groups has tended to buy its own housing: since the first enumeration in 1890, the number of families owning homes stayed at about 45 percent up until World War II, but from 1945 on the rate increased significantly and in the last fifteen years nearly 65 percent of all American families have become homeowners. It is perhaps not surprising then that more than 42 million housing units have been built in the United States over these thirty years—but it is still somewhat shocking to realize that this is more units than there were in the country altogether in 1945, or in other words *a doubling of the entire number of housing units within just thirty years.* And the total amount spent on new construction over that period rose no less than 2,000 percent, from $6 billion in 1945 to $94 billion in 1970 and an estimated $135 billion today, while the total economy was growing by only 500 percent.

Real estate and construction, taken together as a single industry, has today become as significant a part of the national economy as, well, automobile manufacturing—except that it is *eight times* more significant, accounting for more than $100 billion worth of the national income in 1970 (and closer to $150 billion by 1975), as against only $13 billion for automobiles. Real estate and construction, in fact, make up 15 percent of the national income just by themselves—more than any other individual segment of the economy, more than retail trade, state and local government, transportation, communication, banking, or medicine.

No area of the country, of course, has been unaffected by the real-estate boom, but inevitably the Southern Rim, because it has most of the available land and got most of the people, benefited most. This was a region only barely touched by urbanization at the end of World War II and it had enormous open areas where, providing water and people could be supplied, unlimited development was possible; the government supplied the water, the climatic tilt supplied the people, and the developers reaped their profits. The South, which had only a quarter of the housing starts in 1945 and scarcely a third even as late as 1960, had almost half of them by 1972; together with the West, it accounted for 70 percent of all housing starts in the country in 1972, a figure which is supposed to grow to 75 percent by 1980, no matter how the housing market fluctuates. The Northeast, in the meantime, beginning to choke in its megalopolitan mess, declined steadily from 41 percent of the nation's housing starts in 1960 to less than 30 in 1972, in spite of the fact that it had a greater absolute population. Two statistics indicate this shift dramatically: New York City had only 49,000 housing starts in 1971, while Atlanta, a city one-fifteenth the size, had 48,000; the fourteen states of the entire Northeastern part of the country had 382,000 new houses that same year, a figure matched by just the seven states of the southeastern Rim (from the Mississippi east).

Every state in the Rim has been touched by this boom, some mightily.

Naturally such a giant business as this has caught the attention of corporations all over the land, especially those with lots of loose capital, and many a yankee firm has come to cowboy country to make a killing: Republic Steel is a land developer in Alabama, ITT in Florida, Philip Morris in Phoenix and Los Angeles, and Gulf in Texas, California, Arizona, and Florida. But of those corporations whose primary business is land development, the largest ones are native to the Rim: Kassuba Corporation (Florida), the largest apartment builder in the United States; Trammel Crow (Texas), the largest developer of rental housing; Jim Walter (Tampa); General Development Corporation (Miami); GAC (Miami); Gulf States Land and Industries (New Orleans); Major Realty (Florida); McDowell (Memphis); McCulloch (Arizona); John Portman (Atlanta); and countless hundreds of smaller operations. The giants of the construction industry, too, are native to the Rim, which has five of the top ten firms: Bechtel (San Francisco), Halliburton-Brown & Root (Houston)—these are the top two, twice as big as the nearest competitors—Daniel International (Greenville, South Carolina), Fluor (Los Angeles), and McDermott (New Orleans).

An enormous industry, then, this real-estate and construction industry, with an enormous impact on the cowboy economy. Even the recession years, though hard on parts of the real-estate business all across the country, have affected the Rim areas the least—for even if they ain't makin' any more land, they are making more people, and more of them keep moving to the Southern Rim, and buying places to live in.

[Sale's sixth pillar is "leisure," discussion of which has been omitted.]

10. The Federal Rip-off of New York's Money

SEYMOUR MELMAN

While the government and population of New York City were condemned and abused around the world for proposing to operate the City government at an 8% deficit for 1976, President Ford presented a Federal budget for 1976–77 with an 11% deficit. This $42 billion Federal deficit was clearly a record, but one on which Gerald Ford proposes to win approval for popular election to the White House for four more years.

The Federal government can, in the last analysis, inflate the currency by printing more and paying off its debts in money of diminished value. Since that operation is not open to New York City or any other government or private organization within the United States, the Federal government under Ford took advantage of the New York fiscal crisis as an opportunity to organize a great conservative experiment.

For the Gerald Fords and Ronald Reagans of this country, the New York experiment is designed to answer the question: how much reduction in its level of living is a large city population prepared to take? For American conservatives this is a vital issue, because the answer to this question will determine whether the population is prepared to go along with the Federal government's military-oriented pattern of resource use.

For 1976, the tax dollars collected by the Federal government from individuals and corporations (excluding Social Security) were used with overwhelming priority for the Federal government's military enterprises. Thus, 54¢ of each tax dollar has been used to pay for past, present and future military operations. The Ford budget for next year proposes more of the same. The payment for this, in the form of

Reprinted from the *Public Employee Press* (March 12, 1976). Seymour Melman is professor of industrial engineering at Columbia University.

manpower, capital and technology funneled into the military enterprise, must finally come from the rest of the economy and society.

MILKING "CIVILIAN" STATES

The Federal government has been milking the civilian parts of the American economy in order to pay for its military enterprise. The crucial evidence is available to us in the form of the taxes paid from the various states to the Federal government, in relation to the payments made into the states by the Federal government. The pattern is unmistakable. The first years for which data are available on this are 1965–1967. In that period the Federal government took out of New York State $7.4 billion more than it spent here for all purposes. By contrast, California received $2 billion a year more than it paid to the Federal government. The surplus in Virginia was $1.3 billion, and for Texas it was $1 billion each year. New York State was not the only one that suffered a major outflow. The other principal states whose wealth was transferred out were Illinois, Michigan, Pennsylvania, Ohio, Indiana, and Wisconsin. The important common feature of all of these states is that they are all centers of civilian industry and civilian economy.

From 1965 to 1967, New York City paid out to the Federal government $3.2 billion more each year than was received back. Obviously, this is an amount that is far in excess of the record New York City deficit of $1 billion by 1976. But the matter did not stop there.

By 1973, by similar reckoning, the net annual outflow of tax dollars from New York City, in excess of all Federal payments for all purposes into New York City, had increased to $7.5 billion, more than 7 times the estimated New York City deficit for 1976.

Meanwhile, a February series of *New York Times* articles defined the "Sunbelt States" as the location of a Federally-sponsored bonanza being paid for by the citizens of New York City and other northern centers of civilian economy. (The "Sunbelt" includes California, Arizona, New Mexico, Texas, Oklahoma, Arkansas, Louisiana, Mississippi, Alabama, Georgia, Florida, Tennessee, South Carolina, North Carolina, and Virginia.) These states, with a population of 77 million in 1975 (as against 135 million in the rest of the country) have been the concentration point of Federal spending in accordance with the Federal government's priorities of the last 20 years. So in 1974 this region received $13 billion more from the Federal government than the people and firms of this region paid in taxes to the Federal government.

MILITARY MONEY GOES SOUTH

According to the *Times* series, as Federal military outlays increased
—they reached $86 billion in 1975—the Sunbelt region's share in-
creased even faster, rising from 35% in 1960 to more than 40% last
year of prime military contracts alone. This is not considering military
salaries at more than 140 installations, more than in the rest of the
nation combined. Almost 50 per cent of Pentagon research money
also goes into the Sunbelt. In some states—Georgia, Louisiana, Mississippi, Tennessee and New Mexico, for example—the defense industry is the largest employer.

Members of Congress from the southern states have sought out
positions on the Armed Services Committees in the House of Representatives and in the Senate, and have obviously used their positions
as points of leverage for funneling military installations (read *payrolls*)
into their districts and states in a prodigal fashion. As this has proceeded, these states, in turn, became centers of support for military-
oriented policies of the United States around the world. Thus, the
states of this region were the last hold-outs of major support for the
Vietnam War.

I am appreciative of the fact that the people of New York City,
and especially City employees, have had their attention focused on
the New York City budget deficit and the prospect of job and spending cuts in order to try to overcome it. My purpose in underscoring
these wider developments is to establish the framework within which
the New York fiscal crisis has developed.

The New York City problem did not develop in isolation. It is one
effect of a permanent war economy. Here is some crucial evidence
on where our tax dollars have been going, taken from my own last
monthly statement of earning and deductions. Of each dollar of
payroll tax deductions, 69¢ was Federal, 25¢ went to the State of New
York, and 6¢ went to the government of New York City. Of the
Federal amount, 54% or 37¢ was used to pay for government's war
economy. That amount exceeds the combined taxes of New York
State and New York City.

In a letter to the *New York Times,* Professor Roelofs of New York
University asks:

New York, as a cultural and economic entity, is in many ways rich and
powerful. But the City's political institutions appear unable to allocate availa-

ble resources to our social hurts on anywhere near the scale required. Why not? Why the paralysis? What's wrong? The current fiscal crisis is a mask. Where is the root of our discontent?

FEDERAL TAX DRAINOFF

The crucial factor is the drainoff of the New York City tax base to the Federal government. But there is another side that consists of the burden that has been heaped upon the government and the people of New York City by Federal policies.

The Federal government's policies imposed a set of heavy costs on the City and State. Federal subsidies spurred the mechanization of agriculture in the American South after World War II, producing a castoff labor force of poor tenant farmers. The former tenant farmers drifted to the great cities of the North, as did a wave of migrants from Puerto Rico, also seeking opportunity.

The Federal government did virtually nothing to support economic development that would retain, educate and re-employ these people. The "Great Society" program was never implemented, as the needed resources were funneled off for the war in Vietnam. The City school systems and social services gave modest support for people whose traditional lives had been shattered. As a consequence there grew up in New York and other cities a substantial population of jobless and unemployable people. Their depressed condition is accentuated by the racial discrimination toward which the Federal government practices benign neglect.

A permanently impoverished population is costly to a surrounding community. The very poor use more police and fire services, more courts, more jails, more emergency medical care, more social work, and more welfare resources of all kinds than any similar employed population.

For thirty years the Federal government has subsidized the development of suburban communities: by the tax deduction allowed on home mortgage interest; by the Federal highway network that linked the suburbias of the country and gave easy access to central cities. Meanwhile, urban renewal was neglected. So cities like New York developed blighted areas, and city transit was left to decay, deemed unworthy of Federal largesse.

The combination of the tax rip-off of New York City and Federal government irresponsibility for the consequences of its own policies adds up to the New York fiscal crisis.

CONSERVATIVE SOLUTION

The conservative formulation is that the New York fiscal crisis is due
to poor management by the City government, and the conservative
solution is a drastic reduction in City services. The payroll cuts which
have taken place do not represent administrative overheads that
could be dispensed with. Neither are they the fruits of more efficient
re-definition of functions or of ways of performing them. These
reductions represent overwhelming reductions in real services and
hence a real reduction in the level of living for the population of New
York City.

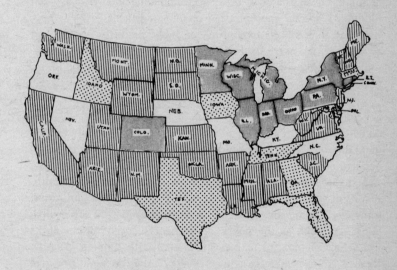

WHERE THE TAXES WENT (1973)

BIG WINNERS:
States which got back more than 100% of their
Federal taxes.

DOING FINE:
States which got back from 80% to 100% of their
Federal taxes.

BIG LOSERS:
States which got back less than 66% of their Federal
taxes.

Source: Research Department, The Dreyfus Corporation.

This is the conservative solution for supporting the Federal exploitation of the City, the State, the other states north of the Sunbelt, and for sustaining the flow of capital and purchasing power into the Sunbelt states which are the concentration points of the Federal military economy.

The effects on the New York economy go well beyond reducing the level of living through reduction of City services. The unemployment that is generated will necessarily have a multiplier effect. Thus, if 44,000 jobs are lost from services provided by the government of the City of New York, then it is prudent to expect not fewer than another 44,000 jobs to be lost as an effect of the diminution of spending power that this causes. The building industry has been suffering a special concentration of unemployment in New York City, and that is likely to continue as public funds for housing and every other kind of construction become unthinkable under the pressure of the City government's effort to cope with the fiscal crisis on its own.

LIVING STANDARDS FALL

Again, I underscore that the pressure on the New York City government and on the people of New York City derives finally from the decision of the Federal government, centered in the White House, to test the degree to which the people of this city are prepared to suffer a massive decline in living standards. This will take many forms, some of them already visible and some that cannot be anticipated.

For example, as the police department reduced various of its forces, enforcement of narcotics laws necessarily suffered. Already, there is strong evidence, as in one report, that on some principal streets in East Harlem the selling of illegal drugs has taken on various qualities of a supermarket hard-sell, with wide open and unconcealed exchanges of large sums for illegal drugs.

Obviously too, the poorest of the poor will be the principal sufferers from the decline in City services. As far back as 1972, the City government established unmistakably that a concentration of poor people, as in the South Bronx and Harlem, required City services of every kind in a ratio 4 times greater (per capita) than the requirement for comparable services in middle-class—let alone more affluent—neighborhoods. Stated differently, this means that economic development for those who need it desperately in New York City is being canceled in favor of economic development for the Pentagon Sunbelt.

None of this is to say that it is not feasible and sensible to effect substantial economies in various parts of the City government.

From industrial experience with problems of administrative overhead, one should expect that substantial reductions in administrative functions and manpower could be made in many City departments. There is no doubt that the Federalization of welfare budgets would remove a considerable burden from the budget of New York City. There is also reason to expect that a serious re-evaluation of City jobs to raise the standards of the lowest and reduce unreasonably high payments would also yield some significant effect. Such job re-evaluation, however, would necessarily require several years for fruition. In the short run, there should also be a meaningful sum of savings that could be garnered by the elimination of ceremonial and honorific "political" jobs whose performance contributes no visible service to the main business and function of the City government.

When all this has been taken into account, however, it would not necessarily eliminate a fiscal problem for a New York City administration which is committed to ensuring the kind of attractive and efficient environment that is worthy of a large American city at the end of the 20th century, and that will provide the kind of infra-structure that is attractive to large and small investors alike.

The rip-off of the New York Cities of the country has the effect of making them less desirable places to work in and live in.

In an article in the *New York Times* of February 6, Municipal Assistance Corporation Chairman Felix G. Rohatyn spoke to the question of economic priority in this society, saying:

A Federal "Marshall Plan" for the reconstruction of our older cities would be both stimulative and, by providing both employment and production, anti-inflationary. Although politically unpopular at present, it is morally right. Shouldn't we rebuild our cities and employ our poor rather than spend billions on nuclear overkill?

When the matter is put in these terms, then clearly the issue is not confined to New York City. That opens the possibility of finding allies for confronting the operators of the Federal war economy, who are, finally, the exploiters of the New York Cities of the country. Rohatyn was right in arguing that "There is at present no prospect for meaningful discussions with the Federal government. We have, however, neighboring states wtih similar problems. One might explore setting up a Regional Development Authority together with Massachusetts, Rhode Island, New Jersey and Connecticut." That is one imaginative approach to the problem which awaits an even broader formulation.

11. Fiscal Problems of Cities

CHARLES L. SCHULTZE,
EDWARD R. FRIED,
ALICE M. RIVLIN,
NANCY H. TEETERS and
ROBERT D. REISCHAUER

While the nation's large cities are plagued by many specific problems—crime, pollution, congestion, and poverty—the overriding urban problem of the coming decade may well be the general inability of large city governments to make ends meet. Although total federal aid to state and local governments has expanded dramatically in the past ten years—from $8.8 billion in 1963 to the $43.5 billion proposed in the 1973 federal budget—it has not been sufficiently concentrated in the central cities to deal effectively with their fiscal problems. As a consequence, pressure has mounted for some form of increased federal commitment to beleaguered urban governments. Revenue sharing, if enacted, will help, but will not channel substantial amounts of funds into central cities. It is clear that a basic decision must soon be made about the nation's interest in preserving the public services and long-run viability of the older central cities.

The cities' fiscal crisis stems from the interaction of two developments. First, the levels of per capita local expenditures are higher and are generally growing faster than those of the surrounding suburbs. While some of the reasons for this lie in deliberate choices made by central city governments, others spring from demographic, economic, and social developments that are outside their control. Second, although the revenue base in most central cities is still somewhat higher than in surrounding suburbs, this advantage is steadily eroding. Retail sales, personal incomes, and property values, which form

Excerpted from Schultze, Fried, Rivlin and Teeters, *Setting National Priorities: The 1973 Budget* (Washington, D.C.: Brookings Institution, 1972), chapter 9. The authors were on the staff of the Brookings Institution when this paper was written.

the basis for taxation, have been growing more slowly in the central cities than in the suburbs.

The interaction of these two developments intensifies the fiscal squeeze on central cities. Public services appear to be deteriorating while tax rates climb. Compared with the suburbs, the central city is becoming a less desirable place to live, to shop, and even to work, especially for middle- and upper-income groups. The resulting change in the city's economic and demographic structure increases its need for public expenditures—for welfare, crime control, and social programs—while reducing its ability to pay for them. Not every central city faces these problems, but virtually every older one does.

There are several possible approaches to dealing with the growing financial plight of cities. Could the central cities become more efficient in delivering public services and discover new sources of public revenue? Would a dispersal of low-income population into the suburbs and a return of high-income residents to the city be a desirable way of reducing financial problems; and even if it were, is it likely to occur? Would a change in jurisdictional boundaries and a move toward metropolitan government provide a solution, and is such a development foreseeable? Should the federal government assume a larger share of the financial burdens of the central cities, and, if so, how—through revenue sharing, increases in current grant programs, or new types of financial aid? Can and should the federal government play a role, through financial incentives or otherwise, in encouraging the development of metropolitan-wide governments and finances?

This chapter analyzes the two major causes of the central cities' financial dilemma—rapid expenditure growth and an eroding revenue base. It evaluates the possibility that these problems could be handled without federal intervention, and then considers alternative federal approaches to the fiscal problems of the cities.

BIG-CITY EXPENDITURES

Two facts stand out from the welter of statistics on urban government expenditures. First, the level of spending is high in central cities —considerably higher, in general, than it is in surrounding areas. Second, central city expenditures have been growing rapidly—usually faster than those of the suburbs.

LEVEL OF EXPENDITURES

As may be seen in Table 9–1, local government expenditures per capita are significantly higher in the central city than in the suburbs.[1] Indeed, in only eight of the nation's seventy-two largest metropolitan areas were expenditures higher in the suburbs than in the central city in 1970. The two major explanations for this are the greater needs and the higher costs in the cities. Cities have much greater concentrations of persons with high needs for public help—especially the aged and the poor—than do suburbs (see Table 9–2). Crime rates are much higher, and the streets and air are dirtier. Density and congestion make the needs for such services as traffic control, sidewalks, street lighting, and street repair far greater than they are in the suburbs. Some of the congestion and need for services is generated by commuters who work and shop in the city, thus increasing its population by day, but go home to the suburbs at night. The higher cost of providing public services in the city is due both to higher wages and to the difficulties of providing certain services under crowded conditions. For example, the sanitation truck in the city may waste a great deal of time stopped in traffic jams or driving to distant disposal locations.

Of course, not all of the indices of need for services show the central city to be on the short end of the stick. For example, although the core areas' children may be more costly to educate, a far smaller fraction of the cities' population is of school age, and an even smaller proportion generally attends public schools than in the suburbs (Table 9–3). Also, dense housing patterns may make certain services easier to provide.

Another source of the expenditure disparity between city and suburbs is that some of the public services of the cities are privately provided in suburban areas. Trash collection is more likely to be in the hands of private carters, houses more likely to have septic tanks rather than municipal sewers and waste treatment facilities, and

[1]The expenditures and revenues referred to in this chapter are computed on a per capita basis to allow useful comparisons between cities and suburbs of unequal and changing populations. The data refer to the consolidated general expenditures and revenue of all of the local governments that operate within an area, whether municipalities, school districts, county governments, or special districts. Where the boundaries of a local government do not lie wholly within either the central city or the suburbs, its revenues and expenditures have been apportioned between the city and the outlying area.

TABLE 9-1. Level in 1970 and Growth, 1957–70, of Local Government Expenditures, per Capita, in Central Cities and outside Central Cities of Selected Metropolitan Areas

Region and standard metropolitan statistical area	1970				Percentage increase in per capita expenditure, 1957–70	
	Per capita total expenditure (dollars)		Per capita state and federal aid (dollars)			
	Central city	Outside central city	Central city	Outside central city	Central city	Outside central city
Northeast						
Washington, D.C.	1,006	425	358	118	321	224
Baltimore	638	349	329	127	221	146
Boston	531	365	224	73	95	102
Newark	735	441	276	102	202	144
Paterson-Clifton-Passaic	381	418	131	56	146	124
Buffalo	528	520	207	226	174	148
New York City	894	644	385	216	248	148
Rochester	699	548	235	238	250	180
Philadelphia	495	325	134	88	200	136
Pittsburgh	450	309	111	95	139	141
Providence	392	265	111	71	145	168
Midwest						
Chicago	478	346	146	86	137	144
Indianapolis	355	306	85	93	99	186
Detroit	474	462	189	131	135	131
Minneapolis-St. Paul	540	520	177	228	192	177

Kansas City	485	347	90	100	161	210
St. Louis	463	292	99	83	211	135
Cincinnati	761	262	171	79	209	124
Cleveland	512	368	187	66	180	91
Columbus	398	290	75	77	140	86
Dayton	456	291	108	83	173	126
Milwaukee	562	486	199	224	145	131
South						
Miami	481	387	137	129	113	129
Tampa-St. Petersburg	372	289	119	108	134	225
Atlanta	554	315	97	95	251	215
Louisville	508	302	108	94	214	165
New Orleans	334	325	100	116	105	171
Dallas	352	279	54	70	91	158
Houston	305	307	61	73	97	64
San Antonio	252	288	89	96	123	177
West						
Los Angeles-Long Beach	624	529	209	227	134	161
San Bernardino	624	529	278	215	111	176
San Diego	484	472	194	202	153	150
San Francisco-Oakland	768	596	298	201	244	159
Denver	502	306	149	94	135	108
Portland	486	328	125	102	139	150
Seattle-Everett	524	471	137	162	201	232

Source: Seymour Sacks and John Callahan, "Central City—Suburban Fiscal Disparities in the 72 Largest Metropolitan Areas" (unpublished paper, January 1972), Tables 14, 28.

TABLE 9–2. Family Characteristics and Crime Rates in Metropolitan Areas, 1970

Item	Central city	Outside central city
Percentage of persons below poverty level[a]	13.4	6.3
Percentage aged 25–29 with less than high school education	25.3	19.2
Percentage of population over 65	11.1	7.4
Female-headed families as a percentage of all families[b]	17.0	8.8
AFDC families as a percentage of all families[b,c]	9.8	2.4
Crime rate (per 1,000 inhabitants)	45.6	21.4

Sources: Poverty level, education, and population data, U.S. Bureau of the Census, *Current Population Reports,* Series P-23, No. 37, "Social and Economic Characteristics of the Population in Metropolitan and Nonmetropolitan Areas: 1970 and 1960" (1971), pp. 15, 51, 76; female-headed families data, Bureau of the Census, *Current Population Reports,* Series P-20, No. 233, "Household and Family Characteristics: March 1971" (1972), pp. 12, 33; AFDC data, U.S. National Center for Social Statistics, *Findings of the 1971 AFDC Study,* Pt. 1, *Demographic and Program Characteristics,* NCSS Report AFDC-1 (1971), p. 13; crime rate, U.S. Federal Bureau of Investigation, *Uniform Crime Reports for the United States—1970* (1971), pp. 104–05.

a. 1969 data. b. 1971 data. c. AFDC = aid to families with dependent children.

TABLE 9–3. Public School Enrollment as a Percentage of Population, Central Cities and Suburbs in Selected Metropolitan Areas, 1969–70 School Year

Standard metropolitan statistical area	Central city	Outside central city
Boston	14.6	26.6
New York	14.3	23.4
Philadelphia	15.1	20.3
Pittsburgh	14.0	21.1
Syracuse	15.4	26.7
Columbus	20.0	26.0
Minneapolis-St. Paul	15.5	27.5
Omaha	16.9	28.9
Louisville	14.5	25.6
Richmond	16.5	27.5
Tulsa	20.9	30.3
Denver	18.8	27.6
Phoenix	20.0	28.3
Salt Lake City	19.7	33.3
San Francisco-Oakland	15.1	24.3
Seattle-Everett	16.0	27.1

Source: Seymour Sacks and Ralph Andrew with Tony Carnevale, "School State Aid and the System of Finance: Central City, Suburban and Rural Dimensions of Revenue Sharing" (Syracuse University, no date; processed), Table 3.

volunteer fire companies more likely to provide fire protection. Expenditure differences may also result from the fact that a greater proportion of city revenues comes from nonresidents than is the case in the suburbs. Residential property tends to account for a smaller fraction of the total assessed value of property in the city; retail sales tax receipts in the city come partly from purchases of nonresidents; and where local income or payroll taxes are levied, taxes are often imposed on commuters. Moreover, state and federal grants often make up a larger proportion of revenues in the city than in the suburbs. The net effect may be to make the city voter less reluctant to increase city expenditures than is the suburban taxpayer-voter, who knows that he himself will have to pay a higher share of the bill.

GROWTH OF EXPENDITURES

While expenditures by all local governments increased rapidly during the past decade, those in central city areas tended to grow more rapidly than those in the suburbs (Table 9–1). There were many exceptions to this pattern, especially in the South, but there were also many instances (for example, in New York, St. Louis, Cleveland, and San Francisco) where per capita local government expenditures in the central city area increased over 50 percent faster than those of their suburbs.

Of the many factors that contributed to the rapid growth of big-city expenditures during the past decade, inflation was probably the most important. The price index for the goods and services purchased by local governments rose at twice the rate of that for consumer expenditures between 1960 and 1971. This exceptional increase was attributable largely to rising labor costs, which make up more than half the current budgets of local governments.

By any measure, the recent rise in the compensation of local government employees has been spectacular. (See Figure 9–1.) Through the mid-1960s, municipal wages roughly kept pace with those in manufacturing, but beginning in about 1966 the rate of increase appears to have been much greater for municipal workers. Along with wage increases, liberalized pension benefits and health plans also contributed to the rising cost of labor. Reductions in the length of the average workday and more generous provisions regarding sick leave, lunch breaks, vacations, and paid holidays further pushed up the hourly cost of labor in the public sector. The importance of such fringe benefits should not be underestimated. For example, the city administrator of New York reported that although the number of policemen increased from 16,000 to 24,000 between 1940 and 1965, the total number of hours worked by the entire force was less in 1965 than it had been a quarter of a century earlier.

There are many possible explanations for the rise in the relative wages of public employees during the past decade. In the generally tight labor market that characterized the 1965–69 period, most wages were rising, but the public may have been disposed to accept greater-than-average wage increases for public employees, who were regarded as being in some sense "underpaid." A more important reason was the increased unionization that made it possible for local government employees to obtain large settlements. Until recently, public employees were largely unorganized. Although professional associations existed, they had few powers. In general, cities, counties, and school districts unilaterally dictated contract terms and wage rates. All of this has changed in the past twenty years as unionization has spread into the public sector. The new unions and the old associations in many areas have gained many of the prerogatives of unions in the private sector. Most important, they often represent their members in collective bargaining. Along with this ability to organize has come an increased willingness on the part of public employees to engage in "job actions" or strikes—even in violation of the law. During the past five years, teachers, policemen, firemen, and sanitation workers have walked off their jobs in ever increasing numbers. (See Table 9–4.) The sudden acceleration of public employee strikes in 1966

TABLE 9–4. Work Stoppages by Local Government Employees, 1958–70

Year	Number of stoppages	Number of workers involved (thousands)	Man-days lost (thousands)	Workers involved as percentage of total
1958–63 average	24	11.3	24.4	0.24
1964	37	22.5	67.7	0.40
1965	42	11.9	145.0	0.20
1966	133	102.0	449.0	1.70
1967	169	127.0	1,230.0	1.90
1968	235	190.9	2,492.8	2.70
1969	372	139.0	592.2	2.01
1970	386	168.9	1,330.5	2.36

Sources: Harry H. Wellington and Ralph K. Winter, Jr., *The Unions and the Cities* (Brookings Institution, 1971), pp. 212–13; U.S. Bureau of Labor Statistics, "Government Work Stoppages, 1960, 1969, and 1970" (1971; processed), p. 3.

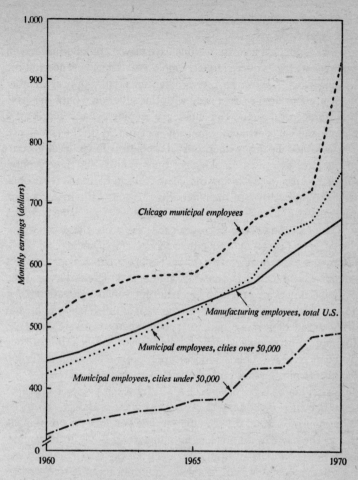

FIGURE 9-1. Average Monthly Earnings of All U.S. Manufacturing Employees and of Municipal Employees[a] in Chicago and in Cities over and under 50,000, 1960–70

Sources: U.S. Bureau of the Census, *City Employment in 1970,* various issues, Tables 2, 3, and 4; U.S. Office of Business Economics, *Survey of Current Business,* Vol. 51 (July 1971), Table 6.5; Office of Business Economics, *U.S. National Income and Product Accounts, 1964–67* (1971), Table 6.5; Office of Business Economics, *The National Income and Product Accounts of the United States, 1929–1965: Statistical Tables* (1966), Table 6.5.

a. Includes highway, police and fire, sewerage and other sanitation, water supply, parks and recreation, library, financial administration, and general control employees.

coincides dramatically with the sharp upsurge in relative wages of municipal employees that began in the same year.

Finally, political factors probably have played an important role in the wage increases offered to city employees. Racial violence and the shifting base of power have created an uncertain political environment in most large cities. Faced with this situation, politicians have tried to keep the support of municipal employees, who represent a potent political constituency in many big cities. With the emergence of blacks and Spanish-Americans as a political force, local governments have expanded employment opportunities for these groups. Often this has meant hiring the "new minorities" in jobs that once were the prerogatives of the older ethnic groups—the Irish cop, the Italian sanitation man, and the Jewish teacher. Large wage increases in some cases may have been designed to placate these groups for their loss of hegemony over public service employment.

The net effect of all of these forces has been that local government employees—at least in the nation's largest cities—are no longer at the end of the pecking order. In the cities for which there are data, it appears that local government workers earn as much per hour as, and often considerably more than, their counterparts in private industry.[2] In addition, they usually enjoy better pension and health insurance plans, more liberal holiday and vacation provisions, and greater job security than do comparable workers in the private sector.

Population changes have been a second major cause of the rapid growth in the expenditures of central city areas. Although the aggregate population of most large cities declined or grew only marginally during the past ten years, there were important shifts in the population mix of most core cities. Persons who rely heavily on services provided by local governments while contributing little to their support—that is, school age children, families with below average incomes, and the aged—became an ever-increasing fraction of the central cities' residents. In some cities, such as Newark and Cleveland, which have been all but abandoned by the middle class, these shifts have been profound.

Stagnant or declining productivity is often mentioned as another cause of the rising expenditures of big cities. Since reliable measures of the output of public employees are lacking, most of the discussion

[2]Stephen H. Perloff, "Comparing Municipal Salaries with Industry and Federal Pay," *Monthly Labor Review*, Vol. 94 (October 1971), pp. 46–50.

of productivity in the cities is speculative. Many have the impression that, although employment has increased rapidly, the quality of municipal services has improved little or has even deteriorated. Local government employment has indeed expanded considerably in many big cities; in New York there is now one full-time local government employee for every twenty residents of the city. But despite the growing work force, many believe that the sidewalks are dirtier, the streets more dangerous, the schools poorer, and city services less reliable than in the past.

While all this may be true, it is not clear that outmoded work rules, labor militancy, or other factors related to the attitudes or effort of the workers are primarily responsible. Increased street congestion and aging equipment may explain why a sanitation crew collects less trash per hour now than a decade ago; the growing proportion of children in the schools who are from disadvantaged homes may present more of an educational problem than even the expanded number of teachers and teacher aides can deal with; the added deterrence of enlarged police departments possibly does not offset the changes brought about by new social mores, the changing economic patterns of the city, and the congested legal process. In short, while output per worker in the public sector may be growing only marginally, or even falling, this may be primarily attributable to changes in the environment in which these services are provided. Furthermore, one should not overlook the "outputs" of public employment other than the provision of services. Traditionally such jobs have served as a kind of antipoverty program—a road for advancement for workers who suffer discrimination in the private job market. They also are used in some instances as mechanisms for keeping the political machine of a city operating smoothly. Perhaps the rapid growth of public employment in the past few years should be interpreted partly as a way of keeping the lid on an otherwise volatile racial and political situation.

Another factor responsible for the growth in big-city expenditures is the proliferation in the number and kind of services provided by urban governments. For example, local programs for pollution control, consumer protection, drug rehabilitation, family planning, day care, and community colleges were almost nonexistent a decade ago. Many such innovations have been spurred by federal legislation. In the case of the Model Cities program, federal dollars were pumped into the central city's budget for new or expanded poverty-related services. Compensatory educational programs are another new serv-

TABLE 9–5. Increase in per Capita Local Government Expenditure and Revenue in the 72 Largest Standard Metropolitan Statistical Areas and in 41 Large Cities, 1962–70

	72 largest SMSAs			41 large cities and their school districts[a]		
Item	Percentage increase, 1962–70	Percentage of 1962–70 increase	Percentage of 1970 budget	Percentage increase, 1962–70	Percentage of 1962–70 increase	Percentage of 1970 budget
Direct general expenditure, total	90	100	100	112	100	100
Education	99	45	43	109	37	36
Highways	24	2	5	14	1	4
Public welfare	258	13	10	264	16	11
Health and hospitals	106	7	6	101	7	7
Police and fire protection	78	8	8	94	11	12
Sewerage and sanitation	55	4	5	56	3	5
Financial administration and general control	75	3	4	81	2	3
Interest on general debt	79	4	4	92	3	3
Other	87	16	16	135	20	18
General revenue, total	94	100	100	108	100	100
Intergovernmental	154	43	35	217	46	36
Property taxes	61	33	42	57	24	35
Other taxes	103	10	9	108	16	16
Current charges and miscellaneous revenues	95	15	15	90	12	13

Sources: Four publications from U.S. Bureau of the Census: *Local Government Finances in Selected Metropolitan Areas and Large Counties: 1969–70*, Series GF70—No. 6 (1971), Table 1; *City Government Finances in 1969–70*, Series GF70—No. 4 (1971), Table 7; *Compendium of City Government Finances in 1962*, Series G-CF62—No. 2 (1963), Table 7; *Census of Governments: 1962*, Vol. 5, *Local Government in Metropolitan Areas* (1964), Table 14. Figures are rounded and may not add to totals.

a. Includes 41 of the 43 largest cities in 1962, and the matching cities in 1970, and 32 matching school districts with budgets independent of their city budgets.

ice that is financed largely by the federal government. The rapid growth in municipal hospital and health expenditures was undoubtedly stimulated by the Medicare and Medicaid programs, which allowed local governments to expand their facilities and care for the poor and aged while charging most of the costs to the state and federal governments. Thus, although all of these programs increased local government expenditures, not all of the burden for raising the necessary revenues fell on the local taxpayer.

The division of responsibility between state and local governments differs greatly from state to state. In many states, welfare is largely a state function, but in some (notably New York and California) a substantial part of the burden is carried by local governments. Some states make major contributions to education; others leave education primarily to the localities. Hence, big cities differ considerably in the distribution of funds by function within their budgets and in the relative growth of expenditures by function over recent years.

If one consolidates the per capita expenditures of the nation's largest metropolitan areas and cities for the period 1962–70, welfare, health, and education emerge as the fastest growing functions. (See Table 9–5.) Although welfare expenditures have risen sharply, they continue to account for a relatively modest proportion of total budget spending in most central cities, mainly because city governments usually finance only a small fraction of welfare costs. New York City is the outstanding exception; welfare costs accounted for almost one-third of the increase in expenditures from 1962 to 1970 and were 23 percent of total city outlays in the latter year. Similarly, although the rate of increase in health and hospital expenditures has been very rapid in most cities, they still constitute a small fraction of total expenditures and contributed only a modest amount to the overall expenditure rise. Expenditures for education, by contrast, grew somewhat less rapidly in most cities than did those for either health or welfare, but accounted for a larger share of the total increase because they were already typically the largest item in the local budgets.

The Revenue Base

For the reasons given above, city expenditures are generally higher and are rising more rapidly than those of the suburbs. If the ability of big cities to raise revenues were commensurably high and rising there would be no problem. But this does not appear to be the case.

In the past, the revenue raising capability of cities far exceeded that of their suburbs—a fact that goes far in explaining how they were able to sustain higher expenditure levels with little assistance from the state or federal government. This superiority stemmed from the fact that real property, sales, payrolls, incomes, and the other bases from which local government revenues are derived were disproportionately concentrated in the central city. Even today, big cities do

Table 9–6. Per Capita Revenue-Producing Capacity, Revenue Collected, and Growth of Revenue Bases of Selected Cities Relative to Their Suburban Areas, Various Dates, 1950–70

City	Ratio, central city to suburban area, per capita basis				
	Revenue capacity, 1966–67 (1)	Local revenues, 1969–70 (2)	Growth of equalized real property values, 1950–70 (3)	Growth of retail sales, 1954–67 (4)	Growth of income, 1964–70 (5)
Atlanta	1.42	1.63	n.a.	0.34	0.67
Baltimore	1.06	1.19	0.30	0.32	0.35
Boston	1.67	1.48	0.16	0.59	0.65
Chicago	1.05	0.93	6.42	0.49	0.84
Cincinnati	1.31	2.65	0.98	0.49	0.93
Cleveland	1.01	1.26	0.76	0.09	1.06
Columbus	1.00	1.31	0.99	0.26	1.51
Dayton	1.30	1.59	0.62	0.37	0.68
Denver	1.68	1.70	0.75	0.44	0.68
Kansas City	1.12	1.64	n.a.	0.41	0.36
Los Angeles- Long Beach	1.15	1.23	1.03	0.88	0.69
Louisville	1.15	1.63	0.37	0.36	0.86
Miami	1.11	1.33	n.a.	0.11	0.78
New Orleans	1.19	1.42	n.a.	0.39	0.74
New York	1.30	1.23	0.69	0.67	1.22
Philadelphia	1.06	1.39	0.57	0.40	0.93
Pittsburgh	1.33	1.53	0.81	1.07	0.94
Portland, Oregon	1.41	1.87	2.96	0.59	0.62
San Diego	1.06	1.07	0.82	0.41	0.74
St. Louis	1.49	1.78	0.50	0.42	0.75
Seattle	1.12	1.42	0.10	0.42	0.54
Washington, D.C.	1.06	2.01	n.a.	0.47	0.92

Sources: Col. 1, Advisory Commission on Intergovernmental Relations, *Measuring the Fiscal Capacity and Effort of State and Local Areas* (ACIR, 1971); col. 2, Seymour Sacks and John Callahan, "Central City-Suburban Fiscal Disparities in the 72 Largest Metropolitan Areas," Table 25; col. 3, based on unpublished data from state boards of equalization; col. 4, U.S. Bureau of the Census, *U.S. Census of Business, 1954*, Vol. 2, *Retail Trade-Area Statistics*, Pts. 1, 2 (1956), and Bureau of the Census, *U.S. Census of Business, 1967*, Vol. 2, *Retail Trade-Area Statistics*, Pts. 1, 2, 3 (1970); col. 5, *Sales Management*, Vol. 94 (June 10, 1965), and Vol. 107 (June 10, 1971).

n.a. Not available.

not appear to be resource-poor in these terms. As the first column of Table 9–6 indicates, their per capita capacity to raise revenue, as measured by an index of the value of their revenue bases, is at least equal to that of their suburbs. In many cases—for example, Boston and Denver—the financial capacity of the city is considerably greater than that of the surrounding areas. Nevertheless, whatever advantages central cities may have in revenue raising capacity are generally outweighed by their greater need for revenue. This can be seen by comparing the first two columns of Table 9-6. Thus, while Atlanta's revenue raising capacity is some 42 percent greater than that of its suburbs, the city area raised 63 percent more revenue per capita in 1969-70 than did its suburbs. Thus the burden was relatively much greater in the city than in the suburbs.

Moreover, the advantages the cities now seem to have in revenue raising ability are rapidly eroding, just when their needs for additional revenues seem to be rising most rapidly. Property values, sales, and incomes, which are the ultimate source of local government revenues, are growing far faster in the suburbs than in the cities.

In the past, cities had higher property values per capita than did their suburbs. Indeed, the flight to the suburbs was partly a flight from the high cost of owning or renting property in the city. However, with the movement of middle-and upper middle-income families to the suburbs and the recent suburbanization of industry, per capita property values—and with them the property tax base—in the suburban ring have grown considerably faster than those in the core areas. (See column 3 of Table 9-6.) Some suburban areas now have higher per capita property values than do their central cities. In a few older cities, such as Newark and Trenton, New Jersey, the aggregate value of taxable property has actually begun to decline. There are of course exceptions to these trends. For example, in Chicago and Portland, where there has been a lot of new construction activity in the core area, the per capita value of property has increased much more rapidly in the city than in the surrounding areas in recent years.

Cities in the past have also had higher volumes of retail sales per capita and hence a greater capacity to raise revenue through the sales tax. Per capita sales are still higher in most cities than in their suburbs, but this advantage is also declining rapidly. (See Table 9-6, column 4.) The suburbanization of higher-income families, the growing use of the automobile in shopping, and the proliferation of large shopping malls used by central city residents have caused the retail sales tax base in the suburbs to grow far faster than in the city. In New York, Detroit, and Philadelphia, per capita sales in the suburbs have already surpassed those of the city.

Income taxes do not play a major role in local finance because the states and the federal government have largely preempted this form of taxation. Even there, however, the cities that tax the incomes of their residents face a growing disadvantage vis-à-vis the suburbs. In most older cities, per capita personal incomes have been lower than in the suburbs for some years. Even in the newer cities, per capita incomes are growing far more slowly than in the suburbs. (See Table 9–6, column 5.) Many middle- and upper-income suburban residents, of course, work in the city. If local governments imposed payroll taxes or communter taxes to tap income where it is earned rather than where the earner resides, the cities would still have the advantage. However, states have not generally permitted cities to tax the incomes of commuters at the same rate as they tax their city residents.

This relative deterioration of the central cities' ability to raise revenue has meant that these areas have had to rely on increased tax rates and on aid from higher levels of government to cover their rising expenditures. While the property tax continues to be the workhorse of the local government revenue system, cities have generally tried to diversify their revenue structures. Many cities have increased their reliance on sales and income taxes. As can be seen in Table 9–5, in the forty-one largest cities per capita property tax revenues grew only half as fast as total revenues during the past decade. Other taxes, many charges, and intergovernmental grants all grew faster. Intergovernmental grants have become especially important. As Table 9–5 shows, roughly half of the recent increase in general revenues came from state or federal grants. Such aid now constitutes more than one-third of the general revenue of local governments in metropolitan areas.

WHAT CAN BE DONE?

The fiscal dilemma of big cities is quite simply that their expenditures for the public services their citizens want and need are outrunning their revenues. Moreover, the situation seems likely to get worse. Obviously, one could attack this problem from either side—by finding ways of reducing expenditures or by finding new revenue sources in the city itself or outside it. The rest of this chapter will be devoted to considering (1) the prospects for reducing city expenditures by cutting back services, by making them more efficient, or by "exporting" some of the cities' more costly problems; (2) the prospects for raising more revenues from nonfederal sources by revitalizing the cities' own tax base, sharing in the growth of suburban revenues, or obtaining state help; and (3) alternative mechanisms for federal assistance to the cities. A final section discusses ways in which the federal government could provide incentives for metropolitan areas to take collective action to solve the fiscal crisis of their central cities.

REDUCING EXPENDITURES

The most direct way of reducing city expenditures is to curtail public services by repairing the streets less often, allowing pupil-teacher ratios to rise, or hiring fewer policemen. Although many large municipalities and school districts recently have cut employment and eliminated certain services, this strategy is likely to be self-defeating, especially if higher expenditures are a function of greater needs. In such cases, service reductions will make the city a less attractive place in which to live or to establish an industry. To be sure, such reductions may often seem preferable to tax increases, but they will surely impair the city's position relative to the suburbs.

The possibility of cutting costs by increasing the efficiency of municipal services has received a good deal of attention in recent years. New management systems, decentralization, technological innovations, and contracts with private firms for the provision of public services have all been proposed as possible ways of cutting costs. Strenuous efforts should certainly be made to improve efficiency, but so far there is little hard evidence that any of these innovations would save significant amounts of money and be politically palatable. For example, although private carters can collect trash in New York for about half what it costs the City Department of Sanitation, this differential would probably not persist if private carters became major suppliers of sanitation services to the city. The sanitation workers union would do its best to eliminate the private sector's lower wages and more onerous working conditions that account for virtually all of the existing cost differential. Similarly, experiments with performance contracting in education—arrangements by which school systems contract with private industry to teach children certain skills—have not offered much hope that this technique will either increase children's performance or save the schools money.

Another way to reduce the level of city expenditures would be to disperse some of the problems that give rise to high expenditures. Since a substantial part of the city's extraordinary expenditures are associated with its concentration of low-income residents, a dispersal of the poor throughout the metropolitan area could help the cities considerably. At least two factors, however, suggest that this is unlikely to happen.

First, there is opposition in the suburbs to the dispersal of low-income families throughout the metropolitan area. While some of this hostility is racial, much of it has an economic basis. Suburbs do not want families who consume more in the way of services than they are able to pay for through taxes. To exclude such families, many have resorted to "fiscal zoning"—that is, restricting the use of their vacant land to single family homes on large lots or to "clean" industry. Any suburb's opposition to low-income housing derives partly from a fear that it would reduce its attractiveness vis-à-vis other communities. If all suburbs were required to accept some low-income housing, the opposition might be reduced. Unless the state or federal government provides an incentive, however, such agreements are hard to obtain. Only in the Dayton and Washington, D.C., areas have area-wide plans to decentralize public housing been approved; and even in these instances, most of the new low-income housing still will be located within the central city.

The second factor working against the decentralization of low-income families is the various advantages the city holds for the poor. First, there is the availability of old and hence cheap rental housing in the core. Of course, this advantage could be reduced if all of the new subsidized housing for low-income families were built outside the city; but even if this occurred, most low-income housing would still be in the city for a long time to come. A second advantage of the city is its accessibility to low-skill jobs. Although this accessibility is declining, it is still superior to that of most suburbs. Finally, the availability of public transportation also makes the city a more rational location for many low-income families.

INCREASING STATE AND LOCAL REVENUE

Some cities could increase their tax rates or impose new kinds of taxes; but, as was pointed out above, the tax effort of the cities is generally high already. Higher tax rates might accelerate the flight to the suburbs of business and middle-income families.

The ability of large cities to revive their failing tax bases by attracting either higher-income residents or new industries is also very limited. This is because the city has little new left to offer. . . . Virtually the only new incentive that the city could use to attract industry or upper-income residents is tax relief. While there is no evidence that either would respond to this lure, it would constitute giving away the very reason for drawing such persons and firms back into the city.

The problem of revitalizing the city and its tax base should not be dismissed as hopeless, but it clearly cannot be done gradually or piecemeal. Massive efforts to rebuild whole sections of cities and provide first-rate services, especially schools, might reverse the exodus to the suburbs. But the funds needed to do this cannot come from the cities themselves.

Although cities may not be able to do much by themselves, most metropolitan areas as a whole do have the capability for dealing with the growing imbalance between the resources and the needs of their core cities. One way is to expand the city's resource base by annexing surrounding areas or consolidating the central city with a larger unit of government, such as the county. In effect, this would allow the city to share in the growth occurring in the suburbs and would shift its demographic makeup toward families that are less in need of local government services. Except in the Northeast, where city boundaries have been fairly static for several decades, annexation and consolidation have been used fairly effectively. In the past decade, such cities as Sacramento, San Jose, Tulsa, Memphis, Toledo, and Omaha have annexed considerable parts of their surrounding areas. City-county consolidation of one sort or another has occurred in Nashville (1962), Jacksonville (1967), and Indianapolis (1969).

Unfortunately, expanding the city cannot be regarded as a likely solution to the fiscal crises of most of the largest metropolitan areas because it has little political appeal. Since annexation usually must be approved by state legislatures or by the residents of the affected jurisdictions, it can easily be blocked by suburbanites who see no reason for giving up their service and tax advantages to help solve the urban problems they have often just managed to escape. Minority residents of the central cities also have begun to oppose annexation and consolidation efforts out of fear that their growing political power base in the core will be diluted by suburban whites. Annexation has generated the least opposition in areas such as the South, where a degree of consolidation already exists because many local public services are provided at the county level. But in such areas, the need for consolidation is least. Elsewhere the effect of annexation often has been seriously blunted because the most important local government

service—education—has been excluded from the unification effort.
Kansas City, for example, which has annexed so much territory that
it now has rural areas within the city boundaries, has preserved a
balkanized school system of seventeen separate districts; San Jose has
fifteen school districts operating within its current boundaries. While
the municipal governments may have solved their fiscal problems
through annexation, the school districts that include the poorer sections of the city are still unable to provide adequate education.

Some of the benefits of consolidation or annexation could be
obtained, possibly with less opposition, through tax-sharing schemes.
A metropolitan-wide tax could be imposed, similar to those that now
finance the operating deficits of some urban transportation systems,
and the receipts could be distributed in accordance with some measure of fiscal need. While the likelihood that suburban residents would
accept such a plan is slight in most areas, an area-wide tax has recently
been levied in the Minneapolis-St. Paul metropolitan area. There
each locality is required to contribute to a common pool 40 percent
of its property tax receipts that are attributable to increases in the
value of commercial and industrial property within its borders. This
common revenue will be distributed among the various communities
on the basis of their population and per capita property wealth. This
distribution formula will provide the central cities of Minneapolis
and St. Paul with only an average share of the common fund.
Whether they are net beneficiaries, therefore, will depend solely on
the patterns of growth of commercial and industrial property within
the metropolitan region. In any case, the central cities' gain from
intrametropolitan revenue sharing schemes will depend on the tax
base used to raise the revenue and the formula chosen for distributing
the receipts.

The same political forces that have thwarted efforts at generating
metropolitan solutions to the fiscal problems of central cities are likely
to preclude action at the state level as well. Although the one man-
one vote ruling has effectively ended the rural domination of most
state legislatures, representatives of suburban areas are now in control. Several decades ago, when the cities and suburbs were joined in
a strong symbiotic relationship, suburban legislators might have supported efforts to have the state aid the central city. However, now
that they are increasingly independent, self-sufficient economic and
political entities, the suburbs often act as though their interests were
opposed to those of the core cities. With the continuation of those
trends and the declining population of the core, the political power

of the nation's large cities is likely to decrease in state legislatures. Since states have given little in the way of special aid to large cities in the past, there is little reason to expect a sudden change in the near future.

THE FEDERAL GOVERNMENT'S RESPONSE

The federal government could respond in a number of ways to the growing fiscal imbalance of large cities. It could expand and modify those grant-in-aid programs that are oriented toward the problems afflicting cities; it could implement new programs, such as general revenue sharing and welfare reform, that are expected to have an important impact on urban areas; or it could provide incentives to induce states and metropolitan areas to come to grips with the problems of the cities in their own ways.

Existing Grant Programs. Federal grants to state and local governments have been increasing rapidly in recent years—by more than 19 percent annually since 1965—and a substantial portion of these funds goes to big cities. For two reasons, however, it seems doubtful that a simple expansion of existing grant programs will do much to alleviate the fundamental fiscal problems of the cities.

First, many of the existing grant programs that channel federal funds into the cities are aimed at alleviating the poverty of individuals rather than that of governments. Of course, higher welfare benefits, better health care, more generous food stamp allowances, and an expansion in the number of public housing units would alleviate the poverty of many low-income city residents; but only in the long run would this alter the city's need for more police, sanitation services, compensatory education facilities, and other municipal services. In the short run, the city would be no more able to support these needs than it is today.

The second reason why a simple expansion of existing grants would probably not help is that many of the programs that are intended to assist local governments in providing services are encumbered by stringent regulations that preclude their use for the support of basic services. Usually these grants were intended to stimulate the provision of new or additional services; in many cases, they require that the recipient government match some fraction of the federal contribution. Hence, rather than providing relief from the fiscal burden of running basic city services, they tend to add to that burden (as well as to the level of services).

New Initiatives. Two major administration initiatives now being debated by the Congress—general revenue sharing and welfare reform—have both been promoted as means of easing the fiscal plight of large cities. ... Revenue sharing will certainly help cities deal with their fiscal problems, but the amounts of money under consideration will not put the cities on easy street. The plans now receiving serious consideration would give large cities an amount equal to between 5 and 10 percent of the revenues they now raise locally. While this contribution is significant, it should be noted that locally raised revenues have been increasing by roughly this amount every year. In effect, then, general revenue sharing would be equivalent to one year's normal growth in revenues.

Revenue sharing is an inefficient means of dealing with the special plight of large cities because much of the money will be distributed among suburban governments that are not facing critical fiscal problems. Of course, such a general distribution may be the price necessary to persuade a nation of suburbs to support increased aid for its cities. Providing resources that allow the city to maintain its existing services, however, will do nothing to enhance the position of the cities relative to that of the suburbs. Unless indices of need are included in the distribution formula, large cities will continue to have a harder time than their suburbs in balancing their budgets while maintaining comparable services and tax rates.

It is clear that welfare reform would do little to ease the fiscal problems of large cities. This is because at present little of the financial burden for supporting the programs that would be replaced by the welfare reform proposals is borne by local governments. In seventeen states, localities contribute nothing to financing the categorical public assistance programs, and in seventeen other states less than 5 percent of total expenditures on such programs derives from local taxes.

Of course, in a few states where welfare expenditures are large, local governments are required to bear a significant share of the costs. New York, New Jersey, California, and Wisconsin fall in this category. But even in these areas the local contribution for supporting the categorical assistance programs is raised at the county level, which generally means that the suburbs within the central county must share the burden of supporting the welfare population that resides primarily within the central city. Only in San Francisco and New York, where the city and county are coterminous, is this not so.

In any case it is not clear that welfare reform as it is being discussed today would relieve the burden even of those localities that do contribute to the support of public assistance programs. Most of these cities and counties are in states that have payment standards considerably above the contemplated federal support level. If, as seems likely, the states either choose, or are forced, to maintain their current levels of assistance through state supplementation, there is reason to expect that they will ask their local governments to continue contributing. If this happened, then the main benefit to the cities of welfare reform would be the federal government's guarantee that the current contribution of states and localities would not rise in the future.

In summary, it is unlikely that welfare reform will provide substantial direct aid for cities; it would not free a major source of funds, primarily because today cities and local governments devote little of their locally raised revenue to welfare. Of course, substantial indirect benefits could flow from welfare reform, but predictions in this area are hazardous. Higher benefit levels would improve the lot of the low-income city residents, and this eventually might alleviate the cities' need for certain compensatory municipal services; a more equal distribution of welfare benefits might reduce the migration of low-income, high-need families into the nation's largest cities; and finally, states might be more willing when their contribution to welfare is frozen to channel their growing revenues into their deteriorating cities.

New Incentive Structures

The preceding section of this chapter concluded that metropolitan areas have the capability of dealing with the fiscal problems of their central cities but lack the necessary will and organization. An appropriate role for the federal government therefore would appear to be that of providing incentives to induce either state action or metropolitan area-wide efforts. To date the federal government has placed little emphasis on this approach. Metropolitan agencies are eligible for federal planning grants and certain other programs, but rarely, if ever, do they receive preferential treatment. Similarly, some capital projects must obtain the approval of area-wide planning agencies to be eligible for federal financing, but such requirements have not touched off major efforts to achieve the coordinated planned development of metropolitan areas.

If the federal government decided to take this approach, several options are available. First, it could provide larger special revenue sharing grants to those areas that were attempting to deal with their problems on a metropolitan-wide basis. In cases where the recipient agency had area-wide authority, the matching requirements and other restrictions of existing grant programs could be reduced or eliminated.

A second possibility would be for the federal government to contribute to any intrametropolitan area revenue sharing scheme or to supplement any state's distribution of urban aid. Another approach would be to underwrite a more balanced distribution of needs within metropolitan areas. This could be done by providing an incentive for suburbs to accept low-income housing or added burdens. Communities could be given grants to cover the cost of the public services consumed by residents of low-income public housing. Suburban school districts that accepted children from the central city ghetto could be provided with bonuses.

Finally, the federal government could provide incentives for full state financing of certain functions that may weigh heavily on cities. For example, the reimbursement formulas for the existing categorical welfare systems could be altered to include bonuses to states that paid the entire nonfederal portion of the welfare bill. Another example of this approach is contained in the report of the President's Commission on School Finance, which suggested that a federal incentive payment be made to states that increased their relative contributions to financing elementary and secondary education.[3]

The difficulty the cities are experiencing in balancing their growing needs with their dwindling resources is likely to intensify in the future. By default the federal government will be required to come to the rescue. Although recent federal initiatives—general and special revenue sharing—will certainly help, the fiscal problems of large cities are not likely to be eradicated by these programs. The basic choice that the federal government now faces is whether to enlist the cooperation of the states and suburbs in improving the condition of the cities or to face the problem alone.

[3]The President's Commission on School Finance, *Schools, People, & Money: The Need for Educational Reform,* Final Report (1972).

12. State and Local Defaults, 1839–1969

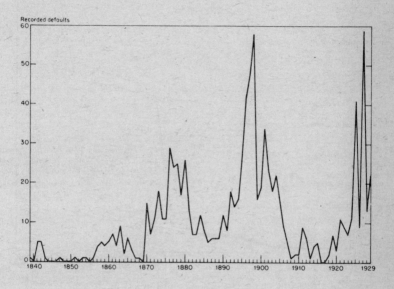

Recorded defaults

CHART 1. Defaults of State and Local Units, by Year Reported, 1839–1929

Sources: NBER compilations from issues of *The Bond Buyer;* Hillhouse, *Municipal Bonds;* Hillhouse, *Defaulted Municipal Bonds;* and Knappen, *Revenue Bonds.*

Charts 1 and 2 and Table 1 (charts 1 and 3 and Table 5 in original, respectively) are reprinted from George H. Hempel, *The Postwar Quality of State and Local Debt* (New York: Columbia University Press, 1971). Table 2 is reprinted from Advisory Commission on Intergovernmental Relations, *City Financial Emergencies: The Intergovernmental Dimension* (Washington, D. C.: Government Printing Office, 1973).

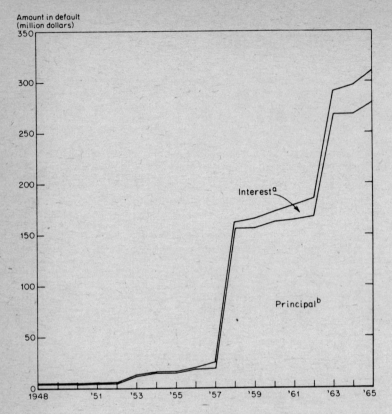

CHART 2. Dollar Amount of Principal and Interest in Default, 1948–65

Source: NBER staff compilations.

[a]Excludes interest on unpaid interest.

[b]Consists of overdue principal and principal upon which interest is overdue.

TABLE 1. Comparison of the Extent of Defaults by State and Local Units in Major Default Periods (dollar figures in thousands)

Period	Average State and Local Debt Outstanding	Total Indebtedness of Defaulting State and Local Units	Per Cent of Debt Outstanding	Past Due Interest and Principal[a]	Per Cent of Debt Outstanding	Loss of Principal and Interest[b]	Per Cent of Debt Outstanding
1837–43	$ 245,000	$ 125,000	51.0	n.a.	—	$ 15,000	6.1
1873–79	1,000,000	245,000	24.5	n.a.	—	150,000	15.0
1893–99	1,300,000	130,000	10.0	n.a.	—	25,000	1.9
1929–37	18,500,000	2,850,000[c]	15.4	320,000[c]	1.7	100,000	.5

Source: Based on data from George H. Hempel, "The Postwar Quality of Municipal Bonds" unpublished dissertation, University of Michigan, 1964, pp. 84–161.

[a]Does not include interest on unpaid interest.

[b]Does not include interest on unpaid interest, interest due after a debt was repudiated or interest lost due to refunding at a lower interest cost.

[c]Overdue interest plus debt upon which interest is in default was $1,355,000 or 7.3 per cent of debt outstanding in 1929–37. This figure is not available for the earlier default periods.

n.a. = not available.

TABLE 2. Recorded Defaults, By Type of Local Government Unit and Geographical Region 1839–1969

	1839 –49	1850 –59	1860 –69	1870 –79	1880 –89	1890 –99	1900 –09	1910 –19	1920 –29	1930 –39	1940 –49	1950 –59	1960 –69	Total Defaults	Number of Local Governments in 1967[a]
By Type of Unit:															
Counties and parishes		7	15	57	30	94	43	7	15	417	6	12	24	727	3,049
Incorp. munics.	4	4	13	50	30	93	51	17	39	1434	31	31	114	1911	18,048
Unincorp. munics.		4	9	46	31	50	33	5	10	88	7	4	26	313	17,105
School districts				4	5	9	11		14	1241	5	23	60	1372	21,782
Other districts				2	1	12	11	7	107	1590	30	42	70	1872	21,264
By Geographical Region:															
New England States[b]	1			1	1	2		1	1	7			4	18	3,045
Middle Atlantic States[c]	1	5	6	19	11	13	13	4	4	251	9	4	10	350	10,437
Southern States[d]			1	32	29	36	25	9	51	1863	16	34	76	2172	9,478
Midwestern States[e]	2	9	28	84	46	89	68	6	18	1152	18	34	76	1630	37,359
Southwestern States[f]			1	19	7	79	27	5	24	707	25	36	112	1042	9,588
Mountain States[g]				2		17	2	8	17	270	6	4	3	329	4,289
Pacific States[h]		1		2	3	22	14	3	70	520	5	1	13	654	7,052
Totals	4	15	37	159	97	258	149	36	185	4770	79	112	294	6195	81,248

Sources: Default Information in *The Daily Bond Buyer, The Commercial and Financial Chronicle,* and *The Investment Bankers' Associations Bulletin:* default lists from Federal Deposit Insurance Corporation, Life Insurance Commission, and U.S. Courts; and Albert M. Hillhouse, *Defaulted Municipal Bonds* (Chicago: Municipal Financial Officers Association, 1935). Number of local government units from: U.S. Department of Commerce, Bureau of Census, *Census of Governments, 1967, Vol. 1* "Governmental Organization" (Gov't Printing Office, 1969).

[a]The number of local government units has changed rapidly. For example, in 1932 there were 127,108 school districts, 8,580 other districts, and 175,369 State and local government units. [b]Connecticut, Maine, Massachusetts, New Hampshire, Rhode Island, and Vermont. [c]Delaware, District of Columbia, Maryland, New Jersey, New York, and Pennsylvania. [d]Alabama, Arkansas, Florida, Georgia, Kentucky, Louisiana, Mississippi, North Carolina, South Carolina, Tennessee, Virginia and West Virginia. [e]Illinois, Indiana, Iowa, Michigan, Minnesota, Missouri, Nebraska, Ohio, North Dakota, South Dakota, and Wisconsin. [f]Arizona, Kansas, New Mexico, Oklahoma, and Texas. [g]Colorado, Idaho, Montana, Nevada, Utah, and Wyoming. [h]Alaska, California, Hawaii, Oregon, and Washington.

Part III
THE NEW YORK CITY

Politics is often like the Theater of the Absurd. Consider the spectacle of the presidential race of 1975–1976. Candidates of both parties campaigned as though they were running against Washington. Even Gerald Ford!

Until the implications of impending default set in, it appeared that New York would have the dubious honor of being the city presidential candidates ran against. Ford seemed so intransigent and so unsympathetic to a New York deeply in trouble that even the conservative *Daily News* was provoked into running this memorable headline: "FORD TO CITY: DROP DEAD."

Washington is the enemy, not, of course, because it houses the Smithsonian or Lincoln Memorial. It is the code word for a mammoth, powerful bureaucracy people increasingly hold responsible—rightly or wrongly—for our social and economic woes. The deep-seated animosity against New York appears to reflect hostilities of long standing: did not Goldwater in 1964 fantasize of New York's being cut off from the rest of the continent to drift out to sea? While Goldwater's pique may in part have been directed at Rockefeller's alleged liberalism, in point of truth New York *is* a deserving symbol of liberality. The unwillingness of the federal government to promote social programs for its less affluent left a vacuum which New York City filled.

In short, with Manhattan setting the tone, New York appears to be more liberal, more cosmopolitan—in a word, more "un-American"—than all but a few intellectual centers like Cambridge, Madison or Berkeley. Still the home of more Jews than Tel Aviv, more Irish than Dublin, and more Italians than Florence, New York is capable of stirring up the darker forces that reside within the American character, its nativism and its racial and religious bigotry. To

FISCAL CRISIS

Middle Americans, then, New York and Washington are much the same, the former a local equivalent of the latter. Both allegedly spend too much money on the "undeserving," on "chiselers" who squander our taxes, and so on.

The roots of racism and the insensitivity and lack of charity that characterize (and victimize) so many Americans lie deep in our history. We are the most capitalist of nations, lacking both a feudal heritage and a contemporary socialist labor movement. Defenders of the "free market" neglect to tell us that single-minded pursuit of economic self-interest results in selfishness, isolation and alienated living. In the final analysis, the culture of American capitalism, viewed most broadly, is responsible for the attitudes that permit the decay of America's greatest city.

This final section of the book pulls together the economic and political factors that affect urban development and shows how the crisis came to a head in New York City. Readers of selection #13 might assume, quite naturally, that they are reading about the contemporary crisis. They are not. As Robert Caro shows in a brief excerpt from his award-winning biography of Robert Moses, New Yorkers in the thirties suffered much the same tribulations as New Yorkers today. And bankers dictated terms then much as they do now, as the following selection on the Bankers Agreement of 1933 makes clear.

The *current* fiscal crisis is the focus of a number of analyses. The first of these (selection #15) is an essay by Matthew Edel, associate professor of urban studies at Queens College, City University of New York, who suggests that to understand the current crisis in New York and other cities, at least two questions should be posed: First, what were the technological developments and institutional arrangements which propelled the postwar boom and what was the role of New York in this process? Second, how did those technological and institutional propagators of the boom generate both the conditions leading to the current general economic crisis and the city's particular role in it? One important aspect of the "postwar economic configuration" was the emergence of a world-wide "American imperial system" as part of the process of the growth and dominance of large U.S. corporations and financial institutions. Like the other postwar developments, this had enormous significance for New York: "America's rise to world dominance had also meant the rise of New York as financial center for the world." Conversely, the erosion of the pillars of postwar profitability has had a particularly severe impact on a New York economy specializing in corporate planning activities and their auxiliary employment, and made even more vulnerable to the business cycle by an overexpansion of construction activity.

Robert Fitch of Cornell University offers an interesting interpretation of just what it is that business has been up to all these years (selection #16). Basing his account on the early works of the Regional Plan Association, he argues that realtors and banks have attempted to weed New York of its small "unkempt" industries and replant in their stead sleek office buildings and luxury apartments conducive to higher real-estate values and more appropriate to New York's international standing. The result was the bankruptcy or disappearance of thousands of small businesses.

Hearings by the U.S. Congress on proposals to aid New York led the congressional Budget Office to prepare a background paper on New York's fiscal problem, excerpts from which are printed as selection #17. As a consequence of the economic deterioration of the city which the Budget Office analyzes, management of New York's financial affairs has been transferred to the Emergency Financial Control Board and the Municipal Assistance Corporation. The most prominent member of these bodies, investment banker Felix Rohatyn, has called for a massive government planning effort to rebuild our threatened cities, a veritable "Marshall Plan" for urban America.

Seemingly unobjectionable planning proposals of this sort make it particularly important to ascertain who will control the planning process. A variety of authors have stressed the point that the city's fiscal ills have in fact been greatly exacerbated by government policies and "planning" in the interests of business. This theme is elaborated by journalist Jack Newfield, whose "How the Power Brokers Profit" (selection #18), focuses on some of the more immediate manifestations. Moreover, as William Tabb makes clear in selection #19, the entire process is partially obscured by a variety of myths that "blame the victims" for the city's problems and sidetrack people from understanding the real causes of the fiscal crisis. Following Tabb is an article by Robert Friedman, which analyzes the reaction of municipal unions and others to the cutbacks engendered by the crisis (selection #20).

At some point readers may be puzzled as to why the much ballyhooed revenue sharing failed to alleviate the crisis. Eli Silverman of John Jay College of Criminal Justice, one of the endangered City University divisions, guides us through the maze of state and federal programs which affect New York's revenue (selection #21).

The penultimate selection (#22) is a satirical note by economist Peter S. Albin, also of John Jay, showing how economic recovery can be stimulated by *dis*urbanization (one example: the employment of a quarter of a million workers to carry the records of business to the hinterlands). The book concludes with a brief essay by David Mermelstein, which places the fiscal crisis of American cities within a broader ideological and political context.

13. Retrenchment Recalled

ROBERT CARO

Even had the city wanted to help its people, it would have been unable to. The Depression had forced New York to total up at last the cost of its Rake's Progress under the Hylan and Walker administrations.

When Hylan became mayor of New York on January 1, 1918, the city's population was 5,872,143. Fifteen years later, when Walker resigned, it was 6,930,446—an increase of 15 percent. During that same period, the city's budget rose from $240,519,858 to $631,-366,298—an increase of 250 percent. The per capita cost of the budget increased by 200 percent. Year in and year out between January 1, 1918, and December 31, 1932, the city's debt increased at a rate equal to $100,000 per day, until, on the latter date, it had reached the staggering total of $1,897,481,478—a figure that was almost equal to the combined debt of the forty-eight states and that required an annual appropriation for debt service (the payment of interest and amortization) of $209,960,338, almost a third of the entire budget.

Since jobs were the fuel of Tammany's political machine, a disproportionate share of the rest of the budget went to purchase that fuel; between the day Hylan entered office and the day Walker left it, the number of city employees almost doubled, and their salaries, paid as political rewards at levels far above those paid for similar work in private industry, almost tripled. In 1932, they totaled $311,937,199.

City officials acted as if they believed that the budgetary gyre could go on widening indefinitely. They based their optimism on the fact that the value of taxable real estate in the city, the base of the city's tax structure, was increasing almost as fast as city expenditures. As a result, even while the city's budget soared, there was only a slight

Excerpted from *The Power Broker: Robert Moses and the Fall of New York* (New York: Knopf, 1974). Robert Caro is a writer living in New York City.

increase in the real estate tax rate. If the Hylan and Walker administrations had erected a huge superstructure of city expenditures, that superstructure was nonetheless resting on a base that they thought was steadily broadening.

Even before the Depression, however, the rate of increase in the base had begun to slow down ominously. The annual percentage of increase in the value of taxable real estate in the city was 12 in 1927 but only 9 in 1928 and 8 in 1929. The Depression forced this key percentage down to 6 in 1930, 3 in 1931, 1 in 1932. And the Depression forced *up* another key percentage, the percentage of real estate taxes which the city was unable to collect; in the years between 1928 and 1932 this percentage was, successively, 11, 13, 15, 18, 26. The uncollected balance of the 1932 real estate tax, the tax which had to finance the bulk of the city's debt service and current expenditures, was $137,613,213. The base on which the top-heavy superstructure of city finances teetered was shrinking, and it was shrinking fast. The superstructure began to topple.

In desperation the city deferred its required annual payments to the Teachers Retirement Fund and expropriated Sinking Fund surpluses already obligated for small-scale public improvements. Unable despite these expedients to meet even its ordinary day-to-day expenses, it was forced to borrow to pay them—at interest rates set higher and higher by bankers increasingly leery of the city's ability to repay. By 1931, even Jimmy Walker was talking about "economizing."

But the city's economizing capacity was limited because one-third of its budget was allocated for an all but irreducible debt service and because of political realities: the city payroll had become the payroll of the Tammany political machine, and while a city might reduce the number of its employees or their salaries, it was less easy for a political machine to throw its retainers off the payroll or substantially reduce their stipends. City construction contracts had become the main ingredient of the rich swill of graft to which the palate of Tammany leaders—including those party leaders who held high city office—had become accustomed; city officials could reduce a city's appropriations for construction, but men accustomed to feeding at a well-filled trough were far less ready to reduce their own portions. Even while talking economy, city officials made clear that they would not economize on construction appropriations or salaries. (There was one exception: one group of city employees—schoolteachers—were not part of the Tammany machine. In 1930 and 1931, the city fired 11,000 schoolteachers.) The 1932 city budget was the highest ever. The city proposed to finance it with a record increase in the real estate tax rate.

But the day of reckoning for fifteen years of Tammany rule was at hand. When, in January 1932, the city attempted to float new loans to meet the payroll coming due at the end of the month, bankers, convinced that the loans could not be repaid if the city spent money during the coming year at the rate it proposed, refused to make them unless the budget was reduced. The city complied by virtually halting all repairs to its physical plant. It refinanced a quarter-billion dollars of subway bonds, which the city had planned to redeem out of current revenues, by selling long-term bonds in their stead—an expedient which loaded future generations of city taxpayers with a monstrous rapid-transit debt.

Still the city's balance sheet reddened. By December 1932, it was forced to go hat in hand to the bankers again, and when new loans were made contingent on further budget reductions, it had no choice but to cut the salaries of city employees by 6 to 33 percent. And hundreds of millions of dollars in short-term revenue notes would be coming due in 1933 and there was no money in sight to pay them.

14. Banks Rescued the City in a Similar Plight in '33

JOHN DARNTON

The fiscal corner that the city has painted itself into recalls the shaky autumn of 1933, in the midst of the Great Depression, when the banks finally bailed the city out, but imposed a series of stringent conditions.

The arrangement between the administration of Mayor John P. O'Brien and the lending institutions, now known as the Bankers Agreement, lasted from 1934 to 1938. It is a singular period in New York City's history, in which banks—long a potent force just beneath the surface—virtually ran the city's business.

Although the financial and political events of the last few weeks have been rapid and confusing, one thing remains clear: the city's prospects for borrowing money to meet its bills and expenses— amounting to $1.5-billion in May and June—are questioned. Some observers, casting about for historical parallels, are wondering whether the Bankers Agreement could serve as a precedent.

In 1933, as in 1975, the city's revenue from tax collections, buffeted by the business depression, fell short of expenditures by millions of dollars. The city had borrowed heavily, because of deficits and capital outlays during a period of prosperity, so that its temporary debt reached half a billion dollars. It was unable to float long-term bonds, and it could obtain only credit over the short-term for limited amounts—at the interest rate of 6 per cent, then humiliatingly high.

Despite tax increases in 1931 and 1932, the general revenues fell $47-million from 1930 to 1932, while expenditures rose almost $100-million. Part of the increase was caused by unemployment relief, which cost $33-million in 1932 alone. In the same three-year period,

Reprinted from the *New York Times* (May 14, 1975). John Darnton is a member of the reporting staff of the *Times*.

the city increased its temporary debt by $147.9-million. Some of it came from pension funds and sinking funds, but most of it came from the banks.

Although the Mayor had instituted stringent budget cuts, the banks were increasingly unwilling to extend further credit; several times it seemed likely that the city would fail to meet its payroll or default on its 4.5 per cent long-term bonds, which were rapidly declining in price. Bad publicity frightened away potential investors.

In early 1932, the bankers, headed by Thomas W. Lamont of J. P. Morgan & Co., at first refused to help the city meet a temporary cash shortage, but then relented. In the fall, asked for another loan, the financiers insisted upon and won, among other things, the promise of a budget reduction of $40-million, of which $20-million was to come from salaries. By the following year, still unsatisfied, they refused to let the city "roll over" its short-term debt.

The Bankers Agreement was born at a tightly guarded series of City Hall meetings, attended by the bankers, Mayor O'Brien, and the city's fiscal adviser, Samuel Untermeyer. Dissent within the then Municipal Assembly was overcome by the two powerful Democrats —Mr. O'Brien and Gov. Herbert H. Lehman—and its approval on Sept. 28 was heralded by a front-page, four-column headline in *The New York Times*.

In essence, the bankers agreed to lend the city money over the following three years, by refunding, at 4 to 4.5 per cent interest, $131-million of outstanding revenue bills issued against taxes in arrears. The bankers also set up a revolving fund for four years against which revenue bills could be issued, and they made two immediate, short-term cash advances.

In return, the city agreed to a seven-point program whose main feature was a four-year limitation on the real-estate tax, frozen at $429-million. The city also agreed to segregate certain tax funds and deposit them in the banks, to budget reserve up to $50-million for delinquent real-estate taxes, and to increase the penalty on tax arrears by 4 per cent.

The city was also forced to drop proposed taxes on stocks, savings banks and life insurance companies.

Key features of Mayor Beame's proposed tax package, disclosed in Albany Monday, are an increase in stock transfer taxes on nonresidents, a 75 per cent rise in the tax on commercial banks and a 50 per cent increase in the tax on savings banks.

One bank official thought the prospect of a bankers agreement, 1975, unlikely.

"In '33, the banks came in and they were the bad guys," he said. "I suspect that in the politics of '75, they just couldn't sustain the political reaction it would engender. It would create enormous levels of deomonstrations, and redirect the demonstrations from City Hall to Wall Street."

In November, 1933, one month after the Bankers Agreement was struck, Mayor Fiorello H. La Guardia was elected. He imposed an austerity program that, together with a gradual improvement in the general economy, finally lifted the city out of its predicament.

15. The New York Crisis as Economic History

MATTHEW EDEL

This paper relates the fiscal crisis of New York City to the general economic crisis arising from the end of the postwar boom.[1] I argue that New York's fiscal problems resulted from the way in which capitalism adjusted to and "recovered from" previous economic depressions in the late nineteenth century and the 1930s, and that the present attack on New Yorkers is part of an attempt by capital to recover from a new crisis.

To link the New York crisis to the broader economic situation should not, in itself, be controversial. Only in the context of press and presidential claims that the specific mismanagement or over-generosity of city officials are to blame for the financial troubles of New York City, is this novel. "New York," says *Fortune* magazine, "is a special case. New York is different because it has had a credit card that enabled it to live beyond its means."[2] This view, which blames New York for its problems, has been promoted for electoral ends or to justify placing the burdens of economic adjustment on urban residents.[3] But many people simply assume New York's uniqueness because they are not used to seeing events within the

Matthew Edel is associate professor of urban studies, Queens College, CUNY. This paper was written in April 1976.

[1] This paper has benefited from my participation in a study group on the Fiscal Crisis run at the New School for Social Research by the Union for Radical Political Economics, but the opinions presented do not represent a group position. I would also like to thank my colleagues Carol Brown, David Gurin and William Tabb and my students in Urban Studies at Queens College for stimulating discussions.

[2] Wyndam Robertson, "Going Broke the New York Way," *Fortune* (August 1975), pp. 144, *et seq.* A similar argument, with stress on New York's uniqueness, was made by William Simon and President Ford in their several statements on New York during late 1975.

[3] See William Tabb's paper in this volume (selection #19).

context of an unfolding history of economic growth and stagnation. This problem also besets some defenses of New York, which blame the city's troubles on a cabal of bankers and federal executives, but which fail to see these manipulators as themselves pushed by the unfolding economic crisis.

If one looks beyond day-to-day policies, New York's "unique" features turn out to be examples of situations that confront other cities, and to be national in cause. New York has been forced to bear many of the nation's costs of coping with economic growth and poverty; its tax base has been weakened by national trends just when financial markets have had to select victims for a restriction of loans. The sacrifice of New York rather than, say, Lockheed Aircraft is an act of policy by banks and government. But the underlying weakness of urban public financing, and the overall recession in the Western capitalist nations, are both rooted in the structure of postwar economic growth.

THE EXPLANATION OF CURRENT ECONOMIC HISTORY

Much of current economic analysis lacks a sense of history. Keynesians and their conservative critics alike see depressions as the result of government error, either in the setting of the national budget or in monetary policy. Even some radicals go no further than to argue that economic contractions are deliberate acts designed to discipline labor through doses of unemployment rather than errors. There is, however, another tradition in political economy, which sees economic cycles as driven by stronger forces than can be controlled by short-run government policy.

Thus, Joseph Schumpeter related periods of rapid economic growth to innovations that allowed an efficient reorganization of economic activity.[4] Innovations generated profits for reinvestment, and created further investment opportunities. Eventually, imitation and reinvestment would exhaust investment opportunities, and a period of stagnation would follow. Such a view explains the boom of the mid-nineteenth century by investment in railroads and power-driven industries, and turn-of-the-century growth by electrical and chemical innovation. The mid-twentieth-century expansion has simi-

[4]Joseph A. Schumpeter, *The Theory of Economic Development* (Cambridge: Harvard University Press, 1934); *Business Cycles* (Cambridge: Harvard University Press, 1939); *Capitalism, Socialism and Democracy* (New York: Harper, 1947).

larly been linked to petroleum-using technologies, including the automobile. Depressions subsequent to these booms are then related to exhaustion of the impetus created by these innovations.

For Karl Marx, a tendency to economic crisis was as much a normal aspect of capitalism as was the drive toward accumulation.[5] Growth gave rise to its antithesis, crisis. The attempt by capital to profit from the proletariat's labor was frustrated by labor shortage and labor resistance, by a saturation of markets or of investment opportunities, or by an unproductive arrangement of existing capital. This crisis of profitability might be countered by institutional changes (including technological ones) which made labor work harder or more productively. If it were not staved off, it would lead to economic crisis, as capitalists either cut back new investments or diverted their investments into speculative adventures and credit extension, which in turn lead to a financial crash. But the crisis itself, by reducing wages and restructuring capital, could help create conditions for new rounds of accumulation.

A view of the business cycle common to Marx and Schumpeter thus sees alternation between periods of declining productivity, economic crisis and social conflict, and periods in which productivity is successfully increased as a result of innovations or institutional reforms made in the depression.[6] This is no mere alternation in time. A depression, in this view, can be "successful" in creating the conditions for new profits and growth. Similarly, a period of growth bears within it the seeds of a new depression. Such a viewpoint has some dangers; it can lead to fatalistic views of cycles. But it can provide a useful framework for analyzing the causes of an economic event. In the present case it focuses us on the role of New York in the

[5]Karl Marx, *Capital* (New York: International Publishers, 1967). The Marxian theories on accumulation and crises are presented in fragmentary form in several places in the three volumes of *Capital*, with different sections stressing different aspects of the theory.

[6]Such a view is presented in Robert Zevin, "The Political Economy of the American Empire, 1974," in *Radical Perspectives on the Economic Crisis of Monopoly Capitalism* (New York: Union for Radical Political Economics, 1975), pp. 131–137, and Ray Franklin, "An Analytic Framework for Understanding the Relationship between Class Conflict and Historical Changes in the American Social Order," paper presented at the New School URPE Conference on Marxist Approaches to History, March 1976. For an application of the Marxian model, see Ben Fine and Laurence Harris, "On the Problem of Analysing Current Economic History." Unpublished paper, Birkbeck College Department of Economics, London, 1975.

institutional arrangements of the postwar boom, and on the way in which the boom and those arrangements affected both the current general crisis and the city's role in it.

KEY FEATURES OF THE POSTWAR BOOM

The postwar boom had several key features. The first was the linking together of the Western powers and the dependent Third World economies into one economic system, under the leadership of United States capital. This "imperial system" allowed the expansion of large corporations and financial institutions, the establishment of a new division of labor at the international level, increased international movement of raw materials and many finished goods, and economies of large-scale production of some goods in the developed areas. It also enforced the production of other goods by low-paid labor in peripheral areas and by relatively low-paid migrants in industrial centers, and it destroyed economic opportunities for much of small business.

A second aspect was the creation of labor-market and social-welfare institutions to guarantee a steady supply of labor and general public order in the capitalist centers. The recognition of labor unions in the United States, their growth elsewhere, and the spread of the welfare state, all were results of the Depression and World War II. Some specific institutions primarily served to mitigate class conflict, to ensure "legitimation" of the system, in James O'Connor's terminology.[7]

However, schools, welfare programs and other government services also sought to channel labor to the needs of industry.[8] The same was true of such institutions as seniority contracts, industrial pensions and federal home-mortgage subsidies, which gave workers specific incentives to maintain continuous employment. The programs thus also served O'Connor's "accumulation" function: direct assistance to capitalist growth. Government macroeconomic policy and Western European planning efforts also served to prevent economic disorder and to reduce competition among capitalists.

[7]James O'Connor, *The Fiscal Crisis of the State* (New York: St. Martin's Press, 1973).

[8]Frances Fox Piven and Richard A. Cloward, *Regulating the Poor: The Functions of Public Welfare* (New York: Random House, 1971); Samuel Bowles and Herbert Gintis, *Schooling in Capitalist America* (New York: Basic Books, 1976).

A third aspect, which interplayed with and reinforced the others, was the growth of the "petroleum-based" and "electronic" technological complex. Petroleum-using means of road, air and sea transportation expanded the international division of labor and allowed the reorganization of urban housing over larger areas. Tractors, fertilizers and insecticides allowed mechanization of agriculture and the introduction of fertilizer-dependent hybrid grains. These major innovations, along with new materials and electronics provided the technical basis for a cheaper production of both some forms of machinery and some consumer necessities. Thus, for at least some workers in the developed capitalist countries, living standards could be increased, while *at the same time* profit rates could recover from the depression and maintain themselves at a high level. The new technologies, including military hardware, also allowed efficient repression of those areas of the world not benefitting by the rising living standards, and of occasional dissidents in the industrial centers.

Related to these three aspects was the ability of the United States to maintain labor discipline by means of opportunities for individual mobility. People worked hard attempting to better their personal or family positions. Education, movement from blue- to white-collar jobs, and migration from farm to city or from city to suburb, all were possible for enough individuals to keep others striving. As long as general productivity grew, administrative work expanded and new technology created jobs for those trained, mobility could remain credible. The system of social control by mobility was less successful outside of the United States, and an attempt to export it to the weaker capitalist nations in the Alliance for Progress failed completely. Even in the United States some groups were excluded, and there was always some tendency for new occupations, suburbs and educational credentials to decline in value as more people came to possess them. By the mid-1960s it became clear that suburbanization, education and new careers would not absorb even the whole U.S. population.

These arrangements and innovations did not "just grow." Many of them had emerged from labor struggles in the late nineteenth century, others in the two decades following 1929. The organization of labor and the demand for relief for the unemployed were met initially by police and vigilante violence against strikers and organizers. Hitler's Germany experimented with forced labor and massive liquidation of labor leadership. Eventually capitalists discovered they could live with and even benefit from some compromise with labor. The compromise was, of course, hemmed in by strict rules, to limit the independent action of labor and preserve the incentive to work, but it also did represent some gains for labor.

Similarly, the adoption of new technologies and the concentration of economic power into large enterprises also emerged from struggle. International rivalry for economic dominance, which earlier had produced World War I, led to the tariff wars of the 1930s and the shooting war that followed. The war's results facilitated the expansion of world-scale enterprises based in the United States and the adoption of new technologies in Europe. Internally, too, new arrangements involved major legislative, legal and economic battles among capitalists, before such "archaic" enterprises as the family farm, the neighborhood store, the trolley line and the independent refinery were defeated, and such alternative forms of rationalization as public housing and public power were limited in scope.[9]

URBAN PROBLEMS IN THE BOOM

Institutional and technological arrangements which emerged from the 1930s' Depression and the war restored profitability and restarted economic growth. They also created a new spatial division of labor with contradictory roles for cities. We can seek the basis for the current crisis of New York by examining these effects.

Starting with the technological innovations, we can easily see the importance of the automobile. Suburbanization increased housing opportunities for workers, but it did so in a way that removed the housing of higher-wage workers, as well as that of professionals and proprietors, from the urban tax base. Boundaries of the older cities were not changed by the institutional reforms of 1930s and 1940s. Only federal subsidies provided new financial support for local government. The result—that suburbanization was one cause of urban insolvency—is well known. However, it is often presented as a tech-

---

[9] A similar battle over forms of rationalization had also occurred in the late nineteenth century, continuing into the "Progressive" era of reform during the turn-of-the-century boom. Reforms attacked utility monopolies as barriers to accumulation, restructured municipal governments and allowed limited unionization and suburbanization for certain strata of skilled workers, as well as setting up institutions for a partition of the Third World among capitalists. This allowed a period of booming investment for the United States, but elsewhere only a briefer boom, whose weakening led to increased competition and international conflict.

nological imperative favoring newer over older cities, rather than as a result of the interplay of technology with policy. Radial highways and suburban mortgages were subsidized instead of public transit and quality public housing, which could have ensured the urban centers' attractiveness.[10]

The connection of agricultural innovation to the New York crisis is less direct, but still crucial. Improvements in agricultural productivity and the use of mechanical equipment and chemicals, assisted by migrant labor at peak seasons, drove large numbers of workers from agriculture. Mechanization and migration were intensified by federal policy for subsidies, government investment and technical assistance that favored larger farms, and by a deliberate mechanization that Southern farmers adopted in response to militancy by black labor beginning in the 1950s. Many of the migrants found their way to cities in the North. The population of skilled and white-collar workers, and of professionals and managers, that the cities were losing to their suburbs was thus replaced by one of minority "internal immigrants."

New York had coped with large migrations of unskilled labor before the postwar era. But the new pattern of growth differed from that of earlier cycles in ways which made migrants' progress more difficult. In this the decline of manufacturing employment from 1,038,800 jobs in 1950 to 766,000 in 1970 was particularly important.[11] Manufacturing had traditionally trained its own workers, drawn from immigrant ranks. And New York's manufacturing sector had been unusually diversified into small firms, allowing some immigrants the opportunity to become small businessmen. But in the postwar boom, opportunities for successful development of small businesses dried up, as capital became more concentrated and larger-scale technologies were adopted. Larger manufacturing firms either migrated out of large cities or automated and tightened their seniority systems, so opportunities both for private job training and for mobility into small business diversity had declined.

With older forms of employment and advancement limited, it fell to government to cope with the migrants, by training them for nonmanufacturing occupations, by providing direct relief, or by repression of discontent. These tasks, being less important at earlier

[10]K. E. Schaeffer and E. Sclar, *Access for All* (Baltimore: Penguin, 1975).

[11]Bureau of Labor Statistics figures.

times, had been left to local governments when major economic policies were transferred to higher levels of government. Although some assistance from state and federal governments became available, city governments were faced with rising costs. As minority communities, municipal employees and other nonsuburbanized workers increased their demands in the 1960s, the concessions made by government were largely left to be financed locally. The local tax base was, however, already weakened by suburbanization and the decline of urban industry. Initially this created a fiscal crisis only in the narrow sense of a need to find national or regional taxing systems to tap a growing economy for local funds. With the end of the boom, the problem grew more serious.

The fiscal problems of New York seemed more manageable, at first, due to the city's unique place in the postwar capitalist system. America's rise to world dominance had also meant the rise of New York as financial center for the world. The location of the United Nations in New York was mostly symbolic; the location of corporate headquarters, international banking establishments, trading companies and a host of auxiliary firms (accounting, advertising, law, etc.) was more crucial. Employment in financial, insurance and real-estate firms rose from 336,200 in 1950 to 459,600 in 1970; employment in headquarters of industrial firms from 76,900 in 1962 to 83,900 in 1968. Taxation of these activities was sometimes difficult, as Mayor Lindsay discovered when he first proposed a stock-transfer tax, but at least they brought some payroll and sales-tax revenues to the city, and kept real-estate values (and taxes) high.

The economic base was, however, inherently unstable. The activities which were expanding in New York were all financed out of profits made elsewhere. As a result New York was sensitive to business cycles. Headquarters and auxiliary employment in New York, as well as high-rise construction employment, expanded throughout the boom. Even in the early stages of recession financial activities retained their profitability at the expense of the smaller companies they were absorbing or financing, and New York remained insulated. But as recession continued, these firms, too, faced crisis and had to cut back. The result was a sudden decline of office employment and a stagnation of tax revenues, just when costs rose most rapidly and loans became hard to get.

THE DOWNTURN AND THE CRISIS

If urban problems multiplied during the long postwar boom, the main causes of the boom themselves also began to erode.[12] First, United States dominance over a capitalist world economy has been weakened. The rebellions of the dependent nations, most dramatic in the victory of the Indochinese revolutions, have raised the cost of maintaining empire; even the most conservative of national leaders have been emboldened to raise prices of natural resources or use tariffs to promote industrial modernization. Even among developed nations, the United States has lost power. The dollar has been devalued. The recovery of Europe and Japan has increased intercapitalist competition on the national level. Rising costs and increasing competition, emerging when corporations have become multinational enough to move capital easily across borders, limits the extent to which surplus can be devoted by corporations or governments to the creation of new jobs and opportunities in the capitalist centers. The increased use of technical economies of scale in production (if any such opportunities still exist) is made more complex by international rivalries.

Second, the technological supports of the boom have passed the point at which increasing productivity can allow simultaneous increases in both living standards and profits. This aspect of the crisis is most clearly seen in the saturation of the automobile market and the congestion of the highways. At first the automobile allowed a rapid expansion of the area of worker housing, and hence a reduction in real living costs. By the late 1960s it was, however, increasing other costs of living by disrupting the environment, and by increasing commuting burdens and driving requirements for maintaining social life or educating children in the suburbs. New land for suburban expansion or highway widening also became scarce, at least around the larger cities.

Agriculture and manufacturing also saw a slowdown of growth. There is still room for increased food production, but the scope for removing labor from the land in the United States is limited by the extent to which farming is already automated. Only a few harvest

[12]For a variety of analyses of the downturn, see *Radical Perspectives on the Economic Crisis of Monopoly Capitalism* (New York: Union for Radical Political Economics, 1975).

operations remain labor-intensive. What is more, technologies to automate production are increasing environmental (and perhaps medical) costs for society. Similarly, manufactured appliances, like the refrigerator and the washing machine, that can save household labor have by now spread widely. The latest consumer items, like the snowmobile and the citizens' band radio are mostly used for recreation, not for saving labor. What is more, except in a few areas of information processing, it is hard to find producers' goods in which costs have fallen during recent years to a degree that could make them leading sectors in a boom.

Third, the labor-channeling institutions that worked well in the first two postwar decades themselves revealed their contradictions. Use of schools and welfare systems to contain large numbers of people temporarily or permanently out of production provoked the response of mass student and welfare-rights movements. Labor unions, content with productivity bargaining when productivity was outstripping the cost of living, demanded gains that kept up with inflation when productivity fell behind. The promise of mobility for all could not be kept, by its very nature, and even small tokens of mobility became more costly as other aspects of the boom faced their difficulties. Individual and group alienation and dissatisfaction began to interfere with production and require new and costly institutions for control, such as drug programs.

Whether one poses the problem in Schumpeterian terms as the end of the electronics/petroleum growth cycle, or in Marxian terms, as an exhaustion of the counteracting forces to falling profit rates, the result is clear. Growth became more difficult for the United States starting in the mid-1960s, and for Western Europe and Japan at the start of the 1970s. This posed, for the capitalist system, a problem which had emerged periodically before in history: how to stave off or cope with an economic slowdown that imposed either declining profits or reduced wages, that increased possibilities of social and international conflict and that threatened financial crisis. There were, to be sure, some differences between this and earlier crises. The economic and political configuration of the period was marked by powerful monopolies in many areas of production, by strong and economically active states mindful of the dangers of international retaliation, and in certain sectors of production, by stronger unions than had existed in earlier economic crises. Perhaps as a result, inflationary finance and competitive devaluations were used, instead of wage reductions and tariff wars, to protect capital from threatened insolvency. These offsets, while delaying financial collapse, did not solve the crisis of profitability. The means of coping with crisis, like the activities that had shaped the boom, had a specific impact on New York.

NEW YORK IN THE CRISIS: IMMEDIATE EFFECTS

That the crisis would have severe effects on New York should have been apparent from urban problems during the boom. As noted above, suburbanization had weakened the fiscal basis of central city governments. Costs of social control through welfare systems, law enforcement or education and mobility were mounting up. The future of city finances and of downtown business districts was, indeed, often debated. But urban renewal to attract white-collar jobs, federal revenue sharing and continued general economic progress were generally counted on to overcome the problems. Even when the economy began to constrict leaving some industrial cities with an immediate crisis, it did so in such a way as to temporarily inflate the particular economy of New York.

As the overall pace of economic expansion slowed down and as insolvency began to threaten businesses, inflationary monetary and fiscal policies were used to stave off financial and social crisis. World capitalist financial arrangements to avoid a liquidity crisis paralleled inflationary financing of the Vietnam war, and of social programs and corporate bailouts in the United States. This inflation of paper wealth, coming at a time in which profitable investment outlets were limited, created pools of mobile financial capital seeking some sort of outlet. Many of these funds found their way into the creation of new conglomerate and multinational enterprises. These served, at first, a function of centralization of capital which in the past had generally been left to bankruptcy during crises: the wiping out and milking of smaller or obsolete enterprises, and the centralization of production into new and potentially more efficient centers. However, the opportunities for increased efficiency through centralization were limited. Conglomerate mergers, national or multinational, could not postpone for long the crisis of profitability. What they did do, at first, was to centralize management functions. This brought to New York even more control over world business than it previously had. As the *Fortune* 500 largest corporations increased the share of business they controlled, New York increased its share of the 500 with head offices in the city.

This consolidation also attracted to New York and other business centers a large amount of capital seeking profitable outlets for investment in real estate. In the late 1960s, office buildings found a ready market among corporate clients and independent businesses that served the major headquarters. Tax loopholes, deliberately designed to increase profits and investment, also helped make high-rise construction a desirable "shelter." As a result, big-city skylines were transformed, and real-estate values generally inflated, leading to speculative stockpiling of older buildings. True, this boom was based on a centralization that was reaching its limits, given the profit opportunities of the productive sector. True, it was financed at the expense of declining property values elsewhere, in older suburbs, smaller cities, and the redlined or "gray" areas of central cities themselves. But this was not immediately apparent. Nor was the cost to the public imposed by the destruction of older neighborhoods in the path of office and highway expansion—and by the resistance these generated. The increase in downtown values—apparently a renaissance of the older central cities—made the cities themselves appear to be good credit risks. Capital in search of profitable investment began to seek out tax-free municipal and state bonds as part of the urban construction boom. Public-sector expansion thus could join with private construction to create an apparent boom in the major cities, including New York, while the economy as a whole slipped into crisis.[13]

The expansion of credit delayed the onset of crisis in New York. As a result, crisis came suddenly rather than as a slow erosion of revenues and the job base. This, in turn, allowed the imposition of lower living standards on New Yorkers to be presented ideologically as a necessary result of local government overexpansion rather than as an incident in general capitalist stagnation. The ideology is one factor which, itself, influences the response to the crisis.

In a sense, any decline of investment can be considered a strike by capital. But such a strike is more clearly seen when the withdrawal of capital is concerted, as in the "redlining" of whole districts to real-estate mortages or in the cutting off of bond purchases to a major

[13]This episode in the business cycle has tended to monopolize the attention of commentators in New York. For the orthodox, city government is the villain for borrowing too much. For some radicals, the bankers who made the loans are the villains. Several pamphlets on the New York crisis have overstressed the role of excessive lending as the prime cause of the crisis. From the perspective of this paper, credit expansion, while important in shaping the forms of the crisis, was itself a response to crisis rather than a prime mover or the central institution of a new stage of capitalism.

city. In the case of New York, elements of both concerted and spontaneous withdrawal of investment were involved at first.

A drain of manufacturing jobs from the city, and to a lesser extent from its environs, has been going on since the mid-1950s. This had, to a degree, conditioned the specific racial unrest of the sixties. But until 1970, it was matched by an increase in office jobs. Construction, transport and commercial jobs also remained buoyant. The first drop in total employment and in total business investments in the city came about when corporations began cutting back on office activities in the city, when overbuilding of office space became apparent and when construction slackened. By 1972, a rapid drain of office, construction and commercial jobs was in effect. Only government continued to increase the supply of jobs. Then, in early 1975, banks and other bond investors triggered the visible fiscal crisis by refusing to buy city bonds. The representatives of capital were able to recognize quickly enough that bargaining between the city and its old creditors or potential new creditors could be carried out. The result has been a political and financial set of bargains between the city and capital since early 1975 which has transferred much of the control over government in the city from elected officials to representatives of capital: the Municipal Assistance Corporation and the Emergency Financial Control Board. The actions of these bodies, as well as observation of why and when individual businesses left New York, indicates some of the demands of capital on the people of New York. As such, they give some indication of potential avenues for solution of the present overall economic crisis that are being explored by capital. But they also indicate clearly that no unique direction for successful solution of the overall economic crisis has yet emerged.

Thus far, two short-term gains have been made by capital through its "strike" against New York. The first is the liquidation of a small amount of the paper wealth of the system in such a way as to differentially harm small investors and workers. The second is a restricting, at least for the moment, of workers' living standards.

The liquidation of paper wealth was accomplished in the 1930s by the stock-market crash, mortgage foreclosures, business and bank failures, and a host of other (mostly unplanned) events. In the New York situation it is attempted through the legal stretch-out of repayment on some city bonds, through the erosion of city real-estate values, and through the tapping of pension-fund assets for meeting current city costs. Although some of the major commercial banks lose by this process, as real estate controlled by their investment trusts declines in value, much of the burden is shifted to owners of homes, smaller office buildings, cooperative apartments and pension rights. The scale of losses is small compared to national monetary aggregates, but the federal government is still, after all, running a moderately expansionist monetary policy. Redlining New York at least allows credit to be directed toward the bailing out of some other threatened institutions in the city's place. And it may give the system's planners some idea of how much small wealth can be liquidated through localized crises, without the need for a contraction of the suddenness of that of 1929–1932. Thus it is useful.

The reduction of workers' living standards is even more essential to capital as a short-term response to crisis, as well, perhaps, as one possible model for a longer-term solution. In the short run, the less paid out in wages or social benefits, the more is available for capital, both as individual corporation's profits which stave off illiquidity and as an investment fund to be directed into any areas of expansion that may emerge. The layoff of headquarters employees, the transfer of manufacturing employment to lower-wage areas of the world, and the reduction of city expenditures on services serve this end in the short run by reducing wage and tax expenses of businesses located in New York. But at another level they seem intended to scare workers elsewhere into acceptance of lower living standards out of fear of "becoming another New York." Due to its role as the nation's largest city and the world business center, New York has a high *visibility,* and its policies have in the past set the tone for demands for unionization, wages or public services, elsewhere in the country and even abroad. The crisis is thus valuable to capital as an object lesson for others.

The crisis has also allowed capital to experiment with new forms of control over government itself. This is at least potentially of some importance. In recent years, national business has not directly controlled local government. Local government power over economic issues was destroyed by the displacement of locally owned by national businesses in the late nineteenth century, and by the shifting of powers to higher levels of government any time that workers had even tried to use local government against the corporations, banks or other capitalist institutions. The major "stakes" left for distribution through local government had thus been contracts, land-use privileges and public jobs. As a result, for the most part running the cities was left by both labor and national capitalist elites to a local "permanent government" of those concerned with these particular prizes.[14]

In the 1960s, when new demands on local government emerged, both the minority communities and national capitalist leaders attacked the response of the "permanent government" and its career bureaucracies. Minority organizing efforts finally took control of several cities, only to find that the weak tax base and lack of control over national industry made city government ineffective as a vehicle for reform. Now major businesses are moving directly for power. The new institutions imposed on New York City by its creditors may be prototypes for more general forms of control, to be used on other cities and states and perhaps even for federal planning. However, it is not yet clear what long-term policies capital wants them to implement!

At present, several different models of how to reorganize the system are being proposed, albeit in confused forms, and contemporary crises like that of New York are being used to propose reforms and new structures which could, perhaps, provide the basis for future growth. Studying the New York crisis thus becomes a study in the design of alternative futures which are being proposed or imposed from different directions.

New York in the Crisis: What Next?

How New York will fare in the further development of the crisis will depend not only on events in the city, but upon what conditions, if any, permit a renewed round of accumulation through increased profits. Recovery within a capitalist framework would seem, based on historical evidence, to require a reorganization of both technology and society. The directions for reorganization are, however, not clear. Recovery from the last crisis did not occur until after a long depression, a world war and many internal changes. Such a catastrophic period is not impossible in the current situation: the "solution" to New York's crisis may yet be atomic war. Assuming there is neither such a catastrophe nor world-wide socialist revolution, a long period of economic stagnation and social conflict is the likeliest outcome. In this event, what is in store for New York and other cities is a further deterioration of living standards, and the imposition of one round of austerity after another.

If there is a capitalist recovery, several different forms of urbaniza-

[14]The term "The Permanent Government" has been used by Jack Newfield in a series of articles on New York in the *Village Voice.*

tion might emerge. The form cities take will depend on the role of labor within the new pattern for growth and on the type of control center required by the centralization of capital. The city currently serves two main functions within a capitalist society—one as a center of production and of control over production, the other as a locus for reproduction, both biological and educational, of the labor force.[15] How each of these functions is handled in any new order will affect the city. It will matter for all cities whether labor is to be reproduced at a reduced level of education and with a reduced standard of living, or whether (as after the crises of the late nineteenth century and the 1930s) it is given an increased living standard in return for higher productivity. And it will matter for New York whether the locus of control of the process is primarily in the hands of those financial institutions which now predominate in the city's economy, in the hands of footloose multinational corporations that will run their activities from other centers, or in the hands of national governments. It may matter also how either production and control or the reproduction of labor is divided among cities and suburbs.

That the choice between these possibilities has not clearly emerged makes prediction about the city's role difficult. The actions imposed on New York can be seen as prototypes for differing programs. Thus the reduction of service budgets may be an attempt to enforce new productivity standards on bureaucracies whose services are still considered necessary for the reproduction of labor power. Such a view is consistent with the notion that a "social-service sector" or a "social-industrial complex" can be a leading sector for a new period of growth, with productivity increasing enough to allow increased consumption by the labor force yet also generate profits, as occurred in earlier booms with agriculture and transportation.[16] On the other hand, the budget cuts may represent an attempt to lower the cost of labor by reducing living standards and using lower "quality" labor in production.[17]

Either strategy is theoretically possible. Increasing service produc-

[15]On the corporate control function, see Stephen Hymer, "The Multinational Corporation and the Law of Uneven Development" in J. Bhagwati, ed., *Economics and World Order* (New York: Macmillan, 1972); on the city as locus of reproduction, see Manuel Castells, *La Question Urbain* (Paris: Maspero, 1972).

[16]Zevin, *op. cit.* and O'Connor, *op. cit.*, raise this possibility.

[17]Carol A. Brown, "The Decline of Urban Services: Who Needs People?" in P. M. Wickman, ed., *Social Problems, Contemporary Perspectives* (New York: Harper, forthcoming).

tivity and utilizing elsewhere the labor displaced by this might have some advantages. Increased exploitation alone would lead only to slow growth for capital, due to market saturation and continuing decline of returns to old technologies. However, a coherent "social-industrial" strategy, with sufficiently productive new technologies, has yet to be devised. For now, decreasing wages and services at home, while directing investment and trade to low-wage countries, offers capital a more immediate solution. The way in which cuts have been implemented suggest that serious productivity innovations are not even being tried experimentally. The only question seems to be whether a hard-line tactic of pay and service cuts, and the promotion of inter-ethnic rivalries, will work more or less effectively than a soft-line appeal to patriotism and an ecological ethos of purported limits to growth in securing acceptance of lower living standards. It would seem, therefore, that in the area of labor reproduction, capital will attempt to stretch out its short-term response into an attempted long-run solution, unless forced by working-class resistance to seek a solution in some other area of innovation.

The role of New York as a center for business is also in dispute. One faction of capitalists still wants to maintain corporate control at a single point in the United States, for which New York still has the advantages of a built-up infrastructure. For this group the fiscal crisis and declining services in New York pose some problems, but they also offer an opportunity to expel the remaining "disorderly" non-business groups from Manhattan. Thus Housing Commissioner Roger Starr has spoken of phased destruction of slums, and MAC Chairman Felix Rohatyn has advocated massive area urban renewal to attract business. For such advocates, the crisis is, as the Pentagon might put it, a chance to destroy New York in order to save it.

However, other factions of capitalists see the future as either an abandonment of location in *any* one center (on the basis of new communication technologies to allow class rule without propinquity) or as a partial decentralization to "sunbelt" or other centers and to New York's own suburbs. Proposals for the automation of stock trading, and for the building of a new bridge linking the Connecticut and Long Island suburbs, stem from this strategy to eliminate dependence on New York. Already a large number of businesses have left. This strategy sees New York as something to be abandoned to the poor, as no longer useful to capital at all.

The conflict over these two possible futures of the geographical city of New York is presented to the city's residents as, at least in part, up to them. Sufficient austerity in local spending and in wage demands, it is said, will help hold business in the city. What is proposed is a short-term sacrifice in the interest of long-run prosperity. However, this proposition assumes there will be a strong capitalist business center to settle either back in New York or elsewhere. This, however, would seem to require a constriction of the working-class standard of living—unless some new technological solution is found. Thus, austerity for the purpose of attracting capitalists back to the city would seem to be a self-defeating proposition for the New York City working class. Rather, the best hope from the working-class perspective is to resist cuts in the standard of living and to hope that this resistance will spark resistance elsewhere as well. Whether resistance ends up forcing capitalists to innovate in new productive areas, or whether it delegitimizes the capitalist system if the capitalists cannot create another boom, it is the only protection the majority of the population has.

16. Planning New York

ROBERT FITCH

In 1929, the same year the Bolshevik party under the leadership of J. V. Stalin prepared to execute the Soviet Union's first Five Year Plan, a group of Manhattan bankers, real-estate men and foundation executives announced the publication of America's first comprehensive regional economic plan. The Soviet plan is the most famous act of economic foresight in the twentieth century. No one can hope to understand Soviet triumphs in heavy industry, its disasters in agriculture, or the present relation between town and country without studying the plan and the conditions that made it necessary. But the Regional Plan of New York and Its Environs, the most ambitious planning effort ever carried out under private auspices, has fallen into almost total obscurity. Urban specialists rarely consult its ten volumes of economic analysis which detail the growth of every industry in the city, chart the rise of its land values, its railroad complex, the highway system, the New York regions' housing, high-rise office buildings, parks, neighborhoods, population movements. And the plan itself, filling two additional volumes of proposals, maps, illustrations and arguments, is largely ignored and unmentioned even by the direct successors of the first plan organization.

What makes this neglect so striking is that the plan has been largely realized in actual physical terms. The proposed highway system, designed like a sculptor's armature to serve as infrastructural support for the desired suburbanization and decentralization of the region—this system, complete with tunnels, bridges, grade separations, was imposed on the region in almost precisely the form specified by the planners. And the same can be said, to a lesser extent, of the post-1929 development of the park system. (The proponents of the Robert Moses Theory of History notwithstanding.)[1]

Robert Fitch teaches at Cornell. This paper was written in May 1976.

[1]See, particularly, Robert Caro, *The Power Broker* (New York: Knopf, 1974).

It is perhaps understandable that the present Regional Plan Association,[2] whose leadership, now as then, comprises the city's core financial and business leadership figures, says so little about the efforts of the previous generation of planners; understandable since for the last fifteen years the focus of the RPA's efforts has been to try to mend the damage done to the area by the first plan. But for anyone who seeks to understand the forces that have shaped the city and the region it dominates, the forces which now grip it in its present agonies, the 1929 plan must serve as a crucial starting point.

CONSEQUENCES OF THE PLAN

The influence of the plan makes itself felt in two closely related ways.

(1) Looking at the New York Metropolitan Region (NYMR) from a very great height, two complementary "cities" stand out, one defined by the other. The first, the most visually striking, called "Slab City"[3] by modern planners, consists of two jagged mounds of high-rise office buildings which emerge from downtown and midtown Manhattan. Total area: 9 square miles. The second, "Spread City,"[4] comprises about 5,000 miles of less intensively developed land which forms the outer ring within a 35-mile radius of Slab City. It is neither agricultural nor truly urban, but rather a sloughing off of key urban functions. Spread City is a kind of negative pole formed as much by the people and industries repelled by Slab City as by those positively attracted to it. This pattern of land use, which appears first on a world scale at about the same time in the London[5] and New York metropolitan regions has a decisive influence not only on distributive questions like taxes and minority jobs, but on the overall development of the region.

[2]Originally called the Committee on a Regional Plan of New York and Its Environs, the organization adopted its present name in 1929, after eight years of plan preparation.

[3]Regional Plan Association, *Urban Design: Manhattan* (New York: Viking, 1969), p. 21. Overbuilding not only creates monotony, but also lowers land values.

[4]Regional Plan Association, *Spread City* (New York, 1962). Crucial analysis showing how low-density development of suburbs undermines urban real-estate values. Financed by Ford, Rockefeller Brothers and Taconic foundations.

[5]In Great Britain, the Town Planning Institute is established under private auspices in 1914 with the aim of controlling land use in the London metropolitan region. An explicit aim is the expulsion of industry from inner urban locations. Peter Hall, *Urban and Regional Planning* (New York: Halsted, 1975), pp. 37–41.

The unprecedented system of highways designed by the RPA in the 1920s, the hub-bound transportation system which makes Spread City possible, massively accelerates the suburbanization of the area, raises land values, increases the overall amount of ground rent paid as a portion of the total regional expenditures. It also helps to undermine the existing transit and transportation system, replacing a single more or less efficient rail network with two less efficient systems: the high-cost truck network and the depreciated, semipublic Conrail operation. This development, of course, imposes hidden costs on production, forcing industry out of the region. Finally, while the wealth of the region grows, an increasing portion is transferred from industry and commodity production to landowners, chiefly in financial institutions, which sink more and more of the region's capital into unproductive investments in real estate.[6] The rate of capital accumulation slows. Signs of regional stagnation appear.

The polarized pattern of land use and its consequences which we observe in the NYMR also characterize other cities in which land is privately owned. But nowhere in the world is the polarization so intense. This intensity cannot be explained as the simple outcome of plans laid by bankers and planning experts in the 1920s. But the proposals drafted at this time, and realized chiefly in the 1930s and 1940s, will, as we shall see, create the essential infrastructure for the development of Spread City and Slab City alike.

(2) Just as the Five Year Plan gave a focus to Soviet leaders' efforts to accelerate the accumulation of state capital in the producer-goods industry at the expense of consumer goods, the plan for the NYMR set priorities for the city's business leadership. The single emphasis was to be placed on the upbuilding of New York City as a "national center."[7] As the National Center or America's Front

[6] I am using the term "real estate" here to refer to private property in land, not to the buildings on the land which are also privately owned. Investment in buildings increases wealth, investment in land does not; it is merely a kind of toll that the capitalists in the construction industry must pay to the landowners in order to commence operations.

[7] *The Graphic Regional Plan,* Vol. I (New York, 1929), p. 173. See also the latest planning effort of municipal authorities, the Lindsay administration's *Plan for New York City* (New York City Planning Commission, 1969). It is entirely based on the concept of New York City as the national center. "As never before, [New York] is the national center of the United States. It is headquarters for a large share of its major corporations; it is the capital of its financial markets; it is the center of its communications . . . Here is the engine. And it is getting stronger." Against those who argue that concentration must be stopped or limited, the plan argues that "concentration is the

Office[8] the city not only added to its skyline, but its leading citizens positioned themselves to serve as landlords and bankers to the growing number of national and multinational corporations that began to locate in the city. Of the surplus value produced nationally and internationally, New York would get its share in the form of rents, mortgages, construction loans on high-rise office buildings, and in the appreciation of the world's highest land values. (This would augment and complement the share of wealth New York received from its unproductive role as money-market capital.) To achieve this grand objective a plan had to be developed that was at least regional in design. The surrounding region was required first as a receptacle for those urban functions that fit poorly into the national-center strategy. New Jersey, for example, was needed, if only as a place to put the fume-spewing chemical industry. In addition, the public costs, if not the revenues prerequisite to the creation and maintenance of the national center, had to be diffused across as wide a territory as possible. Otherwise they would tend to fall exclusively on New York property holders—i.e., on those who directly benefited from the public improvements.

The problem of shifting the infrastructural costs is particularly serious, since investment in real estate depends more heavily on a public, tax-supported economic infrastructure than practically any other sphere of private investment. Moreover, the form which real-estate investment takes in New York—speculative office buildings—imposes unusually heavy infrastructural costs. Now add on to these costs those required to compete with other cities in the urban market for elite office headquarters, to attract top "decision makers" and their white-collar retinues, and the regional focus of the plan becomes more comprehensible.

So, too, does the city's present "fiscal crisis." In the late 1960s and 1970s, downtown and midtown real-estate operators, lured by rents that were increasing as much as 100 percent a year, added more office-building capacity to the city's stock than in any previous period of expansion. The necessary infrastructural expenses rose correspond-

---

genius of the City." The plan is dedicated to Lawrence M. Orton, a former head of the RPA before he became commissioner of the City Planning Commission.

[8]The phrase comes from Citibank's analysis of the New York metropolitan region, "Metro New York" (1974). City Investing Company, a real-estate subsidiary of Citibank, has been a major landlord throughout the last twenty years in Metropolitan New York.

COMPARATIVE FINANCE[1] (thousands of dollars)

48 Largest Cities	New York City		NYC as % of 48 largest
Population, 1973 (est.)	39,444,976	7,646,818	19.3
Revenue, Total	27,342,346	11,872,473	43.3
Revenue, Own Sources	13,740,583	5,460,066	40.2
Gross Debt Outstanding	31,672,250	13,508,723	42.7
Long Term Debt Outstanding	26,301,328	9,808,248	37.2
Housing and Urban Renewal	3,061,363	2,423,645	79.0
Transit	2,046,906	2,024,358	99.0

Source: U.S. Department of Commerce, Department of the Census, "Finances of the 48 Largest Cities in Detail, 1973–1974." September, 1975

[1]Analysis of the city's debt shows that capital borrowings, not borrowing to finance deficits in the expense budget, constitutes the majority of the long-term debt. Housing and transit together constitute almost 50 percent of the total. The extent to which New York "overborrows" on these items can be inferred from the table: New York borrows almost 80 percent of all the money borrowed by the 48 largest cities for housing; 99 percent for transit.

---

ingly: expenses for mass transit to speed suburban-based office workers to and from their residences,[9] subsidized housing for the middle- and upper-middle class office workers which had the economic effect of lowering labor costs for corporate employers,[10] expenses for "industrial development," which removed industry from Manhattan and pushed it into the urban periphery. It was these *capital* expenditures that generated the largest portion of the city's debt, not the more widely known and deplored expenditures for welfare and municipal workers' salaries, which show up on the expense budget.[11] The collapse of the speculative-office-building boom,[12] the shake-out in the

[9]"It must never be forgotten that future growth of the skyscraper community is tied to the mass transit web which serves it." Edgar M. Hoover and Raymond Vernon, *Anatomy of a Metropolis* (Cambridge: Harvard University Press, 1959), p. 112. This study and nine companion volumes were part of the background analysis commissioned by the RPA for the Second Regional Plan and financed by the Ford and Rockefeller Brothers foundations.

[10]"New York City has not faced up to the need for upper and middle income housing for employees of corporate headquarters. That's the reason corporations are moving away." So said the New York regional director of the Housing and Urban Development Department (HUD) prior to the Mitchell-Lama (middle-class, limited-profit) housing boom.

[11]See figures in table above.

[12]The existence of a speculative-office-building boom is a business-cycle phenomenon. It is a sign of a plethora of capital. Surplus capital which can no longer find profitable channels in industry because of limitations in "effective demand" seeks extraordinary outlets. The demand for greater luxury by corporate decision makers

bank-sponsored Real Estate Investment Trust "industry," the absolute fall in real-estate values and the consequent shrinkage of the municipal tax base—all this pressing against the greatly increased infrastructural expenditure ensured the city's financial debacle.

In other words, we can understand the financial collapse of the city and its failure to participate in the modest national recovery of 1976 as a consequence of the peculiar role that the city has sought to play over the last fifty years or so. The national-center strategy pushes out industry, requires an enormous infrastructure, and generates very heavy debt. Let us examine, then, the origins of the national center strategy, the factors that shaped the planners' outlooks, the economic circumstances that framed their need for a plan. Of course it must be realized that the national-center strategy did not arise solely because of the 1929 plan. It arose because of the tripling of office space in the 1920s finally achieved for the real-estate industry a critical mass which enabled it to dominate the local field of economic force. Nineteen twenty-nine, the year of the plan, was also, it should be remembered, the year of the construction of the Empire State Building, the Chrysler Building, and most important of all, Rockefeller Center.[13] The plan may only have been a reflection of the city's overall capital structure, which was so heavily weighted with investments in real estate and finance; the planners themselves may only have been, in Marx's phrase, "personified capital." But it is in the plan that this personified real estate and finance capital finds the most conscious expression of its needs and aims.

---

creates a need for increased office space. At the same time, credit from institutional mortgage makers loosens. Finally, helping to account for the boom was a tax policy which sheltered income from real-estate investments, so that even projects which failed to profit "earned," or more precisely promised to earn, substantial income for high bracket investors through rapid depreciation. Perhaps, too, "syndication" of the equity in these speculative office buildings enabled the developers to attract more capital than would have been otherwise possible.

[13]Comprising now about 9 million square feet of office space and twenty-two individual high-rise office buildings, Rockefeller Center holds about 10 percent of all of Manhattan's midtown office space. It is very probably the largest single investment of the Rockefeller family. With rents of $10 to $15 a square foot, gross income would range somewhere between $100 million and $150 million yearly. Unlike the family investment in oil companies, in which the members' equity is continually diluted, Rockefeller Center is 100 percent family owned. Highly knowledgeable sources say that the family constitutes the city's largest landlord interest.

NEW YORK'S FIRST PLANNERS

What distinguished the New York regional plan from much subsequent and less consequential capitalist planning is that it provided for actual physical planning, not "indicative planning." The New York planners were not content to prescribe general macro targets for the economy, or merely indicate what they believed ought to be the desired level of investment in this or that industry. Instead, they made extremely detailed proposals about the construction of highways, the locations of parks, the redevelopment of neighborhoods.

Ordinary indicative planning lacks authority because the government planners have no legal control over private capital investment.[14] With New York's regional plan, the situation is seemingly the reverse. The private capitalists who sponsored the plan had no legal control over the public investment required for the realization of their highway and park proposals. But the very detailed nature of the plan, the investment in specialized skills, indicates a confidence that leverage could be exerted over the public-investment process not only at a city level, but at state and federal levels as well.[15]

The composition of the original Regional Plan Committee largely justified that confidence. Not in the simple "power structure" frame of reference, which sees power flowing automatically from lists of boards of directors of big corporations and banks. The first planners *were* attached to the city's largest banks, foundations and newspapers. But it is relatively easy to raise committees of this sort. Often, however, their organization guarantees nothing more than an aggregation of well-fed mediocrity. In contrast, the ten-man Regional Plan Committee had several members who embodied the most advanced thinking of their class: men who could read Progressives like Herbert Croly in the original without waiting for the translation into Lippmannese. More than half the directors represented institutions like J. P. Morgan & Co., the Rockefeller Institute and the First National Bank of New York. But even these men, rather than being mere inheritors of wealth, tended to be individuals of ability co-opted into

[14]In Europe, this generalization must be modified to take into account the nationalization of banks and industry. Of the major capitalist countries, the United States has the least admixture of state capitalism.

[15]The staff work was financed by a $1,186,768 grant from the Russell Sage Foundation. John M. Glenn, *et al.*, *Russell Sage Foundation* (New York, 1947), p. 691.

their positions in finance or corporate life after having achieved some success elsewhere. This was certainly true, for example, of Dwight Morrow, the scholarly lawyer who accepted J. P. Morgan's offer to join the firm in mid-life. Morrow's experience in the reorganization of the Interborough Rapid Transit Company (IRT) qualified him as something of a transportation authority; and the knowledge and contacts he gained in 1914, during the effort he led to save the city from its foreign creditors, must have aided the committee greatly.[16]

Within the business "community," Charles D. Norton, of the First National Bank of New York, was probably the key instigator, despite the fact that he died in 1923, six years before the plan was made public. Norton, a transplanted Chicagoan, had been president of the Chicago Commercial Club, the organization which financed and sponsored Daniel Burnham's "City Beautiful" plan in 1909. Norton later wrote to his colleague in the Chicago-plan venture, Frederick Delano: "When I first came to New York in 1911, our efforts for the Chicago Plan were still fresh in mind. The thought kept recurring that New York should have a plan and should take a vital interest in it."[17] What Norton brought from Chicago was the Burnham technique of using parks and highways to transform the class character of neighborhoods in the interest of real-estate values. In addition, there was the germ of regionalism in the Chicago plan despite the fact that it was pretty nearly limited to the lakefront region. In order to increase landholders' monopoly control, the Chicago planners foresaw the need for land-use control within a 30-mile radius of the Loop. The subsequent creation of the Cook County Forest Preserve has to be understood more as a mechanism for preserving land values than for saving trees.

Norton's cohort in the organization of the Chicago plan, Frederick

[16]In the bailout operation of 1914 which was headed by Morgan and supervised by Morrow, the lending syndicate turned a profit of over $2 million, which was shared between the City of New York and the bankers' syndicate. The participating banks refused to accept any commissions for these services. That, of course, was the age of the Robber Barons. But if they were robber barons, what are we to call New York City's present benefactors—David Rockefeller, Felix Rohatyn, *et al.*? Since they undertook to "save" the city last year, debt service has approximately doubled, to an amount in excess of $2 billion a year. (For more on the city's 1914 financial crisis and Morrow's role, see Harold Nicolson, *Dwight Morrow* [New York, 1935], pp. 167–171.)

[17]Norton to Delano, November 24, 1921. Cited in Forbes B. Hays, *Community Leadership: The Regional Plan Association* (New York: Columbia University Press, 1965), pp. 7–8.

Delano, served also as a director of the New York plan committee. An uncle of FDR, Delano worked his way through a series of increasingly responsible executive positions in railroading before becoming vice governor of the Federal Reserve Bank. Under Roosevelt, Delano became, successively, head of the Public Works Administration (not to be confused with the more controversial WPA) and head of the National Planning Board. In these positions Delano was able to give the RPA decisive federal financial help in realizing the plan. In one case Delano stopped Robert Moses from constructing a bridge at the Battery—the RPA plan called for a tunnel, less destructive to Wall Street–Whitehall land values—by persuading the War Department that Moses' bridge constituted a navigation threat.

Along with Morrow, Norton and Delano, who were affiliated with large corporate and financial institutions, there served on the original RPA board several men whose professional backgrounds and political talents made them uniquely valuable. George McAneny earns a place among these real-estate and financial illuminati because of the extremely high order of political skills he displayed in their behalf as anti-Tammany president of the Borough of Manhattan. McAneny's anti-Tammany credentials continued to be highly serviceable to the RPA throughout the 1930s in the struggle for plan fulfillment. What needs to be understood is why Tammany (or the "regular Democratic organization," as it prefers now to be called) and the planners came into continual conflict—a conflict that in the absence of independent working-class activity or movements of oppressed nationalities formed the primary substance of urban politics. Conventional accounts of the antagonism between Tammany and the "good government" and "reform" forces which RPA represented tell only half the story. And the half they tell tends to be told from the reform standpoint or within the framework of reform assumptions. It is true of course that Tammany sought to use the city's budget to generate patronage and repay political favors, and that the "good government" forces developed civil service laws to check the proclivities of Tammany-type formations. The putative reason for the Reform party's antagonism allegedly lay in their "reform ideology"—their Anglo-Saxon values of probity and distaste for the inefficiency of machine politics. While the entire notion of native Protestant ethical superiority is too absurd to discuss, we can get closer to the source of the antagonism if we ignore ideology altogether and look at the municipal budget.

The Tammany-type operation created a budget structure weighted toward service jobs and expenditures for contracts with smaller business. The RPA and the downtown Manhattan financial and corporate interests it represented favored weighting the budget with *capital* expenditures, especially those aimed specifically at realizing their infrastructural plans. The capital budget is sacred; the expense budget is profane. A compromise permitting both types of expenditures was impractical from the RPA standpoint, since it would depress the revenues it aimed to maximize by forcing an increase in the real-estate tax. McAneny, at any rate, was by 1929 a proven field commander in these politico-budgetary battles against the Tammany machine. In that year he resigned his position as executive manager of the *New York Times* to become President of the RPA.

Finally, it is important to recognize the presence of Lawson Purdy and Nelson P. Lewis among the early organizers and board members. Together with McAneny and Edward Bassett, an RPA employee who co-authored the Community Planning Study,[18] their backgrounds help to establish a basis for understanding the circumstances surrounding the formation of the RPA. The authorized history of the organization leaves us with the notion that it was formed as the result of a wonderful convergence of talented Manhattan executives who banded together, something like the Seven Samurai, to save the city from chaos and political banditry.

McAneny, the politician, Purdy, the assessor, Lewis, an engineer, and Bassett, the lawyer, were four of the most prominent leaders of the movement to establish the nation's first comprehensive zoning laws in New York City. What does zoning have to do with planning? According to the "planners oath," "zoning is merely a tool of planning."[19] But historical evidence suggests that this assessment is at least somewhat self-delusory. The first regional plan developed as a broadening of the concerns that led to the establishing of the municipal laws regulating building-size and use restrictions in Manhattan. Both sought to preserve and expand the value of real-estate capital. Planning, at least in its initial stages, can be thought of as zoning across state lines.

[18]*Regional Survey*, Vol. VII, *Neighborhood and Community Planning* (New York, 1929).

[19]Richard F. Babcock, *The Zoning Game* (Madison: University of Wisconsin Press, 1966), p. 120.

ZONING OUT INDUSTRY

The zoning "movement," of which McAneny, Purdy, Lewis and Bassett were the main activists, had as its base the city's wealthiest downtown merchants, bankers and real-estate figures. In 1907 they had formed the Fifth Avenue Association. The impetus for their effort was the desire to preserve the value of their business locations from erosion by the burgeoning garment industry. Understandably, garment manufacturers sought to locate their lofts as close to retail outlets as possible. This led to a problem seemingly more characteristic of Hindu than American society: the indignity high-caste customers had to suffer by coming in close contact with large numbers of garment workers, many of them Jewish. As one representative of the Fifth Avenue Association complained:

These buildings are crowded with their hundreds and thousands of garment workers who swarm down upon the avenue for the lunch hour . . . They stand upon or move slowly along the sidewalks and choke them up . . . and as work ends at the close of the day, thousands of these operators pour out upon the sidewalks within a short space of time, and congest the side streets with a steady stream of humanity that moves its way to the West Side . . . Shopkeepers complain bitterly of financial loss [because many] women shoppers tend to avoid the section.[20]

It was chiefly to escape these crowds of garment workers that the fashionable shops like Tiffany's and Brentano's moved northward along Fifth Avenue into the Thirties, and Forties. But the garment manufacturers and their "hordes" followed. Clearly, the situation required legal remedies. The Fifth Avenue Association first succeeded in winning Borough President McAneny to their side. In 1911 McAneny created a Fifth Avenue Commission to investigate the problem and make recommendations. Of the seven-member commission, six were members of the Fifth Avenue Association. (The seventh, Nelson Lewis, the engineer, later became staff director of the preliminary regional plan investigation.) The commission duly recommended that the garment manufacturers be frozen into their locations, and that, moreover, height and bulk limitations be imposed on the loft buildings used as factories by the garment makers. Publicly they claimed to be seeking measures to solve the health and esthetic

[20]Testimony of Bruce Falconer before the Heights of Buildings Commission, *Report* of the Commission (December 1913), pp. 52–53. Cited in S. J. Makielski, *The Politics of Zoning* (New York: Columbia University Press, 1966), p. 12.

problems caused by congestion; practically, however, they were seeking to make the lofts as uneconomic as possible.

McAneny's next step was to take the report to the Board of Estimate and win approval for the creation of a Committee on City Planning—the first official New York City planning body. The Committee on City Planning, in turn, spun off two zoning commissions. Both the First Zoning Commission and the Second Zoning Commission were headed by Edward Bassett and Lawson Purdy as chairman and vice chairman, respectively. Over the next four years the deliberations, investigations and reports of the commissions failed to generate enough political momentum to overcome the resistance of the manufacturing interest. Finally, in 1916, increasingly distressed over falling land values, the Fifth Avenue Committee gave birth to the Save New York Committee. Full-page ads in the *New York Times* and other papers asked: "Shall we save New York?" New York, they argued, needed to be saved from "unnatural and unnecessary crowding, depopulated sections, from being a city unbeautiful, from high rents, from illy [*sic*] . . . distributed taxation."

With the appeal for public support came threats against individual manufacturers. The head of the Fifth Avenue Association, Walter Stabler,[21] was also comptroller of the Metropolitan Life Insurance Company. Any garment manufacturer, he warned, who tried to cross Thirty-fourth Street would get no credit from the Metropolitan. In spring of 1916, fifty-three financial institutions signed a joint resolution giving "hearty support" to the work and plans of the Zoning Commission. In summer, the recommendations passed into law.[22]

"REFORMING" MASS TRANSIT AND HOUSING

As long as McAneny served as borough president and "Fusion" Mayor John P. Mitchell sat in Gracie Mansion, it was possible for the dominant real-estate and financial interests to work through existing municipal institutions. McAneny had created commissions on transit as well as zoning. He was able to work with Bassett (sometimes

[21]Bassett's book *Zoning* (New York: Russell Sage Foundation, 1936) is dedicated to Stabler as well as to two RPA board members, Frederick B. Pratt and Lawson Purdy. Pratt was the Brooklyn real-estate developer who later founded the Pratt Institute and who initiated Brooklyn's first planning organization.

[22]The real-estate interest had sought to push manufacturing back to Twenty-third Street, but succeeded only in getting the garment jobbers zoned south of Thirty-fourth Street.

called the "father of city planning") and with Lawson Purdy, then the city assessor, and Nelson Lewis to develop a common "reform" approach to the transit question. In the context of the early decades of the twentieth-century progressive movement, "reform" meant trying to limit the development of mass transit—especially its development into working-class neighborhoods. Of course, these progressive reformers did not come out openly against adequate transportation for working people; they declaimed against the congestion that the subways caused and against population density caused by the intensive residential development along subway lines, especially on the West Side. Such intensive development kept large numbers of workers in the city and thus in industry as well. It is no accident that the first regional plan says almost nothing at all about the New York subway system in its ten volumes.[23]

McAneny, Bassett and the other Progressives whose activities presaged the formation of the RPA shared the same objectives in their fight against tenements. Ostensibly against shoddy housing for workers, continually verbalizing about the need for workers' children to get their share of sunlight, the reformers really wanted to eliminate workers' housing on Manhattan Island. Suspicion of their alleged motives here seems quite reasonable, since they were just as much opposed to public housing which replaced the tenements and could not be faulted on the grounds that sunlight was impaired.[24] Nor did they oppose high-density construction when it meant rising land values in the central business district.

At any rate, all this important municipal reform work in zoning, transit and housing stopped dead with the election of the Tammany candidate in 1918. Charles Norton wrote to Delano "everything that

[23]Essentially the subway was built to serve West Side population centers, especially workers engaged in manufacturing. Densities were so great that the subways were built with the anticipation of profit. As industry was pushed out of the city, the West Side emphasis of the subway contributed to its downward-spiraling economics. As the East Side became concentrated with office workers and executives, the RPA began to emphasize the development of a Second Avenue (East Side) subway development.

[24]As late as 1949, the RPA was still publicly fighting tax-supported housing for workers: "There are about 1,125,000 people presently living in about 16½ square miles in New York City's blighted areas. If these areas were rebuilt with the high population densities of our recent housing projects (average 313 persons per acre) they would accommodate 3,333,000 people. This would provide for all the present population in such areas, all the anticipated increase in the entire city for decades to come and an additional 1.5 million people drawn from other parts of the city."—*New York Times* (April 4, 1949).

George McAneny had built in City Hall was swept into limbo."[25] McAneny himself lamented:

> The Mayor . . . Mr. Hylan, was very much against all of these new things. He didn't believe in them. He announced at one of the hearings down there that he didn't believe in the freaks of these "art artists" and so on. I had previously gotten $25,000 a year from the city to run the other commissions (transit and zoning) and it was repeated with this one. Hylan commissioned to have it cut off so that there was nothing left.[26]

The same year that McAneny's transit, planning and zoning funds were cut off by the Tammany mayor, Charles Norton succeeded in getting a directorship on the Russell Sage Foundation—a foundation legally required to dispense a portion of its funds for municipal improvement. Shortly afterward he submitted to the Russell Sage Board his request for major funding for the proposed regional plan. The New York plan was a privately sponsored plan because the Fusion forces had lost their political base. But there was hardly a major city in the United States where planning was not strictly a privately sponsored, privately organized affair confined mainly to business, financial and real-estate circles, with a thin layer of planning professionals that tended to thicken over time.[27] The planning "movement," which was a current in the larger stream of Progressivism, shared with that ideology an impatience with market forces, a desire to transcend them through state regulation. But it was in no sense a popular movement, or a movement directed against big business. As we have seen, planning emerged as a congealing of several separate antipopular intitiatives in zoning, transit and housing. Let us now look at the New York regional plan itself: its objectives, ideology and methods.

[25]Norton to Delano, November 24, 1921. Cited in Hays, op. cit., p. 10.

[26]George McAneny, Reminiscences (New York: Columbia University Oral History Project), pp. 37–38. Cited in Hays, op. cit., p. 10.

[27]According to Walter D. Moody, former director of the Chicago Plan Commission: "Rarely in this country is city planning work initiated by the municipal government. Where this is the case the highest degree of success is not attained. The best results have been had where the city planning movement originated with a group of substantial public-spirited citizens or under the auspices of commercial or civic organizations."—"How to go about City Planning," in The City Plan Quarterly (March 1915). Cited in Harold MacLean Lewis, Planning the Modern City, Vol. II (New York: Wiley, 1949), p. 134.

AIMS OF THE PLAN

Someone looking for a fundamental point of departure to contrast Soviet and New York regional planning in 1929 would be poorly advised to seek it out in doctrinal differences between socialism and capitalism. "Socialism" is nothing more than "a community of free individuals, carrying on their work with the means of production in common."[28] But even so, it is nothing less. For while the socialist society apportions labor according to a definite social plan, the apportionment can only be based on the *democratically expressed needs of the producers*. And while the Soviets rely to a greater extent than the Manhattanites on mobilizing popular support, both plans are formulated and executed in classic bureaucratic fashion. The technical information goes from the bottom to the top, and the planning decisions from the top down. The aims of the plans are not politically debatable because the aims could not survive a free debate. In neither case do we have socialist planning, because nowhere are the producers capable of subjecting the forces of production to an autonomous human law.[29] In the United States, the relations of production, and in the Soviet Union the relatively weak forces of production, compel both sets of planners to emphasize what they must: capital accumulation. The Soviets seek to accumulate state capital; the regional planners seek to use the state to aid them in their efforts to accumulate private capital. But if the mere domination of the state over production makes Stalin's Russia socialist, then we should also unfurl the red banners for Pharaoh's Egypt.

The real point of departure between Soviet and American regional planning is not that one is "socialist" and the other is "capitalist." Both represent presocialist modes of production, with the United States, and the New York metropolitan region in particular, representing a more mature stage of development. The Soviet planners seek above all to expand heavy industry. The New Yorkers desire nothing so much as to expel it from the city. The Soviets de-empha-

[28]Karl Marx, *Capital*, Vol. I, p. 78.

[29]Marx's emphasis on freedom in planning is insistent: "The life process of society, which is based on the process of material production, does not strip off its mystical veil until it is treated as production by *freely associated men*, and is consciously regulated by them in accordance with a settled plan." (*Ibid.*, p. 80.) The essence of pseudosocialism is to alter the phrase "regulated by them" to "regulated by some of them."

size consumer goods and light industry, but the regional planners are only a shade less hostile to these forms of production—or indeed warehousing, wholesale marketing—than they are toward heavy industry. At best, they seek to contain its development through zoning.

An economic plan hostile to manufacturing sounds like a forerunner of the present-day ecology movements, or of those who seek to limit production to the scale of existing "natural" resources[30] according to the slogan "Small is beautiful." These modern movements, whether consciously or not, are objectively opposed to capital which must expand or die. The regional planners, however, are not. They are only hostile to the growth of one form of capital—industry. How can this be true, given the business credentials of the planning board's directors? The answer is that industry is scarcely represented on the board at all. The single industrial representative is an official of the Otis Elevator Company, a corporation not likely to be hostile to the plan's national-center concept. But this raises a further political question: New York in 1929 was not only the country's greatest financial and office-building center, it was also the nation's largest manufacturing center. How is it that manufacturing had no representation in the planning process?

The likely answer here is that the region's truly significant manufacturing interest, the first concentrated and centralized industries, e.g., Standard Oil of New York and Standard Oil of New Jersey,[31] had already, because of their space needs, located not only outside Manhattan, but outside the city.[32] The remaining producers, while economically significant in the aggregate, were made up almost exclusively of small firms. The garment industry is typical of the small manufacturing interest that was hanging on and thriving in Manhattan during the 1920s. In 1919 it was the nation's largest industry in

[30]As if human insight into natural laws and the capability for producing according to to these laws were not also a natural force!

[31]The present Mobil and Exxon, respectively.

[32]Analysis of the chemical and refining industries showed that the factories were pushed out of the city by their need for cheaper land—or attracted to less densely settled areas, to put the matter positively. In 1912, the regional survey showed, almost half the chemical plants employing 20 workers or more were on land worth more than $1,000 per front foot. By 1922 the percentage had dropped to about one quarter. While Manhattan chemical plants were all restricted to less than an acre in size, only 25 percent of those located in New Jersey were so constricted. A sizable percent occupied 100 acres or more.—*Regional Survey*, Vol. IA, *Chemical, Metal, Wood, Tobacco and Printing Industries* (New York, 1928), p. 20.

terms of wage earners. It ranked second to steel in value added by manufacture. It was also the city's largest, with 125,000 employees in the ladies' garment industry alone. Of all city workers engaged in manufacture, one in six worked on ladies' garments. At the same time, the city's share of this growing industry also increased. In 1869 about one third of the ladies' garments produced in the United States were being manufactured in the city. By 1929 the total had reached three quarters. In only one year—the depression year of 1919—did the share not expand. Yet as late as 1922 there were only 3 out of 323 plants in the industry which employed more than 500 employees. More than 45 percent employed fewer than 10 workers. Why the garment industry resisted concentration, why the jobber system prevailed, are questions we cannot take up. But these individual jobbers in the garment industry were evidently felt to be too small to be worth co-opting.

The planners felt the same way about the garment industry that the zoners felt, which is not surprising, since they were the same people. The lofts pre-empted higher-value development; the workers clogged mass-transit lines; housing for workers impeded the development of housing for nonworkers who could afford higher rents, etc. In a word, what was at stake was land use. And if there is one criticism that cannot be made of these first planners, it is that they underestimated the significance of the land question. Here, in fact, is the major positive contribution of the plan: it properly attributed to land use its place as the fundamental question in urban political economy. Indeed, the entire plan rested on the assumption that "the manner in which land is used and in which the functions and bulks of buildings upon the land are distributed . . . lies at the root of all urban problems." Urban problems become those obstacles which develop to prevent land values and the rents upon which the values are based from rising. The outlook of the plan was bluntly expressed: "The area of New York and its environs may be likened to the floor space of a factory. Regional planning designates the best use of this floor space.[33] If we understand "best" as "most profitable," this simile may be understood quite literally. The directors of the regional plan wanted to rent the millions of square feet of available space at the highest possible price.

[33] *Regional Survey*, Vol. I, *Major Economic Factors in Metropolitan Growth and Arrangement* (New York, 1927), p. 18.

But what about manufacturing? Didn't garment manufacturers pay rent for their lofts? Didn't they all, even if they owned the building in which they manufactured, pay ground rent? The answer was yes, but not enough. The planners devoted an entire volume of analysis to showing how much is not enough.[34] What they discovered was that the competitive uses of land in New York assumed the following order of precedence: (1) the financial district, (2) the best retail business, (3) the best residence, (4) inferior retail business, neighborhood shops, (5) wholesaling and some industries, (6) other industries, residences for low-paid workers.[35] Recognition of these priorities in land values prompted the planners to record this observation on the irrationality of capitalism south of Fifty-ninth Street:

Some of the poorest people live in conveniently located slums on high priced land. On patrician Fifth Avenue, Tiffany and Woolworth, cheek by jowl, offer jewels and jimcracks from substantially identical sites. Child's Restaurants [the Chock-Full of-Nuts of its day?] thrive where Delmonico's withered and died. A stone's throw from the stock exchange the air is filled with the aroma of roasting coffee; a few hundred feet from Times Square, with the stench of slaughter-houses. In the very heart of this "commercial" city on Manhattan Island south of 59th street, the inspectors in 1922 found nearly 420,000 workers employed in factories. *Such a situation outrages one's sense of order.* Everything seems misplaced. *One yearns to re-arrange the hodgepodge and to put things where they belong.* (Emphasis added.)[36]

This yearning for rearrangement in the breast of the real-estate man is somehow inserted in the heart of the professional planner as a kind of occupational pacemaker which regulates his ordinary activity. Regardless of subjective aim, planning in New York comes down simply to seeing to it that conditions are created in which land use #1—office buildings—is expanded and maintained, and in which land use #6, various nuisance industries and nuisance classes (i.e., workers), is pushed into the urban periphera.

While the City Beautiful of Burnham gives way to the City Rentable of the real-estate and financial industry, it ought not to be supposed that the ability of a land use #1 to prevail over a land use #6 is strictly a function of planning or urban politics. Given the greater

[34]*Regional Survey,* Vol. II, *Population, Land Values and Government* (New York, 1929).

[35]*Regional Survey,* Vol. IB, *Food, Clothing and Textile Industries, Wholesale Markets and Retail Shopping, and Financial Districts* (New York, 1928), p. 12.

[36]*Regional Survey,* Vol. I, *Major Economic Factors . . . ,* p. 31.

profit potential—in terms of rent per square foot—of a financial district over a district housing workers, it will be impossible over the long run to maintain the land use for workers' housing. Landlords can be bought out, existing structures raised and the premium sales price absorbed through the greatly increased rents and capital appreciation generated by the new land use. Why this should be true is a function of the different ways in which space is utilized by office bureaucracies and manufacturing plants. Take for example the automobile industry and commercial banking. The sixty-five-story Chase Manhattan Bank building (including five below street level) occupies 1 million square feet at its location in lower Manhattan. The Volkswagen Corporation has recently announced that it is seeking 1 million square feet of plant space, all on one level, for a new U.S. assembly plant. If somehow VW were able to get a variance to build its plant in Manhattan, it would occupy nearly 5 percent of the total area south of Central Park. If it were to locate in the immediate area next to the Chase, the cost of land alone would total about $600 million (assuming insuperable technical barriers to the construction of vertical assembly lines).

All this helps to explain some of the familiar preoccupations of twentieth-century urban planning: the passion for the eradication of slums, which is seldom matched in intensity by a desire to erect low-cost public housing on the old clearance site; the inconsistent embrace of high-rise office buildings, and the distaste for high-rise solutions to workers' housing problems; the dedication to public parks, especially those which pre-empt competitive or lower land usages; its appeal to the ecological and esthetic values of the middle and upper-middle classes, who have little stake in inner-city factory and warehouse jobs, to justify industrial displacement.

Whether a more advanced, more democratic society would also decide to concentrate industrial jobs in the suburbs is not the point.[37] What needs to be understood is that behind the planners' expressed concern, however genuine, for urban beauty, workers' health, recreation, sunlight, etc., there lies *necessarily* the pressing need to maintain and expand land values—values whose appreciation requires a thinning out of the existing population of workers, and an expulsion of the the industry which lies south of Fifty-ninth Street. Given

[37]But it would be hard not to improve on an industrial-location policy that shuffles office workers from the suburbs to the city and requires industrial workers to drive from the city to the suburbs, while those who have no cars compete for the remaining jobs.

enough time, it is true that capitalism would solve this problem on its own. Space needs of industry will force it out; lack of jobs will drive out the remaining industrial workers. Supply and demand will finally, perhaps in fifty or one hundred years, equilibriate. The problem of the handloom weavers was "solved" during the nineteenth century in similar fashion.

Just as it was the destiny of the handloom weavers to endure an even more oppressive fate than the rest of their class in the transition from petty production to industrialism, the transition from manufacturing to "postindustrial society" is marked by the special victimization of the Afro-Americans. The black workers, unable to follow the white workers to the suburbs where factory jobs are located, must compete in increasing numbers for the remaining service-industry jobs in the inner city. Relative overpopulation forces these inner-city wages below the socially necessary costs which would enable the worker to sustain himself and his family. "Welfare" necessarily emerges—not truly as a subsidy to the poor, but as an indirect subsidy to the capitalists in the service industry, enabling them to pay below-subsistence wages. To this, the additional humiliation is imposed on the black worker that his children and the mother of his children are rendered ineligible for "welfare" if he is "in the house."

The distorted movements of population, the special burdens imposed upon industry, and the dictation of land use by the capacity to pay rent, all help to show that the regional plan is no more rational than the market process it is designed to accelerate. The planners simply aim to increase the polarization of capital which takes, as we have seen, the form of high-rise buildings at one end and industry at the other. The singular misfortune of the blacks is to have gotten caught between the poles.

THE SWEET MYSTERY OF RISING LAND VALUES

Given the far-reaching consequences of the physical polarization of capital, it becomes crucial to understand something of its dynamics. The regional planners of the 1920s were aware in their own dim way that such a process exists. They observed, for example, that "the best retail merchants have the economic power to capture practically any site outside the financial district"[38] which they deemed desirable.

---

[38]"In New York the concentration of national and international interests has led to pyramiding values in Wall Street which are, on the whole, the highest known anywhere."—*Regional Survey*, Vol. IB, *Food, Clothing . . .* , p. 18.

The luxury-goods merchants, they said, can even "usurp" the residential locations of the very rich. Similarly, just as financial and high-grade retail uses crowd out industry, the planners noted that housing for the rich tends to crowd out housing for the poor. They showed that in the 1920s the south of Fourteenth Street district's population had dropped nearly 160,000, and that the drop consisted entirely of slum dwellers. "Apparently," they concluded, "the well-to-do are not being crowded out; they may be doing some of the crowding."[39]

On the one hand, the planners looked at the polarization process as a kind of providential force which steadily lifted the values of their landholdings, added to the value of mortgages and swept away obstacles to the accumulation of real-estate capital. On the other, they sought to develop a scientific analysis of the "cause" of land values. This analysis, however, was just an agglomeration of empirical factors: street widenings and open spaces increase value, as do large-scale public improvements; crowding and traffic congestion tend to lower values. Most of their hypotheses—unexceptionable as empirical observations—have to do with physical location of the land itself.

While the authors of the regional plan may have grasped only rather weakly the ultimate causal factors in land valuation, they had the tightest imaginable grip on actual Manhattan land prices. This knowledge took the form of a series of meticulously drawn historical maps of the area. Each block in the borough is colored in terms of land values. Mauve-colored blocks are worth $6 to $25 per front foot. Pink indicates $26 to $100, all the way up to the black-colored blocks, which represent land worth over $5,000 per front foot. The maps were placed in historical sequence to show the gradual spread of the black areas and the gradual shrinkage of the low-value mauve districts. The mauve areas are the workers' residential districts and factory areas. The highest peak is achieved in midtown, with land worth $27,000 per front foot. The only exceptions to the general rise in values occurs on the East Side and between 116th and 125th streets "due," said the planners, "to the extension of the negro district."[40]

In fact, the price of land is simply a capitalization of the rent. And the price rises and falls inversely with movements in the interest rate. Thus a rent of $1 million a year is going to give land a value of $10

---

[39]*Regional Survey*, Vol. I, *Major Economic Factors* . . . , p. 35.

[40]*Regional Survey*, Vol. II, *Population, Land Values and Government*, p. 149.

million if the interest rate is 10 percent. If the interest rate falls to 5 percent, the land will be worth $20 million. It is this ground rent which forms the basis of building speculation, not the actual construction of the high-rise office buildings on which the rate of profit is generally subject to the equalization process. The ground rent, or "fee," is the safest and most desirable institutional investment.[41] It is the safest because the "fee" is the first expense paid by the building owner; it is the most desirable because the landowner pockets the fee with even less effort than the capitalist appropriates surplus value. At a minimum, the capitalist must hire managers who refrain from robbing him; workers must be "managed"; fluctuations in raw-material prices can shave profit margins; the weather can interrupt the process of production; and there is always the overhanging problem of realization. With ground rent, the fee holder can look to the future with an unfurrowed brow: producing nothing of value, he is able to appropriate the productivity of others as a consequence of his personal monopoly of a portion of our planet. It is a characteristic of urban landownership that it is increasingly able to appropriate a share of these values, which were created without its assistance, and that an increasing share of the surplus value in the housing and office-building industry is transformed into ground rent. Marx's dictum of one hundred years ago scarcely needs modification: "The sole activity of the landlord is the exploitation of social progress to which he contributes nothing."[42]

What location, population density, etc., help to explain is not rent, but differential rent and rent based on a monopolization of a certain area which enables the owner to extract a portion of the profit which would ordinary accrue to the building capitalist who is renting uniquely located space.[43]

---

[41]William Zeckendorf, *Zeckendorf* (New York: Harper, 1970), pp. 138–152.

[42]*Capital*, Vol. III, p. 639. See also pp. 773–781, "Building Site Rent. Rent in Mining. Price of Land." Also David Ricardo, *Principles of Political Economy and Taxation* (New York: Dutton, 1933), chapter 2: "The rise of rent is always the effect of the increasing wealth of the country . . . It is a symptom, but it is never a cause of wealth; for wealth often increases most rapidly while rent is either stationary, or even falling."

[43]The question of whether a Marxian absolute rent obtains in the office-building industry hangs on the solution to two empirical questions: (1) the organic composition of capital in the office-building construction industry; (2) existence of barriers to an averaging of the rate of profit created by landed property. With respect to the latter question, it is part of the strategy of landowners of urban property to try to get the

ORIGINS OF PLANNING IDEOLOGY

The process whereby the planners rationalized their efforts to decentralize the city helps us to understand the functional importance of American pragmatism in contemporary political discourse, and how it fused self-interest with a particularly shallow concept of science into an ideological amalgam that effectively transcends rational assessment and political responsibility. Here is the problem: in order to accumulate real-estate capital, it is necessary to get rid of workers and industry. But this is not Cambodia. How could the planners justify the process of expulsion in a way that was somehow consistent with America's democratic assumptions? Who makes the decision about who is to go and who is to stay? Who chooses the criterion? How? Here is the solution:

"One of the most stupendous dreams of the social control of civilization concerns the remaking of cities. It is proposed to decentralize them deliberately. By removing obstacles or interposing deflecting factors, the decentralization which is actually going on may be guided, accelerated and focused. This is the meaning of modern city planning. In the process of deliberate decentralization, *science* is ultimately to decide what elements in the present city ought to remain and what ought to go."[44] "Science," however, turns out to be the observation of "the competitive struggle for urban sites." From the results of the marketplace struggle we "glimpse the outlines of an economically ideal pattern or plan." To see what *is* being crowded out of the choice central locations is the same thing as to make the judgment as to what *ought* to be crowded out. Here we have a taut expression of American pragmatism: whatever "works" is good; where "works" is defined as whatever is at least temporarily profitable. That this is too shallow a criterion even for business decisions is revealed every time the cycle turns and what seems to have worked turns out not to have worked at all, and the hot commodities are instantly turned into cold inventory. Still more obviously inadequate is the reduction of science to mere observation.[45]

---

city to create public parks in order to limit the ability of competitors to raise structures on otherwise available land.

[44]*Regional Survey*, Vol. I, *Major Economic Factors . . .* , pp. 31–32.

[45]It might be argued that this is a reductive interpretation of American pragmatism —that this is mere social Darwinism. Leftist pragmatists will point to Dewey the

Science, however, is sometimes an indifferent guide in real-estate matters. Often we observe that the results of competition are unfavorable in terms of what our intuition tells us. Certain activities "belong"; they are congenial to the city.[46] These congenial activities are "managing and administering, buying and selling, financing and risk-bearing, investigating and advising." What does not belong is manufacturing. Do we discover this by an unflinching appraisal of the results of the competitive marketplace? Not precisely. Because when we do, we discover that while some manufacturing activities are indeed being pushed toward outer areas of the city (e.g., metals and tobacco) and others, like the chemical industry, are pushed to the outer reaches of the region, there are still some industries that either hold their own or actually increase their hold, e.g., garments and printing.

Despite the competitive success of the garment industry, however, the planners said, it will have to go. "Obviously," they wrote, "the clothing industry should not be permitted to spoil the choice shopping district by flooding the shopping streets with throngs of non-buying pedestrians. Again it should not be permitted to block the avenues leading to the shopping district with vehicles which prevent the flow of merchandise and shoppers into the shopping center. Further it should not be permitted to pre-empt the transit facilities to the detriment of the shoppers and the employees of merchandising and establishments."

Why trucks carrying bolts of cloth to workshops are inherently

socialist. But here is Dewey, writing on social planning in about the same year as the publication of the regional plan: "Here lies the heart of our present social problem. Science has hardly been used to modify man's fundamental acts and attitudes in social matters . . . To hold that . . . organized planning is possible only in a communistic society is to surrender the case to communism. Were we to forget for the moment the special Russian political setting, we should see here an effort to use co-ordinated knowledge and technical skill to direct economic resources toward social order and stability." (*The Philosophy of John Dewey,* Vol. II, John McDermott, ed. [New York: Putnam, 1973], p. 393; (from *Philosophy and Civilization* [New York, 1931].) Note the similar linkage of science and planning, with Dewey and the regional planners. This is possible because they have a similar pragmatic understanding of the meaning of science. Reason and abstraction are extruded from this activity. In its place we find "experience." Thus science becomes subjectivized to a testing of our individual experience, and the line between what is and what we would like to be blurs significantly. This is perhaps the most important function of the "open philosophy," the "open classroom," the "open society." Anything will fit.

[46]*Regional Survey,* Vol. I, *Major Economic Factors . . .* , p. 33.

more congesting than trucks carrying finished merchandise to retail shops, why the garment workers pre-empt the transit facilities of salespeople and not vice versa is immediately comprehensible only from the standpoint of scientific real-estate consciousness. This same "science" attributes the adhesiveness of the garment industry in the central business district to its Jewish character: it is the nature of the Jew to be clannish; one Jewish businessman goes uptown; they all tend to follow, etc., etc. Not only are the Jewish garment activities undesirable, but the consequent Jewish presence in Manhattan gives rise to the need for kosher slaughterhouses on the East Side which depress real-estate values there.

The Jewish-dominated garment industry thus presents a disturbing challenge to the universality of planning criteria. On the one hand, whatever triumphs in the market is good; on the other, the garment industry also triumphs. (Clearly, this is no time for inane academic talk about Pareto optimality: something serious is at stake—real-estate values.) Here is the way planning science resolves the dilemma: "The forces of competition do tend to approximate the ideal layout and the trends in operation are the surest indication as to what is economically sound. However (here comes the antistrophe)," the trends are the result of the individual decisions of persons in search of dollars of profit. It so happens that unless social control is exercised, unless zoning is fully and skillfully applied, it is entirely possible for an individual to make for himself a dollar of . . . profit, but at the same time cause a loss of many dollars to his neighbors and to the community as a whole, so that the social result is a net loss."[47] Social control must be exercised so that the gains of capitalist A do not take place at the expense of capitalist B—especially in those instances where capitalist A is small and B is large. This is the new meaning of competition. Its tool is zoning and regional planning. These will prevent "the parasitic encroachment of lower functions upon the facilities of higher functions."

Here we have an important result of the scientific analysis of land usage: a reappraisal of the classical bourgeois attitude toward production. The "lower function," according to the analysis, is production; the "higher function" is circulation and financial services. This becomes the nucleus of the modern service economy or postindustrial-state ideology. The modern economist supposes that because finan-

[47] *Ibid.*, p. 44.

cial services, real estate, bureaucracy, etc., take up a larger and larger share of economic activity while national wealth increases, these activities must be the *cause* of increased economic growth, when actually their effect is to retard it. Not being "dependent" on manufacturing, according to the inverted service-economy ideology, becomes a source of strength. As late as 1972, in First National City Bank's 273-page analysis of the New York regional economy, it could be seriously argued that "[The New York region's] strong service orientation cushions it from the strongest effects of business cycles as well as from changing conditions in individual industries. Durable goods manufacturing, cyclically more sensitive, accounts for a significantly smaller share in this region than in the nation as a whole. Similarly, employment in New York City's central administrative offices is more stable than are jobs in the assembly line."[48]

What is the real relation between the evolving "service economy" which the planners seek to nourish and expand, and the productive apparatus which they seek to extrude from the city? Evidently we have nothing to learn from the economists whose wisdom is the equal of the meteorologist who bases weather forecasts on the likelihood that tomorrow will, stochastically speaking, be very much like today. Marx, on the other hand, whose analysis of production is supposed to be outdated by the advent of the postindustrial society, made an analysis which is both highly plausible and chilling in its prescience: he foresaw the service economy quite clearly. Only using the terminology of classical political economy, he described it as the rise of unproductive labor. (Labor exchanged against capital is productive; labor exchanged against revenue is unproductive.) He argued that productivity would grow so that whereas formerly two thirds of the population were engaged in producing the means of subsistence for three thirds; with the advance in productivity, only one third would be required to produce for three thirds. Similarly, whereas one third of the national income was net revenue, a more advanced society would find its net revenue increasing to two thirds (leaving out revenue of the laborers). If labor and leisure were equally distributed, the whole population would have two thirds more time for unproductive activities. Of course capitalism will not divide the leisure equally.

---

[48]*Profile of a City.* Prepared by members of the Economics Department, First National City Bank of New York (New York, 1972), p.10. In fact, the largest single category of job loss showed up in the financial-services sector during the post-1972 decline.

Instead, the two thirds not engaged in production of means of subsistence will consist of owners of profit, rent and interest, and the rest of unproductive laborers. These latter will be poorly paid because of competition. Unproductive laborers will help the capitalists to consume the revenue and in turn give them an equivalent in services. A special stratum of unproductive workers—politicians—will impose their services on the capitalists. "It can be supposed," Marx wrote, "that—with the exception of the horde of flunkeys, the soldiers, sailors, police, lower officials and so on, mistresses, grooms, clowns and jugglers—these unproductive laborers will on the whole have a higher level of culture than the unproductive workers had previously, and in particular that ill-paid artists, musicians, lawyers, physicians, scholars, schoolmasters, inventors, etc., will also have increased in number."[49]

METHODS OF DECENTRALIZATION

We have seen that the outward march of industry and industrial workers toward the economic penumbra of the city takes place at a steady straggler's pace dictated by a real-estate corollary of the law of value. The high-value usage eventually dislodges the low-value land usage. But this process, while inexorable, unfolds too slowly for the real-estate interest. To accelerate the pace of industrial expulsion, there is conceived the strategy of decentralization. The term, it should be pointed out, is something of a misnomer. Industry is targeted for relocation. But there is no intention to decentralize the capital invested in office buildings and commerical property. This notion, attributed to "social philosophers," constitutes unplanned and haphazard decentralization.[50]

The planners thus have a goal—decentralization; they have decided what is to go and what is to stay, and they have a criterion to choose by—science. Or more precisely, the results of the competition for urban space, modified by the real-estate man's intuitive sense of what "ought" to belong in the city. (An intuition which is as uncannily attuned to the uses that afford the highest rent as a dog's ear is to the highest sound frequencies.) There remains the final question of the *methods of decentralization.* Practically speaking, the decentralization of the city is rendered devilishly complex by the fact that

[49] *Theories of Surplus Value,* Part I, p. 212.

[50] *The Graphic Regional Plan,* Vol. II, *Building the City,* p. 34.

the remaining high-value usages—office buildings—have the most serious congestive effects. The planners give some consideration to limiting building bulk—through setbacks, for example; they proclaim a need to limit the number of high-rise buildings that can be built in a given area. But these limits can be defended only during a period like the 1930s, when the real-estate industry is trying to sleep off the speculative binge of the 1920s. As soon as it again becomes profitable to erect speculative office buildings, the planning regulations and zoning laws tumble like the perfectly sound but less potentially profitable structures the new multi-storied surplus-value catchers are designed to replace.

METHOD #1: RICH PEOPLE'S PARKS

How, then, is decentralization to be brought about? By two methods. The first consists in a massive development of the region's highway system, designed to accelerate suburbanization. The second is the extension of the city and regional park system. It strains credulity to see playgrounds, swimming pools and park benches as weapons used by the Establishment in the class war. But it is also utterly naive and one-sided to see the extension of the park system that took place in the 1920s and 1930s in the NYMR as a product of Robert Moses' "nice" period: when the then youthful public servant backed the Establishment into a political corner and forced its members to cough up recreation space for "the people."[51]

Besides the advancement of recreation, park creation has the happy faculty of simultaneously raising the value of surrounding land and creating substantial areas of worker-free zones. The new recreational uses, together with lowering of the density of working-class population tends to attract the middle class to the area, with their bigger rent budgets. The whole rationale, together with park plans, is laid out in Volume II of the plan entitled *Building the City,* in the section entitled "Re-planning the Lower East Side":

> While this whole area can be classified as predominantly residential, it has also for many years been an important center in the garment industry, housing many contract shops of the garment workers. Since the establishment of the new Garment Center on the West Side of Manhattan and the reduction in immigration; the garment industry has tended to move away from this district and many of the smaller non-union shops have been established in Brooklyn and Harlem. It is of great importance to the city that this

[51]See, for example, Caro, *op. cit.,* pp. 458–463.

district be improved as a residential neighborhood. It is as accessible to the downtown business district as Tudor City and Sutton Place are to the midtown district. Sites should be provided for both high class residences and modern low cost housing, leaving space for such industries as would naturally tend to remain in this district.[52]

The plan goes on to state that the factors that stand in the way of the intended transformation include the elevated transit lines; a defective street system, inadequate transit facilities. Of "special importance," however, is the insufficiency of parks, parkways and playgrounds, and means of access to the riverfront. In order to remedy this deficiency "a park of 75 acres, which would be large enough to attract good residences to the neighborhood," is suggested. The dimensions of the RPA park, stretching from approximately Fourteenth Street south, and including the existing Corlears Hook Park and extending west to Governeur Street, are congruent with today's existing park.[53]

The RPA did not expect the park to transform the character of the Lower East Side immediately. The creation of the park though, is aimed at saving the area for future, high-value residential uses.[54] As it happened, the establishment of the parks along the East River Drive finally did have the desired "holding effect" with the creation of Richard Ravitch's Waterside in the late 1960s and the positioning of important institutions like the NYU Medical Center in the vicinity.

RPA park plans for upper Manhattan have to be presented against the twin realities of the black presence in Harlem and the extensive Rockefeller property holdings along both sides of the Hudson River north of Ninety-sixth Street. The RPA shows concern about the

[52] *The Graphic Regional Plan*, Vol. II, *Building the City*, p. 400.

[53] The RPA volume in which the East Side park was outlined appeared in 1931; in 1934 LaGuardia—backed by the RPA—was elected mayor. That year he appointed Robert Moses park commissioner. In the highly unreliable account of Robert Caro, *op. cit.*, pp. 374–375, Moses is made to appear as the originator of the Lower East Side Park.

[54] Failure to move quickly with park creation meant the mislocation of Central Park in the center of the city, where it made traffic congestion inevitable; Central Park ought to have been located on the East Side, according to F.L. Olmsted, Jr. The fact that it was not grew out of short-term real-estate strategies of those who owned the waterfront land and hoped to hold on to it for commercial purposes. Of course, for a long time it languished as a stockyard; not until post–World War II did it recover, through the efforts of William Zeckendorf and the Rockefeller family which resulted in clearing for the UN.

black population. It is one of three "racial elements" discussed in the monograph on population,[55] the other two being Jews and foreign-born. The Jews and the foreign-born are becoming less numerous in Manhattan. But the blacks, who we saw earlier cause property values to decline in the RPA mode of analysis, are actually expanding their numbers. In 1928 the black population was estimated at 250,000, of which 170,000 lived in Harlem, "with a rate of increase," the planners noted, "four times as great as that of the general population."

A map of "Distribution of Negro Population in New York" depicts the concentration in Harlem rather like a swarm of black microbes straining to free itself from its test-tube vial. New York City's blacks are shown to be contained in a triangle, two sides of which form natural barriers to expansion: Central Park to the south and the Harlem River to the east. The side facing the hypotenuse, however, has no physical barrier at all. The creation of parks has the effect of stopping the spread of black population toward the Hudson and the Rockefeller–Columbia-Morningside Heights area, while development of upper Riverside Drive and the improvement of access across Inwood Hill Park—all called for in the plan—stabilize the values in the immediate area. Key to the development of the Upper West Side park system is John D. Rockefeller's gift of Fort Tryon Park—56 acres of it—to the city. And the RPA claims a role in the transfer of this land—once the Billings Estate—to the city. One of the first acts of the organization in 1923 was to get the city to try to buy it. The Rockefeller gift thus helped make possible the overarching plan for the Upper West Side, which was to create parks and parkways along all of the 7½-mile stretch from Seventy-second Street to the Bronx. This plan, which included eliminating commercial land use between 136th and 154th streets, has been completely realized.[56]

[55] *Regional Survey*, Vol. II, *Population, Land Values and Government*, pp. 104–106. Altogether five groups are distinguished. But native-born of native parents and native-born of foreign parents are not discussed.

[56] To what extent did the RPA park planners achieve their overall objectives? The official publication, *From Plan to Reality*, notes in Vol. I that between the presentation of the regional plan in 1929 and December 31, 1932, the city acquired approximately 2,440 acres of park, an increase of about 20 percent. (Note that this progress took place before Moses received his park commissioner's appointment.) "The new parks follow very closely, with few exceptions, locations proposed in the Regional Plan and in the case of Great Kills Park in Staten Island the acreage was greater than that suggested on the Plan" (p. 79.) Succeeding city administrations tended to follow RPA park recommendations concerning location. But a muted controversy developed with Moses over the amount of recreational facilities to be allowed, with the RPA taking

The RPA's plan for transforming the entire Harlem River valley has taken a good deal longer to materialize. By introducing a "liberal spaciousness of street, waterfront, boulevard, parks and parkways," the aim was to turn the Harlem River into a thoroughfare that would play the same role for the surrounding area that the Seine does for Paris and the Thames does for London. No large-scale industry or shipping was desired, but "light industry, business, transportation, marketing and auxiliary economic activities" were put forward as an alternative to the existing residential land usage.

The RPA conceded that "to a person of limited imagination the plan may seem visionary. But looking back on what has happened in twenty-five years in mid-Manhattan, we get some idea of what may happen in Northern Manhattan and lower Bronx in the next twenty-five years." Twenty-five years has proved to be too short a time frame. But recent statements by Housing Development Administration chief Roger Starr and Municipal Assistance Corporation chairman Felix Rohatyn[57] expressing the city's need to obliterate the existing communities of South Bronx and Harlem and create industrial parks in their place, indicate that the real-estate community has not ceased to dream.

METHOD #2: THE HIGHWAY PLAN

The clover-leaf crossings, the under and over-passes, the two storied roads of America, especially in and near New York, will puzzle excavators of the year A.D. 7000 as much as Karnak and Stonehenge puzzle us.

—Nicholas Pevsner[58]

The second and by far the most important—perhaps even historically decisive—method of decentralization proposed by the RPA required the imposition of a regional highway system on the NYMR

---

a "conservation" position and Moses a "recreationalist" position. See *ibid.*, Vol. II, p. V-7; and Vol. II, pp. II-6-7.

[57]Rohatyn was quoted in a recent *New York Times* interview as having said with respect to Harlem and other areas of black concentration: "take a 30-block area, clear it, blacktop it, and develop an industrial park, with the whole package of tax, employment, financing incentives already in place." Rohatyn is a partner in the investment banking firm of Lazard Frères. Lazard is extremely active in the New York City real-estate field (see, for example, Zeckendorf, *op. cit.*, pp. 237-238.) The firm is also the investment banker for the troubled Chase Manhattan Bank–sponsored real-estate investment trust.

[58]*An Outline of European Architecture*, (Middlesex, England: Pelican, 1943), p. 422.

of unparalleled size, density and engineering ingenuity. Admittedly nothing appears less systematic on today's road map than the existing highway agglomeration in the New York area. Nor does the mode of its creation over a period of forty years by the famous "1400 governments"[59] argue well for the notion of a system created once and for all by some central planning authority. Indeed, it is this superficial appearance that buttresses the idea of the existing highway system as either (a) the mindless outgrowth of inexorable technological forces, impacting on the market preferences of millions of auto-happy, mobility-conscious Americans, or (b) more recently, the equally mindless creation of Robert Moses, "The Highwayman," a veritable Medusa who turns everything he looks at into asphalt.

No one would deny that Robert Moses was a powerful official, or that increased auto registrations call forth demands for increased traffic lanes. But it is crucially important to dig beneath these seemingly plausible explanations to the historical origins of the existing transportation system in the RPA plan, not to ridicule Carlylean "great man" theories of history or even more vacuous "great market" theories of the Chicago school of econometricians, but in order to be able to deal with the present historical conjuncture as it is rather than as it appears on the surface.

Here is the general argument. The mood in social science and journalism has shifted from what C. Wright Mills used to call the "great American celebration" to almost a celebration of American crises. There is a fiscal crisis, a welfare crisis, a transportation crisis, a crisis of unemployment, a financial crisis, an urban crisis. And all of these are well reported and researched. The outstanding urbanologist in the country has even conceded that perhaps "the city" is doomed.[60]

The mood changes but the methodology remains: what Mills calls "abstracted empiricism." By abstracting the city from the capitalist environment, i.e., from what gives it its origin, purpose and even its characteristic physical morphology, it becomes possible to save, or at least not to have to confront, capitalism itself. Specifically, in New

[59]The title of an RPA monograph showing the need for regionalism, by Robert Wood.

[60]George Sternlieb, "Is the New York Region the Prototype?" in *Post Industrial America: Metropolitan Decline and Inter-Regional Job Shifts,* George Sternlieb and James W. Hughes, ed. See selection #8 in this volume.

York we learn that there is a transportation crisis, but this transportation crisis is not seen to be in any necessary historical relation to the so-called fiscal or financial crisis, and all these individual crises are kept separate from the collapse of the city's main industry—the renting, constructing and financing of office space; and from the infrastructural demands created by the city's self-imposed role as the national center.[61] Even more specifically, we learn from Robert Caro that Robert Moses imposed the wrong transportation system on the region. He overemphasized the automobile.

> By building his highways, Moses flooded the city with cars. By systematically starving the subways and the suburban commuter railroads, he swelled that flood to city-destroying dimensions. By making sure that the vast suburbs, rural and empty when he came to power, were filled on a sprawling, low-density development pattern relying primarily on roads instead of mass transportation, he insured that the New York metropolitan area would be—perhaps forever—an area in which transportation—getting from one place to another—would be an irritating, life-consuming concern for its 14,000,000 residents.[62]

There is, however, Caro tells us, a phalanx of "reformers," advocates of good government, who have consistently fought against Moses to save us from suburban sprawl and urban congestion: the Regional Plan Association. The RPA leaders appear not as they are, as the designers and motivators of the hypertrophied regional highway system, but as the progressive advocates of mass transit.[63]

It is true that after World War II the RPA began to oppose Moses and his highway programs.[64] But why? Caro gives only one of the

[61]New York City Planning Commission, "Plan for New York City," 1969. The whole plan is based on the city's role as national center. "Concentration is the genius of the city," p. 5. See also pp. 233 *et seq.*

[62]Caro, *op. cit.*, p. 19.

[63]See, for example, *ibid.*, p. 916: "But the awareness was spreading. After July, when the Regional Plan Association published the results of 'investigations . . . to determine the amount, extent and trends of commuting . . . to central New York,' facts and figures were available to document the effect of two decades of neglecting mass transit facilities in favor of highways." Or (p. 897): "These planners had said—the Regional Plan Association had been saying it since 1929 and, after the opening of Moses' creations during the 1930's, with increasing urgency—that the movement of people and goods in a great metropolitan region required a *balanced* transportation system . . ." Caro relies very heavily for his highway material on former RPA officials, e.g., Lawrence M. Orton and Paul Windels.

[64]Moses and the RPA had fought, in the late 1930s, over whether to build a bridge or a tunnel at the Battery. Moses had the support of the mayor and the city council.

reasons—congestion. And he fails to explain satisfactorily why congestion concerns the RPA. David Rockefeller was more convincing in 1952 when he appeared as featured speaker at the seventh annual RPA conference. Arguing for mass transit and a regional transportation authority, he said, "The loss in property values, taxes and human well-being which can result from allowing a bad transportation system to become worse might well exceed the money outlay necessary to correct the situation. Non-action in many circumstances is more expensive than a seemingly high priced program."[65]

Along with the effects of traffic congestion on real-estate values, there is another equally important cause for concern over the hypertrophy of the highway: the competitive effect. The highway system, especially along its radial routes, is generating commercial competition that is having an unsettling effect on downtown real-estate values. Throughout the late 1940s and early 1950s, real-estate figures express concern about suburbanization. In 1953 a kind of real-estate summit meeting was held involving William Zeckendorf, the president of Rockefeller Center, the head of the Chrysler Building, and others. While agreeing that midtown real estate is "fundamentally sound" as evidenced by their heavy stake in the field, they expressed a need to see the region carry out "more adequate long range planning" to deal with the effects of suburbanization, congestion, transit headaches. Recentralization and urban renewal were required.[66]

Thus the upbuilding of suburbia in the interests of decentralization was too successful. Even office buildings were beginning to be attracted to the suburbs. Finally, in the mid-1950s, preparations were begun to develop a second regional plan to counteract the effects of the first. It was the second regional plan which mandated the expenditures for mass transit and middle-class housing[67] foreshadowed by David Rockefeller's speech and actually budgeted by Nelson when he became governor in 1959.

Politically the RPA found it embarrassing, no doubt, to mention

---

The RPA had the support of the financial community which had plans for Battery Park. The RPA won, see Hays, *op. cit.*, pp. 64–67.

[65] *New York Times* (October 1, 1952), p. 32, p. 35.

[66] *New York Times* (November 1, 1953).

[67] Middle-class housing for the office workers was constructed to keep them from moving to the suburbs from where they had to be brought in anyway, and thus clog up the already burdened transit network.

its role as the creator of the region's highway system because of its new role as the pre-eminent advocate of regional transit planning and because of its bitter battles with the "highway lobby." But the theory and empirical work underlying the plan are essential to an understanding of how the political superstructure cemented the region to an infrastructure that steadily undermined, instead of supported, the economic base.

Both the first plan, which emphasized decentralization, and the second plan, which emphasized centralization, had the same ultimate end: tapping state revenues in order to preserve real-estate values, especially downtown values created by the rents from high-rise office buildings. The essential problem faced by both sets of planners was this: the high-rise office building, the source of the rent, is also the source of staggering amounts of traffic and congestion. Exhaustive traffic analysis showed that in midtown Manhattan, while through traffic varied with the number of automobile registrations, "the local traffic will vary as the heights of the buildings."[68]

Banning the automobile, however, was out of the question, since land values depend on traffic, or at least on striking a proper balance between concentration and congestion. Specifically, the RPA says, the value of land depends on (a) "accessibility to the greatest number of people, this accessibility involving ease and facility of movement to and from and within buildings for all purposes; (b) extent of desirable concentration; that is, the highest degree of concentration that is practicable without injuriously affecting health, safety, or convenience of movement . . ."[69]

One conceivable answer to the problem of congestion created by high-rise buildings is to limit the height of buildings. The RPA actually considered this argument, and indeed recommended that in some areas—not in midtown—there ought to be a general limitation of building height and bulk. The planners estimated that if the average height and bulk limits of Manhattan were doubled—they stood at six stories at the time of the survey—no transportation system could be designed that could drain off the resulting congestion. But the financial district and the area around Penn Station and Grand Central Station had already reached an average of ten stories. But they naturally refused to entertain the idea of eliminating conges-

[68] *Regional Survey*, Vol. III, p. 148.

[69] *The Graphic Regional Plan*, Vol. II, *Building the City*, p. 165.

tion by putting limits on the buildings that cause the congestion; the most they would argue for in the way of limitation was the idea of setbacks. Rather than adapt the height of buildings to accommodate the flow of people, the flow of people must be regulated in order to harmonize with the height of buildings. The planners were quite conscious of what they were doing: they realized they were piling new cities on top of old ones. But unlike ancient city builders who raised their structures upon the rubble of dead and deserted cities, modern planners bury the occupants of the existing city underneath the towers of the latest office buildings and then force the occupants of old and new alike to share the ground access.

If traffic cannot be banned and building height cannot be regulated, then the only remaining solution is the creation of a better transportation system. A mass-transit system? The regional plan of 1929 devoted little attention to it. No mention of the New York subway system was made at all. And suburban transit got a ten-page discussion as compared to a discussion of over a hundred pages of the highway system. As the plan said, *"The principal regional need* is the development of wide *radial or arterial highways* with adequate connecting roads in order to provide facilities for greater freedom of movement, *for a rational degree of dispersal,* and for close contiguity of industry and residence."[70]

More than anything else, the regional plan was a highway plan— and a most ingenious one, whose design needs to be more thoroughly understood. Many critics suppose that it was the desire of the highway engineers to flood the city with auto and truck traffic, that no plans were conceived to check auto ingress, that the congestion of the city comes from planlessness and inaction by government. Lewis Mumford, for example, maintains that "arterial roads, ideally speaking, should engirdle the metropolitan area and define where its greenbelt begins; and that failing this they should be planned to go through the zone where relatively high-density building begins to give way to low-density building. Along this perimeter, the through traffic, the traffic not headed for downtown will by-pass the city." Mumford maintains further that there is not a city in the country "whose highways have been planned on this basis."[71]

In fact, New York has been planned precisely this way by the RPA.

[70] *The Graphic Regional Plan,* Vol. I, p. 212.

[71] *The Highway and the City* (New York: Harcourt, 1973), p. 239.

The arterial system Mumford talks about forms the foundation of the entire plan. Only instead of a single artery, the plan calls for three giant circumferential circles—630 miles in total length. The inner circle, called the metropolitan loop, is 117 miles in length. It encircles the main centers of commerce and business in the heart of the region at approximately 14 miles from City Hall. When originally planned, it involved five river crossings. Two of them had been mentioned before the plan, but others—the Bronx–Whitestone Bridge, the Triborough Bridge and the Lincoln Tunnel—were conceived by the RPA. The two other circumferential loops connected (and mightily developed) the suburban communities of Westchester and those in the surrounding New Jersey area.

The extent to which the whole plan was realized to the satisfaction of the RPA we can gauge from this self-appraisal written in 1940:

> The most noticeable change that would strike a visitor who is familiar with the New York Region but who has been absent thirteen years is the extent to which the highway system has been improved. He might be astonished at the amount accomplished but he would have little occasion to wonder at the pattern of routes if he remembered the system of highways proposed by the Regional Plan of New York and its Environs.[72]

Looking at that plan and a highway map today, nearly fifty years later, it seems as if all that was necessary for Moses to do when he appeared on the scene in the 1930s was to pour concrete on the dotted lines.

A final irony illustrates the notoriety of Moses and the obscurity of the RPA. One of the most moving chapters in Caro's book describes the forced relocation of the residents of the neighborhood of East Tremont who must leave their homes to make room for the Cross Bronx Expressway. (Many planners will tell you today that it was the Cross Bronx Expressway that turned the Bronx into what it is today.) Moses, naturally, is given credit for having first proposed it in 1946. The Cross Bronx is described as a "heavy red line slashing inexorably across the delicate cross hatch of streets in the borough's central expanse." Moses is made to appear to have had questionable motives, or worse, perhaps, no motives at all for putting the highway where he did. Just an arbitrary power wielder.

In fact, the regional highway plan designates the entire course of the Cross Bronx Expressway which forms the eastern arc of the

---

[72]*From Plan to Reality,* Vol. III (New York, 1942), p. III-1.

"metropolitan loop." It is hard for a layman to tell where Moses diverged more than a few hundred yards from the course set by the RPA back in the 1920s. The plan called for crossing the Harlem River at approximately 170th Street and then traversing the Bronx easterly to the intersection of Randall Avenue and Ferris Avenue, and thence southerly to Old Ferry Point. "The connection between the Bronx and Queens is by means of a proposed bridge across the East River between Old Ferry Point and Whitestone" (today's Bronx–Whitestone Bridge). In other words, whatever venal or corrupt motives Moses may have had, whatever insensitivity he may have displayed toward the East Tremont residents, the Cross Bronx Expressway is simply another section of the RPA-designed metropolitan loop, which is constructed to enable vehicles from Manhattan or New Jersey which are headed for Long Island to by-pass the downtown commercial center.

In arguing the historical priority of the RPA over Robert Moses, it is not simply a question of blaming the class rather than the man. What is mainly wrong with Caro's effort to explain the role of the transportation crisis in "the fall of New York" is that he fails to locate the transportation crisis in a causal nexus that begins with the high-rise office buildings as the source of congestion. He, like so many others, starts his analysis from the point where the problem becomes insoluble. Because once you have granted the city's real-estate and financial entrepreneurs the freedom to build and rebuild ever greater concentrations of office buildings, to bulldoze and wreck whatever lies in their path—once this has been allowed, five Robert Moseses and a budget many times the size of the existing one would be inadequate to cope with the resulting congestion, industrial location, unemployment, pauperism, etc.

In the age of monarchy it was the practice of allowed critics to attack the king's ministers rather than his majesty himself. More radical critics dared to confront the king in his own person, while the revolutionaries correctly saw the monarchy as simply the last political refuge of hereditary privilege and sought to abolish that. In our era, the role of the allowed critic is reserved for the liberals who limit themselves to criticism of individuals in power; radical criticism comes from those willing to mount an attack on the state apparatus. But the really revolutionary role once again is played by the criticism which strikes at what holds up the state—which is not popular consent, but the institution of capital and its trinity: profit, interest and rent.

The New York regional plan shows how even the most brilliantly conceived and engineered plan can do little more than mirror the existing needs of capital. The plan rather than regulating capital is regulated by it. And each fulfillment of the plan brings a new mismatch between economic base and infrastructure, since, from the moment the plan is initiated, capital has begun to take a new form and demands a new infrastructure. The lesson—for New Yorkers or Moscovites—if you would be a planner: first create the "community of free individuals."

17. New York City's Fiscal Problem

CONGRESSIONAL BUDGET OFFICE

I. Causes of the Problem

A variety of factors have contributed to New York's current fiscal problems. It is useful to distinguish the short-term factors that are responsible for precipitating the immediate crisis from those longer-term trends that have contributed to the city's deteriorating fiscal position.

Short-term Factors. The immediate crisis stems from a loss of investor confidence in the credit worthiness of the city. To some extent the sudden shift in the attitudes of investors towards the city's ability to meet its obligations must be attributed to psychological factors for surely the city's long-run economic outlook, which is what determines its ability to pay off its debts, cannot be much different today than it was one or two years ago.

Any discussion of the factors that affect the psychological attitudes of investors must be speculative. It is possible that investor confidence was eroded by the public debate and confrontation politics that took place between the mayor, the city controller, and the governor over the city's fiscal year 1976 budget. It is also probable that the temporary default of the New York State's Urban Development Corporation and the memories of the Penn Central, Lockheed, and Franklin National Bank collapses have made investors increasingly skittish. Any hint of financial instability may send them scampering away. Investor uncertainty becomes a self-feeding process, for the fewer the number of persons willing to lend the city money, the greater the probability of default and the greater therefore the uncertainty, and indeed, the risk.

However, it would be wrong to attribute all of the loss of investor confidence in New York to psychological factors. Objective market

This is an edited version of a background paper issued by the U.S. Congressional Budget Office, October 10, 1975. The paper was prepared by Robert D. Reischauer, Peter K. Clark and Peggy L. Cuciti.

TABLE 1. Volume of Municipal Borrowing (1967–1975) (Amounts are par values in millions of dollars)

Year	Long-term	Short-term	Total
1967	14,300	8,000	22,300
1968	16,300	8,600	24,900
1969	11,700	11,700	23,400
1970	18,888	17,811	35,999
1971	25,006	26,259	51,265
1972	23,748	24,705	49,018
1973	23,957	24,705	48,662
1974	24,317	29,543	53,860
1975*	30,124	33,932	64,056

Source: Securities Industry Association, *Municipal Market Developments.*

*Annual rate based on January–June volume.

conditions should be considered as well. As Table 1 indicates, 1975 has proven to be an extremely heavy year for municipal borrowing. Therefore, New York has been forced to compete for funds with many other state and local governments with far sounder fiscal conditions as well as with the large borrowing requirements of the federal government. While the volume of issues has grown, the recession probably has diminished the desire and ability of banks, corporations, and individuals to buy tax-exempt bonds. This is clearly the case with commercial banks; during the first quarter of 1975 they dropped out of the municipal bond market almost entirely (see Table 2).

With respect to individuals, it has been suggested that interest rates on municipal offerings have to be raised significantly to entice new buyers into the market. Such buyers must be drawn primarily from middle-income groups which benefit less from the tax-exempt status of municipal bond interest and are less capable of purchasing municipal bonds because these securities generally are available only in large denominations. Furthermore, the market for New York City securities is concentrated largely in New York State where the interest is exempt from not only federal but also state and local taxes. This market may be close to saturated by the large quantities of state and city securities outstanding. To broaden the market to nonstate residents would require interest rates sufficiently high to compensate for the fact that non-New York holders would have to pay state income taxes on the interest earned from their New York City securities.

The recession is a second short-term condition that has con-

TABLE 2. Annual Net Changes in Holdings of Municipal Securities by Major Holder Groups (1970–1975) (Amounts are par values in billions of dollars)

Holder	1970	1971	1972	1973	1974	1975* First quarter	1975* Second quarter
Commercial banks	10.7	12.6	7.2	5.7	5.5	−2.7	6.9
Households	−.8	−.2	1.0	4.3	10.0	13.9	9.3
All other**	1.3	5.2	6.2	3.7	1.9	2.9	4.5
Total	11.2	17.6	14.4	13.7	17.4	14.0	20.7

Source: Unpublished flow of funds data from the Board of Governors of the Federal Reserve System (Processed: August 19, 1975)

*Annual rate.

**This includes corporate business, state and local general funds, mutual savings banks, insurance companies, state and local government retirement funds, and brokers and dealers.

tributed to New York City's problems. Compared to other local governments, New York's revenue system is highly responsive to economic conditions because it relies heavily on cyclically sensitive sales and income taxes rather than on the more stable property tax. While property taxes accounted for 62 percent of the total revenues raised by the local governments serving metropolitan areas in fiscal year 1972–73, they accounted for only 43 percent of revenues raised by New York.

The recession's impact on New York's sales tax base is illustrated in Table 3. Despite a 9.3 percent increase in consumer prices in the year ending June 30, 1975, the volume of taxable sales in the city rose by only 1.7 percent. In New York even the property tax has proven to be unreliable. Delinquencies have risen rapidly from 4.2 percent of collections in fiscal year 1970 to 7.2 percent currently.

The recession has caused high unemployment and stationary incomes which have increased the city's expenditure requirements as well as undercut its expected revenue growth. Not only have the numbers of families eligible for welfare programs increased (see Table 3), but it is also likely that the demand for other city services, such as hospitals, has been boosted by the recession because fewer city residents are able to afford the costs of the alternative private institutions.

The severe inflation of recent years has also had a negative effect

TABLE 3. Measures of the Recession's Impact on New York City

Year	Unemployment Rate[1]	Welfare* Recipients[2]	Sales Tax* Base[3]
1970	4.8	101.5	78.1
1971	6.7	109.5	81.5
1972	7.0	112.9	NA
1973	6.0	106.4	91.9
1974	7.2	101.4	96.7
1974 June	6.9	100.0	100.0
July	7.3	100.2	100.4
Aug.	6.8	99.3	100.2
Sept.	7.3	100.5	99.1
Oct.	7.2	101.3	99.8
Nov.	7.4	101.3	99.6
Dec.	8.5	102.4	100.4
1975 Jan.	10.3	102.8	101.0
Feb.	10.2	102.5	101.0
Mar.	11.0	103.1	101.7
April	10.8	104.3	102.0
May	10.9	104.3	101.9
June	11.7	105.0	101.7
July	12.0		
Aug.	11.0		

Sources: 1. New York State, Department of Labor
2. New York State Department of Social Services
3. Annual figures from New York State Department of Taxation and Finance. Monthly figures from Municipal Assistance Corporation

*Indexes use June 1974 as the base period (Sales Tax Base 100 = $1.6 billion; Welfare Recipients 100 = 949,000). Sales Tax Base is equal to the total value of sales subject to taxation. Index is based on a twelve-month moving average to eliminate seasonal effects.

The Welfare index includes recipients under the AFDC and home relief programs.

on the fiscal position of New York. While in the long run, inflation may increase the value of the local tax base sufficiently to compensate for the decreased purchasing power of the tax dollar, in the short run, expenditure levels tend to be more responsive to inflationary pressures. This imbalance stems from the nature of property tax administration, for it is very difficult to reassess property rapidly enough to keep pace with the continually inflating market values of real estate.

Moreover, the situation is exacerbated by the long time period that transpires between the date at which the property tax levy is set and the dates on which the tax payments are due. In recent years a considerable amount of unanticipated inflation has occurred during these periods. It should be noted that New York's situation with respect to inflation may be better than that of other large cities, because of New York's heavy reliance on sales and income tax receipts which do respond quickly and automatically to price hikes and inflation-induced salary increases.

Long-term Factors. The longer-term roots of New York's fiscal problem are both complex and difficult for the city to change. In part they represent the same forces that have buffeted the other large central cities of the northeast and north-central states. These cities have been called upon to assimilate a new wave of rural migrants into the industrial economy just when the industries offering employment opportunities are shifting their bases of operation out of the cities.

As a result of the immigration from the South, the out-migration to the suburbs, and the natural aging of the existing population, those more heavily dependent on city services—the poor, the uneducated, the aged, the non-English speaking—comprise an ever-increasing segment of the city's population. For example, between 1950 and 1970 the fraction of the city's population over 65 years of age has gone from 8.0 to 12.1 percent while the proportion of the city's families with incomes below the nation's median income level has risen from 36 to 49 percent.

The city's tax base has failed to grow as rapidly as its revenue requirements. This situation can be attributed to shifts in the location of economic activity as well as to the continued suburbanization of middle- and upper-income groups. Many industries are leaving the northeast altogether while others find it more profitable to operate in the suburbs or on the fringes of the metropolitan area. While its population has remained relatively constant, New York has lost jobs at a rapid rate over the last five years (see Table 4).

The city can exert little influence over either the population shifts or the tax base trends. Together they have produced a steady increase in city tax levels which has, in turn, probably affected the types of persons and businesses willing to remain in or move into the city (see Table 5).

An additional factor that has contributed materially to the city's fiscal problems is the manner in which the responsibility for providing welfare and health care services has been divided in New York state. New York is one of only twenty-one states that requires its local governments (e.g., counties) to contribute to the support of cash assistance for the aid to families with dependent children program (AFDC) or to Medicaid payments. Of these twenty-one states, the

TABLE 4. Change in Jobs and Population in New York City

Year	Total Jobs[1]		Private Sector[2] Jobs		Population[3]	
	(in Thous.)	Index*	(in Thous.)	Index*	(in Thous.)	Index*
1960	3,538.4	94.5	3,130.2	98.4	7,782.0	98.6
1970	3,744.8	100.0	3,182.0	100.0	7,895.6	100.0
1971	3,609.4	96.4	3,040.2	95.5	7,886.6	99.9
1972	3,563.1	95.1	2,998.6	94.2	7,847.1	99.4
1973	3,538.4	94.5	2,964.0	93.1	7,664.4	97.1
1974	3,458.4	92.4	2,877.7	90.4	7,567.1	95.8
1975**	3,375.8	90.1	2,802.6	88.1	NA	NA

Sources: 1,2—Bureau of Labor Statistics   3—Bureau of the Census
*Data Indexed using 1970 as base year.
**January—June 1975

TABLE 5. The New York City Tax Burden

Fiscal Year	Personal Income ($ billions)	Taxes* ($ billions)	Taxes as Percent of Personal Income
1963–64	27	2.013	7.6
1964–65	28	2.193	7.9
1965–66	29	2.152	7.3
1966–67	31	2.410	7.7
1967–68	34	2.626	7.8
1968–69	37	2.802	7.6
1969–70	39	2.958	7.5
1970–71	41	3.178	7.7
1971–72	43	3.736	8.7
1972–73	45	4.017	8.9
1973–74	48	4.506	9.4
1974–75	50	5.111	10.2

Source: New York City Finance Administration
*Excludes fees and charges, stock transfer taxes and nonresident income taxes.

local share is the highest in New York, where it amounts to almost one quarter of the total or half of the nonfederal share (see Table 6).

While county governments in New York also must bear half of the cost of the Home Relief Program, New York State's relatively generous general assistance program, this division of responsibility does not differ from the pattern that prevails in the rest of the nation. All told, New York City's welfare-related expenditures amount to some $3.5 billion, or approximately one third of its current spending. One billion dollars of this must be raised by the city. If the city constituted just part of a large county—as is true of Los Angeles, Newark and all but a handful of the large cities located in the twenty-one states requiring local welfare contributions—the costs of supporting the

TABLE 6. Fraction of AFDC Cash Assistance and Medicaid Payments Borne by Local Governments (Fiscal Year 1974)

State*	Percent	State	Percent
New York	23.0	Iowa	4.8
Minnesota	21.8	No. Dakota	4.6
Wyoming	18.5	Maryland	4.2
California	14.5	Montana	2.8
Kansas	11.3	Virginia	0.6
Colorado	9.4	Utah	0.6
Nebraska	8.8	Louisiana	0.2
Nevada	8.3	Oregon	0.1
No. Carolina	8.3	New Hampshire	**
Indiana	6.9	Mississippi	**
New Jersey	6.5		

Source: Department of Health, Education, and Welfare, "State Expenditures for Public Assistance Programs."

*States not listed do not require any local contribution.

**Less than 0.1 percent.

city's income security programs would be shared by some suburban jurisdictions. However, being a city-county, New York must bear the cost alone.

New York's long tradition of providing enriched levels of public services also has contributed to its current fiscal difficulties. The more obvious services in which New York far outdistances most other local governments include the city university system, the municipal hospital system, the low- and middle-income housing programs, and the extensive public transportation network. For many years there seemed little doubt that the city's wealth was sufficient to support its chosen level of services. However, in recent years it has proved difficult politically to reduce services in line with the city's declining relative fiscal ability to afford them or to raise taxes and fees.

Finally, one cannot ignore the city's questionable accounting procedures and loose fiscal management in relation to the current crisis. These procedures masked the fact the New York officials were failing to make the difficult choices that were required if the city's expense budget was to be truly balanced as required by law.[1] The

[1]"Annual budget and financial reports are filed with the Division of Municipal Affairs in the office of the State Comptroller. Budgets are reviewed in substance and legality. . . . Deficit financing is not recognized in the operation of units of Local Government in New York State and can only be legally validated by legislative enactment." Advisory Commission on Intergovernmental Relations, *City Financial Emergencies* (Washington, D. C.: Government Printing Office, 1973), p. 168.

TABLE 7. New York City Compared To Other Large Central Cities

City	(1) Index of Central City Disadvantage	(2) Fraction of Population Receiving Welfare Payments*	(3) Per Capita Expenditures 1972–1973			(4) Local Government Employment Per 10,000 Population 1974		
			(a) City Government	(b) All Local Governments* Serving Central County — Total	(c) Common Municipal Functions***	(a) City Government	(b) All Local Governments* Serving Central County — Total	(c) Common Municipal functions***
New York City**	211	12.4	$1,224	$1,286	$435	517.1	528.2	263.7
Boston	198	16.9	858	756	441	378.0	465.0	249.2
Chicago	245	11.1	267	600	383	140.0	352.5	250.1
Newark	422	14.4	692	827	449	391.1	421.5	304.6
Los Angeles	105	8.0	242	759	408	162.2	401.1	256.0
Philadelphia**	205	16.2	415	653	395	163.8	414.5	301.5
San Francisco**	105	9.1	751	1,073	488	312.5	488.3	244.4
New Orleans**	168	11.4	241	431	260	177.3	357.7	271.3
St. Louis**	231	15.8	310	610	360	241.9	424.6	227.8
Denver**	143	7.2	473	721	375	237.0	410.5	280.9
Baltimore**	256	16.3	806	814	470	434.1	434.1	312.5
Detroit	210	11.1	357	650	396	194.8	354.3	258.6

*Central County.

**Boundaries of the city are coterminous with those of the central county.

***Common Municipal Functions include elementary and secondary education, highways, police, fire, sanitation, parks, general control and financial administration.

| City | (5) Public Employee Average Salaries 1974 | | | | (6) Cost of BLS's Intermediate Family Budget (Index 1974) | (7) Debt Outstanding per capita 1972–1973* | |
	(a) Teacher	(b) Police	(c) Fire	(d) Sanitation		(a) Total	(b) Short-term
New York City	$17,018	$14,666	$16,964	$15,924	116	$1,676	$352
Boston	13,938	14,352	13,844	10,666	117	1,385	334
Chicago	17,409	14,146	15,525	11,956	103	733	169
Newark	13,720	13,282	13,282	8,473	116	616	112
Los Angeles	13,058	15,833	21,180	13,168	98	650	14
Philadelphia	12,800	14,354	13,869	13,337	103	1,015	101
San Francisco	14,855	15,529	17,765	13,023	106	1,225	151
New Orleans	8,715	10,746	10,645	4,170	NA	770	39
St. Louis	14,894	11,748	13,185	9,593	97	731	49
Denver	13,505	12,907	14,198	10,258	95	786	52
Baltimore	10,488	10,098	10,980	13,814	100	609	45
Detroit	18,836	15,636	16,107	13,814	100	658	63

Sources:

1. Richard Nathan, "The Record of the New Federalism: What It Means for the Nation's Cities," Brookings Institution, 1974.

2. Department of Health, Education and Welfare, Recipients of Public Assistance Money Payments and Amounts of Such Payments by Program, State, and County, February 1975, DHEW Pub. No. (SRS) 76–03105 NCSS Report A-8 (2/75). Includes AFDC and general assistance recipients.

3a. U. S. Bureau of the Census, "City Government Finances in 1972–73," GF73, No. 4.

3b, c, 7 U. S. Bureau of the Census, "Local Government Finances in selected Metropolitan Areas and Large Counties 1972–73," GF 73, No. 6.

4. & 5. U. S. Bureau of the Census, "Local Government Employment in Selected Metropolitan Areas and Large Counties 1974," GE74, No. 3.

6. Bureau of Labor Statistics, "Autumn 1974 Urban Family Budgets and Comparative Indexes for Selected Urban Areas" (4–9–75).

* Central County

fault does not rest with the city alone. Many of the "gimmicks" which allowed the budget to appear balanced were tolerated or even suggested by state officials and were certainly not secrets to the banking community. These "gimmicks" produced small deficits which were allowed to accumulate and grow, producing a problem of large and unmanageable proportions.

II. Is New York Unique?

Are New York's problems simply of a larger magnitude or are they qualitatively different from those of other major cities? Much of the public discussion suggests that New York is very different from other cities, that it has an abnormally large welfare population, an unusually large and well-paid public labor force and has expenditure patterns that are significantly higher than other cities. At the same time, there is the belief that the fiscal crisis being visited upon New York soon will afflict other cities. Generally neither of those contradictory sets of impressions is valid.

In recent decades New York has been buffeted by the same socio-economic forces that have affected other large, older urban centers and has responded to these pressures in a fashion similar to that of other cities. According to most measures, New York's situation is far from the worst in the nation. One composite index of central city disadvantage shows New York in better shape than Newark, Baltimore, and Chicago as well as eight other large urban centers not included in Table 7 (see column 1). A smaller fraction of New York's population receives welfare than is the case in Philadelphia, Baltimore, Newark, or Boston (see Table 7, column 2).

Comparisons of the expenditure and employment patterns of New York City with those of other large municipal governments indicate that New York is far out of line with other jurisdictions (see Table 7, columns 3a and 4a). Yet this is a misleading conclusion which stems from the fact that New York City provides services that in other areas may be supplied by a county government, a school district, or another specialized government. If one compares the New York employment and spending patterns with those of all of the local governments providing services to the residents of other large cities, New York appears to be less extraordinary (see Table 7, columns 3b and 4b). While its per capita expenditure and public employment levels are above those of any other major city area, some of the differences with respect to such cities as Boston and Philadelphia can be explained by the fact that welfare is a state function in Massachusetts and Pennsylvania. While New York also spends a great deal more than other cities on higher education, hospitals, and mass transportation, its expenditure on the services commonly provided by municipalities is not out of line with those of other large cities (see Table 7, columns 3c and 4c). With respect to the salaries paid public employees, New York is generous but not the most generous of large cities (see Table 7, column 5). Considering that New York's cost of living—as measured by the Bureau of Labor Statistics (BLS) intermediate family budget—is higher than all but that of Boston, its wages are not particularly out of line (see Table 7, column 6).

However, it should be noted that what little reliable evidence there is seems to indicate that New York City provides its employees with considerably more in the way of fringe benefits—pensions, health insurance, etc.—than is offered the employees of other large cities.

While New York's situation in many ways does not differ markedly from that of other large central cities, some of its problems are clearly not shared with other cities. First there is New York's debt situation. On a per capita basis the city has far more debt outstanding than do the local governments providing services in the other central city areas (see Table 7, column 7). This is particularly true of short-term debt in which New York stands alone in its needs continually to enter the market to "roll over" large quantities of notes. Second, New York, as far as can be told, has been the only major city that has chronically run a large current operating deficit in both good and bad economic years. Finally, as was mentioned previously, New York revenues and expenditures are much more sensitive to the ups and downs of the business cycle. All of these peculiar aspects of New York's situation should make one pause before concluding that the city's crisis is but the forerunner of those that will occur widely elsewhere.

18. How the Power Brokers Profit

JACK NEWFIELD

In Vietnam, an army commander said of the village of Ben Tre: "We had to destroy it in order to save it."

That same deranged logic is now being applied to New York City. Under the three-year financial plan and debt moratorium, the banks have been saved, and the city has been condemned. Behind all the words and all the numbers, the most fundamental fate under capitalism is being played out: The rich are getting richer, and the poor are getting poorer.

The banks are getting their exorbitant interest payments from the city. The brokerage houses are reporting soaring profits—Hayden Stone reported a gain of 130 per cent last week, and Merrill Lynch is up 31 per cent. But half the Bronx is gone.

The clubhouse hacks are still larding the city payroll. The clients and cronies of Pat Cunningham and Stanley Steingut are still getting leases, mortgage closing fees, finder's fees, city contracts, insurance premiums, and other preferments. But there are 65 children in many public school classrooms. And Harlem Hospital is short 149 nurses.

Con Edison reported a 41 per cent increase in operating earnings for the last quarter of 1975. The Port Authority still has a surplus in its bank account. But muggers are going free because the cops who arrested them have been fired, and are not showing up in criminal court.

The budget cutbacks are as stupid and counterproductive, as they are brutal.

Dozens of young, undercover narcotics cops have been laid off. This honest, post-Serpico generation of cops has been fired at a time when a new wave of heroin is flowing back into the slums. So there are more pushers, more junkies, more street crime, and more middle-

Reprinted from the *Village Voice* (April 26, 1976). Jack Newfield is a senior editor of the *Village Voice*.

class whites fleeing to the suburbs. When he was running for mayor, Abe Beame promised to add 3000 cops to the police force.

Out-patient clinics are being closed. So poor people get sicker, and ultimately require treatment at municipal hospitals, and the city has to pay more in Medicaid.

Open admissions and free tuition—the last passage of upward mobility out of the slums—are being destroyed. The one chance to create a black and an Hispanic middle class is being killed by the faceless white men who balance abstract numbers.

Apparently, the last thing Roger Starr or David Rockefeller wants is an educated, unemployed class that has read Marx, Malcolm X, and Robert Caro.

Twenty-eight drug-free rehabilitation centers have been closed, turning 4000 former heroin addicts onto the streets. All last week ex-addicts camped in front of Gracie Mansion, sleeping on mattresses, and in a big yellow tent.

One of them, Wyndal Burt, a member of Project Return, was saying, "Where can I go? Where can I go, man? I was almost there. I have spent almost three years in the program getting an education and preparing for a job. If they cut us, I will have to revert to what I know best—and that is stealing."

James Murphy of Odyssey House said, "The kids out here are not asking for anything like a paycheck. They are pleading for their lives." Most of the squatters seemed younger than 16.

A poster nailed to the fence near the tent said: "This is a forgotten city—these are your forgotten children."

What's really crazy is that many of these "forgotten children" are ex-offenders on probation or parole. If their drug-free programs close, many will have to go back to state facilities. And this will cost more than keeping their drug-free centers open.

The loss of police and fire protection is turning the Italian enclave of East Harlem into a replica of the South Bronx—or Beirut. The city cannot cope with the teenage arsonists in this stable, residential neighborhood.

Around 118th Street and Pleasant Avenue there are families who have been burnt out three times in 18 months. There are burnt-out buildings, where the walls have been ripped open, so that scavengers could strip the plumbing and sinks. One woman, whose family has lived near Pleasant Avenue for 75 years, saw her building stripped by a group of looters "while the ashes were still warm."

Northside is another stable, ethnic community, located in Brooklyn. It is predominantly Polish, and is church and family oriented. But the city is slowly killing this community, bit by bit, year by year.

In 1970, the city closed the 92nd Police Precinct in Northside. In September of 1973, two blocks of homes were torn down so a factory could expand. Paul Levine, the city official who participated in the decision to tear down the homes, now works for the company that owns the factory—the S&S Corrugated Paper Machinery Company. And half the factory expansion has never taken place.

Early in 1975, the city slashed the budget for the well-baby clinic in Northside, and now the clinic is about to close. The budget was also cut for Greenpoint Hospital, and now it may close too. The city cut the budget of the Northside Senior Citizen Center by 15 per cent. And last November, the city closed Engine Company 212 in Northside.

For the last five months, citizens of Northside have been occupying their firehouse to protest the loss of their last municipal service. As a result of the loss of fire protection, the Eaton Allen company has told the city it may have to cancel its planned expansion. This will mean a loss of 300 new jobs to Northside.

What has been accomplished by all this?

The crushing weight of a blood-sucking debt. The new 1976–77 city budget, announced last week, totals $12.5 billion. Of that, $2.4 billion is in debt service costs, almost 20 per cent of the total budget. This figure includes $687 million in interest payments on MAC's obligations. In the 1975–76 budget, debt service was 15.4 per cent. By the 1977–78 budget, interest payments will cost us more than welfare and Medicaid combined.

What else has been accomplished by all this?

In the most crucial area—nothing at all. The bond market is still closed to the city, perhaps for another 20 years, according to the president of Standard and Poor's, the bond rating service. The subway fare was raised to 50 cents "to restore investor confidence." The three-year financial plan was imposed to "restore investor confidence." The experts were wrong. We have sacrificed without reward. The whole city is still redlined by the bankers.

What else has been accomplished?

The loss of representative government—of home rule—to a consortium of bankers, corporate executives, technocrats, and politicians.

Our new rulers blame each other for unpopular decisions and blur all accountability. When the transit fare went from 35 to 50 cents, the MAC directors blamed Beame, Beame blamed the MTA, the MTA members blamed Carey, and Carey blamed the bond market in public and Beame in private.

My own opinion is that as citizens, and as voters, we must hold Abe Beame ultimately accountable. He is elected. He wants to be reelected. And, in fact, he does control day-to-day decisions of the city government.

Beame is responsible for the policy to protect the thousands of clubhouse hacks still on the municipal payroll. Beame is responsible for appointing wretched commissioners. Whatever harsh judgments about other public officials follow in this article, Beame is the worst, and his reelection would be the city's final death sentence.

And what else has been accomplished?

A three-year budget-balancing financial plan that is based on illusions and deceptions. The plan has been thoroughly exposed as a fraud by Percy Sutton, and in this newspaper, by Richard Morris, among many; I cite them only because they are critics of the financial plan, but not proponents of default, an ambiguous position I share. Borough President Sutton has said:

"The fiscal plan says that Medicaid costs will hold steady. Nonsense. Medicaid rates have risen by 25 per cent a year since 1971, and are likely to rise by at least 15 per cent over the next three years.

"The fiscal plan says that welfare rentals will not increase. Nonsense. Experience shows that rents for welfare recipients go up faster than those for the population as a whole, and they are likely to rise by at least 7 per cent per year.

"The fiscal plan says that real estate tax collections will not decline. Nonsense. They have fallen off by 9 per cent over the last three years, and will probably continue to slide. . . ."

Recently I asked an important city official why the financial plan was limited to an impossible three years. He replied:

"You're not going to believe this but in the decisive meeting some of us urged the plan be five years. But some very sophisticated people argued that the public would not accept a five-year plan because it sounded too much like Stalin."

When Robert Kennedy spoke against the Vietnam war, he often quoted what Tacitus said of Rome: "They made a desert, and called it peace."

In my city, they are making a desert, and calling it a three-year plan.

Felix Rohatyn is the best that finance capitalism has to offer. He performed a memorable service in saving the city from default last year. He is a creative theorist, expert negotiator, and mordant wit— the financial equivalent of Henry Kissinger or the young Robert McNamara. Like those two gentlemen early on in their public careers, Rohatyn is now receiving press acclaim. The media has conferred a mystique of class-free, disinterested judgment, and general competence upon Rohatyn.

But Rohatyn, it is useful to recall, was a director of ITT at the time the $12 billion conglomerate, along with the CIA, was "destabilizing" the freely elected socialist government of Chile. He remains a director of ITT today.

Rohatyn insists he has little power over the life of the city. And he does have less influence on specifics than Beame. But he is chairman of MAC. He is Governor Carey's principal adviser on both New York City and economic development. He attends and often dominates the Emergency Financial Control Board meetings. And he has a decisive influence on public opinion through his credibility with newspaper editorial boards and journalists.

Last month, in an interview reported on the front page of the *New York Times,* Rohatyn suggested that poor neighborhoods be bulldozed and converted into industrial parks, with lower business taxes as an incentive. Sounding ominously like Robert Moses, Rohatyn said: "Take a 30-block area, clear it, blacktop it, and develop an industrial park, with the whole package of tax, employment, financing incentives already in place. . . . Get a few of the best people, focus on the problems, figure a reasonable solution, even if we can only afford to get 60 or 70 per cent of the facts, and move."

It was the first insight into Rohatyn's broader knowledge of the city, outside the highly technical realm of finance. Rohatyn talked as if he's never attended a community planning board meeting. He sounded ignorant of neighborhoods and of their value. He seemed unaware that there are today 2000 acres of already vacant land in this city outside Manhattan. There are 150 acres of undeveloped land at the Brooklyn Navy Yard, 200 acres at Howland Hook on Staten Island, 250 acres at College Point in Queens, and 107 acres in the Bronx at the Harlem River Yards.

In fairness to Rohatyn, his thinking seemed more innocent than Roger Starr's abhorrent concept of "planned shrinkage"—the systematic withdrawal of services from poor neighborhoods.

Rohatyn seemed merely out of his depth and overreaching. Starr's darker intention is forced depopulation of certain communities. Starr, at bottom, seems to believe government spends too much money on the poor, and if government would only become more brutal the poor could be driven out of the city. Starr should probably become the housing czar for the Communists in Cambodia, where the urban population is being resettled by the thousands every day.

On February 6, 1976, Rohatyn published a revealing op-ed essay in the *New York Times*. It began with customary eloquence: "New York City is entering a state of siege in a war of survival for its life and soul. Its three-year fiscal plan requires New York City to become Sparta and its managers to become monks."

Rohatyn has a profound sense of history. So he must know that Sparta was a society based on slavery. Its citizens sacrificed, but they had no voice.

Sparta was also ruled by two kings, a board of magistrates, and a council of elders. (Carey, Beame, MAC, and the EFCB?)

As for our managers becoming monks, Rohatyn has so far refused to reveal to the state's Board of Public Disclosure his worldly income, investments, and liabilities. As a partner in the investment banking firm of Lazard Frères Rohatyn earns an annual salary "in six figures." He also sits on the boards of five corporations.

Donna Shalala and Thomas Flynn of MAC, and William Ellinghaus and David Margolis of the EFCB have already complied with all disclosure requirements. But Rohatyn has requested a formal exemption, which the Public Disclosure Board has on its agenda for April 23. Monks should have nothing to hide.

Robert McNamara was the best the technocracy could produce. But he failed in Vietnam because his computers did not know how to take into account the human will of the Vietcong. McNamara, for all his brilliance, could not understand that all his technology, all his firepower, all his napalm, could not kill an idea.

Rohatyn, the best finance capitalism has to offer, will also fail, for several reasons.

One is that he really does not know the city. He has never had to run for office, or relate to ordinary people in the outer boroughs.

Another is Rohatyn's deep pessimism about the nature of man.

Rohatyn grew up under fascism in Europe. He has told me he sees a real prospect for a native American fascism. This fear of the beast in people makes order and stability the overwhelming social objective to Rohatyn. This lends a bias to his thinking—a manipulative, elitist bias, not unlike the bias of another educated refugee from fascism, Henry Kissinger.

A third reason is Rohatyn's profession. He is an investment banker who makes corporate mergers. He believes that only professional money experts can heal the city's cash flow and debt structure. As a result, MAC and the EFCB are totally unrepresentative of the city. There is no resident of Brooklyn or Queens on either board, no community activist, no union leader, no Hispanic. The only black—Robert Weaver—is a trustee of the Bowery Savings Bank and a director of the Metropolitan Life Insurance Company.

All this, I am afraid, prevents Rohatyn from seeing that the cuts are being made in the wrong places. They are being made on the basis of economic class, not merit, reason, or fairness. Everyone admits the cuts are falling disproportionately upon the poor, and Rohatyn has made no visible effort to make the banks and utilities share the sacrifice. Rohatyn, I suspect, thinks of the city first as a vessel for investment, first as prospectus for a bond.

But a city is people, a city is neighborhoods, a city is services. As Secretary of State Mario Cuomo told the tristate regional conference last month: "We are not in the business of declaring dividends, we are in the business of improving lives."

There are many reasons for New York City to exist and endure: We are a port, we are an incubator of ideas and culture, we are a mecca for tourists.

One special reason for our existence should be the quality of life here. Open admissions, fire protection, and health care should be the reasons we exist as a city. So should the exciting diversity of SoHo, Corona, Tremont, Laurelton, Flatbush, Fort Greene, Bay Ridge, and all our neighborhoods.

The cutbacks are accelerating the death of the city. Families and businesses move out of New York because of crime, bad schools, the lack of housing, the loss of amenities.

Each budget cut, whether by the EFCB, Carey, or Beame, leads to more crime, worse schools, less housing, fewer amenities. With each new budget cut we commit suicide as an entity in history.

• • •

Question: How did New York City go into debt?

Answer: One way was letting its politicians waste $1 billion on their clients, contributors, and cronies.

New York City is a victim of federal indifference and national priorities that favor the southern rim at the expense of the older cities of the Northeast.

But New York City did not go broke because it was too liberal. It went broke because its politicians were too cynical.

It wasn't free tuition or the 35-cent fare that broke New York. It was all the patronage boondoggles in the districts of important politicians. It was the wasteful, needless building of construction projects like the Albany Mall and the World Trade Center. Someday they'll build a concentration camp so some county leader can get the workmen comp insurance.

It was reduced real estate assessments for big campaign contributors. It was the award of 99-year no-bid leases to the law clients of Pat Cunningham, who then get favorable court decisions from judges picked by Cunningham. It was pork barrel programs the pols made sure were not audited—like nursing homes prior to 1974. And it was a $500 million bailout of Con Edison.

Politics is business. Most politicians are in it for personal financial enrichment.

Why did Bernard Bergman give the insurance business on two of his nursing homes to Stanley Steingut? Why did Shoup Voting Machine get an $8.5 million city contract as soon as they hired Bill Shea's law firm, when they couldn't sell the city a single voting machine in 37 previous years? Why did the bank controlled by Republican county leader Vincent Albano get more interest-free deposits from the city than any other while John Lindsay was mayor? Why did Leonard Simon's clients get 10 long-term day-care leases shortly after he endorsed Lindsay for reelection in 1969?

This is considered the normal commerce of politics, the trading of influence, favors, and "contracts." But the public pays in the end—for each one.

So let us scrutinize the city and state budgets, and see how much legal graft—politicized waste—there really is, before we close one more firehouse, before we lay off any more cops, before we write an epitaph for open admissions.

Christopher Boomis is a good place to begin. During 1973 and 1974, Boomis—a real estate developer of minor reputation—suddenly lavished $85,000 in campaign contributions upon Abe Beame, Howard Samuels, Stanley Steingut, Malcolm Wilson, and Hugh Carey. He also switched all his insurance business to Grand Brokerage, then owned by Steingut and Brooklyn party boss Meade Esposito. Boomis also mysteriously gave away a 25 per cent limited partnership interest in his company to a Teamster leader named Luis Alimena.

Thereafter, Boomis got a real estate tax exemption for two years —from Roger Starr—for a luxury high-rise he wanted to build at 96th Street and Broadway. He also got a $37 million contract from the city —without competitive bidding—to construct a pier and a refrigerated warehouse at Hunts Point in the Bronx. Boomis also got $20 million in credit from banks and mortgage companies, partly on the word of power broker Bill Shea.

Boomis has been paid $2.1 million by the city so far. But he has not paid his subcontractors, and they have filed civil suit against him. Manhattan District Attorney Robert Morgenthau has impaneled a Grand Jury to find out how Boomis originally obtained the contract from former city officials—EDA administrator Ken Patten and Ports and Terminals Commissioner Edgar Fabber.

But to this day, the city has not canceled its contract with Boomis, or tried to recover the $2.1 million it has already paid him.

Then there's the Bronx Terminal Market rip-off.

In 1972, the city was making a $300,000 profit on the market. The merchants wanted to convert it into a cooperative. But, instead, the city in the person of Ken Patton decided to give a private real estate developer named David Buntzman a 99-year lease to run the market. The lease was amended in October 1973. The amendments gave the New York Yankees two of the market's 31 acres for a parking lot, and Buntzman received 4.2 additional acres the city purchased from the bankrupt Erie Lackawanna railroad for $790,000. In the amended lease, the city also agreed to assume more than $6.5 million of Buntzman's obligations, to make improvements.

In this renegotiation of the lease, the lawyer for Buntzman was Pat Cunningham, then Bronx Democratic party boss, soon to become lawyer for the Yankees. Cunningham has admitted to me to receiving more than $60,000 in legal fees from Buntzman.

City Councilman Henry Stern has said, "The Buntzman lease is absurd on its face. It is as if the city had leased the Brooklyn Bridge for $1 a year, and given the lessee the right to charge tolls on it."

Buntzman has already collected $3 million in rents from the merchants of the market. He has raised rents by an average of 80 per cent. His lease with the city absolves him of paying the city any rent for the first of the 99 years on a building just built for him by the city. Buntzman pays the city 61.5 cents per square foot; Buntzman is charging most tenants $3 per square foot.

Buntzman has also evicted 16 commercial wholesalers from the market, driving 700 unskilled jobs out of the South Bronx, where unemployment is 30 per cent.

The evictions were approved by judges who owed their judicial robes to Pat Cunningham. In the eviction proceeding against Goody Brand Tomato, which I attended last June, Judge Benjamin Nolan rejected motions for a jury trial and ruled himself in favor of Cunningham's client. Nolan had been the regular district leader in the old 85th Assembly District—until Cunningham made him a judge.

Another Bronx judge—Joseph Brust—has been indicted for perjury because of his answers to questions about his disposition of a case involving the Bronx market.

The city's 1976–77 capital budget includes $9 million for the Bronx Terminal Market. The city is also paying debt service on the cost of construction of a $4.1 million warehouse the taxpayers built for Buntzman at the market.

New York City has broken its wage agreement with trade unions, and its covenants with bondholders. But it has not yet broken its contracts with politically connected businessmen like Buntzman and Boomis. Thirty-seven merchants remaining at the Bronx market have signed a petition asking that the market now be turned into a co-op. It is time for the city to start nullifying contracts with the powerful instead of with the powerless.

Another taxpayer rip-off is the Yankee Stadium renovation. Early in 1972, John Lindsay and Ken Patton convinced the Board of Estimate to approve a $24 million "urban renewal expenditure" to improve Yankee Stadium, and the neighborhood surrounding it. Lindsay said the estimate of the cost was based on "hard data."

It is now four years later, and the final cost of the Yankee stadium renovation, according to Comptroller Goldin's office, is $101 million. This includes public money for equipment for the Yankee team, and "catering facilities," carpeting, and private toilets in the VIP boxes.

In contrast to the $101 million cost for renovation, Pontiac, Michigan last year completed a new 80,000-seat stadium at a cost of $55 million.

In the end, $2 million for improving the shops and streets near Yankee stadium was quietly deleted from this year's budget.

Included in the $101 million is $30 million for Kinney Parking to build two garages and rehabilitate a third. The Kinney contract was let without competitive bidding. The city now leases the space from Kinney at $2.4 million a year and shares the parking fees with Kinney as operator. The contract calls for Kinney to get 95 per cent of the first $100,000, 90 per cent of the second $100,000, 85 per cent of the next $200,000, and so on in a complex sliding scale.

The person who helped negotiate this no-bid deal with Kinney for the city was EDA's counsel, Steve Salup. Salup now works for Kinney as a lawyer.

Manhattan Republican county leader Vincent Albano is paid $25,000 a year for "finder's fees and commissions" by the National Kinney Corporation. One of Albano's closest friends is Bronx Democratic boss Pat Cunningham, who is the lawyer for the Yankees.

The insurance on the Yankees is placed by Neil Walsh, the city's commissioner of public events, and a principal in Walsh & Walsh, Inc., of 551 Fifth Avenue.

And so far, it's all legal.

The city's direct lease day-care program is wasting $10 million a year, according to state senators Franz Leichter and Major Owens.

There are 171 direct lease day-care centers in the city. The direct lease system was developed suddenly in 1969. Landlords were offered 15-and 20 year-leases to convert their property into day-care centers. Windfall profits were quickly made on buildings totally inappropriate for day-care centers in terms of space and structure.

What is remarkable is that the average cost per child, per week, in the direct lease centers is three times as high as in community-run centers. Under the 171 direct leases, for example, the city—not the landlord—pays all the real estate taxes and utility bills. Also, the rents per square foot are higher.

As usual, the politicians got the gravy. In 1969, Brooklyn Assemblyman Leonard Simon broke with his party to endorse John Lindsay for mayor. All the good government groups said that was a profile in courage.

Six months later, a construction company represented by Leonard Simon—Getz Construction—was awarded 10 of the first 15 direct leases for day-care.

Simon's client is still collecting rents on his 20-year leases with the city. No doubt Simon has collected a fat legal fee. But 28 community day-care centers—that are cheaper to operate—have been closed in the senseless wave of budget cutting.

Of the 171 direct leases, 83 are held by eight landlords with political connections. Eight leases are held by Ira Belfer of Root Realty. Belfer was also one of the original investors in Bernard Bergman's Towers nursing home.

Investigations Commissioner Nicholas Scoppetta says he can't even get his hands on city records for direct lease centers. "The whole program is a shocking mess," he says. "No one in HRA knows what it's all about."

The nursing home scandal was just the tip of the Medicaid rip-off. In 1973, under Nelson Rockefeller, New York state employed just 16 auditors to supervise 700 nursing homes. In January 1974, a special

---

COST OF LEGAL GRAFT TO NEW YORK CITY

Hunts Point/Christopher Boomis:	*$37 million*
Bronx Terminal Market:	*$15.5 million*
Yankee Stadium renovation:	*$101 million*
Unaudited Medicaid mills:	*$75 million (estimated)*
Nursing home corruption:	*$25 million (estimated)*
Day-care direct leases:	*$10 million*
City leases of private property:	*$87 million*
Reduced tax assessments for landlords:	*$21 million*
Uncollected 1975 real estate taxes:	*$210 million*
Con Edison bail-out:	*$500 million*
	$1.0815 billion

This billion dollars of waste should not be sensationalized beyond its meaning. This is just the sum of all the waste that I know about, because I have written about it in the past. Some of it, like the Yankee Stadium, is not recoverable. There is other legal graft I don't know about, or can't prove yet. The billion dollars is just an example, a symbol of a process that is enriching the few, at the expense of the many.

—J. N.

prosecutor was appointed for nursing homes, and he hired 66 new auditors.

So far, six nursing home operators have been convicted of Medicaid cheating. Eugene Hollander pleaded guilty to billing Medicaid for his Renoir painting. Ten other nursing home owners have been indicted and are awaiting trail. So far, the special prosecutor and the 66 auditors have identified $20 million in Medicaid fraud. They think they will discover $80 million more, with 96 more auditors about to be hired.

And all signs are that Medicaid mills are equally corrupt. There are 426 Medicaid mills in New York City. They are not audited by any agency of government. They are not licensed. They are not inspected. They exist in a limbo beyond scrutiny.

Assemblyman Andrew Stein, who helped break open the nursing home scandal, has estimated that last year there were, "at least $300 million in overpayments to Medicaid mills." The city pays 25 per cent of this cost, the state pays 25 per cent, and the federal government 50 per cent. The total cost to the city last year was $1.6 billion.

The person who is in charge of monitoring Medicaid mills for the city is Assistant Health Commissioner Al Schwarz. This is the same Al Schwarz who had earlier been criticized for his conduct in the nursing home scandal.

Schwarz gave an "A rating" to Bernard Bergman's inhuman Towers nursing home, despite written reports by inspectors who found, "filthy conditions. . . . and irresponsible disregard for the safety, health, and welfare of both residents and employees." Schwarz later admitted he was a close personal friend of Bergman's, and had attended the wedding of his daughter.

City health inspectors testified before the Stein Commission that Schwarz had discouraged unfavorable reports about nursing homes and suggested they write "love letters" instead.

The city's health commissioner—Lowell Bellin—says the reason he promoted Schwarz to this responsible position is that Investigations Commissioner Nicholas Scoppetta has "cleared him." Scoppetta told me: "The matter is still open. I never cleared Schwarz."

The immense profits in the Medicaid mills are split between the landlords and the doctors. The treatment of the patients is notoriously inadequate, and sometimes nonexistent. It is impossible to find out who actually owns the mills, since they are rented from private landlords and the landlord does not have to file any form with the city. There are rumors that powerful politicians, lawyers, and land-lords own mills, but the bureaucracy has made sure there is no document to prove it.

A story of Medicaid computer printouts by the staff of Assembly-man Stein has uncovered:

• A general practitioner who was paid for 1875 sessions of psychi-atric therapy, although there is no evidence he is licensed to perform such work.

• A general practitioner who was paid $91,000 in Medicaid funds; his bills showed that more than 90 per cent of his patients were first visits. Doctors get reimbursed at a higher rate for first visits.

• A pediatrician who was paid $50,000 for doing electrocardio-grams, which he is not supposed to do. Electrocardiograms are mainly performed on adult patients.

With strict auditing the city could recover about $75 million this year in fraud from these storefront swindles.

In defending the city's passive policy toward the Medicaid mills, Commissioner Bellin said that only "5 to 10 per cent" of the Medi-caid-participating physicians could be described as "bandits."

Less than 1 per cent of the public are "bandits," but the city has more than 25,000 cops.

Another area of politicized waste is the city's leases of private property from landlords who are generous campaign contributors. There were 1200 of these leases in the 1975–76 expense budget. They add up to $87 million. Most are at inflated rentals. Many are not needed at all. All are awarded by the Department of Real Estate without competitive bidding.

The City Council, for example, rents two and a half floors at 250 Broadway from builder Sam Minskoff, at $327,000 a year. Most of the 43 councilmen have never used the office space allotted for them, because they don't really need it. They already have office space at City Hall and at 51 Chambers Street.

A summer intern working for Manhattan Councilman Robert Robert Wagner, Jr. has analyzed the rental leases only in Manhattan. The following landlords, who contributed to Abe Beame, now hold no-bid rental leases from the city:

Seymour Cohn of the Sylvan Lawrence Company, holds 12 no-bid leases worth $3 million in annual rent from the city treasury. Meyer Steinberg, who gave the Beame campaign $6,000, holds leases worth

$2.6 million. Issac Silverman gave Beame $10,000, and now holds leases worth $1.1 million from the city.

Kenneth Wilpon, a Staten Island realtor questioned about organized crime connections by the State Commission of Investigations, has seven leases worth $429,000 with the city. Wilpon is listed as a contributor to Congressman John Murphy and Staten Island Borough President Robert Connor.

Ira Belfer, the original Towers nursing home investor, and one of the biggest beneficiaries of day-care direct leases, also has real estate leases from the city. Belfer has three that provide him $541,000 in annual rent. Belfer is also a good friend of Stanley Steingut.

Property owners in the city pay a rate of $8.17 for every $100 of assessed value. The City Tax Commission gives reduced real estate tax assessments to landlords on the basis of proven "hardship." Historically, the landlords who have contributed to the "right" politicians, or have hired the "right" lawyers, find it much easier to make convincing hardship arguments before clubhouse commissioners.

In 1975, the last year for which records are available, the Tax Commission granted 80 per cent more tax reductions than it did the year before. In 1975 the city was in the midst of its fiscal crisis. But the tax commission's generosity to the richest property owners in the city meant that the city collected $21 million less in real estate taxes this year.

Among the recipients of "hardship" tax reductions were: the New York Stock Exchange, the Prudential Insurance Company, Con Edison, Chemical Bank, the American Shipping Company, The New York Telephone Company, the Bank of New York, First National City Bank, and Rockefeller Center.

Last year, Local 371 of the Social Service Employees Union released Research into the pattern of favoritism at the Tax Commission. Their study focused on the real estate empire of Lou Rudin and his family. Rudin is chairman of the Association for a Better New York—a group that employs the rhetoric of boosterism as a cover for landlord self-interest. Rudin and his relatives contributed $15,000 to Abe Beame in 1973 and were significant contributors to John Lindsay in 1969.

The Rudins own 33 buildings in Manhattan. Between 1970 and 1975, Rudin Management made 209 requests for assessment reductions to the Tax Commission. Of that number 137—or 66 per cent —were granted. The total reduced assessment given the Rudins was

$32.3 million. During the same period of time, property owners on the same blocks as Rudin filed a total of 1411 requests. Of this number, only 16 per cent were approved.

For example: 40 Park Avenue is owned by the Rudin family. This building received six consecutive tax reductions in six years. Owners of other properties on the same block made 64 applications for Tax Relief, of which only seven were granted.

On February 19, 1973, the SIC issued a report saying the Tax Commission has "improperly reduced real estate tax assessments by millions of dollars, by blindly acting on incomplete, irregular, and sometimes patently false applications by owners of large properties." In some cases, the SIC report said, "the possible influence of political campaign contributions" might have "tainted" such reductions.

According to the city's Finance Administration, uncollected real estate taxes from property owners for 1975 was $210 million.

Under the law, landlords have three years to pay up before the city can move to collect or foreclose. At the end of three years, many landlords just abandon their buildings, after enjoying the experience of collecting rents while paying no taxes and investing no money in maintenance. It's a racket only the property class can participate in. Tenants get evicted for not paying rent.

A common myth is that most of the landlords in tax arrears are small, marginal types victimized by rent control. But records on file in the Municipal Building provide evidence to the contrary.

For example, Irving Maidman. Maidman owns more than 20 properties in Manhattan. Many of them are massage parlors and porno theatres in the Times Square area that are very profitable. The anonymous sounding 10–42 Corporation owes New York City $584,000 in back taxes. Irving Maidman owns the 10–42 Corporation.

Wellington Associates, part of the Goldman-DiLorenzo real estate empire, is another tax dodger. Wellington owes the city $768,000 on two properties—15 William Street, and The FBI building at 201 East 69th Street.

The New York Bank for Savings owes $450,000 on a property it foreclosed last year. The Times Square Portman Company, owned by millionaire John Portman of Atlanta, owes $885,000 on 200 and 202 West 46th Street.

And the Targee Care Center Corporation on Staten Island owes $362,000. The principal of the company is convicted millionaire nursing home operator Bernard Bergman.

If there are sacrifices to be made on Lenox Avenue and on Fox Street, there is a sacrifice for Con Edison to make.

On May 16, 1974, the state legislature—at the request of Malcolm Wilson—voted to buy and lease back to the utility two partially completed power plants. One was in Astoria, and the other at Indian Point, which is a nuclear generating plant. This bail-out cost the taxpayers of the state $500 million. The deal was made because Con Edison said it was going broke.

In the intervening two years a few things have happened. In November 1974, Con Ed—a licensed monopoly—was granted a 20.3 per cent increase in electric rates by the Public Service Commission. In April 1975, Con Edison reported a stunning 64 per cent ($75 million) increase in profits for the first quarter. In August 1975, Congressman Charles Vanik of Ohio released a study that revealed that Con Edison paid no federal income taxes in 1973. The utility declared an income of $203,319 million but used loopholes and accounting creativity to avoid all federal taxes. And most recently, Con Edison reported a 41 per cent rise in earnings for the last quarter of 1975.

Con Ed has a lot of clout. Its chairman, Charles Luce, sits with Richard Shinn on the board of the Metropolitan Life Insurance Company, and Shinn is also the chairman of the Mayor's Management Advisory Committee. E. Virgil Conway is another director of Con Ed. Conway is also president of the Seamen's Bank for Savings and a member of Shinn's management committee. A third Con Ed director—Richard Perkins—is the former chairman of the executive committee of Citibank. Citibank or Met Life should have bailed Con Ed out in 1974, not the taxpayers.

Con Edison did not really require a bail-out by the state in 1974. But now the utility is reporting soaring profits, and the state is in deep fiscal trouble.

Governor Carey, or the EFCB, should cancel the sale and lease-back agreement, and ask Con Edison for the $500 million back. If Con Edison refuses, their electricity rates should be lowered, and their taxes increased.

Unlike some corporations, Con Edison can't threaten to move to New Jersey.

Do all this, close all the loopholes for the privileged, and all the swindles for the connected, and we still will not end our endless fiscal crisis. The roots of the crisis are structural and historical.

We must remedy all these ripoffs as a defensive action against future erosion of the quality of life. We must stop the legal graft merely to remain in place on the down escalator of history.

But to protect parasites like the Cunninghams and the Maidmans, and powerful institutions like Con Ed and the redlining banks, while a Northside dies, a Pleasant Avenue burns, a Wyndal Burt goes back to prison, is unspeakable. It makes nonsense of the city's claim of austerity. The city's program is one of austerity for the poor and the middle class and profligacy for the powerful.

As long as the city is ridden with waste and corruption, we are vulnerable to the antiurban critics in Washington who want to score debaters' points. Even though Ronald Reagan paid no federal taxes in 1974, and even though James Eastland collects $100,000 a year in agricultural subsidies for his plantation, they are cynical enough to attack us for our waste. And Jerry Brown and Jimmy Carter will find justification in Zen and Christ to win votes off our poor.

It must be repeated once again: The only authentic, long-term solution to our predicament is federal help. New York City by itself does not have the power or authority to tax the suburbs, or control inflation, or print currency.

Out of boredom, out of frustration, out of exhaustion, people might be driven to exotic remedies like default. Or to the hideous ideas of Roger Starr.

But the answers today are what the answers were last year, and eight years ago, when Richard Nixon began his war on the cities.

Pass the Humphrey-Hawkins bill creating jobs and the potential of full employment. Pass the Kennedy-Corman national health insurance bill that will save us $900 million in Medicaid money. Federalize the costs of welfare because poverty is a national responsibility. Enact a new federal housing program and extend FHA guarantees to the rehabilitation of existing housing. And pass the Kennedy-Reuss bill creating an urban bank to extend federal credit to cities.

Union consultant Jack Bigel says: "The single most important act that could save New York would be the passage of the Kennedy bill for an urban bank."

Every day I get a phone call, or a press release, or meet someone who tells a small, personal horror story of the budget cuts. An alcoholism treatment program closes in Queens, and an old man goes to the bars again. A 45-year-old fireman gets a heart attack because he was trying to fight a fire on his second overtime shift in two days. An after-school tutoring program in Bed-Stuy ends, and a chance for college dies. A day-care center closes, and a mother has to give up her job.

The rich get richer, and the poor get poorer.

They made a desert, and called it New York.

19. Blaming the Victim

WILLIAM K. TABB

By now everyone knows how to solve the New York City fiscal crisis: stop giveaway programs and well-meaning but ineffectual social experiments, cut spending, resist unreasonable union demands and roll back past contract gains. "Welfare chiselers and greedy union expectations must be scaled down," say conservatives, and "realism must be the watchword" say liberals. But the conventional wisdom is wrong. These are not the causes of the fiscal crisis. Before we can talk about solutions we must explain what is wrong with the usual analyses of the city's fiscal crisis. We start with the most common answer, welfare spending.

WELFARE

In denying the city aid in late October 1975, President Ford said, "As for New York's much discussed welfare burden, the record shows more than one current welfare recipient in ten may be legally ineligible for welfare assistance." The clear inference is that many people are cheating.

Liberal politicians, however, have not challenged the Administration on its "facts," which are at best debatable. Consider first this matter of the number of ineligibles which seems to so easily upset rank-and-file taxpayers and to win points for conservative politicians. The city's welfare commissioner himself estimates that "50 percent of ineligibility is worker error" rather than client misrepresentation or fraud; the welfare workers' manual is several feet thick with hundreds of new changes each year to be mastered by the welfare workers. The cost of these safeguards against cheating are truly staggering.

The city spends $600 million on welfare (about 30 percent of total

This is an edited version of a paper written in March 1976 which will appear in Larry Sawers and William K. Tabb, eds., *Marx and the Megalopolis* (New York: Oxford University Press, forthcoming 1978). William K. Tabb is associate professor of economics at Queens College, CUNY.

welfare expenditures in the city), yet more than half of the city's share doesn't go to poor people *but to administrative costs.* The petty rules and long forms which must be filled out and checked and computerized take time and money. Given current administrative costs, the cost of eliminating "cheating" would outweigh the savings. The moral crusaders are not, however, interested.

Far more recipients are harassed off welfare or have their cases closed by fiat than cheat the government. As a matter of fact, the state reverses half the appeals brought by recipients against the city agency's actions. The city concedes 30 percent of the cases before the appeal board. Further thousands of others do not even contest unfair decisions. Even the State Department of Social Services readily admits that nearly a third of the welfare families they have called "ineligible" are in fact eligible for some form of relief. They also recognize that the Welfare Department by its own rules underpays clients in more than 18 percent of its cases. The case for cheating by the welfare agencies against the people is far stronger than the other way around. Finally, the overwhelming majority of welfare recipients want work and cannot find it, or have small children and no day care, or are the small children punished for being born in the wrong family. The welfare workers' union says that as a result of staff cutbacks, applicants must wait up to twenty-seven days with a month more before they receive a decision on eligibility.

In early 1976, with the severe cutbacks and an unemployment rate of 12 percent in the city, it was estimated that by the end of the next fiscal year, with unemployment benefits exhausted, day-care cuts, and other services ended, the future welfare roll could be expected to include about a fifth of all New Yorkers.

It is crucial to understand two things about all of this. First, New York City is not the worst problem area in terms of welfare. For example, in terms of Aid to Families with Dependent Children (AFDC), which is what people generally mean by "welfare," the proportion of the population who are recipients is almost 50 percent higher in Baltimore, St. Louis and Boston. But those cities do not carry the financial burden for welfare that New York City does—thanks to payment formulas and rates forced on New York by the state and federal governments.

Second, but more important, the problem is not really the welfare system at all. The real problem is that the United States economy has never produced anything approaching full employment except in time of war. The surplus work force cannot support itself and must turn to government for help. Family pathologies result from no hope and the grueling burden of living below a poverty-income level. The answer is not to throw people off welfare and to cut food stamps but to stop acceding to the current rules of the game. We now accept that the private sector controls investment and job creation, that it can close shops in one area, open them at lower wages elsewhere, no matter what the social costs involved. The government then comes in to ameliorate the poverty created by corporate decisions. That is the current welfare problem's origin. It also suggests where to look for a solution. In my view, the basic problems is how capitalist patterns of investment create poverty.

Similarly fundamental criticisms must be made not just of the Medicaid mills where unscrupulous doctors rake in millions for little or no services, but of the whole U.S. system of health delivery, of the AMA, the drug industry, the whole organization of this highly profitable but socially irrational system which we can ill afford and which offers us low-quality service at unconscionable cost.

In the meantime there are more moderate reforms which could help New York City a lot. The federal government should pay all of the costs of welfare everywhere, of course, but a minimal essential reform would seem to be the state paying all of those costs. In New York State, local government as a whole pays 23 percent of AFDC cash assistance and Medicaid payments. The figure is 6.5 percent in New Jersey, 4.2 percent in Maryland, less than 1 percent in Virginia, Utah, Oregon, New Hampshire and Louisiana. In New York State, cities pay more than in any of the other twenty-one states where a large contribution is required. Most other large cities are part of larger counties which have suburbs as part of the same revenue-generating county district. If New York State had a no-local contribution policy, like Pennsylvania or Michigan do, the city would have saved $366 million in 1974.

SALARIES AND PENSIONS

Well, what about the unions? Municipal wages not just in New York but around the country have been rising fast. So have wages paid to corporation presidents and government officials. How much is too much and is New York far ahead of the pack? It is possible by picking and choosing your numbers to argue it either way. If a fireman's salary in New York averaged close to $17,000 last year, the average was more than $21,000 in Los Angeles, $17,765 in San Francisco. If New York teachers were paid too much at $17,018, what of Detroit's $18,836? And, of course, the higher cost of living in New York gives a real boost of 16 percent to the Detroit teacher.

What is required is some broader measure of total municipal work-force wage differences. A number of comparisons have been offered, and not surprisingly, they differ greatly in their conclusions.

Arguing before a congressional investigating committee against assisting New York City, Treasury Secretary William Simon said that New York spends "in excess of three times more per capita than any city with a population over 1,000,000." He offered a comparison which turns out to be exceedingly misleading. "Looking at the payroll, Census Bureau data shows that New York employs some 49 employees per 1,000 residents. The payrolls of most other major cities range from 30 to 35 employees per 1,000 inhabitants."

The fault lies in Simon's comparing apples and oranges. The Congressional Budget Office, a high-caliber nonpartisan agency, made a serious effort to calculate comparative costs. They found that it was *not* the case that New York spent far more. The major differences arise because New York City provides many public services which in other jurisdictions are paid for by state and county governments.

A stronger case can be made that New York City's pension funds are overly generous. But even here there are a number of relevant matters which are too often swept under the rug.

New York City politicians negotiated generous pension benefits for much the same reason that they borrowed money—they could offer benefits which cost them little. That eventually a day of reckoning would come was not a central consideration given the short-run nature of their calculations. The city's pensions seem generous for two major reasons. First, compared to what the average worker has, they are. Only 25 percent of all companies in the United States pay pension benefits, and according to the Bureau of Labor Statistics, less than half of all corporate employees now covered will ever receive a penny from the money they are paying in (they will not stay with the company long enough), and with benefits averaging $1,605 a year, the private-sector worker has not got such a good deal going.

Since there are a lot of workers, pension funds hold a third of the nation's investable wealth. This is not, however, a source of working-class power, because while pension funds hold (in early 1976) more than 15 percent of all common stock, the largest single block of wealth in the stock market, the trust departments of the large New York banks have control over most of these assets.

The city's pension increases were understood by all to have been negotiated instead of higher wages; that is, if the generous pension provisions had not been accepted, presumably higher direct wage payments would have been forthcoming. Then, too, by concentrating on the twenty-year retirement provision, with payments based on the last year of service, a year artificially inflated with much overtime, the public has been convinced that all pensioners do exceedingly well. Actually not all uniformed retirees are able to inflate their benefits this way, and most city employees are covered by much less generous pension plans. The treatment of the city's police and fire fighters is not any more generous than the twenty-year retirement provisions for career officers in the armed services, and in terms of degree of exposure to danger over the length of working life do not seem all that dissimilar. Focusing on the exceedingly high benefits paid to a small number of city workers rather than the average payments to City Hall file clerks and subway-token sellers is like looking only at executives with $100,000-a-year pensions, plus deferred salary, stock options and other benefits, and saying they represent private-sector workers as a whole.

City pension funds do offer better coverage and benefits than most of the plans ordinary workers in the private sector can qualify for, and do offer hope that when these workers retire, they can live out their lives in some dignity without taking charity from the state or their children. This is not the case for millions of retired Americans. The average benefits retired city workers receive represent a modest but adequate floor for survival in old age. They should be a model for others to strive to attain. The abuses should be curbed, but the principle of adequate income in old age should be fought for by the majority of Americans who have no pensions coming from their employers, and those covered by plans where average payments will not allow survival at anywhere near even the poverty level standard.

The worst aspect of the city pension funds is increasingly being talked about nowadays. The real crime—the city has been robbing these funds for years. The entire pension system is extremely underfunded. Contributions made to it are based on outmoded actuarial tables dating from the beginning of the century when life expectancy was far less (some assumptions in current use date to 1908), so each year it falls further behind. Today, with $7.7 billion in assets, its liabilities are $13.8 billion.

Until the city does realistically change its estimates, the full vulnerability can only be guessed. For the next few years the system may survive, but all too soon the tipping point will be reached and there will be no money for retirees. The process is being speeded along by the city's "curtailing" contributions to the fund above 4 percent of the earnings on the $7.7 billion in assets. While the pension funds actually collect 9 percent on MAC bonds, only 4 percent goes to the pension funds; the city siphons off the remaining 5 percent. The Emergency Financial Control Board knowingly allows this to continue—after all, disaster won't be for a while.

AUSTERITY AND JOB CUTS

It has been argued that the city's fiscal crisis has not been caused by extravagant wages or by overly generous transfer payments. Yet the solutions being imposed have by and large been to fire city workers and cut service levels. Because government employment has been cut so drastically as to seriously affect the overall employment rate and the volume of local expenditures, the cure is exacerbating the problem. While the national economy improves somewhat, the city remains a disaster area. Because services have been drastically cut, crime increases. The urban environment further deteriorates businesses, and the middle class flees. The solution intensifies the problem. This process must be understood because as the nation's commitment to make its urban centers livable diminishes, the deterioration spreads to more and more cities.

City services have reached such low levels that a process of cumulative decay has begun. Fewer city workers means less adequate services, a deteriorated environment, more flight from the city, a smaller tax base, the need to fire more workers. At the national level it has long been recognized that job creation has a "multiplier" effect. Workers hired spend money creating demand for products leading to new workers being hired to produce the increasing demand for goods and services. The reverse cycle is also possible and indeed has begun with a vengeance in New York City, even as politicians at the national level speak of the need for job creation to spur the economy.

The Bureau of Labor Statistics estimates that the city reduced its work force by 48,000 in 1975. The city's new payroll monitoring system says over 34,000 jobs were cut in the seven months preceding

January 31, 1976. In the midst of a national economic upturn, New York stays in the doldrums, the 12 percent unemployment rate persisting due to declining governmental expenditures and the continuing loss of the city's tax base.

What is equally important is that the current austerity program penalizes blacks and Puerto Ricans most heavily. The recent teachers strike in New York ended with 15,000 teachers and paraprofessionals —that's 20 percent of the union—laid off. It is estimated that this reduces the proportion of black and Spanish-speaking teachers from 11 percent to 3 percent of the total number of teachers employed by the city, although two thirds of the students are either black or Puerto Rican. Between the fall of 1974 and the winter of 1976 the city work force lost half of its Spanish-speaking workers, 40 percent of black male employees and a third of its female employees. Deputy Mayor Kenneth Gibson said that minorities who were 31 percent of the city payroll suffered 44 percent of the cuts. Given the seniority system, the 13 percent decrease in the work force was not shared equally by race or sex, due to past discriminatory hiring. In areas most recently "broken," cutbacks were more severe. For example, the number of women police officers was reduced by 55 percent.

Estimates of expected job loss in the private sector due to city layoffs showed the importance of the public sector in generating income in the private sector. Harvard's Otto Eckstein, through his consulting firm Data Resources, Inc., estimated that 75 private-sector jobs would be lost for every 100 public employees "retrenched." Since many of the 40,000 laid-off government workers lived outside of New York City, not all of the ripple or multiplier effect would be felt within the city. Eckstein still estimated a minimum of 15,000 jobs would be lost in the city's private sector. Benjamin Chinitz, head of the Social Policy Institute of SUNY Binghamton, offered as his estimate more than 30,000 jobs lost as a result of the city cutbacks (close to a 1:1 ratio). As the city's unemployment rate rose to almost 50 percent above the national average, further cutbacks threatened to accelerate this downward cycle—layoffs and unemployment resulting in the need for still more services the city could less afford to provide—and a self-generating downward process seemed to be devastating the city. The New York Office of Data Resources, Inc., estimated that for 1975 a 1 percent cut in actual city expenditures with a 7 percent inflation rate would result in more than 8,000 lost service-sector jobs. The mayor's experts said another 8,000 jobs would be lost in construction due to the austerity three-year emergency budget (28,000 jobs had already been lost in that industry as building had virtually ceased in the city).

For every dollar cut in city payrolls, the federal government must spend 50 cents more in unemployment compensation, welfare and other expenses. The three-year plan Mayor Abraham Beame recently submitted to the city's new governing body calls for no pay increases until after June 1978, and despite increasing need and inflation, a cut in aggregate expenditures—$12.1 billion in 1976, $11.9 billion in 1977, and $11.7 billion in 1978. While the plan is a joke, its estimates totally unrealistic and its results unattainable, the plan is being used to try and bludgeon city workers into taking massive cuts in their real income, and service recipients to accept the need for the closing of hospitals and police stations.

PRODUCTIVITY AND PAYOFFS

The whole issue of cutbacks must be considered on two levels. First, the downturn in the economy caught everybody. The banks had made bad loans to airlines flying half-empty planes, to builders of supertankers now starving for business, to Real Estate Investment Trusts with unsold vacation homes and empty hotels, and to Zaïre and the generals in Chile. The federal government copes by running an $80 billion deficit, the corporations by borrowing even more short-term, but the banks were perilously close to illiquidity. Only New York is told to pay up. Quite simply, New York is the only place the banks can get their money, raise their rates. They negotiate reductions with their other bad risks. Lockheed, as New York, was a social decision made by the powerful. There was nothing ordained by God about the choice. Austerity in New York is a lesson to all. It helps nationally to transfer resources away from social needs, weakens municipal unionism, and redistributes capital to the corporate sector.

But there can be little argument with substituting civilians for police officers in clerical and desk jobs to get more cops on the street, or with vandalproof hydrants (this would save about $1 million in fire loss a year resulting from water-pressure problems), or with hoist compactor containerized garbage trucks. If high-expansion foam fights fire better, fine. If ten-ton garbage trucks are more efficient, OK. These are not in a real sense the issue, except to the extent that innovations displace large numbers of workers who are simply fired.

If such improvements were added gradually and labor saved through attrition, savings could be made without the price being paid by city workers. Unions resist such changes because their workers are asked to pay a heavy price for such savings. Cutting abuses, such as convenience arrests made at the end of a cop's workday so that booking and going to court is on overtime pay, should be stopped but there really is a difference between stopping abuses on the one hand and speed-ups and firings on the other. Around the edges there is room for honest disagreement, but the layoffs we are witnessing do not curb abuses; they cut needed services and demoralize workers and citizens alike.

Most of the proffered improvements are not exactly new ideas. They've been around for years but the city has systematically underinvested in such innovations. Before new garbage trucks, compactors, containerized carting and such are brought in, the management experts might allocate money for mechanics to fix the 25 percent or more of the existing fleet waiting for repairs. The city has less than one mechanic for more than twenty-five vehicles. In the private sector, one mechanic services on the average only eight vehicles. Three years ago on any one day, 8 percent of the fleet was in for repairs; today it is more than a quarter and rising fast. Since the budget for new trucks had by September (1975) been reduced 88 percent and existing trucks are worked double and triple shifts, all this talk of new breakthroughs in collection methods seems to have an air of unreality.

The public sector does so poorly because it is expected to do everything cheaply. Short-run "economies" are instituted but at greater long-term cost. There are two other important and related truths here. The first is that politics is a business. It is a question *not* of mismanagement within the system but of the system resting on payoffs, bribes, favors and milking the public. This is not the aberration, but the rule. As the middle class has left the city, the degree of pure rip-off has qualitatively increased. Second, the business community rakes off far more from the city through subsidies and favors than politicians do, so to set them in charge in the public interest is fraught with contradictions.

The big winners from the system are not the party faithful who have highly paid elevator-starter jobs in public buildings, but those who profit from construction subsidies or who receive the interest on the bloated bond borrowing. Consider that the office buildings in

lower Manhattan have a 30 percent vacancy rate in part because
some years back David Rockefeller (head of the Lower Manhattan
Association and of the Bond Council that sets the rates the city must
pay) pressured the Port Authority (headed over part of this period by
William Ronan, who accepted hundreds of thousands of dollars in
gifts from the Rockefeller family) to build the World Trade Center.
This billion-dollar tax-exempt structure (it was supposed to cost $350
million) would be yielding the city some $45.2 million in taxes if it
paid what it would as a privately owned structure. Even so, the towers
could not rent all their space. Fortunately a concerned governor (later
Vice President) moved in numerous state agencies to help out. The
state is the largest tenant (2.4 million square feet). It costs more to
rent space in the World Trade Center, of course. It also contributed
to the 30 percent vacancy rate in lower Manhattan office buildings.
This leads to lower tax assessments and tax abatements and thus to
revenue loss. The World Trade Center itself runs an $8 million
deficit, which citizens also pay for. Payoffs, subsidies and false billings
come to billions and account for much of the city's debt.

I am arguing, then, that it is not welfare or the unions which are
to be blamed for the city's fiscal crisis, nor is it mismanagement in
the sense the term is usually used. The World Trade Center is far
from an isolated incident. In fact, the city's capital budget debt owes
far more to the banker–real-estate-developer agencies—the Housing
Finance Administration, the Urban Development Corporation—
than it does to helping the poor, more to subsidizing commuters than
to helping the unemployed get jobs.

If the New York economy is crumbling, as headline writers like to
suggest, the city is not going downhill alone. While New York City
lost nearly 16 percent of its jobs between 1965 and 1972, Philadelphia
lost 17 percent and New Orleans nearly 20 percent. The recessions
of recent years have had dire effects in most of the nation's older
cities and regions like New England and the Middle Atlantic. In
longer-run terms, the economic epidemic has been decline in the old
manufacturing areas and growth in the West, Southwest and parts
of the South and Northwest. But the decline in quality of life in the
older areas is spreading to their newer suburbs, and the rot of deteriorated infrastructure, housing stock and public services is spreading.
It cannot be contained by punishing New York. Such a course only
accelerates the problem.

In July 1973 the Advisory Commission on Intergovernmental Relations issued a report entitled "City Financial Emergencies." Well before the New York fiscal crisis exploded, the commission found an "incredible and seemingly insoluble array of financial difficulties" facing urban governments due to a long-standing array of deeply structural problems: outmoded capital facilities, inability to increase the tax base and a seeming irreversibility in soaring demands for public services. Debt ceilings, tax-payer rebellion and competition with other jurisdictions placed limits on ability to raise funds, yet the basic needs of the citizenry were not being met at all adequately. The "general inability to make the revenue sources stretch to fit the expenditures mandated by the state and demanded by the people" had, in the commission's view, reached "emergency" proportions. A year later the New York crisis burst upon the popular consciousness. The commission's warning had gone unheeded, however, as had countless earlier warnings. In a real sense, the New York fiscal crisis had not been a surprise.

As so often happens, the way the New York City crisis is being solved lays the groundwork for the next crisis. The federal government has been unwilling to make a real full-employment policy a first priority and instead relies on greater subsidies to the private sector as the major method of stimulating the economy. As a result our older cities continue to deteriorate.

Ironically, New York may, as a city, come out far better than most others. In the long run the city has more resources than other large cities and remains the nerve center of the U.S. economy.

There are those, such as Herbert Bienstock, regional commissioner of the Bureau of Labor Statistics, who expect New York to continue its upward trajectory as world headquarters in the 1980s. He sees development and expansion of the "undisputed center of the nation's knowledge-oriented industries" with job growth in publishing, advertising, merchandising and expansion in both business services and cultural facilities—theater, dance, art. But such a bright future is perhaps a decade away and there is no guarantee that the majority of the city's current population will participate in it.

The trauma the city is currently undergoing is to scale down services to the working poor, who, since the manufacturing base continues to be destroyed, are no longer needed, and to make room for more workers in communications, media, finance and corporate-sector jobs. The hope is that the overbuilding of offices in the mid-1960s was temporary and that a safer, lower-cost city will once again attract corporate headquarters. Who pays the cost of this continuing transformation is clear.

For the city, what is in store is not one set of sacrifices but real and continued severe cutbacks in service, a cycling downward into further decay to be ended only when "planned shrinkage" gets rid of the poor, and unionization among municipal workers has been beaten back. American social scientists are fond of denying that there is such a thing as class struggle. Certainly, in the case of the New York City fiscal crisis they speak in value neutral terms of increasing efficiency. Politicians urge us all to pull together, share the burden, bite the bullet. The perspective offered in the current analysis suggests that in fact class conflict lies at the heart of why the city crisis exists, why those in power choose the scapegoats they do and seek to impose the "solutions" they do. Alternative answers exist which do not involve blaming the poor and working class for the existence of the crisis. The conventional analyses, when subject to scrutiny, have been found incorrect and misleading. The simplest of class analysis strongly suggests which forces are in fact to blame and how to conceptualize alternative answers to the crisis.

20. Pirates and Politicians: Sinking on the Same Ship

ROBERT FRIEDMAN

In a ninety-day period, from the beginning of September to the end of November 1975, there were 45 demonstrations in lower Manhattan—an average of one every other day—in response to New York City's fiscal crisis. There were untold more throughout the five boroughs, protesting the closings of fire stations, police precincts, hospitals, day-care and old-age centers. Many of the demonstrations, like a gathering of 10,000 old people at City Hall in October, were never reported in the press. Others resulted in sit-downs, traffic tie-ups and arrests. According to a spokesman for the 1st Police Precinct in lower Manhattan, "There hasn't been anything approaching this level of protest since the days of the antiwar movement when there were demonstrations down here almost every day."

Despite this extraordinary level of activity, there was no organized, sustained resistance to the budget cutbacks, no strong leadership or viable programs presented by the city's municipal unions, by its liberal Democrats or by the radical left. This default by those in a position to oppose the "solutions" imposed by city, state and federal governments was grounded in the widespread acceptance by most New Yorkers of a myth: that there wasn't enough money to go around. Once people accepted this myth, it was inevitable that their response would be one of acquiescence.

But there *was* money to go around. The banks were taking nearly a sixth of the city's budget for debt service on their loans; the federal government was siphoning more money out of New York in taxes than it was paying back in services; the politicians were soaking the treasury for millions of dollars in salaries for patronage jobs; and the landlords owed over half a billion dollars in unpaid real-estate taxes.

A similar version of this paper appeared in *Working Papers for a New Society* (Spring 1976). Robert Friedman is a writer living in New York City.

It is not surprising, then, that the banks, the federal government, the city politicians and local business interests—all of whom had significant investments to protect—should attempt to spread the illusion that there wasn't enough money. The public would have to make sacrifices, they cried, and the city's media broadcast the distress signals, blaming the victims for the sinking ship.

Public unions were a favorite target. Said the *Daily News*, which claims as its audience more than a million New York City workers: "For at least ten years, the city government has been . . . knuckling under to virtually every demand, no matter how piratical, of the bosses of the civil servants' unions."

Barry Feinstein is one of New York's "piratical" union bosses. Like most pirates, he is something of a folk hero. In June 1971 Feinstein, president of Teamsters Local 237, called a two-day strike that virtually paralyzed the city. Local 237, the fifth largest Teamsters local in the country, represents 15,000 municipal employees, including school security guards, hospital cooks, sewage maintenance workers and drawbridge operators. When union members walked off the job in 1971, they left the city's drawbridges raised. Traffic backed up for miles.

The strike was a dramatic move for Feinstein. A pension benefit that had been agreed to by Mayor John Lindsay was avoided by the state legislature, usually given to rubber-stamping such matters. By showing a little muscle, Feinstein's union won a partial victory; though the legislature refused to change its position, another benefit, bringing members an equivalent amount of money was negotiated.

In October 1975 Feinstein once again fired the public imagination: he called for a general strike of city workers. Feinstein and other municipal union leaders had just emerged from a meeting with Mayor Beame where they had been informed of further layoffs and a three-year wage freeze. "I'm in favor of a general strike in this city at this time," he told reporters. "We have given our blood. The unions are bleeding to death."

General strikes are not a common phenomenon in this country. They require union solidarity, some degree of class consciousness, and effective leadership. The last major general strike crippled the city of San Francisco in 1934 and resulted in several workers being killed by the police. In New York the closest thing to a general strike occurred during the summer of 1872, when some 70,000 workers from thirty different trade associations went out on strike for an eight-hour day. (The *New York Times*, showing remarkable editorial consistency over the years, opposed the strike on the grounds that an extra two hours of leisure time would have a deleterious effect on the working classes.)

So, it was something of a surprise to read in the *New York Times* the morning after Feinstein's meeting with Beame: "City Unions Weigh a General Strike." For the municipal unions, it was one of the few signs of militance in the eleven months since the first layoffs were announced—eleven months characterized by a pattern of threatened cutbacks by the mayor, vocal opposition by the unions, negotiations, then eventual compromise. But talk of a general strike turned out to be only more rhetoric. Other leaders backed off; and the headline the next day read: "Labor Chiefs Here Unreceptive to Call for General Strike." A spokeswoman for Albert Shanker, president of the United Federation of Teachers (UFT), which had recently settled a week-long strike of its own, said that the general strike "is a weapon used by Communists to achieve political change and is not a suitable weapon here in New York City."

A few days after he first suggested a strike, Feinstein brought the matter before the Municipal Labor Committee, a loose federation of most of the city's municipal unions. A resolution was passed unanimously and tacked on, almost as an afterthought, to a four-page statement about the fiscal crisis. The resolution concluded that the city was on a "collision course: a course towards inevitable conflict and a general strike." The strike proposal died there.

NO BARGAIN

Local 237's headquarters are on West Fourteenth Street in Manhattan; the building's façade is sheathed in aluminum as if to blend in with the neighboring merchants' metal gates that are rolled down every night to prevent burglaries. The offices are just what a Hollywood set designer might have come up with: they are neither prosperous nor dingy; a large board lists meeting times; a strike by another Teamsters local representing private carters is being run out of a littered room; the president's office is paneled in dark wood and cluttered with sports trophies and pictures, including one of a dollar bill that hangs at a 45-degree angle.

Feinstein, dressed in tailored denim pants, an open shirt and patent-leather shoes, and smoking a large cigar, is about forty and loves to talk. He has been with Local 237 for the past nineteen years; his father founded the union in 1952, and he started working there as a $60-a-week organizer in 1956. At the time there was no such thing as collective bargaining for municipal employees unions. Salaries were fixed by City Hall—a ceiling of $2,400 a year was set for members of Local 237—and though requests for raises could be made to a review board, the unions had little power. All that began to change in 1957 when Mayor Robert Wagner instituted collective bargaining. Ten years later, when Feinstein became president of Local 237, the municipal unions were at the height of their strength, winning new benefits and wage increases with each new contract.

Now the tables are turning the other way again. "There is no doubt," he said, "that the municipal unions have been the losers in this fiscal crisis. We went down a path which none of us thought we'd go down; we gave stuff away that none of us dreamed we would ever give away."

Why didn't Local 237 and the other municipal unions go out on strike when they were threatened with losing some of the very things they had gone out on strike to win? Feinstein says it has to do, in part, with the special relationship between Mayor Beame and the unions. "Most of us grew up with Abe. [Beame was a personal friend of Feinstein's father and still calls the Local 237 president "kid."] We all supported him in his run for mayor and when he was elected it was like having a friend in office. No other mayor could have sat us down and had us agree to giving away pieces of our contract. If it had been Lindsay or anyone else, the unions would have been more militant. I trust Abe Beame. When he says something about a budget gap, when he says there isn't enough money, I believe it.

"Everything we did was to prevent default," Feinstein went on. "We would have lost 50,000 jobs overnight. So we negotiated. Look, it's the easiest thing in the world for a union leader to call a big meeting, tear up a contract and call a strike. When times were good, we got good contracts. Now things are bad and we expect our members to accept the fact that these are hard times. We're in for four or five tough years. And anyone who says we've made our last concession is a fool."

"We will accept no further sacrifices than we've already made."
"The unions have to give up some of the crap they got at the bargaining table. They never should have gotten some of it."
The first statement was made in May 1975 by Victor Gotbaum,

head of the 110,000-member District Council 37 of the American Federation of State, County, and Municipal Employees, after Mayor Beame proposed that city workers forgo a 6 percent salary increase that was due them July 1. The second statement was made by Victor Gotbaum in a speech two days later.

District Council 37 is the largest municipal union in the city, and Victor Gotbaum is the most powerful municipal union leader. The union, which he has headed since 1965, represents most white-collar civil servants and blue-collar laborers in the city government. Though unions like DC 37 have been portrayed as pirates, its members are not exactly getting rich off the city treasury. While benefits are generous, the average salary of a DC 37 worker is only $9,200 a year, below the U.S. Department of Labor's figure of $9,852 needed to support a family of four in New York at a "lower than intermediate" standard of living. Some employees make considerably less: typists average $6,432 a year; keypunch operators $6,992.

Over the years Gotbaum has earned a reputation as a tough negotiator. Yet when faced with layoffs and cutbacks, he decided to compromise rather than fight. It was Gotbaum, more than anyone else, who set the strategy for the municipal unions; leaders of smaller unions, like Feinstein, tended to follow along. Of course, Gotbaum affected the style and rhetoric of an angry labor leader: he railed against the banks, organized a rally of 10,000 in front of First National City Bank in June, attacked Ford for not providing federal aid to the city, and threatened job actions. But throughout, he was motivated both by a desire to avoid default and by a belief that the unions would have to make sacrifices.

In December 1974, when the first round of layoffs was announced, Gotbaum wrote in the DC 37 newspaper, the *Public Employee Press:* "This union will not allow permanent civil service employees to be laid off." Six months later, when nearly 10,000 permanent civil service employees were laid off, Gotbaum took no action. In August, three months after a proposed wage freeze led him to declare that there would be "no further sacrifices," Gotbaum agreed, during a three-day negotiating session at the Americana Hotel, to accept a partial deferral of wage increases.

One particularly instructive example of Gotbaum's style of leadership was the fight over summer working hours. Back in the days before air-conditioned offices, city employees won the right to quit work an hour early during the summer months. In July 1975 Mayor

Beame announced that summer hours would be ended as an economy measure. Gotbaum chose to draw the line over this relatively archaic custom, though he had taken no action on the layoffs ten days earlier. He called for arbitration on the issue and told reporters, "It's a unilateral, antilabor act and he won't get away with it." The following day Beame rejected the arbitration proposal and Gotbaum fumed: "The guy wants war. This is really what he's asking for and he's going to get it." He fired the first shot, advising his members to leave work early the following Monday, despite the mayor's order.

But there was no war. Over the weekend Beame agreed to arbitration if Gotbaum would abandon summer hours until the issue was decided. Gotbaum went along, ordering his members to stay the extra hour on Monday. Ten days later the arbitration board ruled in Gotbaum's favor. But his victory was short-lived. In the Americana meetings a week later, each union leader agreed to give up one work rule. Gotbaum gave up summer hours.

Perhaps Gotbaum knew all along that he was going to give up summer hours and shrewdly manipulated the near-confrontation with Beame to make it appear a more crucial issue than it really was, thereby enhancing the value of his concession. But the net effect of his actions was to undermine his own position: to draw the line one place one week, then retreat the next. Shortly after backing down from the fight over summer hours, Gotbaum explained to a *New York Times* reporter, "I once read an interview with Mao or Chou and he said, 'Before we had the bomb, we had to talk like we did, but now that we have it, we don't have to talk that way.' When a union has power it doesn't have to be militant."

In choosing to exercise power rather than militance, Gotbaum no doubt won the admiration of Mayor Beame, Governor Carey and the businessmen, like Felix Rohatyn, who sit on the Municipal Assistance Corporation (MAC). He won some special concessions for DC 37 members; and from his point of view, the city owes him a lot for his cooperation. But his power may be illusory. By agreeing to contract regressions and layoffs, Gotbaum set a dangerous precedent, undercutting the municipal unions' power of collective bargaining. Far from making the city administration indebted to him, it could be an invitation to push the unions into giving up even more. And he further sowed dissension among the municipal unions, which are never known for their solidarity anyway. UFT president Albert Shanker remarked after the Americana sessions, "Vic Gotbaum got a good deal and in the process he stabbed a lot of other people." Ken McFeeley, head of the Patrolmen's Benevolent Association, said, "We're never going to have labor unity. . . . I can't sell out my guys. I know there's collusion between Victor Gotbaum and City Hall, and police and fire are going to pay for it."

The Americana marathon was the most high-powered of a series of meetings between city, state and union officials to convince the union leaders that they simply had no choice: there was no money forthcoming from Washington or from the banks unless the unions cooperated. And if the unions didn't cooperate? The city would be plunged into default. Once Gotbaum and the other union leaders accepted this commonality of interest, they really had no choice but to make concessions.

Perhaps the most significant thing to come out of the Americana meetings was the agreement by the unions to invest $140 million from their pension funds in MAC bonds. It was an investment that sealed the common destiny of City Hall and the unions. A month later another $100 million in pension money was invested, and in November the unions agreed to put up an astounding $2.3 billion over the next three years. No doubt the union leaders believe that the city will be eternally grateful for their benevolence but in effect, the pension-fund investments lock the unions into a treacherous position. According to a recent state study, most of the pension funds are dangerously underfunded. This gives the city leverage: raise the specter of default and of vanishing pension funds, and the unions will have little choice but to bend.

Despite the sniping at Gotbaum by other labor leaders, the municipal unions, down the line, rolled over in the face of the fiscal crisis. In September 1975 the 80,000-member UFT went out on strike over the issues of salaries and increased class sizes. Shanker had opposed the strike, he said after it was over, but went along with the more militant rank and file for fear of losing control of his union. When it came to settling, Shanker negotiated a freeze on class size but sacrificed the jobs of nearly 9,000 teachers and school personnel.

Similarly, in July, when the entire membership of the Sanitationmen's Association went out on a wildcat strike to protest the layoffs of 1,400 workers, the union leadership had encouraged the men to go back to work. A deal was finally negotiated whereby the union treasury gave the city $1.6 million to pay the wages of the rehired men. A few weeks later the $1.6 million was exhausted and the garbagemen were collecting unemployment checks. Jack Janoff, who handles the union's public relations (he works for the same firm, Howard Rubinstein Associates, that formally represents Beame), explained the antistrike position to me: "What is the point of striking? The people of New York who would suffer from a garbage strike are not the cause of the problem. The problem is caused by a handful of individuals who do not live in the city, and a strike doesn't affect them. So, what can you win by striking?"

The unions clearly preferred layoffs to contract concessions, preferred to have some of their members out of jobs than all of them suffering a little. After all, a worker who is laid off no longer belongs to the union, while a disgruntled membership can elect new leaders. That the unions agreed to make a choice at all, however, indicates that they came to believe that they had to give up something—the "crap" won at the bargaining table, as Victor Gotbaum called it. The municipal unions hovered too close to the flames of political power in New York: they were blinded into thinking that the workers and the bosses had the same interests, and in the end, they got burned.

MUNICIPAL TRIAGE

Richie Galgano and Frank Bruno are two New York City cops who were laid off in June 1975. Galgano is twenty-seven, waited out a six-year hiring freeze to become a cop, then worked for sixteen months walking the streets of the 19th Police Precinct on the Upper East Side of Manhattan. ("I had eighteen Rockefellers living in my district.") Bruno is younger, twenty-three years old, recently graduated from Queens College; he spent a year working the 28th Precinct in Harlem before being laid off.

Both men like being cops and want their jobs back. Both think the Patrolmen's Benevolent Association should have gone out on strike to protect their jobs. "The PBA was unresponsive to the needs of three thousand laid-off cops," Galgano said. "They are ineffective as a labor force in this city and are not representative of the majority of the people in the union. We tried working with them for five weeks after the layoffs, then they told us they couldn't do anything more."

Galgano was not happy. He sat around his house in Bayside, Queens, for a week, then decided to call a meeting. More than 2,000 ex-cops turned out and formed the Former Police Officers Association (FPOA), which Galgano now heads. He opened up an office in the ornate Woolworth Building across the street from City Hall, started publishing a newsletter called *Off The Job* (its logo is a cracked police shield), and organized a 41-bus caravan of laid-off cops to Washington to lobby for more federal aid to New York. "The PBA does not like having us around," Galgano said, "but we've had a definite effect on them. We want to be a thorn in their side, not a knife."

Though he has organized an effective rank-and-file movement among policemen—one of the few such organizations to come out of the crisis—Galgano is conservative. His newsletter carries endorsements of such conservative politicians as Vito Battista and Mario Biaggi; he thinks that the unions "milked the city" and are largely to blame for the fiscal crisis; and he sees the solution to layoffs in the unions' giving up contract benefits in exchange for rehiring workers. But his anger reaches to the banks as well: "I hate the banks. I'd like to see them suffer a little along with the rest of us."

Frank Bruno, secretary of the FPOA, is somewhat more radical—he calls himself a socialist, regularly reads left-wing publications like the *Guardian, Dollars and Sense* and the *Progressive,* and took part in antiwar demonstrations at Queens College. He and Galgano humor each other, but their viewpoints coexist within the FPOA. Bruno sees the organization as a vehicle for defending the interests of younger cops and of blacks and Puerto Ricans who were hardest hit by the layoffs. He blames the city's fiscal crisis not on the unions, but on the increasing debt load, the misuse of funds for political patronage, and an unfair tax structure. Like Galgano he, too, is angry at the municipal-union leadership, but for different reasons. "People like Victor Gotbaum are full of shit," he said. "He makes all these radical statements, then goes off and makes deals. Labor is definitely not standing together. I wish we could reach out to other groups of city employees, but I don't see it happening."

Co-op City is the largest housing project in the world. Sixty thousand people live there in forty high-rise apartment buildings built on a 300-acre tract in the Bronx that used to be the site of Freedomland amusement park. The project was financed by the state to provide low- and middle-income housing. Most of Co-op City's population flocked there from the decaying East Tremont section of the Bronx; 80 percent are white and working class, and a good number of those are Jewish and elderly. In the five years since the project opened, rents had increased 60 percent. In April 1975, as a result of the continuing financial troubles of the State's Housing Finance Agency, rents were again raised, this time by a third.

But this time something happened. The tenants organized a rent strike. At first no one really thought it was possible to have an effective rent strike in a housing project with some 15,000 families. But the results of a trial run in June were astonishing: the strike was more than 80 percent effective. More than 13,000 families had sent their rent checks not to the rental agent, but to the Strike Steering Committee. Over the next months, as the strike continued, more than $20 million in rents was collected by the committee, even though the state brought legal action against the strike leaders.

Charlie Rosen, a thirty-two-year-old printer for the New York *Post*, is the chairman of the steering committee. He comes from an old-left background and was active in the civil rights and antiwar movements. He has been the principal engine behind the strike. Though what is happening at Co-op City is not directly related to New York City's fiscal crisis, it is an instance of people in the city resisting the imposition of extraordinary financial burdens.

"This strike has provided an opportunity for working people to resist encroachments," Rosen said. "It shows that people will fight back if they are given a program and a winnable struggle. It's a reform struggle, not a revolutionary struggle. But what's important is that people are liberated by their ability to fight. And it's that kind of change in people that will alter history."

The biggest obstacle Rosen and the steering committee faced that spring was cynicism. "The whites said the blacks wouldn't support it, the young people said the old people wouldn't support it. No one believed it would work. But when those first results came in, that was the death of cynicism. You can't coerce people into resisting, you have to convince them slowly, you have to tell the same story thousands of times, you have to go back again and again to explain to them that they won't be evicted as long as they are united."

Once it was clear that the strike could work, hundreds of people were mobilized: committees were set up in each of the forty buildings, weekly meetings were held in every building, leaflets turned out almost every day. "We borrowed from left-wing and trade-union movements," Rosen said. "The strike is run on the principles of democratic centralism. We have a broad-based steering committee which is able to function because people set aside their different interests for the sake of unity."

Charlie Rosen does not believe in the myth of a money shortage and he has worked hard to convince the people of Co-op City that in periods of economic recession "there must be money for people, not only for the bankers." And the only way to ensure that, he says, is by "fighting back against depression."

The municipal unions were not alone in being acquiescent in the face of disaster. New York's liberal Democrats were, with a few exceptions, immobilized by their fear of default, by their poverty of ideas and by their steadfast allegiance to a Democratic mayor.

City Council president Paul O'Dwyer is the godfather of liberal Democrats in New York. He has several times been an unsuccessful candidate for mayor and has long been associated with union activities in the city. In the 1930s he led a brewery strike, and later he represented "Red" Mike Quill's Transit Workers Union when his brother Bill O'Dwyer was mayor. O'Dwyer was thoroughly pessimistic about the fiscal crisis: "There are no radical solutions to the problem. If circumstances suggest that you only have so much money, you have to do the best you can with that and use it wisely. For a while I thought we should consider default as an option. But if you go into default, you are faced with the proposition that this city will never be able to get its credit back. Maybe, at the end of a year, we'll find out that it would have been better to go into default. We might find ourselves in a hell of a kettle of fish. We might find that we're still not out of the woods and have nothing but ten more years of misery ahead of us."

O'Dwyer explained why neither he nor the municipal unions struck a more militant pose: "There's an old trade-union policy that you keep the boss in business. I was brought up with that philosophy. During the brewery strike, the first thing we did was to make sure that the mash was kept hot. Because sooner or later you go back to work."

It's not clear that as City Council president, there was much O'Dwyer could have done. But his timidity leads him only to gloom: "I'm not optimistic about the future. We're going to suffer from these restrictions for a long time. The last banking agreement in 1933, when the banks stepped in to run the city's fiscal affairs, left us without paint on the hospital walls for fifteen years. I see a similar period ahead."

The left, for its part, did not step in to fill the void. Both organized groups and individuals who had entered the ranks of municipal em-

ployees as teachers, social workers and city planners were hampered
by a reluctance to tackle economic issues and by a sectarianism that
weakened their potential for leadership. "The left has totally ignored
the issues of New York over the last twenty years," said Jack Newfield, who did some of the best, most radical reporting on the fiscal
crisis for the *Village Voice*.

Yet the fiscal crisis in both New York and the nation has been an
opportunity, unequaled since the Vietnam war, to organize a broad-
based movement for economic change. And the left has put forward
the clearest analysis that sees the fiscal crisis in New York not as an
aberration—not as a temporary cash shortage—but as a sign of fundamental, long-range crisis in the capitalist system in which wages and
social service spending are being cut to protect corporate profits.

As the crisis intensifies over the coming months, it will inevitably
touch more and more people, threatening the survival of many. Jim
Haughton, head of Fight Back, a rank-and-file movement of minority
workers within New York's construction unions, put it this way:
"When people understand that they aren't responsible for the fiscal
crisis, that it's really the voraciousness of the corporate structure, they
will begin to act. People have been crippled by depending on the
establishment to help them. That may be okay when times are good,
but it doesn't serve them now to be dependent on those who are
exploiting them. People have been passive so far, but it will change."

Despite what the crisis mongers say, New York's problems are far
from over. The $2.3 billion federal loan program that President Ford
finally agreed to in November is tied to the further torpedoing of New
York's social-service expenditures and the jettisoning of an additional
40,000 employees. Far from being a rescue of New York, as city
officials, bankers and the federal government would have us believe,
it is, rather, a policy of municipal triage. And what is most alarming
is that everyone, including the victims, believes that there just aren't
enough lifesavers to go around.

21. New York City Revenues: The Federal and State Role

ELI B. SILVERMAN

New York City's revenues are influenced by federalism in a number of ways. First, America's federalism permits individual and industrial mobility among its numerous jurisdictions. While the bulk of economic research indicates that industrial location decisions are based more on wages, access to raw materials, energy and other costs than they are on tax variations, these studies have focused on interstate differences. Within a metropolitan area, however, these factors tend to be fairly comparable (although New York City is at somewhat of a disadvantage even in the cost areas) while tax differentials within the New York and other metropolitan areas can be substantial.

A second impact on city revenue originates in national economic forces. As the city has become increasingly reliant upon such non-property taxes as sales and income levies (32 percent of its tax receipts), its revenue has become increasingly subject to overall economic conditions. Of course, the city's unemployment rate is also affected by recessionary forces. The combination of a sensitive tax system and a high unemployment rate has led one congressional study to conclude that "New York has probably experienced greater revenue shortfalls than three-quarters of the 24 largest cities as a result of the depressed state of the American economy." The property tax, the city's major income source, has been especially hard hit by increasing delinquencies resulting from inflationary cost increases, recessionary forces and, some would add, rent control.

The third major area in which federalism has affected the city's revenue is more direct. Federal and state aid increased significantly from 1965 to 1972, growing from approximately 25 to 45 percent of

This is an abridged version of a paper written in March 1976. It will appear in a somewhat different form in *Empire State Report*. Eli B. Silverman is chairman and associate professor of government, John Jay College, CUNY.

city expense spending, and thereby partially compensating for the revenue gap in the city budget during this period. Since 1972, however, both federal and state aid have leveled off and declined as a percentage of city revenue. An assessment of the state and federal aid impact and future prospects rests on an examination of the underlying state and federal forces. Although state and federal aid are part of the same intergovernmental revenue mosaic, we will first present an overview of state aid to the city.

STATE AID

Historically, localities have, to varying degrees, depended upon their mother states for substantial portions of their revenues. In New York State, about 60 percent of the budget is funneled to localities, although this percentage represents a slight dip from previous years. The vast bulk (about 85 percent) of New York State aid to localities is in the form of categorical grants designed for specific programs and levels of services which are either mandated or encouraged by the state. Aid to education constitutes the greatest portion of this categorical aid, followed by social services, and then health, housing, highways and other items. The remaining 15 percent of state aid is in the form of general-purposes state aid, of which revenue sharing constitutes the largest portion.

As in other large urban, industrial, competitive two-party states with substantial urban-rural-suburban differences, the allocation of the state pie to these competing jurisdictions is perpetually subject to deliberation, reports, negotiation and bargaining. The outcome of these political exchanges has often been unfortunate for New York City compared to the state's other jurisdictions. On an overall basis, while state aid to the city between 1959 and 1975 increased 600 percent compared to 300 percent for the rest of the state, half of this increase was for state-mandated welfare programs. Excluding this welfare assistance aid, the city receives less aid per capita than the rest of the state.

As the basis for over 50 percent of all state aid to localities, the education formula is a classical example of the Albany budgetary ritual. The formula's reliance on assessed property valuation as the only measure of community wealth, and on public-school attendance rather than registration as the prime measure of need, favors suburban and upstate communities and affects the city adversely. As a result the city, with over 30 percent of the state's public-school registration, receives about a quarter of general state education aid.

Parallel inequities also emerge, strangely enough, in the area of higher education. Although the City University of New York has become a prominent lightning rod for critics of excess city spending, it is important to note that the state contributes considerably more to the State University of New York than it does to CUNY. The combination of disparity in state higher-education aid and the city's financial burdens has intensified demands for state takeover of the City University.

As the major component of general-purposes state aid, state revenue sharing has been studied ad infinitum. The present state revenue-sharing program, enacted in 1970, built upon previous aid programs. It ties per capita aid to the state's most elastic revenue source, the personal income tax, thereby hopefully promoting long-range local-government fiscal stability. Originally 21 percent of the state income tax was promised and scheduled for revenue sharing. Before the program was operational, however, the percentage was reduced to 18 percent because of the state's own financial problems. These three percentage points represent substantial funding levels—$100 million this fiscal year alone, of which the city would have received a considerable portion.

Despite superficial equality in state revenue-sharing aid to cities, the program actually discriminates against cities like New York. This gap between appearance and reality is displayed in the revenue-sharing program's two major components—regular (or general) revenue sharing and the special city aid program.

Under the regular aid program which constitutes half of revenue sharing's 18 percent income-tax distribution, cities receive the largest share, followed by towns, villages and, finally, counties. The inequity in this formula stems from its equal per capita funding to all cities regardless of size even though only 23 percent of the state's cities have populations exceeding 50,000, while about 54 percent have populations less than 25,000 and about 12 percent have less than 10,000. Despite the formula's inclusion of a "fiscal capacity modifier," aid to all cities is very similar on a per person basis. But there are glaring disparities in financial hardships confronted by large and small cities, the types and ranges of services provided, the impact of size on per capita costs, and the extent to which cities can and have taxed themselves. Many observers have noted that the regular aid formula does not take these differences into account. One Temporary State Commission recommended that

> in order to put State aid to New York City on a more rational basis, the formula should be modified to provide aid on the basis of need, capacity and effort, and should incorporate such factors as: 1) the percentage of persons with incomes below the designated poverty levels; 2) personal income; 3) the percentage of persons in the population over 65 and under 18; and 4) population density.

The other half (9 percent of the state income tax) of revenue-sharing funds is disbursed by the special city aid program. While this program was originally targeted for financially pressed cities, it was altered to generate equal per capita grants to *all* cities. Treating unequal cities equally has led a Temporary State Commission to conclude that the special city aid program

> exacerbates the inequities of the jurisdictionally-based formula [since it] provides large amounts of aid to a number of jurisdictions whose needs are not great, whose fiscal capacities are relatively high, and whose taxing efforts are relatively low, simply because they are called cities. Some jurisdictions called cities receive disproportionately large shares of aid, regardless of need, capacity or effort.

While cities and other jurisdictions have, for several years, been pressing for reform in the state revenue-sharing program and a restoration of the 21 percent in income-tax dispersal, the prospects do not appear hopeful. Hard pressed by state revenue shortages, the governor's budget seeks a reduction in state education aid and other forms of local assistance. If the likelihood of increased state aid is bleak, can New York City rely more heavily on the federal government? To address this issue, we must review federal aid to America's cities.

FEDERAL AID

Compared to New York State's assistance to New York City, the federal government is both a junior partner and a Johnny-come-lately. In 1964–1965, when the state was contributing almost 20 percent to the city's expense budget, the federal government was providing 6 percent. It was only during the Johnsonian "Creative Federalism" period in the latter part of the 1960s that federal aid to New York and other cities mushroomed, followed, however, by a decline in federal aid during the Nixon-Ford "New Federalism" of the 1970s. An understanding of the city's changing fortunes during these two periods requires a brief review of the contrasting approaches.

The history of federal grants-in-aid to state and local governments is long and varied. Some assistance predates the Constitution, and in the 1860s the federal government donated public lands to states to encourage agricultural and mechanical arts schools followed by grants for books for the blind, agricultural extension and veterans services. It is important to note that during the early period of cash grants, a formula of equal per capita amounts to each state, matched on a dollar-for-dollar basis, was applied fairly generally.

During the Depression of the 1930s, however, when state and local governments experienced severe fiscal problems, the concept of "financial need" in grant formulas was introduced. In order to provide incentives for poorer states' expenditures, federal aid was generally based on per capita income which, of course, redistributes income from the wealthier to the poorer states. This type of formula was equitable in the 1930s, when most of the nation's poor lived in the rural Southern states. But today, when most low-income families reside in the same urban centers as the wealthy, per capita income remains high for these areas. Consequently, formulas based on per capita income adversely affect states such as New York whose urban poor receive less than their rural counterparts. In the past, low-income states also extracted more of their own resources in relation to personal income than did higher-income states. The opposite is true today with greater tax efforts exerted by some higher-income states such as New York.

Thus, federal aid for programs like maternal and child care, crippled children's services and child welfare services have a rural bias. New York State receives only 5 percent of crippled-children and maternal and child health services funds despite the fact that infant mortality rates are higher in more densely concentrated urban areas than in rural areas.

Per capita formulas have not only been incorporated into other programs (i.e., comprehensive alcoholism, developmental disabilities and comprehensive health services), but their adverse impact on New York and other urban states has been compounded through the income squaring formula. The Hill Burton (hospital construction) Act of 1946 and the Vocational Rehabilitation Basic Support Program, for example, square each state's per capita income percentage. The consequences of this complex formula are illustrated in Table 1.

The so-called poverty level is another formula measure utilized to indicate financial need for federal assistance programs. The very large

TABLE I. Impact of Income Squaring-Vocational Rehabilitation Basic Support Program, Fiscal Year 1975

	State Allocation as a Percentage of National Average with Income Squaring	State Allocation as a Percentage of National Average w/out Income Squaring	Percentage Difference	Amount Gained/ Lost under Income Squaring (in Millions)
Alabama	2.55	2.08	+.47	+3.2
New York	5.19	6.75	−1.56	−10.6

funding levels in the Elementary and Secondary Education Act of 1965, for example, were based, in part, on the number of children in families with incomes under $2,000, children in foster homes and children in families whose incomes exceeded $2,000 only as a result of AFDC payments. Many problems arise from this formula—the difficulty of updating census income data to reflect geographical shifts in low-income families, the lack of recognition of family size, regional and urban-rural disparities in cost of living and hence poverty levels. The consequence of this formula is to skew aid in favor of rural states. In 1971–1972, for example, the national average was 7.1 percent federal/state receipts; for states more than 30 percent rural it was 10.8 percent; and for states less than 30 percent rural it was 6.5 percent.

The impact on selected states, including New York, is graphically illustrated in Table 2.

TABLE 2. Revenue Receipts-Elementary/Secondary Schools by Selected States, 1971–72

State	Total	Federal	Percentage Total
*Alabama	$ 481,819,000	$ 88,047,000	18.3
*Alaska	137,214,000	23,880,000	17.4
*Arkansas	278,343,000	48,100,000	17.3
#California	4,376,291,000	267,118,000	6.1
#Connecticut	911,729,000	28,004,000	3.1
*Mississippi	369,564,000	96,000,000	26.0
#New Jersey	1,942,000,000	84,000,000	4.3
#New York	5,346,071,000	286,483,000	5.4
*South Carolina	487,756,000	80,381,000	16.5
Totals and Average	$46,644,623,000	$3,305,707,000	7.1

Key: *indicates states more than 30 percent rural

#indicates states less than 30 percent rural

This negative impact of "poverty level" formulas is further compounded in additional ways. The Education Amendments of 1974, for example, adopted the so-called Orshansky index of poverty. This formula includes only 40 percent of the children receiving aid under the AFDC program. In addition, the act limits aid for New York State by imposing a ceiling on per pupil expenditures (heretofore not in the act) which the federal government will recognize. The Orshansky index of poverty also determines eligibility for the school lunch program.

Not only is the shift to formulas not helpful to New York, but the increasing use of formulas that base their definition of need on per capita income, poverty levels or equalization rates, as compared to formulas which reflect tax efforts, further aggravates the impact. The differing impacts of these formulas are illustrated in Table 3.

CREATIVE FEDERALISM

It was against this backdrop of disproportionate federal aid to rural as opposed to urban areas that President Johnson's Creative Federalism was launched. While slogans of any national Administration often embrace more rhetoric than rationality, the Johnson program basically emphasized the setting and implementation of national goals and priorities through categorical project grants for which jurisdictions must compete. These grants, targeted for specific needs, were given higher priority than the automatic dispersal of federal funds to all jurisdictions based on population and per capita income formulas.

As a consequence, there was an increased crisscrossing of interrelationships between the national and other levels of government, quasi-governmental groups and private-sector organizations. The objective was to utilize the most pragmatic mix of interorganizational units in order to address pressing social needs. (Medicare, however, proved to

TABLE 3. Illustrative Allocation of $1 Billion Under Various Allotment Formulas: General Support Grant

	Population	Population plus 10 percent Equalization	Population and per capita Income	Population and Tax Effort
New York	93,221	83,899	76,359	108,917

Source: Selma J. Mushkin and John F. Cotton, *Sharing Federal Funds for State and Local Needs* (New York: Praeger, 1969), p. 160.

be an exception to the reliance on the intergovernmental mechanism). The swishes and swirls of the revenue marble cake became even more variegated. Most of these grants were project grants in which specific program purposes and eligibility requirements often raised the discretionary level of federal granting agencies.

Creative Federalism lent a special recognition to the importance of and previous lack of attention to urban problems. Consequently, many grant-in-aid programs were introduced which increased direct relationships between the federal and local governments, thereby circumventing state governments. There were some seventy such programs in 1969, tripling the funding level to local governments. By the end of the Johnson period, 90 percent of the central cities in the largest metropolitan areas were receiving more per capita federal aid than their suburban neighbors.

NEW FEDERALISM

President Nixon's New Federalism (which Mr. Ford has consistently supported) was posed as a more desirable alternative to Creative Federalism. As originally articulated, New Federalism had a somewhat alluring, perhaps seductive, logic. Instead of perpetuating the multitude of duplicative and overlapping narrow categorical grants ("hardening of the categories" it was called) which hamstrung state and local program management, New Federalism sought to decentralize power and responsibility from the federal to state and local governments. State and local governments would be provided program and administrative discretion through the vehicles of revenue sharing and more general block grants.

Nevertheless, the fiscal impact on large urban areas has been nothing short of disastrous and, in large part, explains the leveling off in federal aid to the city. New Federalism's fiscal tourniquet consists of the revenue sharing program, the levels of federal aid, and the changes in the grant program.

REVENUE SHARING

Revenue sharing, with its virtually unrestricted funding and absence of matching funds, was proudly proclaimed as the hallmark of the Nixonian New Federalism. Revenue sharing provides approximately $30 billion over a five-year period to state and local governments. The extent to which revenue sharing should be or has been a supplement to or substitute for other federal aid is a controversial issue.

In addition to the possible link between revenue sharing and the decline in federal aid, New York City has also been affected by certain provisions in the revenue-sharing program itself. Under revenue sharing's complicated mechanism, the amount available to each "state area" (the fifty states and the District of Columbia) is divided into two parts. One third is distributed to the state government, and the remaining two-thirds for local distribution. This division, however, implicitly assumes uniformities between the fiscal roles and responsibilities of state governments vis-à-vis local governments in the fifty states. In reality, however, there is considerable disparity in the relative distribution of fiscal roles and program responsibilities between state government and their local governments throughout the nation. As a city which assumes a more substantial fiscal role than most cities, New York would have much to gain under a provision which varies the state-local proportion according to the relative fiscal roles of the two levels of government. As it stands today, revenue sharing's fiscal benefits are distorted. Of all the fifty states, local governments in New York State receive the smallest percentage of revenue funds compared to their general expenditures.

A second unfortunate aspect of revenue sharing is that it distributes aid to many local jurisdictions with insignificant urban problems and inconsequential governmental responsibilities, thereby dissipating the amount of funds available to New York and other jurisdictions most in need. The two thirds of revenue sharing distributed to general-purpose local governments include over 3,000 counties, over 18,000 municipalities, almost 17,000 townships, or over 38,000 eligible governments in addition to Indian tribes and Alaskan native villages. Although the blanketing in of all these local governments was strategically calculated to elicit wide support for revenue sharing's legislative enactment, the broad coverage embraced governmental units spanning a wide spectrum of responsibilities and roles. In some states, either counties or townships do not exist. Where they do exist, their population size, level of revenue raised, functions and range of responsibilities vary. Part of this disparity is attributable to the variety of state arrangements for the financing and operation of public schools. In some states, public schools are the responsibility of independent school boards while in other states public-school systems are associated with counties, municipalities and/or townships.

A third revenue-sharing issue relevant to New York City stems from the funding percentages allocated to localities. Many have called for elimination of the provision which limits the per capita amount of shared revenue for county areas and individual municipalities and townships to 145 percent of the statewide average. In the opinion of one respected study of revenue sharing, the elimination of this provision

would benefit the most hard-pressed local jurisdiction, [i.e., New York City], curtail the law's bias in favor of multilayered local government [of which New York City is not an example], simplify its administration and make the resulting allocations far more understandable to concerned officials and the public.

STATE AND FEDERAL AID: CURRENT PROSPECTS

While the state and federal governments have, over the years, made significant contributions to the city's ever-expanding revenue needs, we have seen how this external assistance has leveled off and declined as a percentage of city revenue raised from its own sources. The immediate prospects for increased external aid (excluding such assistance as loans) are quite dim.

New York State, long the senior partner in external assistance to the city, has extended itself during New York City's much publicized financial crises with advances in state aid, and legislation creating the Municipal Assistance Corporation and the Emergency Financial Control Board. Nevertheless, with the State facing its own critical budgetary problems, there is little expectation of increased regular and sustained aid to the city.

On the national level, New Federalism has turned out to be a new hoax for the nation's urban centers. Emphasis on decentralization of program priorities and administration only makes sense if it is accompanied by commensurate resource increases to those areas with the most pressing needs. New Federalism thrusts down program responsibilities without supplying the requisite funding levels. Similarly, the new state budget is pushing the cost of these programs down to its local government. Unfortunately, New York City has nowhere else to go. Nowhere, except to the taxpayers' wallets.

22. Disurbanization and Economic Recovery

PETER S. ALBIN

The Ford Administration has been accused of stodgy conservatism in economic matters, yet it has received little recognition for its fiscal innovation in creatively linking economic recovery to the stimulus of progressive disurbanization. The cornerstone of this policy is a finding in a yet-to-be-released Treasury study which proves that private expenditures of over $20 billion a year will be required for the next three decades in order to recover from the dislocations caused by the final dismemberment and bankruptcy of New York City. These expenditures, when amplified by multiplier effects, would be more than sufficient to hold the economy at full employment and would eliminate the need for inflationary extensions of existing programs.

The basic Treasury finding is expressed in a series of calculations on what private industry and free enterprisers would have to spend if driven out of the city by its collapse and the resultant cancellation of luxury services. For example, the moving of business offices and records alone would give jobs to more than 250,000 American workers, while the dispersion of population would require a minimum of $2 billion in annual needs. In fact, there is every reason to treat the $20 billion figure as a conservative estimate; one can easily argue that a figure two or three times as large approximates the value to the nation of the trade and commerce uniquely generated in the city. Whether $20 billion, $60 billion or even $80 billion is the correct figure, the great appeal of the disurbanization plan is that the government can generate the requirement for these private expenditures by not spending as little as $500 million from public funds (the amount of intergovernmental transfers that would finance the current deficit

Peter S. Albin is professor of economics, John Jay College, CUNY. This paper was written in the fall of 1975.

from federal funds). In fact, by not spending only slightly more, the Administration could extend the policy to cities throughout the nation.

A virtue of the disurbanization program is its simplicity. No elaborate plans are required to implement it, nor need American citizens cede additional discretionary authority to an already swollen federal bureaucracy. The time frame for the plan is ideal as well, given uncertainty as to the momentum of the current recovery. The disexpenditure peak in education programs is scheduled for the fall election campaign at just the instant of time that federal disexpenditures in other recovery programs will run out, while the writedown in the value of the city's paper resulting from eventual default will, of itself, eliminate a considerable portion of excess debt at the forecast moment of a peak in credit requirements.

Americans have tended to suspect down-to-earth nuts-and-bolts practicality such as that embodied in the disurbanization program, so that there is some need to show that the policy is theoretically sound and consistent with the most advanced thinking of scholars in the field. Just as the outmoded Keynesian analysis had its *accelerator* principle and the neo-Friedmanian inflation theory its *escalator* principle, the Simonian disurbanization theory is founded on its own dynamic principle of mechanical ascension, the *elevator* principle. A homely example will convey some insights as to the power of this conception. Imagine yourself waiting for an elevator, watching the indicator arrow as it rotates across the dial measuring the slow progress of the lift toward your landing. The elevator can move at its appointed speed or you can seize the initiative, leap up, and by grasping the arrow in your own free hands, pull the elevator to your floor. Simonian disurbanization theory works through an analogous mastery of the linkages between the financial system (the indicator) and the real economy (the elevator). The value of the major urban centers to the national economy has long been known, but only through the creative application of the *elevator* principle can this now be realized as a *need* for private activity. We should note that the theory and primitive versions of the *elevator* principle have been tested in other connections with appropriate success. One can cite the support given to the OPEC cartel so that profits of domestic oil companies could rise to a high enough level to finance a national energy policy which might otherwise not be carried out at government expense—or the use of bilateral arms and food deals to anticipate a breakdown of free multilateral trade. These steps plus other innovative moves taken to bring the rate of economic progress more in line with diminished national expectations encourage the belief that the disurbanization policy will be enormously successful in creating new national needs. Remember that if all else fails, the disurbanization program will bring the nation one step closer to the main long-term planning goal of national transportation policy—the need to fill the gap between the Jersey Turnpike and the Long Island Expressway.

23. Austerity, Planning and the Socialist Alternative

DAVID MERMELSTEIN

Few Americans pay sufficient attention to the business press. For those who do, *Business Week* sounded an ominous warning in November 1974:

Finally, and most distressing of all, it is not at all certain how graciously Americans, or any other people for that matter will accept what is plainly today's (and history's) economic reality: that there is no such thing as perpetual plenty and no party that does not eventually end.

Not everyone, of course, had attended the gala affair. Poor people at home and abroad were generally excluded. Millions of others had their lives devastated by a faraway war in Vietnam which did much to create the party in the first place. However, most Americans, both black and white, *did* prosper during the sixties and had expectations that good times would never end.

Sadly they did. The "depression" of 1974–1975 was steep enough to challenge the euphemistic nomenclature fashionable in the post-war epoch. In spite of an economic recovery that at present writing is more than a year old, unemployment at 7½ percent still exceeds past recessionary highs. National averages by definition understate the hardships of particular localities and groups in the population.

The level and pervasiveness of current unemployment flow from an emerging corporate strategy of forced austerity. Its roots lie in the crisis of profitability.[1] By potentially reducing property taxes (or at

---

David Mermelstein teaches economics at the Polytechnic Institute of New York.

[1] See the discussion in the Preface to this book, pp. xiv–xviii. Some students of capitalism believe we are in the early stages of a reorganization of the world capitalist order under the aegis of the multinational corporation, following which a new prosperity may emerge. Others hold that capitalist development leads to permanent stagnation. Another view is that we are "simply" in a cyclical downturn, albeit one of serious proportions. These are not necessarily mutually exclusive approaches. Whatever proves

least not permitting the increases of the past), by making loanable funds more readily available to private enterprise and by dampening wage rates and labor militancy through unemployment, it is hoped that cutbacks will eventually aid in restoring the health of the economy, in particular its rate of profit. In short, in the peculiar world of capitalism, bad news is good news: cutbacks are necessary for recovery, while a slow-paced upturn is welcomed as a brake on inflation and an indicator of a prolonged expansion.

As necessity is the mother of invention, the "need" for austerity creates an appropriate ideology. For example, at the very moment pollutant controls are being removed in the name of economic recovery, ecological principles themselves are being harnessed (in distorted fashion) to justify lower standards of living. Among politicians, Zen Master Brown of California is only the most flamboyant of the purveyors of this new ideology of "declining expectations."[2] Carter rose to prominence as one untainted by a spendthrift Washington connection. Budget cutting is currently the mood of the nation, whether engaged in by true believers Ford and Reagan or reluctantly accepted by pragmatists Carey and Beame.

The question arises, Why do people accept this ideology of sacrifice? In good part the answer lies in the simple fact that they are in no position to do otherwise. Given a capitalist economy, there is truth to corporate slogans that "What's good for General Motors is good for the country" or Mobil Corporation ads proclaiming that jobs and "progress" (or at least rising levels of production—the two are not synonymous) are dependent on corporate health. The latter, in turn, requires substantial profits. Whether one views them as justifiable returns to risk or a rake-off which the wealthy impose for providing us with jobs, profits are the prime financial source for new investment. In short, profits *are* the incentives corporate propagandists say they are. Without the prospect that investment will turn a healthy profit, the wheels of industry will, as they say, grind to a halt, and to some extent in 1974–1975, did. Their livelihoods and well-being thus dependent on the health and viability of the corporate system, workers are ideological captives of the capitalist class. It is hardly surpris-

---

to be the case about the long-run workings of capitalism, the point here is that the present epoch is one of hard times and economic austerity.

[2]The phrase is from Felix Kramer, "The Revolution of Declining Expectations," unpublished manuscript.

ing, then, that many tend to see events in accordance with capitalist nostrums which emphasize the essential benevolence of the institutions of private property and the profit system. They dismiss its defects as exceptions. To challenge those institutions, to see them as essentially malevolent and the source of our problems is to destroy the comforting set of values most people live by. Such understanding is difficult to develop. The result is that most Americans have no conception of economic disorder resulting from a myriad of forces in which the role of the private corporation is decisive.

In effect, workers are in a double bind. If they fight for increased wages and full employment, they undermine corporate profitability and run the risk of pushing the nation into a depression. To do otherwise—cooperate with capital—is to cooperate in wage cuts and layoffs. Held over such a barrel, it is no wonder that workers are demoralized and divided. Separated on other levels as well, by skill, occupation, race, region, sex, ethnicity, and so on, workers have learned they must look out for themselves. They forsake joint endeavors because by and large, historical experience teaches them that to do otherwise is personally costly. Not expecting to win, few want to be suckers.

PLANNING FOR PROFITS

There is, to be sure, one powerful alternative to this double bind. Workers can opt out of the system altogether. A remote prospect, perhaps, but there *is* precedent for a radical response to hard times. The Great Depression, for example, unleashed forces that overcame repression in defense of an open shop and a previous generation's reluctance to bargain collectively. The hardships of the late nineteenth century gave birth to Debs and the considerable socialist movement of that era. There is no immutable law of capitalist development that requires workers to remain forever divided any more than there is a law of class cohesion.

The dialectics of history are not unappreciated by far-seeing defenders of capitalist class interest. They know that too brutal a dose of austerity risks a counterattack by those whose backs are forced against the wall. Thus it is no surprise that an alternate strategy has emerged for revitalizing profits and achieving capitalist prosperity. It calls for *increased* economic planning and an *enlarged* role for the state rather than the diminished one contemplated by the budget cutters.

Congressional expression of this viewpoint is incorporated in the Humphrey-Hawkins bill promoting full employment and the Humphrey-Javits bill on behalf of balanced growth and economic planning. Although Democrats presumably are preponderant, the New Planners include luminaries from both parties: Thomas B. Watson of IBM, Henry Ford II, perhaps Arthur F. Burns, who has been advocating some form of wage-price controls, and Felix Rohatyn. The latter is chairman of New York's Municipal Assistance Corporation, a director of such corporate titans as ITT and partner in the influential investment banking house, Lazard Frères. He has explicitly called for state planning and the creation of a new Reconstruction Finance Corporation which would serve as an "instrument of both rescue and stimulus."[3]

These men and others want to extend the system of capitalist planning beyond the Keynesian regulatory framework, which is general in nature, to *individual* controls on prices, wages and resource allocation. They hope to create new federal agencies, like Rohatyn's RFC, to mobilize huge agglomerations of capital for needed private investment that otherwise might not be made, especially in the development of new sources of energy.

This movement for overt corporate-government planning appears to be in conflict with the dominant ideology of free enterprise promoted by the budget cutters. In reality, this ideology has veiled a vast system of government subsidy and waste designed to promote profits and prosperity. In this fashion, corporations can have their cake and eat it too: a government thoroughly oiled and geared to their needs, yet a populace concerned with government restrictions on business and with handouts squandered on the undeserving poor. The following captures what is at issue:

When the state is used surreptitiously to socialize the costs of businesses which appropriate the benefits for themselves, it proves that the benefits from state actions are invisible relative to the burdens of its costs. When the prime resources of the nation are used for private purposes, the leftovers available to the state cannot serve as demonstrations of the state's potential. In this way, the business system has killed two birds with one stone: it achieves its guaranteed survival through the needed and enlarged state and then can appear as an underdog and champion of efficiency in the ideological

[3]See Rohatyn's article in the *New York Times* (December 1, 1974), reprinted in David Mermelstein, ed., *The Economic Crisis Reader* (New York: Vintage Books, 1975).

attack on the wastes and bureaucratic inefficiencies that are visible and allegedly inherent in underfinanced and over-used state activities. . . . When the economy falters, it can be blamed on the errors of government policies; when the economy succeeds, it is due to the dynamic qualities of the private sector.[4]

Nonetheless, such past ideological obfuscations may not be possible in a regime of planning. From the capitalist point of view, planning like austerity carries grave risks (not least of which is the politicalization of income distribution through a system of imposed wage schedules). More important, capitalists are also placed in a double bind: if controls work badly, all of the problems of unemployment, inflation and profitlessness continue apace. But if they work well, the working class may begin to reassess its bias against socialism so carefully cultivated all these years by the culture of capitalism.

THE SOCIALIST ALTERNATIVE

Many papers in this volume suggest that a meaningful and progressive solution to America's urban and economic problems cannot be achieved within a capitalist framework. Those who reject the corporate solutions of austerity or capitalist planning generally believe that ultimately America's ills require a socialist transformation. Similarly, in response to a question about solutions to the most recent crisis of capitalism, Joan Robinson told of a traveler who stops by the side of the road to ask the way to Oklahoma. "I don't know the way to Oklahoma," the guide replies, "but I sure wouldn't start from here." Since the notion of socialism tends to be bandied about and loosely used, some elaboration is needed.

Socialists are of the belief that like the economic systems which preceded it, capitalism, too, is a transitory phenomenon which sooner or later will be forced to give way to more rational forms. As Marx wrote more than a hundred years ago,

The growing incompatibility between the productive development of society and its hitherto existing relations of production expresses itself in bitter contradictions, crises, spasms. The violent destruction of capital not by relations external to it, but rather as a condition of its self-preservation, is the most striking form in which advice is given to be gone and to give room to a higher state of social production.[5]

[4]Mark Rosenblum and Raymond Franklin, "New York: A Case of Ideological Bankruptcy," unpublished manuscript.

[5]Karl Marx, *Grundrisse* (Baltimore: Penguin Books, 1973), pp. 749–750.

Ideologues like Ayn Rand would have us believe that the contemporary capitalist system is a mixed economy, part capitalist and part socialist, that somehow we have departed from "true" capitalism, which is some kind of perfect political state, like the notion of God transferred to politics. True capitalism is a hypothetical laissez-faire construct, one which never has existed in reality and never will. Eternal, and "existing" only in the mind, this approach is totally ahistorical.

It ignores first of all the brutal origins of capitalism. As Marx put it, "If money . . . comes into the world with a congenital blood-stain on one cheek, capital comes dripping from head to foot, from every pore with blood and dirt." It also ignores the entire history of its development, one in which the capitalist class itself increasingly made use of state power to increase its profits and ensure its survival. If it is silly to believe that Richard Nixon—a reactionary Republican of long standing, with close ties to big business—became a socialist on August 15, 1971, when he promulgated a wage-price freeze to solve the problems of capitalism, it is absolutely ludicrous to call state planning under Nelson Rockefeller "socialism." We'll know that socialism has arrived when we see Nelson enter a cab and sit down behind the wheel!

Social complexity being what it is, it is hardly surprising that no single definition of socialism can command the allegiance of all who advocate it.[6] Socialists have in mind the transformation of existing capitalist society into something more genuinely democratic, more egalitarian and more humane. At the very least, this implies that society's property and technological-productive apparatus cannot be owned, controlled and developed by the few (the capitalist class) in the interests of their own private profit. These resources must be owned by all and democratically controlled to create a sane and healthful pattern of existence, compatible with real human needs, and with the environment as well. Moreover, decisions made at the workplace and in government must be democratic not just in name, but in the fundamental sense that everyone to the extent humanly possible participates as an equal. At the same time, the right of minorities to freely dissent from majority rule must be cultivated and safeguarded.

[6]The following material was developed in collaboration with my colleague Louis Menashe.

Socialism, then, is not only an economic mode of production and distribution but a social-cultural system in which social, political and economic privilege has been eradicated (or at least the direction of movement is continuously toward this ideal). The socialist goal is that everyone should live up to potential or at least not be denied the opportunity to do so because of an inegalitarian system of power and stratification.

No one seriously denies the enormous obstacles standing in the way of achieving such a goal. One immediate problem is the strength of capitalist ideology already alluded to, especially its ability to create divisions within the working classes (all those who labor for wages). Behind this lies the immense repressive apparatus the capitalist class can bring to bear against those who seek fundamental social change. Given this context of political struggle, socialists have usually hesitated to present blueprints of how socialism will work, believing that any future revolutionary condition will be considerably different from what now exists.

The idea that socialism can only be introduced after "the revolution" is not without challenge. On the other hand, many question whether it is possible to introduce socialism piecemeal: perhaps "socialized" medicine here, public housing there; perhaps the nationalization of energy here and of transportation there. Such efforts may result in more massive and oppressive state bureaucracies. Workers may make gains, but in ways that reinforce the capitalist ideology (co-optation). The piecemeal approach to socialism is therefore viewed skeptically since it fails to destroy a state apparatus dedicated to maintaining capitalist forms, capitalist privilege and a capitalist class structure. Nevertheless, some socialists (the Communist party of Italy, at least implicitly) believe that this state apparatus can be effectively neutralized by a strong working-class movement during a period of transition. If so, socialist modes of thought and socialist structures can take root and be partially introduced within the context of electoral politics. The danger here is that capital will go on strike, so to speak, sabotage such efforts and cause such a socialist party to discredit itself by moving too quickly (or not moving at all).

Regardless of the route taken to *achieve* socialism, certain key and unresolved issues present themselves. For example, how centralized or decentralized shall decision making in the economic sphere be? Some insist that decisions be made locally in small units. Decentralized decision making is considered preferable, since it reduces the number of intermediaries between the people and their leaders. Yet a New England town-meeting style of socialism is probably not feasible in a modern industrial nation of more than 200 million people. For example, a local decision to produce more steel may adversely affect the river life of another area. This suggests that some kind of democratically elected national economic council with the power to veto projects of subunits is needed. Centralization may also be needed on the morrow of the revolution to counter patterns of sexual and racial discrimination in those spheres where capitalist ideology still holds sway.

Another question is that of incentives. Since it is not likely that centuries of capitalist conditioning can be erased overnight, it is unrealistic to expect that people will initially work out of sense of socialist commitment. On the other hand, there is no justification for wage differentials of the magnitude we are accustomed to in capitalist America. In the end, the line between moral and material incentives will undoubtedly be pragmatically drawn. Related to this is the role played by small-scale capital, such as the family farm, neighborhood grocery or small manufacturer. Small businesses—even those motivated by self-interest and greed—may be necessary for the flexibility they provide, not to speak of the fact that they are repositories of distributive and productive know-how. This may be tolerable as long as the socially controlled large-scale productive forces are used to narrow sharply differentials in income. To the extent that creativity, equality and democratic participation is socially encouraged both on the job and off, individuals may less feel the need to own their own business. Also, to the extent that investment is directed more toward social and communal consumption—for example, parks, recreation facilities, dining areas—there is less need for individuals to have the extra income that private enterprise offers.

This discussion also poses the question of what role the market should play in contrast to that of a central plan. Complex industrial economies are not easily planned in the absence of a market for goods and labor—even with computers and such economic techniques as input-output and linear programming—without creating serious problems relating to inefficiency, bureaucracy and coercion. (A case in point: the Soviet economy.) On the other hand, the capitalist market gives rise to the inefficiency and coercion of advertising, sales pressure, monopoly, imperialism and an economy misdirected away from human needs. In the long period of readjustment, there may be a realistic place for the market mechanism as long as it exists within a socialist framework, one in which investment is controlled by the people at large, and the fruits of progress are largely directed to those most needy.

Socialists are also committed to democratizing the work place. Here, too, a compromise must be fashioned between the interests of society as a whole and the rights of workers to make decisions affecting their lives. Workers' control must inevitably be a part of a national plan—a plan, moreover, having the flexibility to tolerate strikes or errors of judgment by workers themselves. Within such a framework, concrete decisions on wages, working conditions, pensions, etc., must be made. Another problem: years of capitalist oppression do not prepare workers to be confident, independent participants in new forms of industrial democracy. For this reason, workers' control is not a panacea. Problems that arise from the spiritually destructive form of society we now have are from a socialist point of view essentially *transitional* problems, likely to diminish as the new socialist ethic emerges.

In the last analysis, these remarks on how socialism works, or can work, rest upon a faith that humankind need not live in the kind of societies which have to now dominated existence, that once people get fed up with the malfunctions and disasters of capitalist modes they have the intelligence and capacity to create a better social order. In this sense, *socialism represents a qualitative step forward, not utopia.* By the same token, economic issues are not fundamental barriers. They are more in the nature of technical problems, surmountable by a people energized enough to want to create something better for themselves and posterity.

For those who reject socialism because of its negative features where it already exists (or in countries describing themselves as socialist), I would counter with an old, yet valid argument: these experiments in socialism have taken place in backward countries where the need was to build a modern industrial economy on an underdeveloped, agricultural base. These were countries lacking traditions of democracy and civil liberties; moreover, they were surrounded by hostile and aggressive capitalist powers.

The United States is hardly economically backward—many would call it *over*developed. We are also a people who cherish our civil liberties and democratic processes, however much we have permitted them to erode. Should America become socialist, no hostile capitalist power of any consequence is apt to threaten our existence.

American socialism, then, when and if it arrives, will necessarily be qualitatively different from what now exists. Its specific features are of course unknown at present, but it will obviously reflect our level of development. Socialism, though, is no more around the corner than Hoover's prosperity. The question is whether or not the economic crisis will be used to reorganize capitalist society along increasingly regimented lines, or alternatively, whether the crisis can be used to build a popular, socialist movement which will in the short run protect the living standard of working people and in the long run prepare the way for the eventual reorganization of our society along more humane lines.

About the Editors

ROGER E. ALCALY was born in New York City in 1941. He received a B.A. from Amherst College in 1962 and a Ph.D. in Economics from Princeton University in 1969. Mr. Alcaly taught economics at Columbia University (1966–1974) and the University of Montana (spring 1973) and has been a member of the economics department of John Jay College of the City University of New York since September 1974. He is a member of the editorial board of the *Review of Radical Political Economics*, and has contributed articles to the *American Economic Review*, *Econometrica*, the *Journal of Regional Science*, the *Journal of Business*, the *Journal of Economic Issues*, *Land Economics*, the *Bell Journal of Economics*, the *Economic Crisis Reader* and *Radical Perspectives on the Economic Crisis of Monopoly Capitalism*, among others.

DAVID MERMELSTEIN is a native of Baltimore, born in September 1933. A graduate of Amherst College, he received his Ph.D. in economics from Columbia University. He is the editor of *Economics: Mainstream Readings and Radical Critiques* (New York, Random House, 3d ed., 1976), co-editor (with Marvin E. Gettleman) of *The Great Society Reader: The Failure of American Liberalism* (New York, Random House, 1967 [2d ed., 1970, entitled *The Failure of American Liberalism: After the Great Society*]) and *The Economic Crisis Reader: Understanding Depression, Inflation, Unemployment, Energy, Food, Wage-Price Controls, and Other Disorders of American and World Capitalism* (New York, Random House, 1975). His articles and reviews have appeared in such journals and magazines as *Monthly Review*, *Science & Society*, the *American Economic Review* and the *Quarterly Review of Economics and Business*.

A member of the Union for Radical Political Economics, Mr. Mermelstein is an associate professor of economics at the Polytechnic Institute of New York. He lives with Cindy and his daughter, Julie, on Manhattan's Upper West Side.